THE NEW MIDDLE CLASSES

MAIN TRENDS OF THE MODERN WORLD

General Editors: Robert Jackall and Arthur J. Vidich

Propaganda
Edited by Robert Jackall

Metropolis: Centre and Symbol of Our Times
Edited by Philip Kasinitz

Social Movements: Critiques, Concepts, Case-Studies
Edited by Stanford M. Lyman

The New Middle Classes: Life-Styles, Status Claims and Political Orientations
Edited by Arthur J. Vidich

The New Middle Classes

Life-Styles, Status Claims and Political Orientations

Edited by
Arthur J. Vidich
Senior Lecturer and Professor Emeritus
of Sociology and Anthropology
New School for Social Research
New York

MACMILLAN

First published 1995 by
MACMILLAN PRESS LTD
Houndmills, Basingstoke, Hampshire RG21 2XS
and London
Companies and representatives
throughout the world

ISBN 0–333–61758–4 hardcover
ISBN 0–333–61759–2 paperback

A catalogue record for this book is available
from the British Library.

10   9   8   7   6   5   4   3   2   1
04 03 02 01 00 99 98 97 96 95

Printed and bound in Great Britain by
Antony Rowe Ltd
Chippenham, Wiltshire

Contents

Series Preface

Main Trends of the Modern World is a series of books analyzing the main trends and the social psychology of our times. Each volume in the series brings together readings from social analysts who first identified a decisive institutional trend and from writers who explore its social and psychological effects in contemporary society.

The series works in the classical tradition of social theory. In this view, theory is the historically informed framing of intellectual problems about concrete social issues and the resolution of those problems through the analysis of empirical data. Theory is not, therefore, the study of the history of ideas about society, nor the abstract, ahistorical modeling of social realities, nor, as in some quarters, pure speculation often of an ideological sort unchecked by empirical reality. Theory is meaningful only when it illuminates the specific features, origins, and animating impetus of particular institutions, showing how these institutions shape experience and are linked to the social order as a whole.

Social analysts such as Karl Marx, Max Weber, Émile Durkheim, Sigmund Freud, Georg Simmel, Thorstein Veblen and George Herbert Mead, whose work we now consider classics, never consciously set out to construct paradigms, models or abstract theories of society. Instead they investigated concrete social phenomena such as the decline of feudal society and the emergence of industrial capitalism, the growth of bureaucracy, the consequences of the accelerating specialization of labor, the significance of religion in a scientific and secular age, the formation of self and the moral foundations of modern society, and the on-going rationalization of modern life. The continuing resonance of their ideas suggests the firmness of their grasp of deep-rooted structural trends in Western industrial society.

Later European and American social thinkers, deeply indebted though they were to the intellectual frameworks produced by the remarkable men who preceded them, faced a social order marked by increasing disarray, one that required fresh intellectual approaches. The social, cultural and intellectual watershed was, of course, the Great War and its aftermath. The world's first total war ravaged a whole generation of youth. In Europe it sowed the seeds of revolution, militarism, totalitarianism, fascism and state socialism; in both Europe and America it signaled the age of mass propaganda. On both continents the aftermath of the war brought economic and political turmoil, cultural frenzies, widespread disenchantment and disillusionment, and social movements of every hue and description that led eventually to the convulsions of the Second World War. These later social thinkers grappled with issues such as:

- The deepening bureaucratization of all social spheres and the ascendance of the new middle classes.
- The collapse of old religious theodicies that once gave meaning to life and the emergence of complex social psychologies of individuals and masses in a rationalized world.
- The riddles posed by modern art and culture.
- The emergence of mass communications and propaganda as well as the manufacture of cultural dreamworlds of various sorts.
- War, militarism and the advent of totalitarianism, fascism and state socialism.
- The deepening irrational consequences and moral implications of the thoroughgoing rationalization of all life spheres.

Emil Lederer, Hans Speier, Joseph Schumpeter, Kenneth Burke, Robert MacIver, Harold Lasswell, Walter Lippmann, Robert Park, W. I. Thomas, Florian Znaniecki, George Orwell, Hannah Arendt, Herbert Blumer and Hans H. Gerth are only a few of the men and women who carried forward the theoretical attitude of the great classical thinkers in the course of working on the pressing issues of their own day. In this tradition, social theory means confronting head-on the social realities of one's own times, trying to explain both the main structural drift of institutions as well as the social psychologies of individuals, groups and classes.

What then are the major structural trends and individual

experiences of our own epoch? Four major trends come immediately to mind, each with profound ramifications for individuals. We pose these as groups of research problems.

BUREAUCRACY AS THE ORGANIZATIONAL FORM OF MODERNITY

- What are the social and psychological consequences of living and working in a society dominated by mass administered bureaucratic structures? How do mass bureaucratic structures affect the private lives of the men and women exposed to their influences?
- What is the structure and meaning of work in a bureaucratic society? In particular, how does bureaucracy shape moral consciousness? What are the organizational roots of the collapse of traditional notions of accountability in our society?
- What is the relationship between leaders and followers in a society dominated by a bureaucratic ethos? What are the changing roles of intellectuals, whether in the academy or public life, in defining, legitimating, challenging or serving the social order?

THE TECHNOLOGIES OF MASS COMMUNICATION AND THE MANAGEMENT OF MASS SOCIETY

- What role do public relations, advertising and bureaucratized social research play in shaping the public opinions and private attitudes of the masses?
- What is the relationship between individuals' direct life experiences (with, for example, family, friends, occupations, sex and marriage) and the definitions that the mass media suggest for these individual experiences? What illusions and myths now sustain the social order? What are the ascendant forms of this-worldly salvation in our time?
- What are the different origins, dynamics and consequences of modern political, social and cultural mass movements with their alternative visions of justice and morality?
- What social, economic and cultural trends have made many

great metropolises, once the epitomes of civilization and still the centers and symbols of modern life, into new wildernesses?

THE ON-GOING SOCIAL TRANSFORMATIONS OF CAPITALISM

- What are the prospects for a transformed capitalism in a post-Marxist, post-Keynesian era?
- How has the emergence of large bureaucratic organizations in every sector of the social order transformed the middle classes? What is the social and political psychology of these new middle classes?
- What transformations of the class and status structure have been precipitated by America's changing industrial order?
- What are the social, cultural and historical roots of the pervasive criminal violence in contemporary American society? What social factors have fostered the breakdown of traditional mechanisms of social control and the emergence of violence as a primary means for effecting individual or group goals?

THE CLASH BETWEEN WORLDVIEWS AND VALUES, OLD AND NEW

- How has science, particularly in its bureaucratized form, transformed the liberal doctrines of natural rights, individual rights and concomitant conceptions of the human person, including notions of life and death?
- How have the old middle classes come to terms with mass bureaucratic institutions and the subsequent emergence of new classes and status groups? What social forces continue to prompt the framing of complicated social issues in terms of primal antagonisms of kith, kin, blood, color, soil, gender and sexual orientation?
- What are the roots of the pervasive irrationalities evident at virtually every level of our society, despite our Enlightenment legacy of reason and rationality and our embrace of at least functional rationality in our organizational ap-

paratus? To what extent is individual and mass irrationality generated precisely by formally rational bureaucratic structures?

In short, the modern epoch is undergoing social transformations every bit as dramatic as the transition from feudalism to industrial capitalism. The very complexity of the contemporary world impedes fixed social scientific understanding. Moreover we may lack the language and concepts necessary to provide coherent analyses of some emerging features of our social order. Nonetheless this series tries to identify and analyze the major trends of modern times. With an historical awareness of the great intellectual work of the past and with a dispassionate attitude toward contemporary social realities, the series tries to fashion grounded, specific images of our world in the hope that future thinkers will find these more useful than speculation or prophecy.

Each volume in this series addresses one major trend The book in hand analyzes the new middle classes. In particular it explores their origins, their relation to bureaucracy and capitalism, their life-styles, their status insecurities and their political orientations.

ROBERT JACKALL
ARTHUR J. VIDICH

Introduction
Arthur J. Vidich

This volume is designed first to provide a theoretical orientation and historical perspective on the rise of the middle classes in modern civilization, and second, to portray the social and political roles these classes have played and continue to play in the United States over the past century, with particular reference to the American class structure and political economy. Our method is necessarily both historical and sociological and offers an orientation for understanding contemporary American society. The essays included here were written between 1926 and 1982: they reveal both the genealogical development of sociological thought about the middle classes and the substantive content of these classes' life-styles, status claims and political orientations. The present work stresses empirical studies and puts forth neither a theoretical interpretation nor a conceptual taxonomy; rather it delineates the emergence and the social and political significance of the new middle classes in relation to the classes, above and below, that preceded them.

An analysis of the social and political psychology of the new middle classes is necessary because the issues contained therein go to the heart of historical as well as current discussions within Marxism, debates between Marxists and Weberians, and the conflicting points of view among Weberians of different persuasions. These same issues have been central to discussions of the American class structure as described by Thorstein Veblen in the *Theory of the Leisure Class* and later by Hans H. Gerth's student C. Wright Mills. In the United States, where the new middle classes emerged only during and after Roosevelt's New Deal and the Second World War, its life-styles and political mentality served as a model during the Cold War for the new middle classes throughout the world. These discussions began in the early decades of this century when Marxist-oriented social analysts endeavored to grasp the social implications of a newly emergent stratum of white-collar workers and to incorporate their

1

struggles and interests within their older perspective.

Marx's expectation of an increasing polarization between capitalists and workers had not accounted for the emergence of a vast new middle stratum employed in administrative, service and bureaucratic positions. These new white-collar workers – salaried employees – were not capitalists but neither did they correlate with earlier conceptions of factory or industrial workers. The social-scientific examination of this new class was taken up by a new generation of investigators who discovered that its political significance could not be explained within the frameworks of Marx or Weber: the new middle *classes* (for there were more than one) were simultaneously distinguishable from the older bourgeoisie and substantively a new social phenomenon. They had arisen as a result of the growth in size and scale of industrial, commercial, labor-union and state bureaucracies.

The landmark study of these new middle classes was written by Emil Lederer and published in Tübingen in 1912 as *Die Privatangestellten in der modernen Wirtschaftsentwicklung*, later this work was republished in part in an English translation entitled *The Problem of the Modern Salaried Employee: Its Theoretical and Statistical Basis*. By 1926, when Lederer in collaboration with Jakob Marschak published the essay that appears in this volume under the title "The New Middle Class" (Chapter 2), Germany had already suffered a major defeat in the First World War, had established the precariously democratic Weimar Republic, and was in the throes of such severe economic difficulties that the job and income security of many sectors of the new middle classes was threatened. "The New Middle Class" carefully analyzes the occupational, organizational, status, political and personal identity problems of the middle sectors of German society at a time when the rumblings of fascism were already being heard. For this reason their essay has acquired a classic status: Lederer and Marschak perceived in raw detail the political implications of middle-class occupational insecurities.

Val Burris's "The Discovery of the New Middle Classes" (Chapter 1) reviews and evaluates the entire spectrum of classical literature on the middle classes, including that of Marx, Karl Kautsky, Eduard Bernstein, Carl Dreyfuss, Theodor Geiger and others.[1] Burris also shows the genealogical connections between these earlier discoverers of the new middle classes and such later students of the subject as C. Wright Mills, Daniel Bell, Alvin Gouldner and James Burnham. Burris provides not only a summary of the literature on the new middle classes but also an estimation of that literature's most critical historical moment: the era of German national socialism and Hitler's rise to power.

The unabated preoccupation of much of modern social science with Hitler and the rise of fascism testifies to the unease that is still felt by many analysts about the stability of Western democratic institutions. Is a fascist political economy yet a possibility in modern mass democracies? If so, under what circumstances might it come into existence? What leaders, parties and classes would be most attracted to such a solution? In a period of severe economic dislocation (inflation, budgetary deficits, high unemployment and/ or an international banking and credit crisis) and great political instability (racial tensions, tariff wars, foreign competition and weak or directionless presidential leadership) could the constituencies of a Western democracy conclude that their society was ungovernable except by a totalitarian leader ruling without democratic checks, civil and political liberties, and procedural restraints on power?[2]

The justification for asking such questions is established in a major analysis by the late Hans Speier. Written by 1932 but not published for almost 50 years, Speier's book[3] (three chapters of which are included in this volume as Chapters 3, 6 and 7) examines and gives deeper sociological and political significance to the work of his predecessors and teachers, Lederer and Marschak, anticipates the work of C. Wright Mills, and is crucial for the continuing debates over the psychology and political orientations of the middle classes. Because Speier's book is not addressed in Burris's essay, I wish to point to its significance for this volume.

In spite of the fact that Speier wrote about the new German white-collar classes in 1932, his ideas have relevance for any contemporary discussion of the middle classes. His chapter, "Middle-Class Notions and Lower-Class Theory" (Chapter 3) presents a general empirical framework for understanding those social, status and economic factors that separate blue- from white-collar workers. Speier was the first to point

to the uneradicated differences between the social and psychological predispositions of the new middle classes and those
of blue-collar workers despite the effects of the 'proletarianization' of the former – a process that began in Germany
during the Weimar period and continued until January 1933,
when Hitler took office. He noted the persistence of autonomous and historical conceptions of prestige that were carried over into these new middle classes. In part, the autonomy
of the prestige factor was based on the acceptance by the
new middle classes of the status ideologies of the old middle
classes – the premodern bourgeoisie. Such status claims were
held onto by the new white-collar middle classes even after
white-collar work had been devalued by the mechanization
of office procedures and the emergence of nonegalitarian,
hierarchical, bureaucratic relations. Moreover these status
claims were held onto even in the face of the increasing
political power and concomitant prestige of Weimar's blue-
collar classes in Weimar Germany, due largely to their in-
corporation into the socialist trade-union movement. Speier
analyzes these new-middle-class prestige aspirations and their
concomitant status defensiveness as they manifested themselves in specific industries and occupations, providing what
are virtually ethnographic portraits of higher and lower administrators, foremen and workers, technicians and engineers,
sales clerks in large and small outlets, typists, secretaries,
bank tellers, mine inspectors, insurance officials and civil
servants, each at different levels of the respective hierarchies.
The analytical path provided by Speier's analysis served as a
model for later studies of the American middle classes by
C. Wright Mills, Joseph Bensman and myself, some of which
appear in this volume.

The substantive focus of Speier's book, like that of many
of the works reviewed by Burris, is on the new middle classes'
contribution to the rise of Hitler. Here he analyzes the various
professional and occupational associations to which the middle
classes belonged and through which they were organized,
noting especially the attitudes these organizations held toward the free, blue-collar trade unions. Speier points out
that the status defensiveness and nationalism of the new
middle classes contributed to the necessity of their acceptance of some limited trade-union goals; while at the same

time they remained primarily committed to gaining and maintaining political and economic privileges over the blue-collar classes. Of particular importance in this regard was the middle classes' strident opposition to the internationalism of workers' organizations and their vociferous affirmation of a *Volksgemeinschaft* nationalism. In the arena of education, conflicts between white- and blue-collar classes centered on the claims of white-collar workers to cultural superiority over blue-collar workers on the basis of the superiority of humanist over technical education. At the level of social, political and economic programs and public policies, middle-class occupational associations were connected to the various conservative, nationalist and traditional political parties, including the National Socialist Party and the conservative wing of the Social Democratic Party. In dealing with the ideological stances of specific occupational associations, as well as their claims to educational superiority, Speier came close to providing a complete description of the inner differences and complexities of these classes, an accomplishment that since that time has not been repeated anywhere in studies of the middle classes.[4]

Since the emergence of the new middle classes in Germany, observers have noted the enormous growth in this sector of the class structures of other Western democratic societies. The historical shift away from the radical bipolarization in class structure expected by many later Marxists is the subject of Chapter 4 of this volume; Anthony Giddens' "The Growth of the New Middle Class," shows that each of the histories of the new middle classes in Germany, France, England, Japan and the United States follow unique trajectories and are guided by each country's cultural, economic and political uniqueness. Yet in spite of such differences, nowhere does it appear that a "merging" of white- and blue-collar workers is taking place. Even where white-collar unionization has occurred, it does not "involve any major process of interpenetration of middle and working classes." With respect to the United States specifically, Giddens concludes that even within the so-called new middle class – proletarianized white-collar workers – there is no evidence of political radicalization or acceptance of status equality with blue-collar workers.

Part II of this volume, "The Status Sphere and the Psychology of Classes," focuses upon the relationship between status claims and the grounds upon which such claims can be made. In the essays by Hans H. Gerth and C. Wright Mills (Chapter 5) and Hans Speier (Chapters 6 and 7) is to be found a rejection of the idea that there exists a one-to-one relationship between social status and economic class. These sociologists examine the complex ways in which claims to social status are related to descent, race, education, occupation, politics and religion. They note that modern societies contain many hierarchies of prestige and that these hierarchies are subject to continuous change, resulting in an instability in the bases upon which such status claims are either made or recognized by others. Of special importance is the relationship between individual claims to prestige and the organizations with which individuals are affiliated. Prestigious organizations may lend status to their individual members, just as prestigious individuals may elevate the prestige of an organization by joining it. Such forms of borrowed status, however, may conceal or mask the actual economic status of those persons whose social prestige is enhanced by this process of borrowing. As Speier notes, such practices lead to multifarious forms of hidden class membership and result in the otherwise unexpected neutralizations of social and class conflicts.

In the final essay in Part II, "Economic Class, Status and Personality" (Chapter 8), Joseph Bensman and I analyze changing patterns in status structures as they relate to both changes in forms of capital and fluctuations of economic values, all of which tend to occur in inflationary and deflationary business cycles. Noting that such changes represent economic opportunities for some and economic losses for others, we describe three possible directions of movement for classes and individuals: up, down or stable. The essay illustrates how the social psychology and world views of classes and individuals are affected by economic change and suggests that, over longer periods of time, status claims and class psychologies are primarily determined by economic considerations.

Part III brings us to a consideration of the specific dimensions of the new and old American middle classes in the larger class and political systems of the United States. Our focus is upon the new middle classes and their political orientations, as described by C. Wright Mills and Arthur S. Evans, Jr in Chapters 9, 10 and 11. In Chapter 9 Mills, in work carried out in the 1950s, documents the shift from the dominance of the older middle classes to the growth of the new middle classes in the immediate post-Second-World War era. In Chapter 10 he attempts to discern the social and political directions likely to be taken by these new classes. His speculations are reminiscent of those of Lederer and Marschak and are also informed by those of Hans Speier. In Chapter 11 Arthur S. Evans, Jr provides us with a description and analysis of the old and the new black middle classes. Noting that the new black middle classes are a product of recently acquired occupational opportunities in white-collar administrative and bureaucratic organizations, Evans examines the implications and meaning of this for the political orientations of these new classes: in contrast with the older black middle classes, the new ones find themselves socially distanced from the black ghetto communities and in some cases ethnically estranged from their social and economic problems.

In Chapter 12 Bensman and I, writing more than 15 years after C. Wright Mills' seminal discussion of the subject, discuss the massive growth of the new middle classes in the 1950s and 1960s and the emergence of their brand of political liberalism, one based on economic advance, occupational success and class ascendancy. Our essay on the "Changes in the Life-styles of American Classes" examines the varieties of life-style created by the middle classes and points out the raw materials from which these styles were cut.

Our discussions of the new class system in the United States in Part IV includes an examination not only of the middle classes, but also of the upper, upper-middle, lower-middle, working and poverty classes. The politics and political psychology of the middle classes must, of course, always be seen in relation to the classes above and below them. Enacting a given life-style depends upon individual preferences and priorities and the economic wherewithal to support them. Increasingly the ability to support many of the life-styles associated with a given level of achievement is dependent upon political measures and social policies, all of which are legislated at the state and national levels of government. Class and political attitudes therefore are increasingly conditioned by legally defined sanctions and by the capacity of each of the respective classes to influence the political process to its own advantage – often enough at the expense of other groups or classes.

In "Liberalism and the New Middle Classes" written in 1968 for the second edition of *Small Town in Mass Society*, Bensman and I describe the political orientations of these newer middle classes in such settings as small rural hamlets, university towns, suburban communities and urban enclaves. It then appeared that the liberalism of these classes had become a dominant force in the country – as exemplified by the elections of John F. Kennedy and Lyndon Johnson and the weakening of the Republican Party. But with the beginnings of the economic recession in the 1970s the newer middle classes, by then middle aged, began to move in a conservative direction that we had not then anticipated. In our conclusion, however, we noted that an open conflict between the opposing orientations of the new middle classes and the older populist classes would "have to be avoided if the United States hopes to cope with its other problems." It now appears that that confrontation is taking place in the political arena over such issues as abortion, school prayer, pornography, sexual moralities and the very definition of Americanism.

Over the past 20 years, as the post-Second-World War new middle classes have aged they have also become more conservative. This turn away from the liberalism of the new middle classes in the 1960s is analyzed by Michael W. Hughey in his essay, "The New Conservatism: Political Ideology and Class Structure" (Chapter 15), which identifies the older economic and social values that the new middle classes have begun to absorb as their own. Hughey's essay captures the political mood of the 1980s as it was given form during the presidency of Ronald Reagan. A critical instance in this history of American politics occurred before the Reagan era: the Watergate scandal that culminated in the resignation of President Nixon in 1974. My essay, "The Politics of the Middle Class in a National Crisis: The Case of Watergate" (Chapter 16), analyzes the reactions of three strata – the older middle classes, the industrial and factory working classes and the new middle classes – to this political crisis. Threatening the legitimacy of government itself, these classes' reactions to Watergate were critical to Nixon's ability to retain the presidency in the face of scandal. The withdrawal of consent accorded to Nixon by the middle sectors during the Watergate period turned on such issues as political immorality, betrayal of trust and rejection of hard-headed political realism by the various sectors of the classes. This withdrawal of support by the middle classes led to Nixon's resignation, and it was their willing acceptance of an appointed president that led to the relegitimation of the government itself.

When the middle classes are the beneficiaries of economic prosperity and abundance, as they were during the Reagan presidency, their sense of buoyancy and self-satisfaction seems to express the dominant mood of society as a whole. Their political and social activism thus transcends that of their economic needs and turns in the direction of environmentalism, political corruption and immorality, and uplifting humanitarian causes. Published in 1980, "Class and Politics in an Epoch of Declining Abundance" (Chapter 17) draws a portrait of class responses to the shrinkage of economic opportunity. Its argument is applicable to the current economic situation in the United States. The prosperity of the 1980s, stimulated by President Reagan's deficit spending and vastly increased budgetary deficits, has come to haunt the United States in the 1990s: the recession of the early 1990s appears as a re-enactment on a larger scale of the recessions of the 1970s. This essay provides a portrait of the actual and possible reactions of the various classes to declines in America's historic abundance and to the increasing dependence of the American economy on an internationalized and more competitive world economy. Major political and social issues facing the middle classes in the 1990s focus on tax and welfare policies and threats to their employment in business, government, cultural and philanthropic institutions. The economic vulnerability of the white-collar administrative, clerical, bureaucratic and technically employed middle classes raises once again the question of how their electoral choices will shape the political agenda of their leaders. Should economic growth be precluded as a means to their political

cooptation, America's leaders will be under pressure to find
other more novel solutions to the problem of assuring their
political loyalty.

Notes

1. Full citations to Lederer's and Marschak's work are given in this essay.
2. See my foreword to Hans Speier, *German White Collar Workers and the Rise of Hitler* (New Haven: Yale University Press, 1985), p. xi, for a further discussion of these issues.
3. At the moment it should have gone to press in 1933, the Nazis came to power and his publication contract was cancelled. The book was first published in German under the title *Die Angestellen vor dem Nationalsozialismus: Ein Beitrag zum Verstandnis der deutschen Sozialstruktur 1918–1933* (1977) and later published in English translation as indicated in the preceding footnote.
4. Speier's method included the use of surveys conducted by occupational organizations and the analysis of pamphlets, broadsheets, journals, newspapers, books, and speeches by leaders and intellectuals. His use of secondary data and of 'unconventional' sources makes the book a methodological classic. Current studies of national socialism, such as that by Richard Hamilton (*Who Voted For Hitler,* Princeton University Press, 1982), concentrate on election statistics, but no matter how statistically refined these may be, they can only yield gross results because election districts include voters of different occupational and socio-economic statuses: distinctions by this method can only be made on the basis of gross economic characteristics.

Bibliographic Notes

Jurgen Kocka's *White Collar Workers in America 1890–1940: A Social – Political History in International Perspective* (Beverly Hills, CA: Sage Publications, 1980) provides a detailed and comprehensive history of the various sectors of white-collar workers in the United States, including sex and gender differences, earnings, union affiliations and political orientations. Studies of the American middle classes that appeared in the 1930s before C. Wright Mills' *White Collar* tend to reflect the more radical ethos of that decade: Lewis Cory, *The Crisis of the Middle Class* (New York: Lovici, Friede, 1935); Franklin Charles Palm, *The Middle Classes: Then and Now* (New York: Macmillan, 1936), which utilizes literary studies to capture the flavor of middle-class social psychologies. Loren Baritz's *The Good Life: The Meaning of Success for the American Middle Class* (New York: Alfred A. Knopf, 1989) is a history of the life-styles of earlier immigrant groups and the mobility strivings, successes and cultural values of the generations that followed them. E. Franklin Frazier's *Black Bourgeoisie*

(New York: W. W. Norton, 1950) captures the social psychology of the black middle classes before the civil rights movement when they were still socially and culturally segregated. Bart Landry, *The New Black Middle Class*, (Berkeley, CA: University of California Press, 1987) takes account of changes in the occupational and class psychology of a new generation of Afro-Americans. Except for the work of Ray Lewis and Angus Maude, *The English Middle Classes* (New York: Alfred A. Knopf, 1950), which celebrates the contribution of the middle classes to Anglo-Saxon civilization, middle-class studies by other English authors take their point of departure from Marx: Andrew Grant, *Socialism and the Middle Classes* (London: Lawrence and Wishart, 1958) and Roger King and John Raynor, *The Middle Class* (London: Longman, 1981, 2nd edn), Anthony Giddens, *The Class Structure of Advanced Societies* (New York: Harper Collins, 1973) retains a Marxian perspective by introducing the concept of "class awareness" as a replacement for Marx's "class consciousness."

Part 1

Emergence of the New Middle Classes: Theoretical Problems and Historical Changes

1 The Discovery of the New Middle Classes*

Val Burris

Few topics in political sociology have received as much attention as the nature and politics of the new middle class. Among Marxists the class position of salaried mental workers has been an issue of controversy for nearly a century. Concern with this question can be traced back at least as far as the revisionism debate of the 1890s. It was a major focus in Marxist analyses of fascism in the 1930s and today remains one of the most hotly debated issues within the Western socialist and communist parties. In non-Marxist circles the rise of the new middle class has inspired no less fascination. From the technocratic prophesies of Thorstein Veblen and James Burnham to the "new little man" of C. Wright Mills's *White Collar* to the post-industrial theories of Daniel Bell and Alvin Gouldner, each generation of social theorists has based its vision of the emerging social order on the rediscovery or reinterpretation of this class. In the words of one recent commentator, "an entire history of political sociology could be written on the theme of the new middle classes. Whether in the guise of the 'managerial revolution,' 'white collar,' the 'new working class,' or the 'new petite bourgeoisie,' the emergence of intermediate strata in advanced industrial societies has been rediscovered more often than the wheel."[1]

The reasons for this preoccupation with the new middle class are not hard to identify. As salaried professionals, most social theorists are themselves members of the new middle class. Their concern with this group is thus motivated by an interest in self-understanding, if not by an inflated sense of their own importance. Apart from this are reasons that derive from the distinctive characteristics of the new middle class.

* Reprinted from *Theory and Society*, vol. 15, pp. 317–49. (Dordrecht: Martinus Nijhoff Publishers, 1986).

Because of its heterogeneous composition, the new middle class poses the most difficult problems for the classification of persons according to their place within the social relations of capitalist production. Disagreements over the nature of the class structure have therefore focused on this stratum. On account of its intermediate location the new middle class is often the pivotal class in the formation of political alliances. It has therefore occupied an important place in the investigation of patterns of political alignment and cleavage. Finally, because of its increasing size relative to other classes, the new middle class lends itself to speculation about the transformation of the class structure. Critiques of earlier theories of class and projections of the future of class society have therefore placed the new middle class at the center of the analysis.

As is common in sociology, different theories of the new middle class have often served to bolster different political viewpoints. Social democrats in Weimar Germany cited the supposed lack of proletarian consciousness among white-collar employees as a justification for their reformism. In the United States during the same period, social critics like Veblen used the purported frustrations of salaried technicians to advance a populist attack on big business. From the 1930s onward Marxist explanations of fascism as a panic reaction of the lower middle class served to deflect attention from the strategic failures of working-class parties. Mainstream sociologists used similar theories to absolve capitalists of any responsibility for fascism. Theories of "managerial revolution," developed during and after the Second World War, reflected different political reactions to the expansion of large-scale state and corporate bureaucracies. Conservatives depicted the rise of a new managerial class as a totalitarian threat from which capitalism must be saved; liberals welcomed it as the initiator of a new era of class harmony and corporate responsibility. In American sociology of the 1950s the growth of an affluent new middle class was celebrated as a sign of the "end of ideology" and an assurance of the permanent stability of capitalist institutions. New Left theorists of the 1960s reinterpreted these intermediate strata as a "new working class" in order to account for (and further) the unanticipated revival of political radicalism. Since the 1970s the efforts of European socialist and communist parties to establish new forms of political alliance have prompted renewed debates among Marxists in which opposing views of political strategy have been expressed as disagreements over the proper conceptualization of these intermediate classes.[2]

In this article I examine some of the earliest theories of the new middle class – namely, those that originated in Germany prior to 1933 and were transplanted to the United States following the rise of fascism. These early writings on the new middle class are interesting today for several reasons. By their sheer volume they constitute one of the most extensive bodies of literature on social class yet produced. As the first studies in this area, they have also been influential in establishing the basic directions later theorists would follow. Indeed, Mills's statement in 1951 that "the range of theory had been fairly well laid out by the middle 'twenties, and nothing really new has since been added" is almost as true today as it was thirty years ago.[3] Finally, because of their origins during a period of crisis and their close connection to strategic debates taking place within the German Social Democratic Party, these early writings provide a clearer focus on the political implications of the new middle class than many subsequent accounts.

This political dimension of class theory provides the main focus for the present article. In the pages that follow I seek to do three things. First, I attempt to clarify the historical circumstances in which various theories of the new middle class originated. Second, I aim to evaluate these theories on the basis of the most recent empirical evidence. Third, and most important, I seek to elucidate the political motives and interests that have shaped (and sometimes distorted) the development of theory in this area.

As the range of theories covered is rather broad, it is helpful to begin with a brief summary of the different theories to be examined and the general nature of my argument. Because most of the early theories of the new middle class were intended as revisions or refutations of Marxism, I begin with a short discussion of Marx's views on intermediate classes. This is followed by a discussion of the pre-1933 German debates over the class position of salaried employees. The main protagonists in these debates were the "orthodox"

Marxists, who viewed all white-collar employees as proletarian and therefore potentially revolutionary, and the "revisionists," who viewed all white-collar employees as middle class and therefore resistant to revolutionary appeals. Reviewing the empirical evidence, I conclude that neither of these theories provided a very accurate account of class alignments in Weimar Germany. As a group, white-collar employees were sharply divided in their relation to the proletarian movement, casting doubt on the assumption that all such employees should be considered members of a single class or class fraction. Examining the political context of these debates, I speculate as to the factors that prevented either side from developing a more differentiated analysis. In the following sections I discuss the theories of the new middle class that were prompted by the rise of fascism – in particular, theories that identified lower white-collar employees as a leading force in fascist movements. Reviewing the available evidence, I conclude that these theories were also largely unsubstantiated. While fascist movements drew considerable support from certain intermediate strata, the lower ranks of white-collar employees were not among these. Here again I speculate as to the political factors that encouraged the acceptance of such theories despite their lack of empirical support. In the concluding section I examine the continuing influence of these classical theories of the new middle class and discuss the implications of my analysis for contemporary debates over the nature of the class structure.

MARX AND THE NEW MIDDLE CLASS

The most common reading of Marx attributes to him a simplistic theory of class polarization in which the disappearance of the old middle class (the petty bourgeoisie) prepares the way for a direct and final confrontation between the two remaining classes: the proletariat and the bourgeoisie. According to this interpretation, Marx totally ignored the emergence of a salaried or new middle class.

Despite the frequency with which these views are attributed to Marx, it is doubtful whether he ever held such a conception of the class structure. As evidence for the simple polarization thesis, commentators typically point to selected passages in the *Communist Manifesto* in which Marx and Engels speak of the increasing division of bourgeois society into "two great hostile camps, into two great classes directly facing one another: bourgeoisie and proletariat." The specific passage that seems to provide the strongest support for this view comes where Marx and Engels describe the decline of the petty bourgeoisie.

> The previously existing small intermediate strata – the small industrials, merchants and rentiers, the artisans and peasants – all these classes sink down into the proletariat, partly because their small capital does not suffice for the carrying on of large-scale industry and succumbs in competition with the larger capitalists, partly because their skill is rendered worthless by new methods of production. Thus the proletariat is recruited from all classes of the population.[4]

Just a few pages later, however, Marx and Engels acknowledge not only a counter-tendency toward the continual renewal of small-property ownership, but also the replacement of petty-bourgeois intermediaries by intermediate groups of another kind: the growing number of salaried managers, overseers, and other capitalist functionaries.

> In the countries where modern civilization developed, a new petty bourgeoisie was formed, which hovers between the proletariat and the bourgeoisie and continually renews itself as a supplementary part of bourgeois society. The members of this class, however, are being constantly hurled down into the proletariat by the action of competition; indeed, with the development of large-scale industry they even see a time approaching when they will be replaced, in commerce, manufacturing and agriculture, by labor overseers and stewards.[5]

The historical growth of these salaried intermediaries is discussed at greater length in Marx's later writings – leading some to argue that Marx was actually an advocate, if not the originator, of the concept of a "new middle class."[6] This interpretation, while closer to the truth, is also something of an oversimplification. Admittedly there are passages in which Marx used the term "class" or "middle class" when speaking of salaried intermediate groups. In *Theories of Surplus Value*, for example, Marx argued that the displacement of workers by machinery not only opened new areas for productive employment in other branches of industry (as Ricardo had maintained), but also enabled capitalists to hire increased numbers of unproductive employees, which Marx referred to as "middle classes."

> What he [Ricardo] forgets to emphasize is the constantly growing number of the middle classes, those who stand between the workman on the one hand and the capitalist on the other. The middle classes maintain themselves to an ever increasing extent directly out of revenue; they are a burden weighing heavily on the working base and increase the social security and power of the upper ten thousand.[7]

Marx included in this "middle class" category "the horde of flunkeys, the soldiers, sailors, police, lower officials and so on, mistresses, grooms, clowns and jugglers," as well as "ill-paid artists, musicians, lawyers, physicians, scholars, schoolmasters, inventors, etc."[8] That Marx addressed these disparate groups as "middle classes," however, should not be taken to mean that he attributed to them the same economic and political significance that he ordinarily implied by the term "class." Despite his obvious awareness of these sectors, and his belief in their likely expansion, at no place in his writings did Marx attempt to incorporate them within his general model of capitalist society as a class on a par with the proletariat or the bourgeoisie.

Marx's reasoning on this point would no doubt have been clarified in the famous unfinished chapter on "Classes" that concluded the third volume of *Capital*. It was precisely this problem, in fact, that Marx was beginning to address at the point where the manuscript breaks off. Marx noted that even in England, where capitalism achieved its highest state of development, "the stratification of classes does not appear in its pure form. Middle and intermediate strata even here obliterate lines of demarcation everywhere."[9] Nevertheless Marx affirmed that there were three distinct groups – wage-laborers, capitalists, and landlords – that constituted the three major classes in capitalist society. "What constitutes a class?"

Marx then asked. "What makes wage-laborers, capitalists and landlords the three great social classes?"

> At first glance – the identity of revenues and sources of revenue. There are three great social groups whose members, the individuals forming them, live on wages, profit and ground-rent respectively, on the realization of their labor-power, their capital, and their landed property. However, from this standpoint, physicians and officials, e.g., would also constitute two classes, for they belong to two distinct social groups, the members of each of these groups receiving their revenue from one and the same source. The same would also be true of the infinite fragmentation of interest and rank into which the division of social labor splits laborers as well as capitalists and landlords – the latter, e.g., into owners of vineyards, farm owners, mine owners and owners of fisheries.[10]

Here the manuscript ends without Marx explaining why physicians and officials – or, more generally, professionals, civil servants, and similar groups – should not be considered as an intermediate "class" between the proletariat and the bourgeoisie. From the arguments of preceding chapters, however, we can surmise the general line of Marx's reasoning. In the previous chapter Marx distinguishes between production relations and distribution relations and argues that it is the former that uniquely determine the character of a given society. In bourgeois society, the capitalist and the wage-laborer are the "personification" of the dominant production relations. It is for this reason, according to Marx, that they embody objective contradictions that drive capitalist society forward.[11] As a tool for historical analysis, classes are therefore defined from the standpoint of their position within the social relations of production of a given mode of production. This was the criterion, presumably, by which Marx rejected the concept of a salaried middle "class." As categories of unproductive laborers, such groups as professionals and civil servants are alike only in the limited sense that they are all supported out of capitalist revenue – a relation of distribution rather than one of production. From the standpoint of the mode of production they have no common place or function. In Marx's view, therefore, they are not compelled by systemic forces to organize around distinctive economic interests; they lack the objective basis for solidarity and social unity. For these reasons they do not constitute a "class" in the strict sense of the term, but merely a heterogeneous grouping of intermediate strata.

Exactly which wage and salary employees Marx would have classified as belonging to such an intermediate stratum and which he would have classified as part of the working class is a question he never adequately addressed. As a first approximation, Marx identified the proletariat with productive labor – i.e., with labor hired by capitalists for a wage and producing surplus value in the process of commodity production. There are numerous passages, however, where Marx admitted that a strict application of the productive/unproductive distinction was inadequate to define the boundaries of the proletariat. On the one hand, not all unproductive workers are necessarily excluded from the working class. Commercial employees, for example, although unproductive, were considered by Marx to occupy positions equivalent in all important respects to those of other wage-laborers.

> The commercial worker produces no surplus value directly. But the price of his labor is determined by the value of his labor-power, hence by its costs of production, while the application of this labor-power, its exertion, expenditure of energy, and wear and tear, is as in the case of every other wage-laborer by no means limited by its value . . . He creates no direct surplus-value, but he adds to the capitalist's income by helping him to reduce the cost of realizing surplus-value, inasmuch as he performs partly unpaid labor. The commercial worker, in the strict sense of the term, belongs to the better-paid class of wage-workers.[12]

On the other hand, not all productive workers are unambiguously members of the proletariat. Marx interpreted the category of productive labor broadly to include "all those who contribute in one way or another to the production of the commodity, from the actual operative to the manager or engineer."[13] The latter, however, stand in an uncertain relation to the majority of wage-laborers. The labor of supervision, for example, is both productive and unproductive. In *Capital* Marx distinguished between two aspects of supervision: that "made necessary by the cooperative character of the labor process" and "the different work of control, necessitated by the capitalist character of that process and the antagonism of interests between the capitalist and laborer."[14] Salaried managers and supervisors, insofar as they perform coordinating functions of the first type, are simply "a special kind of wage-laborer." However, to the degree that they also enforce the expropriation of surplus-value, they stand in an antagonistic relation to other workers as the direct agents of capitalist domination over the labor process.

The same ambiguity applies to engineers. Marx noted that not only the relations of cooperation, but the forces of science and technology are "capitalized," i.e., they appear as a form of development of capital and thus as a means for the exploitation of labor. The labor of science, once it is separated from the skill and knowledge of the immediate producers and incorporated in the capitalist, his machinery, and his "intellectual understrappers," confronts the workers "as something *alien* . . . existing without their intervention, and frequently hostile to them."[15] Engineers are thus, at one and the same time, both productive workers and the bearers of capitalist relations of domination. They are part worker and part capitalist. Like salaried managers, they appear to occupy an intermediate position between the proletariat and the bourgeoisie, although nowhere does Marx provide a detailed analysis of the precise nature or significance of this intermediate location.

Marx had little to say about the politics of salaried intermediate strata; however, his occasional comments regarding these groups suggests that he attributed to them a pattern of contradictory political tendencies similar to that of the petty bourgeoisie. As propertyless employees they experience conditions of economic dependency not unlike those confronting the working class. For this reason they can be expected to identify with certain aspects of proletarian ideology. On the other hand, as servants of the bourgeoisie, they are inclined to identify with their masters and look down upon the working class. The fact that they are paid out of capitalist revenue, and therefore dependent for their livelihood on the existence of a high level of profits, may also lead them to side with the bourgeoisie.[16] Like the traditional petty

bourgeoisie, they are thus pulled in contradictory directions. Nothing definitive can be inferred about their political orientation other than it is likely to be varied and
changeable.

THE SALARIED EMPLOYEE IN WEIMAR GERMANY

If Marx avoided any rigid definition of class boundaries or
iron-clad pronouncements about the politics of intermediate strata, his immediate followers were inclined toward more
categorical formulations. In the latter part of the nineteenth
century, two alternative interpretations of Marxist theory competed for authority – each of which presented a more sharply
defined view of class relations. The first, which was already
prevalent in Marx's time, identified *industrial* wage-earners
as the exclusive base of the socialist movement. Relative to
this industrial proletariat, all other classes and strata were
viewed as "a single reactionary mass." In his *Critique of the
Gotha Program* Marx rejected this formula as being either a
prescription for defeat (because it unduly restricted the
potential base for socialism) or a license for opportunism
(because it made no distinction between the more progressive
and more reactionary of potential allies).[17] These views were
nevertheless incorporated in the 1875 program of the German Social Democratic Party, because they corresponded
to the organizational needs of a fledgling movement that
based its initial appeal more on its proletarian form than
on its socialist content.

The second interpretation proposed a much broader conception of the working class. As socialist parties moved toward
a more exclusive reliance on electoral tactics, the doctrine
of socialism as a movement by and for a narrowly defined
industrial proletariat became an increasing liability. Rather
than abandoning their proletarian identification, the more
orthodox parties sought to correct this problem by simply
expanding their definition of the proletariat. The 1891 Erfurt
Program of the German SPD provides the classic illustration
of this tendency. It is here, rather than in the writings of
Marx, that we first encounter the simple polarization view
of class structure. The proletariat, defined as all who work

for a wage or salary, is described as the overwhelming majority of society. "In all countries the mass of the population has sunk to the level of the proletariat . . . The condition of the proletariat [tends] to become more and more that of the whole population."[18] The few remaining small-business owners and farmers are dismissed as a "disappearing middle class" whose "days of independent production are numbered."[19] Over against the proletariat we find only "a small group of property holders – capitalists and landlords" – the last remaining defenders of the established economic order. These formulations allowed the SPD to retain a rhetorical identification with the proletariat while presenting itself as the legitimate representative of all but a small minority of the population. By combining this expanded definition of the proletariat with a deterministic conception of the "laws" of capitalist development, the party affirmed the inevitable polarization of class society and the imminent victory of socialism.

The concept of a "new middle class" originated in opposition to the official Marxist theories of this period. The term was first popularized by anti-Marxist theorists of the 1890s as a designation for the increasing number of civil servants, technical employees, supervisors, and office and sales personnel. Gustav Schmoller, the founder of German academic socialism (*Kathedersozialismus*), was one of the first to designate these salaried employees as a "new middle class." Standing Marxism on its head, Schmoller saw this new middle class, rather than the downtrodden proletariat, as the embryo of a future ruling class that would embody the general interests of society.[20] Other theorists held more modest expectations for the new middle class. Although it might not rise to independent power, the new middle class would become an important stabilizing force in the overall balance of social classes. In opposition to Marxism, the advocates of this view preferred to see society as an organism in equilibrium in which the new middle class, together with the old middle class (the petty bourgeoisie), played the role of mediator between the opposing interests of capital and labor. The rise of the new middle class, by compensating for the decline of the old, was to put an end to the instability of capitalist society.

Social-democratic leaders were divided in their response

to these theories. The dominant tendency within the party vigorously opposed the concept of a "new middle class." Reaffirming the orthodox Marxist viewpoint, they continued to speak of salaried employees as part of the proletariat, often referring to them as a "stiff-collar proletariat" (*Stehkragenproletariat*). Pointing to the increasing oversupply of educated labor and the progressive rationalization of commercial and clerical occupations, Karl Kautsky predicted that "the time is near when the bulk of these proletarians will be distinguished from the others only by their pretensions."[21] He did not fail to notice that the class awareness of these "proletarians" often lagged behind their objective condition. "Most of them still imagine that they are something better than proletarians. They fancy they belong to the bourgeoisie, just as the lackey identifies himself with the class of his master."[22] Nevertheless, because their material situation was becoming more homogeneous with that of the proletariat, their eventual union with the proletarian movement would follow as a matter of course.

> As much as they cling to bourgeois appearances, the time will come for every one of the proletarianized strata of the white-collar groups at which they discover their proletarian heart. Then they will take an interest in the proletarian class struggle and finally they will participate in it actively.[23]

A second group within the party was more receptive to the concept of a new middle class. The advocates of this "revisionist" view had never accepted the orthodox theory of class polarization or the proletarian strategy that was based on that theory. They denied that the middle class was disappearing and maintained that socialism could succeed only if it abandoned its identification with the proletariat and redefined itself as a multi-class movement appealing to universal ethical principles. Eduard Bernstein, the leader of the revisionists, was one of the most outspoken critics of the theory of class polarization. According to Bernstein:

> Far from society being simplified as to its divisions compared with earlier times, it has been further gradated and differentiated both in respect of incomes and of economic

activities. . . . If the collapse of modern society depends on the disappearance of the middle ranks between the apex and the base of the social pyramid, if it is dependent upon the absorption of these middle classes by the extremes above and below them, then its realization is no nearer . . . today than at any earlier time in the nineteenth century.[24]

In modern capitalism, Bernstein argued, the petty bourgeoisie was not a disappearing class, but one that "increased both relatively and absolutely."[25] As for salaried employees, Bernstein stopped short of labeling these groups as a separate "new middle class," but he also denied that they were being reduced to a common level with other wage-earners. In Bernstein's view, the increasing number and variety of white-collar employees reflected a more general tendency toward the internal differentiation and economic improvement of the working class as a whole.[26] From this he concluded the unlikelihood of class polarization leading to a revolutionary rupture and therefore advocated a gradualist strategy of social reform.

Other revisionists went beyond Bernstein by explicitly excluding salaried employees from the ranks of the proletariat. One of the first social-democratic theorists to argue for the non-proletarian status of salaried employees was Emil Lederer, editor of the influential *Archiv für Sozialwissenschaft und Sozialpolitik.* In a work published in 1912, Lederer argued that the orthodox Marxist interpretation "oversimplifies the stratification of the classes. The formula 'capitalist-proletarian' blurs all contrasts within the economic order and thus obscures all distinctions outside of and within the process of production."[27] According to Lederer, salaried employees – specifically, salaried technicians and commercial employees – should be classified as occupying "a middle position between the two classes." This intermediate position was defined less by any specific economic or technical characteristic than by its distinctive social *status.*

The grouping of . . . technical and commercial employees under the heading of "salaried employees" is traceable to the analogous social positions which at least the great majority of each group occupies. In neither of these groups is social esteem, which determines their peculiar position, based upon the nature of their technical or economic work; on the contrary, their social valuation is chiefly decided by their relationship to the important classes, the employers and laborers. This middle position between the two classes – a negative characteristic – rather than definite technical functions, is the social mark of the salaried employees and establishes their social character in their own consciousness and in the estimation of the community.[28]

Lederer documented the important changes taking place in the German class structure. Contrary to Bernstein's expectations, he showed a continuing decline in the proportion of independent entrepreneurs: from 28 percent of the economically active population in 1882 to less than 20 percent in 1907. The proportion of manual wage-earners increased only slightly during this period. Thus the decline in the old middle class was compensated primarily by an increase in the number of salaried employees. From 1.8 percent of the workforce in 1882, their ranks increased to 6.7 percent in 1907. In Lederer's opinion, similarities of economic interest inclined these employees toward some form of alliance with the working class; however, their distinctive social status precluded any identification with proletarian ideology. The implicit political message was clear: the socialist movement could appeal to these employees only if it played down its proletarian character.

The economic impact of the First World War gave additional impetus to the growth of the new middle class. The war economy accentuated tendencies toward economic concentration and bureaucratization, expanding the ranks of salaried employees. By 1925, the year of the first postwar census, the number of salaried employees had increased to about 10.9 percent of the employed population.[29] The same conditions that brought into being increasing numbers of salaried employees, however, also tended to lower their standing on the social and economic scale. The widespread unemployment at the beginning of the war brought home to salaried employees the insecurity of their market situation. The temporary economic stagnation that followed the outbreak of war also led to salary cuts for many employees.

Salaries increased once again during the course of the war, but far less than the rise in wages and prices. By the end of the war many salaried employees were earning considerably less than skilled workers.[30]

The economic decline of salaried employees during and after the First World War caused Lederer to reverse his earlier position. In an article on "The New Middle Class," written in 1926 with Jacob Marschak, he rejected the possibility of an intermediate position "between the classes."

> The great majority of salaried employees have come to recognize the fundamental incompatibility between capital and labor, between employer and employee, but they are in no position to bridge this gap; they cannot stand between the two warring classes, and must therefore choose that side which best serves their interests.[31]

Postwar changes in the organizational and political behavior of salaried employees seemed to confirm the orthodox Marxist predictions. Membership in white-collar unions increased four-fold between 1917 and 1923. Collective bargaining, previously rejected by employees as inappropriate to their standing, became the norm after the war. White-collar employees engaged for the first time in strikes and participated in workers' councils alongside manual workers. The adoption by salaried employees of the aims and methods of organized labor convinced Lederer and Marschak that "a single stratum of all gainfully employed (if not a single organization) was in the process of formation."[32]

By the time Lederer and Marschak's article appeared, however, the pendulum had already begun to swing in the other direction. The defeats suffered by the socialist movement during the crisis of 1923 marked the turning point in the development of a unified working class. Although the economic position of salaried employees continued to decline throughout the 1920s, the anticipated fusion of wage and salary workers did not materialize. With the "return to normalcy," salaried employees who had joined socialist trade unions after the war began to shift their allegiance to the more conservative employee associations. The socialist *Allgemeine freie Angestelltenbund*, the largest employee federation in 1923, lost almost 30 per cent of its members by the end of the decade, while the conservative *Gesamtverband Deutscher Angestelltengewerkschaften* grew to become the largest and most powerful white-collar association.[33]

This rightward shift in the politics of salaried employees gave new credence to the concept of a "new middle class." By the mid-1920s few theorists thought that such a concept could be defended on the basis of the economic condition of salaried employees. Instead, following Lederer's original formulation, they sought to conceptualize the distinctiveness of white-collar employees in terms of their peculiar social *status*. Otto Suhr documented the distinctive "life-style" of salaried employees – exemplified in their white-collar mode of dress and unique consumer habits.[34] Fritz Croner described the powerful hold of occupational ideologies that were based less on the objective position of salaried employees than on romantic analogies with the similar tasks once performed by independent enterprisers.[35] Hans Speier pointed to the special status salaried employees derived from their greater contact with employers and the conservatizing effects of their physical isolation from other workers.[36] In one of the most insightful studies of the conditions of white-collar employment, Carl Dreyfuss emphasized the status consciousness created in salaried employees by the artificial differentiation of the rank order in bureaucratic enterprises.

> Employees in various occupations and in different social positions, such as bank clerk, salesgirl, traveling salesman, stenographer and manager, seem at first glance to have authority and responsibility in the artificial economic pyramid. All are swayed by a great many false conceptions as to their positions and functions in the process of distribution and by illusions as to the importance of their particular work and their social status in general. We have seen how little these employees differ from laborers in their economic and social position and in their activities, but what greater possibilities their occupation offers for the formation of ideologies, and to what extent this situation is taken advantage of by the employer in the exercise of ideological influences. Although the various grades of the business setup are sham and only a few occupations are unaffected by the extensive process of mechan-

ization and standardization, nevertheless, in the consciousness of the majority of employees, their activity and position, in other words their occupation, appears to
differentiate them fundamentally from the worker.[37]

In this manner there developed the notion that white-collar
employees occupied conflicting positions on two different
dimensions of social stratification. In economic terms they
were indistinguishable from the proletariat. In terms of social
status they formed a separate group. The question of whether
salaried employees belonged to the proletariat or the middle
class thus came to be understood as a question of the relative importance of economic relations versus status relations
in the determination of political consciousness.[38]

During the last years of the Weimar Republic a fierce debate
raged in socialist circles on this issue. Revisionist theorists
viewed the status preferences of salaried employees as un-
alterable and proposed to modify the party program. The
party should accept the non-proletarian aspirations of these
workers and commit itself to the defense of their special
interests. Orthodox theorists continued to regard the status
preferences of salaried employees as a transitory phenomenon. Sooner or later material interests would prevail over
ideology; class consciousness would replace status consciousness as the basis for political action. The party, they argued,
should encourage this "inevitable" process by holding firm to
its proletarian line.

These debates were given a special urgency by the economic crash of 1929 and the rise of National Socialism.
Between 1928 and 1930 Nazis increased their vote from
2.6 percent to 18.3 percent of the electorate, making them
the largest political party after the Social Democrats. Theodore
Geiger, who by the early 1930s was one of the leading advocates of the revisionist position, interpreted the rise of fascism as a panic reaction of the economically endangered
middle strata – including the lower levels of salaried employees. In an influential article on "Panic in the Middle
Class," he argued that the proletarianization of the middle
strata, rather than leading to their alliance with workers,
was having just the opposite effect.[39] The more the socioeconomic differences between themselves and manual workers

diminished, the more actively white-collar employees struggled to preserve their status differences. Fearful of the loss of status, but incapable of organizing economically to defend their interests, these middle strata were especially susceptible to the appeals of fascism. The success of the Nazis, Geiger maintained, was in part the result of the failure of the Social Democrats to reformulate their ideology and political style.[40] Appealing to salaried employees to acknowledge their proletarianization only heightened their status anxiety. Greater moderation was called for in order to avoid driving the middle strata into the arms of reaction.

SOCIAL DEMOCRACY AND CLASS THEORY

Two opposing theories of class structure thus emerged out of the debates of the Weimar period. According to orthodox Marxists, the proletariat consisted of all (or nearly all) of those who worked for a wage or salary. According to the revisionists, the proletariat was restricted to manual wage-earners, while white-collar employees at all levels belonged to the middle class. Although the evidence is sketchy, it does not appear that either of these theories provided a very accurate account of class alignments in Weimar Germany. Orthodox theorists were probably correct to classify at least the lower levels of salaried employees as members of the working class, but their reasons for this classification and the conclusions they derived from it were highly misleading. By positing nonownership of the means of production as a sufficient criterion of proletarian status, orthodox theorists eschewed any attempt to develop a more detailed analysis of the social relations of capitalist production. In a typically economistic fashion, orthodox Marxists also assumed an automatic correspondence between membership in the proletariat as an economic category and the adoption of a class-conscious proletarian politics. Their analysis denied any independent role for political and ideological struggle in the process of class formation.[41] Most importantly, the theory and ideology of the SPD leadership were totally at odds with the nature of their political practice. While posing as representatives of the common interests of all workers in the establishment of socialism, the party actually functioned as an interest group *within capitalism* for the relative advancement of a particular sector of the proletariat: unionized industrial workers.[42] In the pronouncements of socialist leaders, white-collar employees were as often a target of derision as the object of appeals to proletarian unity.[43] Given the SPD's indifference (if not hostility) to the immediate interests of white-collar workers and the declining credibility of their commitment to a socialist alternative, it is not surprising that, once the revolutionary hopes of the immediate postwar period began to fade, salaried employees also sought to organize themselves on an interest-group basis for the defense of their relative economic standing. The fact that many white-collar workers joined non-socialist employee associations is probably less an indication of their opposition to socialism than a reflection of the greater militancy with which these associations defended the immediate economic interests of white-collar employees.[44]

Revisionist theorists presented a more sophisticated analysis of the social position of salaried employees. Their innovative studies of authority structures, occupational ideologies, and cultural patterns constituted a definite advance over the crude assertions of orthodox Marxists. Nevertheless, the basic thesis of the revisionists – that status distinctions prevented white-collar employees from identifying with the proletariat – was as much of an oversimplification as the orthodox assertion that the lack of property ownership insured the development of proletarian consciousness. While orthodox theorists exaggerated and oversimplified the influence of economic factors, revisionists were too quick to reify the ideological differences between manual and non-manual employees into a fixed and qualitative class division. In fact, the status differentials from which they deduced the greater conservatism of salaried employees – consumption patterns, position within the bureaucratic rank order, paternalistic contact with employers, isolation from other workers – cut across the basic manual/non-manual division as much as they were aligned with it. By these criteria, the higher ranks of salaried employees were at least as different from the lower ranks of white-collar workers as the latter were from the average manual worker. The political conclusions that revisionists derived from their theories were also inconsistent with the actual pattern of political events in Weimar Germany. The militant posture of the socialist movement in the years between 1918 and 1923 did not drive salaried employees into the arms of reaction. On the contrary, it polarized large numbers of them toward the side of the working class.[45] It was only with the defeat of the German Revolution, the break-up of the workers' councils and the adoption of a more defensive posture on the part of the SPD that salaried employees began to drift away from the socialist movement.

What was obscured by both the orthodox and revisionist theories was the significant cleavage within the ranks of salaried employees. Judging from the available evidence, salaried employees as a group did not identify with either the proletariat or the bourgeoisie, but divided down the middle. The higher level of salaried employees (professionals, managers, engineers, higher civil servants) generally opposed the goals of social democracy. It is significant that during the heightened polarization of the early 1920s these strata moved rapidly to the right while other salaried employees moved to the left.[46] The politics of routine white-collar employees were much closer to those of manual workers, even though they were separated from the latter by a combination of status pretensions and organizational antagonisms. These divisions were not sufficient to prevent routine white-collar workers from identifying with the proletariat during periods of political polarization. Between 1918 and 1923 over 40 percent of white-collar employees (at all levels) were organized into socialist trade unions.[47] Approximately 40 percent of urban white-collar employees continued to vote for socialist or communist parties until the end of the decade.[48] During less revolutionary periods, however, the weakening of the socialist movement, together with the revival of interest-group competition, served to heighten sectional differences within the proletariat, including the division between manual and non-manual workers.

Orthodox theorists thus exaggerated the size of the proletariat and underestimated its political and ideological divisions, while revisionist theorists minimized the size of the proletariat by reinterpreting status differences as class divisions. Although opposite from one another, these two tendencies derived from a common source: the internal tension within social democracy between its revolutionary theory and its reformist practice. Both subordinated questions of class struggle so as to redefine socialism as a *national* rather than a *class* movement. Orthodox theorists did this surrepetitiously by expanding the category of the proletariat to include virtually the whole of society. There are places where Kautsky even goes so far as to include within the proletariat "the majority of the farmers, small producers and traders" on the grounds that "the little property they still possess today is but a thin veil, calculated rather to conceal than to prevent their dependence and exploitation."[49] While the commitment to class struggle was retained in theory, the meaning of this commitment was obscured when upwards of 99 percent of the population was defined as proletarians. Recognizing the inconsistency of this position, revisionists called for a more open break with the theory of class struggle. They responded to the logic of the orthodox argument by seeking to demonstrate the minority status of the proletariat. Their inflated conceptions of the new middle class were motivated by their desire to show that social democracy could succeed only if it renounced its identification with the working class.

FASCISM AND THE LOWER MIDDLE CLASS

On 30 January 1933, Adolf Hitler became Chancellor of the German Reich. A month later the Reichstag fire provided the excuse for the invocation of emergency powers. By the summer of the following year the German parliament had been abolished, opposing political parties dissolved, trade unions and other democratic organizations smashed, and power firmly concentrated in a totalitarian one-party state. The rise of fascism in Germany had an important influence on the development of sociological conceptions of the new middle class. Geiger's article on "Panic in the Middle Class" anticipated what would become one of the most popular theories of fascism. According to this view, it was the middle class – particularly the "marginal" or "lower" middle class –

that constituted the social base of fascism. In this interpretation, fascism represented a reactionary protest of intermediate strata that were threatened by the expansion of
capitalist industry on the one side and the rising power of
the working class on the other. Combining a populist attack on big business with a hostility to organized labor, fascism presented itself as a third alternative to capitalism or
socialism, which promised to protect the position of the
middle classes through the establishment of an all-powerful
corporatist state.

This interpretation of fascism was actually first suggested
in the Italian case by Luigi Salvatorelli in the early 1920s.
"Fascism," Salvatorelli asserted, "reflected the class struggle
of the petty bourgeoisie that was wedged between capital
and the proletariat as a third combatant between two
others."[50] In the early 1930s, social democratic theorists like
Geiger adapted this theory to account for German fascism.
National Socialism, they argued, was an autonomous movement of the old and the new middle classes. These constituted an independent "third force," opposed to both capital
and labor. After 1933 this became the accepted social-democratic theory of Nazism and laid the basis for the interpretation of fascism in power as the "dictatorship of the
petty bourgeoisie."[51]

Communist theorists of the Third International also stressed
the middle-class nature of fascist movements, although they
rejected any suggestion that the petty bourgeoisie was capable
of acting as an autonomous political force – much less of
exercising a dictatorship over the proletariat and the bourgeoisie. According to the official Comintern theory, ex-
pounded by Georgi Dimitrov at the Seventh Congress in
1935, fascism in power represented "the most reactionary,
most chauvinist and most imperialist elements of finance
capital."[52] The middle classes, although they provided the
primary recruitment base of fascist movements, were viewed
as little more than the paid mercenaries of the bourgeoisie
and the large landowners. Individual communist theorists,
however, attributed a greater significance to the middle classes
in the rise of fascism. Antonio Gramsci and Clara Zetkin
both argued that fascism originated as a partly autonomous
mass movement of the petty bourgeoisie and cautioned against

the Comintern's propensity to reduce fascism to a simple capitalist conspiracy.[53] Leon Trotsky also emphasized the decisive role of the petty bourgeoisie in the genesis of fascism, although he granted that fascist movements came into power only through the support of the bourgeoisie and, once in power, represented the dictatorship of monopoly capital rather than that of the middle classes.[54]

Perhaps the best-known Marxist account of the rise of fascism was that presented by the French Trotskyist, Daniel Guerin, in his 1936 study, *Fascism and Big Business.* Guerin placed the major blame for fascism on the treachery of the bourgeoisie; however, he also argued that fascism would have been impossible if it had not had a genuine base of support among the discontented middle classes. Guerin explicitly included white-collar employees as part of the social base of fascism.

> The "white-collar proletarian," whose employer has imbued him with "a false feeling of bourgeois respectability," is likewise hostile to the industrial workers. He envies them for earning more than he, and tries at the same time to differentiate himself from them by every means. He does not understand why proletarian socialism speaks of destroying classes; he trembles for his illusory class privileges. Wishing to escape at any price from the proletarianization that lies in wait for him, he has scarcely any sympathy for a socialist regime which, according to him, would complete his proletarianization. He is ready, on the other hand, to listen to those who promise to save him from that fate.[55]

According to Guerin, these salaried employees, together with the urban and the rural petty bourgeoisie, provided "the backbone of the fascist troops."

The thesis of an intrinsic relation between fascism and the middle classes was introduced into American social science by Harold Lasswell in 1933. In an influential essay on "The Psychology of Hitlerism," Lasswell defined National Socialism as a "desperation reaction of the lower middle classes," who were increasingly overshadowed by both the workers and the upper bourgeoisie and who sought to gain revenge. According to Lasswell, nationalism and anti-semitism were peculiarly suited to the emotional insecurities of the petty bourgeoisie. "Rebuffed by a world which accorded them diminished deference, limited in the opportunities afforded by economic reality, the members of this class needed new objects of devotion and new targets of aggression."[56] Anti-semitism provided a rationalization for ethnic competition within the petty bourgeoisie and also enabled the middle class to discharge their hatred toward both the proletariat and the bourgeoisie. The prominence of Jews within the socialist movement allowed the petty bourgeoisie to ration-alize their animosity toward the wage-earning class as oppo-sition to the "Jewish doctrine" of Marxism, while the historical role of Jews as the money-lenders of tradition allowed them to work off their hostility toward the bourgeoisie as hatred of "Jewish capitalism."

Two years later, the historian David Saposs advanced a similar thesis in an essay that emphasized the continuity between fascism and earlier forms of middle-class radical-ism. Saposs argued that the basic ideology of the middle class was populism.

> Their ideal was an independent small-property-owning class consisting of merchants, mechanics and farmers . . . From its very inception it opposed "big business," or what has come to be known as capitalism . . . Their slogan has been "Bust the trusts" and tax the rich, so as to keep the wealth distributed.[57]

Although anti-capitalist in its demands, populism was also opposed to socialism – the basic ideology of the working class. Whereas socialism accepted the concentration of econ-omic life and proposed to socialize large scale industry, populism opposed the trend toward economic concentra-tion and wished to regulate, rather than abolish, the system of private property and profit. In Saposs's interpretation, fascism represented "the extreme expression of middle-classism or populism" in the same sense that communism represented the extreme expression of socialism.

> Just as the strained conditions and economic chaos have given birth to communism as an extreme expression of socialism, so have these same conditions brought forth fascism as the extreme expression of populism . . . In the

desperate attempt to cope with the present chaotic social situation, one represents the proletariat and the other the petite bourgeoisie.[58]

Frankfurt School emigrés Erich Fromm and Franz Neumann were also influential in promoting the middle-class theory of fascism. In *Escape from Freedom,* written during the late 1930s, Fromm echoed many of the themes of Lasswell's essay. "The Nazi ideology," he argued, "was ardently greeted by the lower strata of the middle class, composed of small shopkeepers, artisans, and white-collar workers."[59] The reasons for this were two-fold. In economic terms, the middle class, squeezed between the workers and the bourgeoisie, was the most defenseless group in society and the hardest hit by both the inflation and the depression. In psychological terms, their situation was aggravated by the destruction of "primary bonds" that tied the individual to society. The defeat in war and the downfall of the monarchy struck down the traditional symbols of authority upon which, psychologically speaking, the petty bourgeoisie had built their existence. The monetary inflation undermined the principle of thrift as well as the authority of the state. The greater prestige of organized labor meant that there was no longer anyone for the middle class to look down upon. Rapid social change weakened the authority of parents and shattered the family as the last stronghold of middle-class security. As a result, Fromm argued, the lower middle class "moved into a state of panic and was filled with a craving for submission to as well as for domination over those who were powerless."[60] Hitler, who "combined the characteristics of a resentful, hating petty bourgeois, with whom the lower middle class could identify... with those of an opportunist who was ready to serve the interests of the German industrialists and Junkers" was able to mobilize this panic and direct it in the service of German imperialism.[61]

Franz Neumann agreed with Fromm that the Nazi movement was essentially "a middle-class and lower-middle-class movement." Sketching what would later be known as a theory of status inconsistency, he emphasized the contradictory situation of white-collar employees as a contributing factor in their support for fascism.

It is a well known fact that in every industrial society the new middle classes increase much faster than the industrial workers. It is equally known . . . that the material compensations of the huge bulk of this group are below those of the industrial workers . . . Thus, we have a stratum, growing in numbers, economically below the skilled industrial worker, but whose social aspirations are diametrically opposed to its economic status. It is this dichotomy between economic status and social prestige that provided the soil for Nazism.[62]

Following the Second World War, the interpretation of fascism as an essentially middle-class movement was popularized in American sociology by mainstream theorists like Talcott Parsons, William Kornhauser, and Seymour Martin Lipset.[63] Of the modern versions of this theory, probably the best known is that outlined by Lipset in *Political Man*. Expanding on Saposs's typology, Lipset divided political ideologies into three types – left, right, and center – representing the class interests of the working, upper, and middle classes respectively. Depending upon the political and historical circumstances, each of these classes could espouse an ideology that was either moderate or extremist. Social democracy and communism were the moderate and extremist ideologies of the working class; conservatism and right-wing radicalism were the corresponding ideologies of the upper class; liberalism and fascism were the ideological variants of the middle class. Fascism was thus designated by Lipset as "extremism of the center." Fascism was "basically a middle-class movement representing a protest against both capitalism *and* socialism, big business *and* big unions."[64] Taking German National Socialism as the ideal-typical fascist movement, Lipset marshalled three types of evidence to corroborate his thesis. First, shifts in the electoral statistics between 1928 and 1932 were interpreted to show that the Nazis increased their vote mainly at the expense of the non-Catholic liberal parties of the middle class. Second, ecological studies were cited that showed a correlation between the proportion of Nazi voters in particular regions and the percentage of intermediate strata. Third, he noted that the membership and elite of the Nazi party were disproportionately drawn from the urban middle classes. In opposition to Marxist theorists, Lipset maintained that the German bourgeoisie played a relatively minor role in the rise of National Socialism.

On the basis of this interpretation of fascism, there developed in American sociology of the 1950s a broad consensus affirming the reactionary potential of the "lower middle class." Theories of lower-middle-class "status panic" were applied to explain a variety of right-wing political movements from the Know-Nothings to the Ku Klux Klan, and were also central to liberal interpretations of McCarthyism.[65] In these theories the term "lower middle class" acquired a new and distinctive meaning. In its original Marxist usage, the "lower middle class" was merely another term for the petty bourgeoisie. In this schema, the term "upper middle class" referred to the bourgeoisie proper, while the term "upper class" was reserved for the landed aristocracy. Proponents of the lower middle class theory of fascism broadened the meaning of the term to include elements of the new as well as the old middle class. The terms "lower" and "upper" were also modified so that they came to be understood as representing two distinct levels or strata between the bourgeoisie (now designated as "upper class") and the proletariat. Top managers, professionals, and government officials were classified as "upper" middle class, while small-business owners and lower-level white-collar employees were defined as "lower" middle class. In American sociology of the 1950s, reactionary tendencies were attributed primarily to the latter group, while the more educated and affluent members of the upper middle class were portrayed as the champions of political tolerance and democracy.

PLACING THE BLAME FOR FASCISM

From the efforts to provide an explanation of fascism there thus came a third theory of the new middle class, distinct from both of the dominant theories of the Weimar period. White-collar employees were neither an ally of the proletariat nor a mediating force between the classes, but an inherently reactionary class. Like the Weimar theories, however, this middle-class theory of fascism was as much a product of political rationalization as it was the result of solid empirical research. The chief weakness of this theory is its inability to explain why *lower* white-collar employees, in particular, should have supported a movement that was explicitly anti-labor and anti-socialist. In the case of the old middle class, it is easy to identify the material interests that might produce a hostility toward labor and socialism. These include their attachment to the rights of private property, their fear of unionization that increases the wage costs of small employers, and their opposition to taxation for the support of employment and social insurance programs from which the self-employed receive little benefit. The higher ranks of salaried employees – salaried managers and professionals – might also have reason to oppose the egalitarian aims of labor out of an interest in preserving their considerable power and privilege. But such factors would seem to be of limited applicability to the routine white-collar employees who are the focus of most middle-class theories of fascism.

Two reasons are usually given to account for the fascist leanings of white-collar employees. The first posits a rapid decline in the economic standing of salaried employees relative to manual workers. This decline, it is argued, produces a "status panic" among white-collar employees, which is directed against those whose economic position is improving relative to theirs. The problem with this explanation is that its initial premise is empirically false. Generally speaking, the ratio of salaries to wages declines in periods of economic expansion, while the *relative* standing of salaried employees typically improves in periods of recession – the periods in which fascism arises. In Germany, for example, the real incomes of salaried employees increased by an average of 13 percent between 1929 and 1932, while those of manual workers declined by 7 percent.[66] Between 1927 and 1932 the rate of unemployment among salaried employees increased from 2.4 percent to 13.6 percent, while unemployment among manual wage-earners increased from 4.5 percent to 38.4 percent.[67] Relative to manual workers, the economic position of salaried employees deteriorated much more during the First World War and the postwar inflation. It was during this period, however, that white-collar workers were polarized most sharply toward support for social democracy and organized labor.

A second explanation attributes the fascist leanings of white-collar employees to certain psychological traits: their "authoritarian personality," ideological confusion, emotional insecurity, etc. Such factors may indeed be important in explaining why some individuals are attracted to fascism. It is doubtful, however, whether such traits are unique to salaried employees and other members of the "lower middle class." In the classic empirical work on the subject, Theodore Adorno and his colleagues report little in the way of a consistent relation between class background and such "pre-fascist" character traits as authoritarianism, ethnocentrism, and anti-semitism.[68] More recent studies of the class correlates of authoritarianism, racial prejudice, and political intolerance yield similarly inconclusive results.[69]

An examination of the empirical evidence on the support for National Socialism raises considerable doubts as to the validity of theories that view white-collar employees as uniquely susceptible to the appeals of fascism. In the German case, studies have produced considerable evidence of Nazi support within the old middle class, but have failed to document a comparable level of support among white-collar employees. Analyses of Nazi membership lists by Hans Gerth and Karl Bracher showed independent proprietors to be the most overrepresented of all occupational groups.[70] Charles Loomis and J. Allan Beegle reported high correlations between the support for the NSDAP and the proportion of independent producers in rural areas.[71] Samuel Pratt reported similar correlations with the proportion of independent proprietors in urban areas, but found less consistent evidence of Nazi voting among the salaried sectors of the middle class.[72] The strong inverse correlation between the National Socialist vote and the size of community also contradicts the assumption of high levels of Nazi support among white-collar employees, because the majority of these employees were concentrated in the larger urban centers.[73] In the most recent and comprehensive ecological study of Nazi voting, Thomas Childers found a much stronger pattern of support for the Nazi Party within the old middle class than among the ranks of salaried employees. According to Childers, "while

a hard core of support for the NSDAP persisted throughout the [1924–1932] period within the old middle class, Nazi
electoral sympathies within the white-collar labor force were
marginal before 1930 and surprisingly weak thereafter."[74]

Outside the old middle class, the support for National
Socialism appears to have come less from the lower ranks
of salaried employees than from groups much closer to the
top of the social hierarchy. Contrary to Lipset, historical
research provides extensive evidence of capitalist support
for Hitler and his party.[75] Studies more refined than Lipset's
have also shown that the Nazi electoral upsurge in 1930,
which made it the largest non-Marxist party, was based primarily on the defection of supporters of the ultra-conservative Nationalist Party – the traditional party of the bourgeoisie
– together with the influx of new voters.[76] Richard Hamilton, in a detailed study of Nazi voting in fourteen large
German cities, found that the highest levels of support for
the National Socialists came from the residential districts of
the upper and upper middle class, while working-class and
lower-middle-class districts showed no pronounced pattern
of fascist voting.[77] Daniel Lerner's study of the Nazi elite
corroborates the relatively high class standing of Nazi supporters. Lerner found that 73.6 percent of Nazi leaders
consisted of university-trained civil servants, business managers, and members of the liberal professions.[78]

In the face of such evidence, it is remarkable how many
social theorists continue to view lower white-collar workers
as a leading force in the rise of fascism. To understand the
reasons for this belief, in the absence of supporting evidence,
it is necessary to examine the political and ideological functions these theories have come to serve. For different reasons,
various groups have found in the lower-middle-class interpretation of fascism a convenient vehicle for advancing their
own political views or for avoiding the need to reexamine
their most cherished political beliefs. Reformist social democrats have cited the supposed "status panic" of white-collar
employees in order to accuse those to their left of adventurism
and as proof of the correctness of their appeals for political
moderation. Left-wing socialists and communists have interpreted the same theories as confirmation of their *ouvrierist*
prejudice in favor of industrial workers and as a demonstra-

tion of the folly of attempting to woo the reactionary middle classes. Both sides have been absolved from having to confront their own political and theoretical errors, while the working class (minus its white-collar elements) has been given a clean bill of health. Conservative apologists, on the other hand, have utilized similar theories to shift the responsibility for fascism from capitalists onto the middle class. Distinctions between "upper" (good) and "lower" (bad) middle class have been added so as to exonerate the more privileged professional and managerial strata as well. The "lower middle class" has thus served as a common scapegoat for both the left and the right.

The real causes for the rise of fascism are too complex to deal with adequately here.[79] It appears clear that fascism originated as a largely autonomous movement with deep roots in the traditional petty bourgeoisie (especially its rural, Protestant fraction). Certain groups of salaried employees were also strongly attracted to fascism, although these were mostly concentrated among the upper levels of professionals, managers, and civil servants, rather than among the lower levels of white-collar workers. By itself, however, this initial base of middle-class support is insufficient to account for the success of fascism. Two additional conditions were necessary. First was the hostility of the German ruling classes to the democratic institutions of the Weimar Republic. While the majority of German industrialists probably preferred the Nationalist Party to the Nazis as late as 1932, their intense fear of social democracy made them only too willing to embrace Hitler's installation as Chancellor if that was necessary to block the spread of social democratic influence. And once the anti-socialist intentions of the new Chancellor became clear, capitalist support for Hitler and his party increased dramatically, thereby insuring his consolidation of power.[80] Second was the disunity and weakness of the working-class movement, which invited such an anti-socialist offensive. Part of the blame for the success of fascism must be placed on the intense sectarianism of the German socialist and communist parties. On more than one occasion, Social Democrats in Germany allied themselves with reactionary forces in order to bloodily suppress the uprisings of revolutionary workers. The German Communist Party, for its part, grossly underestimated the seriousness of the fascist threat and devoted most of its effort toward attacking the SPD. It is in such factors, and not in the "status panic" of white-collar employees, that an explanation for the rise of fascism is to be found.

CONTEMPORARY PERSPECTIVES ON THE NEW MIDDLE CLASS

The theories examined in this article have continued to influence the direction of sociological thinking on the new middle class. Because they reflect the strategic dilemmas of social democracy, the debates of the Weimar period have been re-enacted, at one time or another, in virtually every Western social democratic party. In the wake of the Nazi defeat, the controversy over the class position of salaried employees resurfaced within the German SPD. This time, however, the revisionist position prevailed, resulting in the adoption of the so-called *Mittelklasse Strategie* under the leadership of party chairman Kurt Schumacher.[81] In the British Labour Party during the mid-1950s, similar debates were waged between the left-wing supporters of Aneurin Bevan and the revisionist "Gaitskellites." New Fabian theorists like Anthony Crosland made the non-proletarian status of white-collar employees a central theme in their critique of Marxism and their argument of the need for a reformulation of Labour Party strategy.[82] With the election of Hugh Gaitskell as party chairman in 1955, these theories provided the justification for downplaying the rhetoric of class struggle, abandoning the commitment to public ownership, and redefining the goals of socialism in terms of income redistribution and the expansion of the welfare state. Similar debates have also taken place within the social democratic parties of Norway, Sweden, and other European countries.[83]

To the present day, orthodox Marxists (and many who are not so orthodox) continue to insist that non-ownership of the means of production is a sufficient criterion for membership in the working class. By this criterion, Charles Loren estimates that the United States' population is "approximately 90 percent working class, eight percent petty producers, and two percent capitalists." Analyzing historical trends in the

U.S. class structure, he concludes that the middle class "has practically shrunk to nothing, leaving the working class and the capitalist class face to face."[84] Francesca Freedman agrees that the working class "has grown to include the overwhelming majority of the United States' population." With an optimism reminiscent of Kautsky, she maintains that:

> The objective unity of the [working] class – that is, the unity of its wage-relation to capital – creates the potential for a broad-based mass socialist movement. A socialist revolution in the United States would not face the problem of a multiplicity of classes that characterize many third-world countries.[85]

On the other hand, revisionist theories that define the new middle class as consisting of the entire range of white-collar employees have found a prominent place in academic sociology – particularly in the United States.[86] Applied to modern American society, these theories have been used to predict the disappearance not of the middle class (as the orthodox Marxists predicted) but of the working class. Daniel Bell, for example, writes:

> The classical proletariat consisted of factory workers whose class consciousness was created by the conditions of their work. But even at its most comprehensive definition, the blue-collar group is an increasing minority in advanced or post industrial society... For the paradoxical fact is that as one goes along the trajectory of industrialization – the increasing replacement of men by machines – one comes logically to the erosion of the industrial worker himself... The manual and unskilled worker class is shrinking in the society, while at the other end of the continuum the class of knowledge workers is becoming predominant.[87]

Bell concludes, with obvious satisfaction, "not only are we a white-collar society, we're quite definitely a *middle-class* society."[88]

Theories of lower-middle-class "status panic" are still one of the favorite sociological explanations of reactionary right-wing movements. In his recent book on Reaganism and the "New Right," for example, Alan Crawford interprets the rightward shift in American politics as a neopopulist "revolt of the lower middle class."[89] Like earlier sociological accounts of fascism, Crawford is careful to distinguish between the irrational extremism of the lower middle class and the "responsible conservatism" of the upper and upper middle classes.

This is not the place to present a fully developed alternative to the theories examined above.[90] Nevertheless, the preceding analysis yields several conclusions that are relevant to such a task. In the first place, I would argue that an adequate model of the class structure of contemporary capitalist society must come to terms with the fact that the major political cleavage in such societies is one that cuts through the middle of the white-collar ranks. There are any number of possible class models consistent with this finding: lower white-collar employees might be classified as working class and upper white-collars as middle class; both might be classified as an heterogeneous intermediate stratum, while recognizing the propensity for political polarization within this group. What is not consistent with the empirical evidence is any theory that treats *all* white-collar employees as members of a *single cohesive class* – whether as part of the working class or a separate new middle class.[91] Second, the evidence is equally clear that, however one conceptualizes the cleavage within the ranks of salaried employees, it is the lower segment of white-collar employees that has historically been most supportive of a democratic, egalitarian, or socialist politics, and the upper segment that has been most easily mobilized in opposition to these political goals. This is not to say that the concept of "status panic" is entirely without merit or that there are not circumstances in which those of moderate privilege sometimes resist more fiercely the advancement of those beneath them than do those of even greater privilege. But generalizing from these concepts to the conclusion that lower white-collar employees constitute an inherently reactionary class is a form of sociological reasoning that deserves to be relegated to the dust-bin of history.

In addition to these substantive points, the preceding analysis yields several conclusions of a more general kind. One of the aims of this article has been to highlight the ideological distortions that have plagued the discussion of the new middle class from the very beginning. Two such distortions have been especially pronounced. First is the tendency for arguments about the composition and relative size of the proletariat and the middle class to serve as a substitute for the concrete analysis of political trends and strategies, as if the assignment of persons into classes were sufficient to determine the nature and outcome of political struggle. In this manner, class analysis has been reduced to a mere rationalization of the political hopes and preferences of different theorists. Second is the tendency for boundaries between classes to be created and adjusted in an effort to neatly isolate any undesirable political traits from whatever class with which one holds an ideological identification. Inherent in both of these tendencies is a kind of "class reductionism" that ignores the complex political and ideological differentiation *within* classes and the contingency of the political and ideological practices through which classes are organized, or fail to be organized, behind specific political agendas. Contemporary social theorists would be wise to reflect on the influence of these tendencies on their own conceptions of the new middle class.

Notes

1. George Ross, "Marxism and the New Middle Class," *Theory and Society*, 5 (1978): 163.
2. For a survey of some of the more recent Marxist debates on this topic, see Alan Hunt, ed., *Class and Class Structure* (London: Lawrence and Wishart, 1977), and Pat Walker, ed., *Between Labor and Capital* (Boston: South End Press, 1979).
3. C. Wright Mills, *White Collar* (New York: Oxford University Press, 1951), 290.
4. Karl Marx and Frederick Engels, *The Communist Manifesto*, translated from the original 1848 text by Hal Draper, *Karl Marx's Theory of Revolution, Volume II: The Politics of Social Classes* (New York: Monthly Review Press, 1978), 616. The choice of translations is not without consequence. As Draper shows, much of the evidence for attributing the simple polarization view of class structure to Marx comes from revisions made in the English translation of the *Manifesto* in 1888 – five years after Marx's death.
5. Ibid., 618.
6. Martin Nicolaus, "Proletariat and Middle Class in Marx," in James Weinstein and David Eakins, eds., *For a New America* (New York: Random House, 1970).

7. Karl Marx, *Theories of Surplus Value*, Part 2 (Moscow: Progress, 1968), 573.
8. Karl Marx, *Theories of Surplus Value*, Part 1 (Moscow: Progress, 1963), 218.
9. Karl Marx, *Capital*, Volume 3 (New York: International, 1967), 885.
10. Ibid., 886.
11. Ibid., 880.
12. Ibid., 300.
13. Marx, *Theories of Surplus Value*, Part 1, 156–157.
14. Karl Marx, *Capital*, Volume 1 (New York: International, 1967), 332.
15. Karl Marx, "Results of the Immediate Process of Production," Appendix to *Capital*, Volume 1 (New York: Vintage Books, 1976), 1054.
16. Karl Marx, *Capital*, Volume 2 (New York: International, 1967), 410.
17. Karl Marx, *Political Writings*, Volume 3 (New York: Vintage Books, 1974), 348–349.
18. Karl Kautsky, *The Class Struggle* (New York: W.W. Norton, 1971), 35–42.
19. Ibid., 8–17.
20. Gustav Schmoller, *Was verstehen wir unter dem Mittelstand?* (Göttingen: Vandenhoeck und Ruprecht, 1897).
21. Kautsky, *The Class Struggle*, 40.
22. Ibid., 40.
23. Karl Kautsky, *Bernstein und das sozialdemokratische Program* (Stuttgart: J.H.W. Dietz, 1899), 133.
24. Eduard Bernstein, *Evolutionary Socialism* (New York: Schocken Books, 1961), 49–72.
25. Ibid., 48.
26. Ibid., 103.
27. Emil Lederer, *Die Privatangestellten in der modernen Wirtschaftentwicklung* (Tubingen, 1912), translated as *The Problem of the Modern Salaried Employee* (New York: Department of Social Science, Columbia University, 1937), 2.
28. Ibid., 8.
29. Hans Speier, *Social Order and the Risks of War* (New York: G.W. Stewart, 1952), 70.
30. Jurgen Kocka, "The First World War and the Mittelstand: German Artisans and White-Collar Workers," *Journal of Contemporary History* 8 (1973): 107.
31. Emil Lederer and Jacob Marschak, "Der neue Mittelstand," *Grundriss der Sozialoekonomie* 9 (1926), translated as *The New Middle Class* (New York: Department of Social Science, Columbia University, 1973), 21–22.
32. Ibid., 8.
33. Peter Gay, *The Dilemma of Democratic Socialism* (New York: Columbia University Press, 1952), 210–211; Kocka, "The First World War and the Mittelstand," 122–123.
34. Otto Suhr, "Die Lebenshaltung der Angestellten," in *Untersuchungen auf Grund statistischer Erhebungen des allgemeinen freien Angestelltenbundes* (Berlin, 1928), 30–31.
35. Fritz Croner, "Die Angestelltenbewegung nach der Wahrungs-

stabilisierung," *Archiv fur Sozialwissenschaft und Sozialpolitik* 60 (1928), translated as *The White Collar Movement in Germany Since the Monetary Stabilization* (New York: Department of Social Science, Columbia University, 1938).

36. Hans Speier, *The Salaried Employee in German Society* (New York: Department of Social Science, Columbia University, 1939).

37. Carl Dreyfuss, *Beruf und Ideologie der Angestellten* (Munich, 1933), translated as *Occupation and Ideology of the Salaried Employee* (New York: Department of Social Science, Columbia University, 1938), 133–134.

38. Interestingly, the German theorist whose name is today most associated with the distinction between economic (class) and status relations – namely, Max Weber – was rarely cited in the literature on salaried employees. Apparently, this distinction was such a commonplace in German sociology that no one at the time would have thought to identify it with Weber in particular.

39. Theodore Geiger, "Panik im Mittelstand," *Die Arbeit* 7 (1930): 637–653.

40. Theodore Geiger, "Die Mittelschichten und das Sozialdemokratie," *Die Arbeit* 8 (1931), 619–635.

41. Adam Przeworski, "Proletariat into a Class: The Process of Class Formation from Karl Kautsky's *The Class Struggle* to Recent Controversies," *Politics and Society* 7 (1977): 350–351.

42. Adolf Sturmthal, *The Tragedy of European Labor* (New York: Columbia University Press, 1943).

43. Richard Hamilton, *Restraining Myths* (Beverly Hills, Ca.: Sage Publications, 1975), 136.

44. Richard Hamilton, *Who Voted for Hitler?* (Princeton: Princeton University Press, 1982), 58–59.

45. Lederer and Marschak, *The New Middle Class*, 25–31.

46. Lederer and Marschak, *The New Middle Class*, 41.

47. Ibid., 28–31.

48. Hamilton, *Who Voted for Hitler?*, 48–49.

49. Kautsky, *The Class Struggle*, 43.

50. Luigi Salvatorelli, *Nazionalfascismo* (Turin, 1923), quoted in Renzo De Felice, *Interpretations of Fascism* (Cambridge: Harvard University Press, 1977), 129.

51. G. D. H. Cole, *A History of Socialist Thought: Volume 5, Socialism and Fascism* (New York: St. Martin's, 1960), 5.

52. De Felice, *Interpretations of Fascism*, 48.

53. Martin Kitchen, *Fascism* (London: Macmillan, 1976), 1–11; John M. Cammett, "Communist Theories of Fascism: 1920–1935," *Science and Society* 31 (1976): 149–163.

54. Leon Trotsky, *The Struggle Against Fascism in Germany* (New York: Pathfinder Press, 1975); Martin Kitchen, "Trotsky and Fascism," *Social Praxis* 2 (1974): 113–133.

55. Daniel Guerin, *Fascism and Big Business* (New York: Monad Press, 1973), 47.

56. Harold Lasswell, "The Psychology of Hiterlism," *Political Quarterly* 4 (1933): 374.

57. David Sapoos, "The Role of the Middle Class in Social Development:

Fascism, Populism, Communism, Socialism," in *Economic Essays in Honor of Wesley Claire Mitchell* (New York: Columbia University Press, 1935), 397.

58. Ibid., 395–401.
59. Erich Fromm, *Escape from Freedom* (New York: Avon Books, 1941), 235.
60. Ibid., 244.
61. Ibid., 244.
62. Franz Neumann, "Introduction," to Daniel Lerner, *The Nazi Elite* (Stanford: Stanford University Press, 1951), vi.
63. Talcott Parsons, *Essays in Sociological Theory* (Glencoe, Ill.: Free Press, 1954), 124–141; William Kornhauser, *The Politics of Mass Society* (Glencoe, Ill.: Free Press, 1959), pp. 194–211; Seymour Martin Lipset, *Political Man* (New York: Anchor Books, 1960), 127–179.
64. Lipset, *Political Man*, 131.
65. Daniel Bell, ed., *The Radical Right* (New York: Anchor Books, 1963); Martin Trow, "Small Businessmen, Political Tolerance, and Support for McCarthy," *American Journal of Sociology* 64 (1958): 270–281; Seymour Martin Lipset and Earl Raab, *The Politics of Unreason* (Chicago: University of Chicago Press, 1970).
66. Hamilton, *Restraining Myths*, 145.
67. Calculated from statistics presented in Hans Speier, *Die Angestellten vor dem Nationalsozialismus* (Göttingen: Vandenhoeck und Ruprecht, 1977), 72–73.
68. Theodore Adorno, Else Frenkel-Brunswik, Daniel J. Levinson, and R. Nevitt Sanford, *The Authoritarian Personality* (New York: W.W. Norton, 1950), 172, 267.
69. See Hamilton, *Restraining Myths*; Nevitt Sanford, "Authoritarian Personality in Contemporary Perspective," in Jeanne N. Knutson, ed., *Handbook of Political Psychology* (San Francisco: Jossey-Bass, 1973); G. J. Selznick and S. Steinberg, *The Tenacity of Prejudice: Anti-Semitism in Contemporary America* (New York: Harper and Row, 1969); John L. Sullivan, James Piereson, and George E. Marcus, *Political Tolerance and American Democracy* (Chicago: University of Chicago Press, 1982).
70. Hans Gerth, "The Nazi Party: Its Leadership and Composition," *American Journal of Sociology* 45 (1940): 527; Karl Dietrich Bracher, *The German Dictatorship* (New York: Praeger, 1970), 233–234.
71. Charles P. Loomis and J. Allan Beegle, "The Spread of German Nazism in Rural Areas," *American Sociological Review* 11 (1946): 724–734.
72. Samuel Pratt, *The Social Basis of Nazism and Communism in Urban Germany* (M.A. Thesis, Michigan State University, 1948), 148.
73. Hamilton, *Who Voted for Hitler?* 37–38.
74. Thomas Childers, "The Social Bases of the National Socialist Vote," *Journal of Contemporary History* 11 (1976): 30.
75. For one of the best summaries of this evidence, albeit one that seeks to downplay its significance, see Henry A. Turner, "Big Business and the Rise of Hitler," *American Historical Review* 75 (1969): 56–70. Turner shows that "Hitler received considerable support from small- and middle-sized business" (69). With a few notable exceptions, big business leaders were more reluctant to support Hitler, primarily because of

their fear that the National Socialists might eventually live up to their name by turning out to be socialists of some kind. Once Hitler became Chancellor, however, he demonstrated that he was, as he had always reassured them, not a socialist. From that point onward, Turner reports, Hitler "had no difficulty in extracting large sums from big business" that aided him significantly in the consolidation of his power (68). For further evidence on this point, see Arthur Schweitzer, *Big Business in the Third Reich* (Bloomington, Ind.: Indiana University Press, 1964), 89–109; David Abraham, *The Collapse of the Weimar Republic* (Princeton: Princeton University Press, 1981), 281–327; Guerin, *Fascism and Big Business*, 33–40.

76. Karl O'Lessker, "Who Voted for Hitler? A New Look at the Class Basis of Nazism," *American Journal of Sociology* 74 (1968): 63–69.
77. Hamilton, *Who Voted for Hitler?* 219.
78. Lerner, *The Nazi Elite*, 7.
79. Among the best recent treatments of this question are Hamilton, *Who Voted for Hitler?*; Abraham, *The Collapse of the Weimar Republic*; Kitchen, *Fascism*; and Pierre Aycoberry, *The Nazi Question* (New York: Pantheon Books, 1981).
80. Turner, "Big Business and the Rise of Hitler," 68.
81. William E. Paterson, "The German Social Democratic Party," in W. E. Paterson and A. H. Thomas, eds, *Social Democratic Parties in Western Europe* (London: Croom Helm, 1977).
82. Anthony Crosland, *The Future of Socialism* (London: Cape, 1956); Richard Crossman, ed., *New Fabian Essays* (London: Turnsteil, 1952). For an orthodox Marxist rejoinder, see Andrew Grant, *Socialism and the Middle Classes* (London: Lawrence and Wishart, 1958).
83. Adam Przeworski, "Social Democracy as a Historical Phenomenon," *New Left Review* 122 (1980): 36–44.
84. Charles Loren, *Classes in the United States* (Davis, Ca.: Cardinal Publishers, 1977).
85. Francesca Freedman, "The Internal Structure of the American Proletariat," *Socialist Revolution* 26 (1975): 76.
86. During the late 1930s, the New York State Department of Social Welfare, together with the Department of Social Science at Columbia University, jointly sponsored a WPA project of translations of foreign social science monographs. Among the works translated and deposited at Columbia University were many of the revisionist writings on the salaried employee, including the major essays of Emil Lederer, Fritz Croner, Carl Dreyfuss, Hans Speier, Erich Engelhard, and Hans Tobias. From here the ideas of the Weimar revisionists found their way into he writings of Columbia sociologists like C. Wright Mills, Seymour Martin Lipset, and Daniel Bell.
87. Daniel Bell, *The Coming of Post-Industrial Society* (New York, 1973), 125, 148, 343.
88. Daniel Bell, "The Coming of Post-Industrial Society," *TWA Ambassador* (January 1976): 38.
89. Alan Crawford, *Thunder on the Right* (New York: Pantheon, 1980), 290–310.

90. For my own views on the new middle class and its place in the contemporary class structure, see Val Burris, "Capital Accumulation and the Rise of the New Middle Class," *Review of Radical Political Economics* 12 (1980): 17–34; and Val Burris, "Class Structure and Political Ideology," paper presented at the meeting of Pacific Sociological Association, March 1981.

91. For further evidence on this point, see Robert O'Brien and Val Burris, "Comparing Models of Class Structure," *Social Science Quarterly* 64 (1983): 445–459; Reeve Vanneman, "The Occupational Composition of American Classes," *American Journal of Sociology* 82 (1977): 783–807; and Hamilton, *Restraining Myths*, 99–146.

2 The New Middle Class*
Emil Lederer and Jacob Marschak

The collective term "new middle class"[1] goes back in its origin to prewar days. It purports to designate a large number of wholly distinct occupational groups with a catchword, which at the same time suggests a theory of historical development. This theory maintains that capitalism, by reason of its inherent tendencies, irresistibly leads to a concentration of commercial and industrial enterprises with the consequent reduction in the number of independent business men and women and the distintegration and loss of importance of the old middle class. The historical theory also maintains that the existence of a rapidly growing class of dependent workers, containing no manual workers, checks the spread of proletarianization and acts as a buffer between capitalism and labor. This new class is also supposed to take over certain social functions that the "old middle class" is no longer able to fulfill, because it lacks the necessary numerical strength and to some extent also the requisite social and cultural qualifications.

The hypothesis, too, calls more or less for a cooperation between the old and the new middle class. Furthermore it expresses an optimism that takes, as a matter of course, the bridging over of class contracts and the balancing of class interests. This optimism was so strongly entrenched that its adherents, completely failing to appreciate the existing conditions of political power, expected the new middle class to play the role of social mediator between capital and labor in industrial disputes and to help in furthering the principles of industrial democracy. Accordingly the new middle class was to put an end to the instability of the social system and to strengthen the inner cohesion between the classes. Entrepreneurs occasionally interpreted these hopes for the new middle class, here sketchily indicated, with a call for it

* Translated from the German "Der Neue Mittlestand" by S. Ellison and originally published in *Gundriss der Sozialekonomik*, IX, Abteilung I. Teil (Tübingen: J.C.B. Mohr (Paul Siebeck), 1926).[†]

to absorb the upper layers of the workers: thus merged with the workers socially, the new middle class would be in a position to act as the economic and social vanguard and as the connecting link between the proletariat and the other social classes. Such ideas are inherent in all theories of social solidarity: the new middle class was supposed to mitigate the conflict between capital and labor, and between employer and employee, which might imperil the existing economic order. The advocates of social solidarity must be particularly sensitive to those tendencies that help span the gulf of social inequalities. No doubt such tendencies toward equalization are to be found in the capitalistic economy; but the question is whether the new middle class can be regarded and construed as a real factor in the development of social solidarity.

The term "new middle class" and the definitions applied to it must, perforce, be rejected by all those who see in capitalism an unavoidable intensification of class contrasts and expect from such a heightening of contrasts the ultimate sweeping change in the conditions of production and political power. This group, voicing socialistic doctrines, speaks of the new middle class simply as part of the proletariat, often referring to it as "white-collar proletariat" (*Stehkragenproletariat*). Its interests, the group claims, are identical with those of the proletariat and its eventual union with the general proletarian movement, both in its political and associational policies, would follow as a matter of course. The white-collar proletarian is primarily identified with rank and file salaried employees and civil servants, while a thin upper layer from these strata is socially assigned to the entrepreneur class.

It is only natural that whenever an attempt is made to define and explain this rising group as an independent phenomenon, its characterization should be determined by the interests of the existing historical classes. The peculiar position of the new middle class – which cannot be regarded as an isolated social stratum, but as an intermediate position between other classes of a well-established social and economic status – has made it extraordinarily difficult to develop a uniform character and a common consciousness in these new strata. It is natural that the entire group of occupations that make up the new middle class should be judged according to the viewpoint of the individual observer and the interests of the various classes; that is to say, on the basis of those component parts that might serve to prove this or that interpretation. But perhaps of still greater importance are the attempts of the old historical classes to influence the active policy of the new middle class. Accordingly we find that within the new middle class specific groups follow a policy that corresponds to one or the other of the above mentioned fundamentally different concepts. In addition, a third school seeks to explain the peculiar position of the employee "between the classes" as well as its postulates as independent of the organizations and the idealistic and materialistic ideologies of the entrepreneur and the labor classes. The proponents of this theory regard the new middle class, particularly private employees, as a group *sui generis* and strive to emancipate it from the policies of the other classes.

Although there is unanimity that the new middle class is separate from the other classes, it is nevertheless difficult to devise a universal criterion that identifies the groups that belong to it. Ordinarily the new middle class is identified with salaried employees and civil servants. But it is extremely difficult to say which of the "gainfully employed" can be considered salaried employees and civil servants. The definition given by social-insurance legislation, that brain work is the decisive characteristic of these two groups, cannot be accepted since the new middle class, that is, salaried employees and civil servants, includes numerically important occupational groups whose activity is not mental but which are classed below that of skilled labor in terms of their qualifications. In the case of public employees and officials, the line of demarcation is indicated by their official designation and legal status. Concerning salaried employees, it can only be said that their activity is either purely manual, like that of the laborer, except that a certain mental performance stamps the occupation with a special character (technical employees), or their activity is not at all mental and has nothing to do with production, only with distribution (commercial employees). These are the borderline types of the group. Within, we find the purely mental activity of the higher official in industry and commerce; outside is the essentially manual work of the laborer. An amalgamation of these highly heterogeneous groups cannot, then, be based upon some technical or economic function common to all of them, but rather upon their common social position. Still, the criterion of this social position is anything but positive. Rather, the fact that the position of the new middle class is an intermediate one between the classes makes the criterion a negative one.[2]

Although its position between the classes is recognized as the social criterion of the new middle class, the social position of its constituent groups is not uniform. Indeed it is as variable as in the other classes, which likewise exhibit considerable lateral extension: the entrepreneurial class includes the small manufacturer and the commercial entrepreneur, as well as the industrial magnate. The manual-laborer class includes the unskilled proletarians of the lowest strata (*Lumpenproletarier*), low-paid and unskilled female wage-earners, as well as skilled, regularly employed and well-paid male wage earners. But the employee group has a particularly broad range, and it can be comprehended as an entity only in contradistinction to the other classes. Within it predominate the differences between the various subgroups; still, it may be asserted that there is hardly another social stratum that, even though composed of so many heterogeneous elements, presents such a relatively united front insofar as common interests are concerned.

THE NEW MIDDLE CLASS IN MODERN ECONOMIC DEVELOPMENT

The manifold and complex causes that account for the rise and growth of the new middle class of salaried employees and civil servants in the last few decades might, above all, be ascribed to general economic development, and, in the case of civil servants, also to certain changes in the state and its functions.

Private Employees

The intimate relationship between economic evolution and the growth of the salaried-employee class is best illustrated by the case of the technical employee. Technical employees did not exist in either handicrafts or industry during their infancy. The master craftsman of old, like the independent proprietor of a factory, was totally different from the technical official of today's mammoth concern. These modern industrial concerns have devised a whole superstructure, or mechanism, of which the technical employee must form an integral part. This mechanism removes from the shopfloor; all brain work and centralizes it in the planning and laying-out department. In this systematized business technical employees play an important role, and will play an increasingly important role the more big business displaces small undertakings. At the same time, with the growth of the industrial enterprise the individual role of the technical employee tends to become less important, for as an individual he or she is easily replaced. Thus the rise of big business has created the technical employee of today and put him or her into a distinct category. It has also brought into existence a rapidly growing class of clerical employees working in factory offices. Their numbers are increasing all the more rapidly as the introduction of American business methods requires a minute cost-accounting system and, in consequence, a large personnel. These clerical employees of industry are not in touch with individual, technical aspects of the business. They typify, perhaps better than any other group, the present-day employee, who, in carrying out a particular task, has lost all contact with the process of production as a whole.

As in the case of the technical and clerical employees of industry, the rapid increase in the number of clerical employees must likewise be attributed – although less directly – to economic evolution and the transformation of business. The salaried employee has long been known to the large as well as to the small business. Trade is the special domain of the employee. All those employed in it, even in positions where no mental work is required, are known as salaried employees and not wage earners. Therefore the transformation of business did not prepare the ground for clerical employees, it only caused their numbers to be greatly augmented. This increase was far more rapid than that of the independents engaged in commerce, while in the modern, large, commercial concerns it made possible an extensive division of work and the employment of persons without special training.

The First World War gave a tremendous impetus to the growth of the salaried-employee class. The conscription of all men able to bear arms, and the rush of war orders, coupled with the simultaneous aggravation of the general economic situation, caused the emergence of new groups of gainfully employed, in the majority women. Whether those groups belonged to the old middle class or came from families of salaried employees and public functionaries, they took such positions in the economy as were best suited to their education and social background. In other words, they performed the functions of salaried employees. The appearance of these new groups was intensified by the fact that the transformation of the national economy, in response to war needs, had greatly fostered the tendencies that favored the growth of this class of employees; for a war economy means the expansion of big business, as well as extensive "organization," or bureaucratization, which multiplies the functions of the salaried employee. But neither the termination of the war and the demobilization of the army, nor the abandonment of the war economy reestablished the social stratification of the prewar period. In the first place the tendencies of industrialization and of organization, even though the latter was now to be found not in the exigencies of a state engaged in a war but in large, private corporations, were not checked. Secondly, the disintegration of the old middle class was accelerated at an unprecedented pace with monetary devaluation and the wiping out of private fortunes. As a result, those who had been reduced to dependence turned to the socially kindred occupations of the salaried employee, although these, too, showed a steady deterioration of economic status and an approximation to (if not an actual drop below) the living standards of the wage earners. On the other hand consideration of class and tradition turned the young generation away from manual occupations. One must admit that this hypertrophy of employees is bound to lead to a reaction under the pressure of unfavorable labor-market conditions.[3] In particular, monetary stabilization must cause a stringent reduction of personnel in overstaffed commercial and industrial enterprises and, especially, banks. Still, inasmuch as the number of the new middle class will remain the same, the composition of the social body will be completely changed compared with the prewar period.

Public Employees

The number of public servants in the last decades shows an extraordinary increase due, in the first place, to the fast pace of the development of the industrial state and its growing functions, which require a large staff. The number of governmental employees was bound to increase faster than the population, precisely because industrialization and changes in the geographical distribution of the population necessarily multiplied the tasks of the various governmental agencies. Not only the internal administration proper, but also the administration of justice has witnessed an enormous expansion of its calendar, while the functions of the civil service have become increasingly complex. This is also true, if not more true, of the administration of municipal governments. Furthermore both state and municipalities have extended their activities by operating certain industrial enterprises (chiefly in transportation) under direct management. These tendencies towards municipalization and nationalization have brought into being legions of public servants, who, properly speaking, are another consequence of the capitalistic system and of the industrialization of the national economy.

The war stimulated these tendencies considerably. The far-reaching state regulation of national production and distribution, the systematic organization of the state on a "war-economy" basis, added new functions to the machinery of administration. In addition there was a large expansion of the manifold functions that the modern service state performs. To be sure, in the years after the war a reaction set in against the emergency economy and statism. In Germany and elsewhere, a retrenchment of the army of civil servants and a definite return to private life of public servants was urged and partly carried out.[4] But this does not mean that there was a return to prewar conditions. The fast absorption during the war of former independents by the large and complex economic organizations could not be undone. Moreover it should be noted that it is becoming increasingly difficult to draw the line of demarcation between "civil servant" and "salaried employee" from a sociological standpoint, though not from a legal standpoint. For, on the one hand, the salaried employee's relationship with the impersonal, complex business organizations, which in many cases extend over generations and arrogate to themselves the position of public corporations as to power and purpose, approximates that of the civil servant; on the other hand the relationship between the public servant and the state has changed. The public servant does not exhibit the same loyalty towards the state as of old; the grip of the state's authority over the civil servant has relaxed and a contractual relationship is sought instead of one of public law. The convergence of these two groups of the new middle class (which before the war already followed in the wake of a rapid increase of employees in state-operated enterprises in contrast with the officials exercising functions of the sovereign state) explains why the return to private life of many public servants and the contracting out of the state's range of activity cannot seriously affect the social stratification favoring the new middle class that was produced during and after the war.

The general economic developments accounted not only for the tremendous increase of employees and civil servants, but also for a qualitative change in the social composition of both these groups, before as well as after the war. New types of undertaking and state function appeared and, simultaneously with them, new categories of employees and civil servants, whose position differed in many respects from that of their "old-time" colleagues. It is these new categories of employees and civil servants who have started the salaried-employee and civil-servant movements and have drawn the entire class from its relative peace and security into the turbulent currents of social movements.

The foregoing points to those forces that are of significance in the salaried-employee and civil-servant movements. In their aggressive aspect, these movements are the reaction of the great masses of employees whom the new economic system has driven into an unfavorable position and kept there. It is true that employees of old were also dependent workers; still, the door remained open to each one of them, as an individual, to become economically independent or to rise to a position that, economically and socially, put him or her on the same level as the independent. For a large majority of lower-rank employees and civil servants this had become impossible even before the war. The salaried employee and civil servant of today move through life in a rather small circle; they can neither rise to a higher post, nor can they even hope to improve their economic and social status. The very conditions that have brought into being the great armies of employees and civil servants also tend to keep them down in the social and economic scale. Just as the labor movement is a rebellion against the insecurity of existence and the insuperable obstacles that are placed in the path leading to independence and adequate incomes, likewise similar conditions facing the employee of today give rise to social movements of which we shall say more presently. Transformations within these strata took place rather slowly before the war, for there were still large groups whose status had suffered little, if at all, and whose interests and sympathies prompted them to adopt a cold and unresponsive attitude toward the new movements; but after the revolution abrupt changes set in as economic collapse, social degradation, the dissolution of traditional bonds and insecurity of existence particularly affected salaried employees and civil servants.

STATISTICS

Salaried Employees

The number of salaried employees increases in absolute as well as relative terms faster in industry than in commerce. In industry the most rapid increase is found in clerical staff – a consequence of a technically more-thorough organization, the continuing rationalization of business and the introduction of American cost-accounting methods. Thus the center of gravity shifts, as far as numbers are concerned, from commercial to industrial employees, the more so as the latter are for the most part concentrated in large-scale industries where their massive strength gives them a decided economic and social advantage.[5] The same tendency is manifest in the relatively large proportion of employees in the big cities.

The rapid growth of the salaried-employee class must be regarded as a consequence of continuous economic development, particularly of big business, and of the new methods of business organization. This rapid swelling of the number of such employees, which runs parallel to a decline in the number of independents, prevents the great majority of them from shifting to the independent class and forces them, collectively as well as individually, to remain permanently as salaried employees. The rapid increase in the number of salaried employees enhances their effective power and activity as a group, particularly in the larger cities where we find them concentrated in large numbers. Lastly, salaried employees, by their sheer numbers, offer a counterweight to the increasing numerical strength of the laboring class. In the social and political field, and elsewhere, salaried employees could adopt a policy aimed against the excessive concentration of business and against the elimination of the small independent from the economy – a policy that might be supported by the various groups of employees in the national economy. Similarly, salaried employees could infinitely strengthen the position of wage earners in the struggle between capital and labor, and considerably imperil the power of the entrepreneur. The following survey will show the lines along which these possibilities have been realized.

Civil Servants

In the occupational census the civil servant is not given a distinct place. Official statistics ignore civil servants as a separate group, and therefore do not permit unambiguous determination of their numbers. The determining factor in classification is the nature of their occupation, therefore public and private officials (or civil servants and salaried employees) who are engaged in the same activity are grouped together. Still, it is perhaps right that a line of demarcation should be drawn between the two categories. The occupational census of 1907 contains the following data. Grouped together are:

1. Civil servants in the diplomatic service and in federal,

state, county and municipal administrations; administrators of the domains of the upper nobility and of other large estates; officials in the administration of justice, including inspectors and the service personnel of prisons, other penal institutions and reformatories, and of poor houses and welfare institutions, and so on (group E2 of the occupational census):

(a) Higher officials, lawyers, notaries 55,038
(b) Other functionaries in the middle civil-service
    class, inspectors and office personnel,
    calculators and clerks 257,347
(c) Service personnel, messengers, office porters 77,620
                                                                        390,005

2. Teachers in universities, *Gymnasien, Realschulen,* grammar schools, trade and technical schools, orphan asylums; proprietors of private schools and their teaching staff, boarding schools, institutes for the blind, deaf and dumb; private teachers and tutors and so on (group E4 of the census):

(a) Managing and teaching staff 277,153
(b) Administrative personnel 4,127
(c) Service personnel, institutes included 18,116
                                                                  299,396

Both of the following large groups include also salaried employees, as is evident from the enumeration:

3. Civil servants in the postal, telegraph and
   telephone services 232,571

4. State railway employees (1908) 276,312

These four groups, taken together, comprise about 1,200,000 persons. But these figures do not take into account civil servants in other public and municipal enterprises. For government employees employed as forecasters and gamekeepers, in mining, blast furnaces and foundries, salt-works, waterworks, as well as in building, road, harbor and pilot services and so on, were allocated to their respective occupations together with private employees working in the same fields. Likewise the data given for civil servants employed in the postal, telegraph and railway services do not seem to be accurate; the figures given by the authorities are in every case considerably higher than those of the occupational census. At any rate, for 1907, the year of the occupational census, the number of civil servants may be placed at 1,500,000; but since then this number must have increased appreciably. Let it be added that the rate of increase in the number of civil servants, particularly in enterprises operated by the government, has been extraordinarily rapid.

Our studies of the statistical data show that the numerical importance of old-time civil servants performing purely governmental functions and representing governmental power and state authority is constantly diminishing. By far the greater majority in the civil service are employees in public undertakings, and here the growth has been most rapid. As far as their occupational activity is concerned, civil servants in state enterprises cannot be distinguished from salaried employees doing the same kind of work. Their status as civil servants rests rather on an historical and legal basis. The term civil servant and its related social position were originally associated with the functions of the civil servant of the old school, but were later transferred to the large groups of governmental employees in state enterprises. To be sure, these new categories of civil servants have no absolute power; nevertheless a modicum of authority, deriving from the power invested in the old-time public official, still clings to their positions. Similarly the legal status of civil servants who exercise governmental power[6] affords them a certain security of tenure, giving them an advantage over salaried employees in private business; but it also implies a restriction of their freedom of movement and a hindrance to the assertion of their economic power by independent action. Hence the appearance of special problems in the civil-servant movements, of which we shall say more later.

SOCIAL POLICY

Salaried Employees

The social policy of salaried employees must be studied in the light of their peculiar social position. Salaried employees represent a new stratum of the gainfully employed, the bulk of whom find themselves in circumstances that are in sharp contrast with the traditional position of the salaried employee. To be specific, their permanent dependence on employers; the fact that they are at the mercy of the labor market; the development of a remunerative system based on the prevailing economic and financial situation; and the ever-growing practice of compensation being proportionate to efficiency, which means that employees' pay decreases the older they grow – all these factors help to undermine the social and economic status of salaried employees, who thus finds themselves exposed to the danger of proletarization. When salaried employees first became conscious of their numerical strength and the importance of their function in industry, they entertained the notion that they would be able to play the role of mediators between capital and labor and to reconcile the conflicting interests of employer and wage earner. But this illusion was given up long ago and in its place we now find social pessimism. The great majority of salaried employees have come to recognize the fundamental incompatibility between capital and labor, between employer and employee, but they are in no position to bridge this gap; they cannot stand between the two warring classes, and must therefore choose that side which best serves their interests.

The problem of finding his or her right place was rendered still more difficult to the salaried employee by the fact that the class is composed of highly heterogeneous elements. Salaried employees, for the most part, come from the independent class or, at any rate, from the bourgeois stratum. Before the collapse of 1918 their income was considerably higher than the average income of wage earners. Compared with the latter, their work is generally characterized by definite qualifications; it enjoys higher social prestige and brings them into direct contact with the entrepreneur class. Moreover, recently, it was possible for the salaried employee to attain a position consistent with his or her abilities or to become an independent. Such considerations foster among salaried employees those tendencies that seek to check the material and social degradation of their class and to preserve their middle-class standards of living and their social prestige. The situation has given rise to claims that, if realized, would improve the condition of salaried employees as individuals, particularly with regard to making their positions more secure and relatively permanent, despite their dependence upon the entrepreneur. Naturally the policy of the salaried employee is a labor policy, but apart from this it has an unmistakable middle-class character, which distinguishes it from the policy of the proletariat.

To indicate the essential identity of class interests, it is interesting to note that the demands of the various employee groups, as a whole, coincide. This identity of interests should eventually lead to a common orientation of many strata of employees. This united front was especially evident, prior to the revolution, in the demand by salaried employees for old-age insurance, which was deemed to be the counterpart of the civil-service pension. Similarly, other demands aimed at a minimum-salary provision, the abrogation of any clause in employment contracts that prevented (with a view to obtaining long-term contracts) the employee from entering the service of a rival concern, the safeguarding of employees' rights to their own inventions, the regulation of apprenticeship, the establishment of uniform discharge notices and so on. These and other claims stamped the policy of salaried-employee organizations with a distinctive mark, thus differentiating it from the social program of wage earners. Nevertheless salaried employees adopted the main points of labor's social program, particularly emphasizing the unqualified right to organize, claiming also, with suitable modifications, the extension to them of those protective measures that were already enjoyed by wage earners. The middle-class character of the employees' policy is clearly brought out by a modification of those demands, that is, by the effort to make the employment of the individual salaried employee secure and stable and thus to realize, as far as possible, the principal demands of the middle-class policy within the framework of dependent occupations.

Within this general program, which characterized the salaried-employee movement before the war, important differences existed between the component groups. In the organization of commercial employees, conservative class tendencies prevailed and the traditional notion of one united mercantile class made it possible for employers to become members in many employees' unions and effectively precluded the adoption of all trade-union policies (strikes, collective bargaining and so on). In contrast technical employees, who first appeared as a compact group in the centers of mass production, were strongly influenced by modern labor policies. The combating of these ideas by the entrepreneur was not in the least responsible for the adoption of a radical program. Still, up to the time of the collapse in 1918 even radical salaried-employee organizations would uncompromisingly reject any cooperation with the workers' trade-union movement; nor would they accept its socialist ideology (apart from a few insignificant exceptions, whose failures were conspicuous). Indeed, even in the radical wing of the salaried-employee movement one could easily detect a fundamentally middle-class character with all its social and traditional earmarks, namely, that individual stamp which stood as symbol for the preservation of the salaried employees' place "between the classes" and which shunned a fusion with the worker as well as the employer class.

The situation changed fundamentally after 1918.[7] The middle-class character of the salaried employee had to capitulate before the growing notion of the mere wage earner. Proletarianization of the middle-class stratum, which went on at an unprecedented pace, and the raising of the social status of the manual worker steadily closer to that of the salaried employee, proved stronger than any class tradition. These economic conditions, the political changes, the recognition of trade unions and the abolition of all traditional conceptions of the social order forced salaried-employee associations to adopt the aims and methods of the labor unions. Consequently numerous groups of employees rallied under the new banner.

The transformation of the whole employee movement after 1918 also shifted the balance of power to the more radical salaried-employee associations and caused further changes in their policies. These changes include the replacement of the policy of "harmony" by a trade-unionist policy in conservative associations and the infiltration of formerly rejected socialistic doctrines into the radical organizations. Employers were no longer eligible as members of these associations. Responsibility for the well-being of the individual, employment bureaus – which formerly presupposed a cooperation between the commercial employees and the entrepreneurs – and promotion of sociability were relegated to the background. What is still more important, characteristic activities of labor unions – such as collective wage agreements and "organized labor's last resort," the strike – were fully adopted and practiced in the manner of labor organizations. In fact the whole machinery of the associations was overhauled in order to adjust it to these new functions.

Membership in the various salaried-employee unions from 1911 to 1921 was as follows:

	Total membership	*Employees*	
		Total	*Women*
1911	830,870	739,291	70,789
1912	941,343	830,441	73,118
1915	531,609	470,285	82,200
1917	425,928	376,382	105,087
1919	1 436,780	1 400,568	342,026
1920	1 571,337	1 543,310	375,597
1921	1 671,796	1 642,913	351,289

The rapid increase of members before and, especially, after the war may be attributed partly to the growth of the employee class and partly to the dissemination of the idea of organization, especially in its post-revolutionary, union type. The complete disappearance from the associations of those members who were not salaried employees (among whom employers figured prominently) is characteristic of the new order of things. Noteworthy also is the large increase in female members, from 17.7 per cent in 1913 to 23.8 per cent in 1919.[8] This latter fact is also very important in the transformation of the salaried-employee movement.

The expansion and organic changes of the salaried-employee associations are concurrent with a tendency towards amalgamation. Formerly independent unions, after the removal of certain obstacles, were absorbed by larger ones, or they became affiliates. More important yet is the rise of national federations, which aim to include salaried employees of all occupations. Their general policy is somewhat colored by the policy of the German trade-union movement (social-istic, liberal, Christian). Thus we find today in Germany three federated associations of salaried employees, which, together with the federations of civil-service employees, borrow both their ideology and organization from kindred labor federa-tions. The role of legislative pressure group, which the vari-ous unions played in the past, has now been assumed by the top federations, which as a result must now be regarded as important political forces.

The grouping of the salaried-employee unions within these three federations and the distribution of their respective mem-bers among them should by no means be considered final. In 1923 the most important groupings were as follows (taken from the *Jahrbuch der Berufsverbande*, 1925).

First, the *General Independent Employee Federation* (Afa-Bund). This top federation, which is affiliated with the free trade-unionist, the National Federation of Labor Trade Unions (ADGB), as a cartel member, has its parentage in the Com-mittee on Uniform Employee Legislation, which was founded before the war, and the Conference of Independent Em-ployee Unions, which came into being during the war. Even before the war the member organizations of the Confer-ence stressed their unmitigated and unqualified viewpoints. After 1918 the principal points of trade unionism of the ADGB, which included, among other things, "a collective system of economy," were incorporated in the by laws of the Afa-Bund. In some matters, for example that of coop-eration with employer associations, the Afa-Bund adopted a decidedly more radical attitude than the ADGB. This is another characteristic of the movement. In 1925 the Afa-Bund had about 658 000 members. The most important unions affiliated with the *Afa-Bund* are as follows:

Organization	Approximate membership
General Federation of Salaried Employees (commercial, office, insurance employees)[9]	310,000
German Foremen Alliance[10]	160,000
General Federation of German Bank Clerks[11]	31,000
Guild of German Stage Members	15,900
Union of Salaried Employees in Agriculture and Forestry	12,300
Union of German Construction Foremen	13,200

Second, the *Federation of German Salaried Employee Unions,* which is patterned after the Christian National German Federation of Unions and had 460,000 members in 1923. The most important organizations associated with it are as follows:

Organization	Approximate membership
German National Federation of Business Employees[12]	285,000
Association of Female Commercial and Office Employees	102,600
National Federation of Administrative Employees in Agriculture and Forestry	13,000

Third, the *Federation of Salaried Employee Unions* (300,300 members), which embraces several separate organizations that are now contemplating a merger. This top federation proposes to unionize its members "along strict labor lines and in a liberal–national spirit." It describes the range of its interests as "the social policy of the employees and the entire field of unionized labor, including employment service and support of strikes and defense against arbitrary measures of employers." The federation is affiliated with the National Cartel of Labor and employee federations that are headed by the Hirsch-Duncker unions.

We may consider the attempt on the part of the salaried-employee associations to cooperate on an international scale as also symptomatic of the new trends. Thus the German employee associations of the Afa-Bund are now linked to the International Association of Private Employees, which was founded in 1920. This association, which in 1924 comprised 35 unions with 825,000 members in 15 countries, is like its prewar and now defunct predecessor, the Employees Division of the International Trades Unions, a member of the Amsterdam International Trades Union Federation. Salaried-employee associations with different trends similarly cooperate with more or less closely knit organizations of an international character.

The Social Policy of Civil Servants

As a result of the mounting cost of living, the civil servants of Germany and elsewhere had become an active social group even before the war. The diminished purchasing power of money unleashed forces that irresistibly led to a social organization among the civil servants. This, no doubt, was accentuated by the growing exigencies of the standard of living and by the advance of the other classes, which, through social organizations, sought to protect their special interests, irrespective of the common welfare. To be sure, the position of civil servants is, in this respect, a difficult one. Their oath of office binds them to their employer – the state – far more effectively than in the case of salaried employees. Their privileged status (permanent tenure of office, right to pension and higher salary with advancing years) imposes upon them limitations that are unknown to private employees in their relations with their employers. Any demands on the part of civil servants must be submitted to the public as employer. And so the highest tribunal to which civil servant can generally appeal is, at the same time, their foremost opponent.

Despite these difficulties we see widespread organized movements all over Europe pursuing a two-fold aim. The first is to secure an improvement in the economic situation of civil servants, specifically the introduction, in the face of rising prices, of a system of remuneration built upon a higher basic salary, and a reduction in the number of years required to enter higher-salary groups in order to guarantee an adequate standard of living as civil servants grow older and their family needs increase. Their second aim is an improvement of their status in relation to the higher officialdom and a greater security of their civil position and civil rights.

It is the nature of the hierarchical system of the civil service that any demands on the part of civil servants are not submitted by them as a body to the state but are first condensed into complaints of the lower ranks filed with their superiors. It would be a bold and radical form of petitioning if the associations of civil servants appealed directly to parliament. Such procedure is discouraged as much as possible by higher government officials. A further consequence of the hierarchical system of officialdom is that the policy of the civil servants is essentially a "group policy." In other words, their demands represent the interests of one service group and not those of the whole body of public servants that is indirectly represented by this official group. It may be asserted that the more civil servants are conscious that they represent state authority (something to which even the lowest grades of civil servants are keenly sensitive), the more they feel that they are the representatives of a higher order with regard to the public at large; and the more, therefore, they are aware that their special functions flow from the sovereignty of the state, the more they are inclined to realize their demands through a service group policy. On the other hand, when large groups of subordinate officials become aware of the impersonal character of their official functions, the ground is prepared for a common course of action on the part of the different categories of civil servants; their demands now appear as the expression of a common policy of the entire civil service. Thus before the war it had already become possible in Austria and France to work out a common policy on a broad basis, whereas in Germany the group policy was by far the more predominant.[13] Only the revolutionary events of November 1918 brought about a radical change of conditions.

In its initial stage the civil-servant movement had an economic basis. Above all it aimed at improving the economic status of civil servants. Civil servants have always pointed out that since they devote themselves exclusively to the state's business, the state is duty-bound to provide them with a livelihood that is commensurate with their position. In accordance with this view, even prior to the war they had advanced a demand for more pay to meet the rising cost of living. In addition, the principle was laid down by them that the pay of every government employee should not depend upon the discretion of his or her superiors, nor should it be contingent upon promotion to a higher post. Pay should be independent of official classification and increased for each individual with each passing year, so that every public servant would have the means to meet the new obligations imposed upon him by his advancing years and by the more expensive maintenance of growing children. As a result of the new economy and of the fewer opportunities for promotion due to the overcrowding of all government positions, it was a matter, then, of granting offsetting benefits: the safeguarding of the social and economic middle-class position of civil servants and the warding off of the proletarianization of their class. Such terms must be deemed essentially conservative, for the policy toward civil servants – viewed from an economic viewpoint – in reality strove to save the threatened status of the middle class, just as the conservative middle-class policy of the independents tried to do the same, although, as was to be expected, by different means.

The events of 1918, which shook the autocratic state to its very foundations, made more imperative the necessity of organized resistance against the threat of wholesale pauperization and were responsible for a radical change of policy in the civil-servant movement.[14] Group policy had to give way to a common policy, which could now readily follow the pattern of trade unions, as the latter had by this time lost their former epithet "enemies of the existing order" and had gained the recognition of employers and become one of the most important factors in political life and in the formation of government. An active trade-union policy, however, presupposes a change of the traditional and legal basis of civil servants' status; it involves the unimpeded exercise of their civil rights and, especially, a more or less liberal granting to civil servants of those conditions under which private employment contracts are entered. This implies a loosening of the ties that bind civil servants to the state, but also the loss of certain privileges contingent upon these ties.

These demands for a change in the status of civil servants are at the same time closely related to the types of organization: the independent occupational unions, which negotiate the question of pay and so on directly with the state, if need be taking strike action; and staff representation, a public law organization attached to the various administrative departments (civil-service committees). The analogy between those two forms of organization and those in the labor movement (trade unions and shop committees) is obvious. But although the demands for unrestricted right of association and for a "democratized bureaucratic structure" go back to an earlier period, they became real issues only after the civil-servant movement had approximated the labor movement, and after the civil-service code had adopted the main points of the new labor code.

Since Article 130 (paragraphs 2 and 3)[15] of the German constitution has recognized in principle both these claims, without, however, clearly defining civil servants' rights in relation to those of other workers, the issue in the present struggle for these nascent rights revolves around determining their limits. The maximum extent of these rights or warrants of civil-servant associations is epitomized by the slogan "employment of all the means of organized labor;" the rights of civil servants' departmental committees are summarized by the demands for an extensive application of the "principles of collaboration." In practice the former means recognition of civil servants' right to strike; the latter is supposed to protect civil servants as employees (in questions of salary, appointment and discipline), but it also calls for an active cooperation between the state and civil servants for the proper discharge of administrative functions (which finds its analogy in the dual task of the workers' council in industry – settling of social questions and promotion of production).

Two distinct questions emerge clearly from the above. First, there is the question of how far the state, on the basis of existing laws, may ask civil servants to abandon certain union policies or to limit the right of "collaboration" in exchange for the privileges granted to them.[16] Secondly, what are the present-day tendencies in the evolution of the civil service? Do they lead to a strengthening of the mutual ties binding the state and the public servant (which would increase their mutual dependence but also widen the gap separating the civil servant from the free worker), or does it lead to a weakening of the traditional bond of loyalty and to a social fusion of civil servants with salaried employees? Conceivably the answer to these questions will not be the same for higher and lower officials, for officials exercising governmental power and for officials in the state's business enterprises.

The aims of the present-day civil-servant movement culminate in the aforementioned demands, at least insofar as their objective is not exclusively confined to the improvement of their economic status. Spearheading these demands, as well as the campaign for more pay, are the various civil-servant organizations, which today are members of large federations. Questions of economic self-help (for example consumers' cooperative associations, insurance, savings systems and so on), which once stood to the fore, have been eliminated from the program of the unions and have been taken over by the Association for the Protection of Economic Interests of German Civil Service Employees (Deutsche Beamtenwirtschaftsbund), the offspring of the now defunct Federation of German Civil Service Associations (Verband Deutscher Beamtenvereine), while the organized movement of the civil servants has called into existence new federations.[17]

As in the case of salaried employees, it has not been possible to consolidate the various unions of civil servants into one single federation. Besides the Federation of German Civil-Service Employees (Deutsche Beamtenverband), which is supposed to be politically neutral, we find the following organizations whose policies are based on one or other of the three main policies of the worker and employee movements. These are the General Federation of German Civil Service Employees, which is affiliated with independent unions; the General Federation of Civil Service and Appointive Employees' Associations, which leans toward the Christian National Federation of Salaried Employee Unions; and the national–liberal National Cartel of Labor and Employee Federations, with its own units.

Things, however, are still in a state of flux. In 1923 the

German Association of Civil Servants had 826,000 members, including 43 professional associations and 19 state associations. The most important organizations affiliated with this federation are as follows.

Organization	Approximate membership
Union of the Salaried Employees of the National Railroad Corporation	80,000
National Federation of Postal and Telegraph Employees	120,000
German Police Officers' Association	106,000
German Teachers' Association	152,000
National Association of Municipal Civil Servants	166,000

These figures have undergone certain changes since the end of 1922 as a result of the establishment of the independent General Federation of German Civil Service Employees following the failure of the German Association of Civil Servants and the General Federation of Labor Trade Unions to come to an agreement. The position of the General Federation of German Civil Service Employees in the whole movement of free organizations is supposed to be analogous to that of the Afa-Bund. In 1923 the General Federation of German Civil Service Employees comprised 20 associations, including many important ones, some of which had their origin in the German Association of Civil Servants. It had 354,000 members (of which 200,000 came from the National Unions of German Railroad Employees and Substitutes). Somewhat less important than these two federations is the Christian National Federation, the General Federation of Civil Service and Appointive Employees Association, with 390,000 members, the majority of whom are in the railroad service. The civil-servant units of the liberal National Cartel of Labor and Employee Federations number about 174,000 members (of whom 82,000 are in the Railroadmen's Association).

Until recently only associations of civil servants working in the technical departments of government enterprises, such as postal and railroad employees, had international affilia-tions. The other groups (organized on a trade-union basis) succeeded in forming an international association only in the spring of 1925; the International Union of Government Employees, Civil Servants and Teachers in Public Service was founded during a congress attended by 400,000 civil servants from nine countries. Obviously an international collaboration of associations poses certain difficulties, given the nature of the relationship between the public servant and the state.

HIGHER OFFICIALS AND EMPLOYEES: EMPLOYEES OF LIBERAL PROFESSIONS

The radical turn in the movement of the great masses of the "new middle class" prompted, on the other hand, a con-solidation of the traditionally conservative tendencies in certain higher-ranking salaried-employee and civil-servant or-ganizations. We might point out, for example, the prewar German Association of Civil Engineers (Verband Deutscher Diplomingenieure), which strove to secure a privileged po-sition for technicians who had received their education in the higher institutions of learning. Several other organiza-tions of a similar, although less outstanding, character clearly showed that, precisely because of the growing number of salaried employees and civil servants, certain groups with a higher social, intellectual and financial status sought to sep-arate themselves from the masses and pursue their own aims independently. These groups endeavour for the most part to assure a privileged status to civil servants of higher rank or possessing academic training. Accordingly these organ-izations clearly reveal a distinctly middle-class, conservative tendency. This explains why, after the revolution, the associ-ations of higher-salaried employees and public officials were practically the only ones that had nothing to do with a trade-unionist policy. The organizations of higher-salaried employees might be said to have taken the position of the former "har-mony associations," while the National Association of Sal-aried Employees in Elevated Positions (Reichsbund hoherer Beamten) pursues to a large extent a "group policy."[18] But the groups in question are numerically unimportant and not thoroughly integrated; consequently their organizations will probably not decisively shape the policies of the large body of salaried employees and civil servants.

Besides civil servants and technical and commercial employees, the new middle class includes a number of other groups, which here will be listed without any attempt to define their character: private teachers and nurses of both sexes; the higher employees of economic associations, of occupational societies, and of trade-unions and consumers' cooperatives; secretaries of labor organizations; the employees of insurance companies; actors, singers, musicians, chorus personnel and so on; employees of drug stores; and employees and editors of newspapers and periodicals. In short, chiefly all those who belong to the liberal professions, insofar as they are gainfully employed in a subordinate capacity, and the lower employees in the establishments of the liberal professions. Finally, we must mention the last of the larger groups of salaried employees, namely those engaged in agriculture.

All these groups have an entirely heterogeneous character. Sometimes they are the humble servants of a huge business organization and, quite naturally, they feel that their social status is under threat (for example technical employees). But there are also occupations in which salaried employees are able to maintain their traditional and historical position (especially in agriculture), or in which the number of available posts has in recent times considerably increased, so that these groups do not consider their economic status to be unfavorable. In any case, although conditions in one and the same group vary, it may be asserted that these groups, in the aggregate, are not of primary importance insofar as the general character of the new middle class is concerned, despite their rather considerable numerical strength. Moreover the practical demands of the several groups vary too much in fundamentals and, at times, have so little in common with those of the great masses of technical and commercial employees that one could hardly expect an organic connection among all these groups; in fact such an alliance is perhaps felt to be not imperative. Sometimes interests actually clash, as in the case of executive salaried employees and higher public officials, who in reality are called upon to perform a great many of their employers' functions. It must be pointed out, however, that the critical years of the revolution, because of the extensive proletarianization and leveling down of the new middle class and because of the urgent necessity of economic self-protection, stirred into action those occupational groups that had not been drawn into the general movement of salaried employees and civil servants. To some extent these groups (for example editors) appropriated the aims and methods (collective salary agreements) of the larger federations. In addition there are cases on record in which certain "liberal professions" formed a direct affiliation with the general federations of salaried employees and public officials (for example actors, musicians). These phenomena can be of lasting importance only if they are based on a changed position of the respective professions in the social scale, and not simply on a temporary dislocation of income levels.[19]

SUMMARY

It may be said that before the war the term new middle class (in accordance with the change that had already set in among the groups in question) was not very appropriate; after 1918 it became still less felicitous. Before the war all these social strata might have been called new middle class insofar as they endeavored to secure for themselves the economic status of the old middle class; in other respects they exhibited a tendency to form a stratum *sui generis,* and as such remained independent of the other social classes. At that time it was apparent that, should they ever attach themselves to some social class, it could be only the class of organized labor. This view was further strengthened by the conduct of employer associations. As a result of the postwar collapse this alliance has now become a fact. Urban society is constantly organizing itself on the principle of group interests, and the contract between employer and employee is more and more accentuated. An intermediate position between the classes is no longer possible and the fact of being employed in a dependent capacity triumphs over all class and traditional restraints. The adoption by salaried employees and public officials of the aims and methods of labor (collective salary agreements), and the tendency among civil servants to change their relationship with the state from a subordinate one determined by public law into a contractual one fixed by civil law are expressive of the fact that a single stratum of all gainfully employed (if not a single organization) is in the process of formation.

Compared with the prewar period social grouping has become much simpler. In the old days there was an extensive stratification of social groups, also within the new middle class, but much stratification was based on ideological rather than economic differences. The collapse of 1918, no less than the ensuing period of inflation, swept aside the last vestiges of economic differentiation and enhanced the social importance of organized labor to such a degree that, in the case of salaried employees, the most serious objections to an organic alliance with the trade unions disappeared. Accordingly salaried employees and civil servants followed the trends of the three principal trade unions. The undeniable tendency in recent years toward a return to the social stratification and distribution of power that existed before the war has been without effect upon the organic connection between salaried-employee and labor organizations. This statement implies that the grouping of the population according to class interests has made great progress since the war, and that the notion of social harmony is only a utopian ideal of some writers, the realization of which in a system of social forces and counterforces has remained a pious hope.

Notes

† Published in English in 1937 by the State Department of Social Welfare and the Department of Social Science, Columbia University, as a report on Project no. 165–97–6999–6027, conducted under the auspices of the Works Progress Administration. Edited and corrected in its present form by Abby Scher and Harry Dahms.

1. For lack of space, our account of the new middle class has of necessity been limited to essentials. Therefore historical explanations that would be especially appropriate in our discussion of civil servants have been entirely omitted.
2. The legal definition of the term salaried employee was attempted in the Employees' Insurance Act (Versicherungssgesetz fur Angestellte) of 1911, and recently in the Works Councils Act (Betriebsrategesetz) of 1920. In Section 1, Paragraph 1 of the former, the following groups in particular are mentioned:

    – Employees in executive positions, when such activity is their chief occupation.
    – Factory officials, foremen, and other employees in a similar high position, regardless of their training; office employees who are not occupied with small or routine tasks and when such activity is their chief occupation.
    – Commercial clerks and drug clerks.
    – Musicians and actors, regardless of the artistic merit of their performance.
    – Teachers and educators.
    – Captains, deck officers, engineers of German seagoing vessels and of craft engaged in inland navigation; also pursers and their assistants and other members of the crew who are likewise engaged in some high capacity, without regard to their training, and when such activity constitutes their chief occupation.

    On the other hand the Works Councils Act, Section 12, extends the lower limits of salaried employees by including office employees in the lower grades and apprentices, while it restricts its upper limits by excluding "business managers and department heads who are empowered to hire or discharge other employees in their business or in one of its divisions and upon whom partial or full power of attorney is conferred."
3. Commercial and office employees basically suffer from an overcrowding of their occupation. Thus in 1921 the commercial occupations, in comparison with others recording a satisfactory economic position, showed one of the most unfavorable conditions of the labor market; there were 319 male and 183 female applicants for every 100 available positions. Technical employees, thanks to the requirements of a specialized training, have fared better.
4. Incidentally these demands formed an important part of the economic program of Italian fascism, but they also characterize the policy of other countries in times of economic slackness and other sociopolitical instability.
5. In the large concerns (these with more than 50 employees) of the four industrial groups (machinery, textiles, food and the building industry, which employ the largest number of employees), we find 34 per cent of all industrial employees. On the other hand only 22 per cent of the total number of gainfully employed in industry are employed by large concerns.

6. The terms "civil servants exercising governmental authority" (*Hoheitsbeamte*) and "civil servants of governmental business enterprises" (*Betriebsbecamte*) appear to be gradually finding their way into current literature, although their use, especially of the former, is not consistent.

7. During the war the unions of salaried employees – particularly the radical ones – showed a decrease in membership. In spite of this these unions gained in importance inasmuch as they were integrated into the wartime organization together with the trade unions and employers' association. Besides, even before the collapse of 1918 the depreciation of the national currency had stimulated their campaign for more pay. Nevertheless it was only through the revolution of 1918 that the movement received its essentially new orientation and attained its present success.

8. The influx of women applies primarily to radical unions. For the rest, the most important and consistently conservative union, which characterizes itself as "Christian," the German National Federation of Business Employees, admits no women as members. Women employees who identify themselves with similar conservative trends have their own organization, the Association of Female Commercial and Office Employees.

9. Resulting from the amalgamation of three unions, one of which was even before the war affiliated with the independent trade unions, although it played no great role. Membership in these three unions increased ninefold from 1913 to 1919; the proportion of women rose from 33.3 per cent in 1913 (the average percentage of women in employees' unions amounted to 7.7 per cent) to 47.8 per cent in 1919.

10. Compared with the 62,000 members at the end of 1913. Prior to the war the organizations of foremen were unquestionably not regarded as trade unions. Their program was primarily one of mutual welfare. The development of the principle of trade unionism among them compared with that of other technical-employee unions was rendered difficult by their peculiar social position; although they came from the wage-earner class they were nevertheless representatives of the employers. One of the factors that served to transform their unions into trade unions was the introduction of the system of functional management in the large factories and plants. The functional foreman is no longer supposed to manage the whole shop and to represent the employer among the workers. Thus the entire activity of the old-style foremen is subdivided into eight functions (route clerk, speed boss, inspector, repair boss, gang boss, instruction card clerk, cost and time clerk, shop disciplinarian), which under the new system are exercised by as many separate individuals. The functional foreman, then, appears as a replaceable member of the entire organism. The ordinary or military type of organization in the workshop is abandoned and the single gang boss loses his identity as the symbol of the entrepreneur.

11. This association came into being in 1919 as a result of the amalga-

mation of the National Federation of Technicians with the more radical and younger Association of Technicians in Industry. In the new organization it was the latter's basic policy that prevailed. In a joint statement both proclaim the "unbridgeable gap between capital and labor" and express their intention "to continue unswervingly the fight against capitalism in common with all labor unions having similar aims, until the German technical employee has attained a position in the economic and political life that is compatible with his services."

12. One of the largest and oldest employee unions and at the same time the outstanding representative of the conservative wing. In the Federation of German Salaried Employee Unions there are other unions that do not share so pronouncedly this conservatism and the members of which could not in every case acquire membership in the German National Federation of Business Employees. The latter had, however, an "entente cordiale" with the Catholic Guilds, which are composed of clerical employees and independent merchants. Still, the fight against all "yellow" organizations is characteristic of all unions.

13. A very important exception was the Bund der Festbesoldeten (Civil Service Association).

14. As regards the living conditions of civil servants, we are currently informed by the statistics of income and standards of living that are published, for example, in *Wirtschaft und Statistik* (Economy and Statistics) or in the *Wirtschaftskurve* (Economic Curve) of the *Frankfurter Zeitung*. Cf. also Zeiler, *Der Beamtenschaft Not und Reggung* (Munich 1918). For the period before the war see Dannell, *Preussiche Jahrbucher*, 1908.

15. "Freedom of political opinion and of association are assured to all civil servants." "The civil servants will receive special representation in accordance with the more detailed provisions of a national law."

16. The equalization between the privileged position of the civil servant and his curtailed freedom of action in the economic struggle is, for example, embodied in a decree by the Federal Ministry of Transportation, on the occasion of the railroad strike of 1922, as follows: "Just as the Federal Government is not in a position to abrogate the appointment of the civil servant without disregarding protective legislation, so the civil servant has not the right to refuse to work." It is true that this mutual restriction is capable of different interpretations.

17. Since the German Federation of German Civil Service Employees has now made its own provisions of mutual help and the facilities of the Christian Federated Unions are open to civil-servant unions of similar trends, the Association for the Protection of Economic Interests of German Civil Service Employees has probably lost its importance.

18. The associations of higher-salaried employees – but not all – are federated in the Association of Executive Employees (Vereinigung der leitenden Angestellten), which had 21,000 members in 1922,

while those of public officials in the upper grades are organized in the National Association of Civil Servants in Elevated Positions (Reichsbund hoherer Beamten), which had 100,700 members in 1924.

19. On the so-called "brain worker," see Ludwig Sinzheimer, Ernst Francke and W. Lotz, *Die geistigen Arbeiter* (Munich, 1923); paper read at the meeting of the Verein fur Sozialpolitik (Social Policy Association), 1922; articles on writers, doctors, lawyers and actors in the *Handbuch der Politik*, 1921, vol. IV. But in our discussion only the "subordinates" (teachers, editors, actors and so on) claim our attention.

3 Middle-Class Notions and Lower-Class Theory*
Hans Speier

In the Weimar Republic two different views of white-collar workers gained currency: the lower-class theory and the middle-class theory. The lower-class theory was advanced by socialist intellectuals and politicians and by the Afa-Bund, (Allgemeinerfreier Angestelltenbund) while the middle-class view enjoyed great popularity among white-collar associations not connected to the Afa-Bund—principally the GdA (Gewerkschaftsbund der Angestellten) and the DHV, (Deutschmationaler Handlungegehilfen-Verbond) whose combined membership far exceeded that of the former. The middle-class view also found spokesmen among politicians in all political parties from the Democrats to the National Socialists. The most radical formulations did not originate with the members or functionaries of the associations, but with ideologists, whose center of work was neither the factory, the office, nor the shop, but the realm of political rhetoric. They wrote or spoke with passion, interpreting a reality they seldom knew through their own experience. What did Rudolf Borchardt, the poet, really know of the life of white-collar workers, or Ernst Jünger of the worries of laborers? What concrete observations lay at the bottom of Hans Freyer's fantasies about the "Volk"?

In all middle-class views, the salaried employees were assigned a position between the upper and lower strata, between the capitalists and the proletariat. It made no difference whether specific types of employees (commercial clerks, technicians) were singled out for special attention, as they were among the Christian-national organizations, or whether all the different types of white-collar workers were considered together as an "estate," as was characteristic of the GdA

---

* Reprinted from Hans Speier, *German White Collar Workers and the Rise of Hitler* (New Haven: Yale University Press, 1985).

87

conceptions. Such divergent emphases reflected the different organizational principles on which the functionaries of the various associations formulated their "sociologies." They all agreed, however—and this is decisive—that white-collar workers belonged to an intermediate "estate."

The line separating salaried employees from the strata above them was always less distinct than the boundary separating them from those below. For example, advocates of the proletarian theory followed the example of both legal practice and official census categories in excluding employees with executive functions from the stratum of white-collar workers, considering them instead as "economically independent," while the middle-class theoreticians tended to designate such persons as salaried employees.[1] (A parallel may be seen in the independent artisan stratum. Attempts were repeatedly made to include semi-industrial large-scale handicraft production as part of the handicraft economy, in consequence of which "handicraft" appeared to comprise a larger stratum than it actually did.) The lines of distinction that set white-collar workers apart from the lower strata, from blue-collar workers and employees operating office machines, were sharply drawn. The customary principles of this delimitation must be briefly considered.

Blue-collar workers were engaged mainly in production, white-collar workers chiefly in the distribution, planning, and preparation of work and in administration. Occasionally the social superiority of white- over blue-collar workers was derived from these functional differences,[2] but this derivation was generally untenable. Functional differences did exist between the two kinds of gainfully employed persons, but they were not always even recognizable in the activities of the individual employee or worker and therefore could not be the manifest basis of social rank. More importantly, economic function never determined social rank and prestige in society. If distributive functions had conferred superior rank upon those who performed them, the owner of a village dry goods shop, active in distribution, would have been superior to the artisan and even to the captain of industry, both of whom were active in productive functions. Social distinction could be conferred by the performance of distributive, planning, or preparatory functions only if they were superordinate to those which were exercised in the sphere of production. But inasmuch as economic necessity demands the cooperation of all these activities, and since none can be more easily dispensed with than any other, there simply is no autonomous rank order of functions. As a result, the different economic functions were not translated into a social hierarchy of the persons performing them.

The same reasoning applies to the notion that the distributive, preparatory, or administrative quality of their work helped to forge a special occupational consciousness among white-collar workers. Quite apart from the fact that such a consciousness would have been functional rather than occupational, the persons who performed white-collar tasks were not characterized by any special set of attitudes or distinctive social prestige. A broker, a woman selling flowers on the street, and a correspondent in a wholesale firm might share a general distributive function, but they differed widely with respect to rank, attitudes, and social consciousness. Social attitudes and ranks are evidently not grounded in economic functions, which are identified for other, analytic purposes, namely, the theoretical understanding of the larger economic process (distribution, production) or of the processes within the enterprise (administration, preparation of work). Even the negative definition—that the white-collar worker is in any case not "productive" like the blue-collar worker—is of little use, because many other social strata resemble white-collar workers in this respect without sharing their special rank or prestige. On the other hand, peasants and agricultural workers are productive in the same sense as workers without forming a social unit with them.

Of perhaps greater relevance, most salaried employees differ from workers in how their work activities are related to economic goods. The workers encounter goods as a concrete substance which they extract, refine, and transport. The salaried employee handles them in an abstract form as names or numbers, symbols or designs, measurements or patterns, or in their technical character or composition, or in respect to their economic cost, price, or profit. An important exception is the salesperson, but she or he distributes goods to people (customers) in a way the manual worker does not. This difference between salaried and manual workers did not confer a privileged rank on the white-collar worker. Indeed, no one could imagine that it did, except by erroneously equating it with the difference between physical and mental labor, and thus by disregarding the well-known difficulties in cleanly and serviceably distinguishing mental from physical work. This error was incorporated even into legal codes, which defined the salaried employee in terms of work activities that must not be "predominantly physical."[3]

The DHV always insisted that the work of commercial employees be regarded as "delegated" by the entrepreneur. As we shall see, this view came closest to a correct understanding of the superior rank occupied by the white-collar worker. The DHV claimed that commercial employees ranging "from the assistant bookkeeper to the responsible executive participate in the commercial direction of the enterprise."[4] And since entrepreneurs had delegated certain functions to these employees, they differed not only from manual workers but also from technical employees and foremen, whose work was thought "to resemble rather that of highly qualified workers."[5] Thus, the rivalry between commercial and technical employees within the enterprise was reflected in the opinions of their functionaries. A view from the employer's camp did not support the DHV:

> In the large (industrial) establishments . . . the work of the engineers is valued more highly. In one establishment the technicians enjoy special esteem, in the other the commercial employees. In general, the higher esteem of the technician may be due to the fact that he is engaged in the primary activity . . . upon which the secondary, distributive function of the merchant is based. A contributing cause of his high esteem is the fact that the technician has acquired more knowledge through longer education. Finally, the fact cannot be disregarded that, in general, the scientific education of the merchant is concluded with his apprenticeship and his attendance at a commercial school, whereas the technician, owing to this activity, must continuously try to enlarge his scientific knowledge.[6]

The middle-class thesis that entrepreneurial functions were delegated to commercial employees was not generally tenable. I. Silbermann, in his own middle-class theory of salaried employees, objected that numerous artisans and merchants combined the work of entrepreneurs, white-collar workers, and manual laborers in their activities, and that even many blue-collar workers could regard their functions as part of the entrepreneurial function. The thesis of the DHV was therefore "neither complete nor correct."[7] This criticism was also supported by the fact that entrepreneurial functions had changed with the historical development of the economic system. Was the self-employed owner of a shop the prototype for the entrepreneur in trade and commerce? Did the large, lowest strata of salaried employees in industry perform functions which once were contained in the work of a master craftsman? If the DHV argument were valid, delegated entrepreneurial activity would be found not just in the work of the commercial employees, nor, as Silbermann added, in the activity of many blue-collar workers, but also in the activities of *all* laborers, including those of the lowest-ranking unskilled workers. But it was already stretching the point to describe the work of auxiliary bookkeepers, office-machine operations, card-file keepers or money counters— in short, the work of the subordinate personnel in the office—as delegated entrepreneurial activity. The DHV explanation of social rank held neither for the workforce as a whole nor even for all salaried employees, but at best for only a small upper layer of white-collar workers.

The merit of the DHV thesis, however, is that it did not attempt to understand the white-collar workers' social privileges exclusively as a consequence of their economic tasks, but rather as a product of their ability to decide how these tasks were to be performed. This decision-making capability was actually controlled by those few persons who were dominant within the enterprise. The social rank, powers and prestige of white-collar workers were delegated to them by these persons. This derivation, which incidentally does not do justice to *all* principles of the social rank order, will be given more comprehensive and detailed treatment in Chapter 6 of this volume. Here it suffices to observe, in the interest of precision, that the issue is not one of delegated control but of the delegated prestige of the entrepreneur and employer—in short, of "the capitalist." In his entrepreneurial activities, the capitalist deals with such outsiders as competitors and consumers; as employer, he faces the employees within the enterprise. The capitalist (as a sociological type) thus derives his rank and prestige from both external and internal sources. Similarly, the rank and prestige of the salaried employee depends not only on his position within the hierarchy of the enterprise, but also on the importance of the enterprise in which he is employed. Thus, for instance, the bookkeeper in one of the many medium-sized enterprises is less highly esteemed—despite equal pay—than the bookkeeper who works for a "prominent" firm. The social self-esteem of the white-collar worker is also influenced by this difference.

The notion that commercial employees performed entrepreneurial functions was often closely associated with the view that they differed from manual workers in their possession of an occupation and a corresponding occupational consciousness. This view, however, could not provide the basis of a middle-class theory of white-collar workers.

A superficial effort was required to look for consciousness, pride, and honor of occupation among white-collar workers but not among laborers. In fact, for several reasons, consciousness and pride of occupation were more prominent among highly qualified workers than among clerks. For example, guild traditions had remained powerful in the occupations of various workers, because the corresponding craft participated strongly in the training of the young. Moreover the organizations to which manual workers belonged originated as occupational associations, whereas the many associations of salaried employees had, from the beginning, an organizational basis that cut across several occupations. Finally, changing from one type of economic enterprise to another was a constant possibility for salaried employees because their function was not specifically confined to any single occupation.

Occasionally, the term "occupation" was used to convey a somewhat different meaning. In plans for an occupational restructuring of society, "occupation" was meant to convey an obligation to serve in a given type of enterprise without regard to its social rank. This and associated conceptions of "occupational estate" and the "occupational order of society" were of fascist origin and were no less opposed to the lower-class theory than was the middle-class theory of the white-

collar workers. Yet, even working with the fascist conception of an occupational estate, the DHV attempted to justify the social privileges of white-collar workers by claiming
that commercial clerks still constituted a special "occupational group."[8] Every occupation comprises people of different social positions and ranks, the DHV contended,
including employers, white-collar, and blue-collar workers.
If commercial and technical employees formed a special estate,
it certainly was no occupational estate. Technical employees
belonged to their "estate organization" not because of their
occupation, but because of their social position within that
occupation. Workers and entrepreneurs of the same occupation could not join. Werner Sombart was quite right in
saying that an association of employers and an association
of employees were not two occupational associations, but
none at all.[9]

In modern society, with its highly developed division of
labor, people engaged in the same occupational work seldom form a community. The content and form of social
life are determined primarily by equality of occupation only
in a few circumstances, which include continuity of work in
a given occupation, apprenticeship leading to work as a skilled
master, and the chance to tie the meaning of life to one's
occupation. These circumstances did not exist for white-collar
workers in the Weimar Republic, least of all for those of
low and middle rank.

Every salaried employee was in danger of losing his job
regardless of his performance, so that it was not possible to
speak of the continuity of his work in a given occupation.
Even the elite employees in executive positions were vulnerable to the business cycle. The decisive facts in their
professional life, as in that of the mass of lower-placed
employees from whom they tried to distinguish themselves,[10]
were not merit and performance but the collapse or takeover of an enterprise, or a technical innovation. In 1929
Vela, the organization of executive employees, investigated
the reasons for dismissal of 537 unemployed members. The
causes in 174 cases were bankruptcy, liquidation, or closing; in 93 cases contraction of work or personnel; in 54
cases rationalization or reorganization; in 42 cases change
of ownership or takeover; and in 102 cases such varied reasons

as "too expensive," "too old," illness, or intrigue. Only 12 of 537 executive employees were dismissed because of dissatisfaction with their performance.[11]

A large majority of white-collar workers did only fragmented work, with the consequence that "he who performs only a small fragment of the work can hardly develop a lively interest in the whole work process."[12] The occupation had thus disintegrated. Nowhere was this fact more visible than in the professional training of the young. Only in exceptional cases were apprentices instructed in such a way as to become acquainted with all aspects of their occupation, and only in exceptional cases did they gain the ability to understand the work process as a whole.

In 1925 in Prussia, 9 percent of white-collar workers employed in industry and handicraft were apprentices, as were 14.5 percent of those employed in trade and commerce. In subsequent years significant changes occurred at the expense of adult workers. In 1930 one girl was employed as an apprentice for every adult female employed in trade; in small retail trade only every fourth salesperson was not a female apprentice![13] As the economic crisis deepened, the inclination grew stronger to regard the apprentice not as someone in training, but simply as someone who worked cheaply. In 1932 many smaller establishments had more "apprentices" than employees.

The DHV declared that the apprentice's familiarity with merchandise had decreased as the size of enterprise increased. A GdA survey in the fall of 1931 established that many apprentices were no longer trained in important areas of their occupation. The extent of their shortcomings was almost incredible, as table 6.1 indicates. It seems impossible in the light of these figures to regard apprenticeship as a time during which young people were trained to know their occupation and to recognize it as a lifelong task. The extraordinary efforts of the white-collar workers' associations to enhance the occupational training of their young members was always justified by pointing to the inadequacy of training on the job.

In sum, the middle-class theory could be derived neither from a special function in the economic process nor from occupational qualities. Even "delegated entrepreneurial activity" was to be found only among a small minority of white-collar workers. The stratum as a whole comprised many employees of very different ranks so that only those at the top were in social proximity to the entrepreneurs. Moreover, even the social prestige of this small minority at the highest rungs of the social ladder—like the prestige of the middle strata—had been founded only in part on the delegation of prestige in the enterprise.

Table 3.1   Training of GdA apprentices in their third year of apprenticeship (percentages)

Not trained in	Retail trade	Wholesale trade	Industry
Simple correspondence	77	47	29
Correspondence according to dictation and instruction	83	52	36
Simple bookkeeping	84	66	63
Complex bookkeeping	93	96	78
Treatment of goods	58	42	31
Wage calculation	95	96	52
Independently serving customers	13	–	–

Source: GdA (ed.), *Die kommende Angestellten-Generation,* (Berlin 1933), p. 103.

Before turning to the bases of social prestige, we must still briefly consider the theory which attempted to explain the social prestige, political actions, and opinions of white-collar workers in terms of their class situation. This theory offers greater initial insight into the economic conditions of life of salaried employees than does the middle-class theory, but it encounters considerable difficulties in its explanation of the social prestige and political orientations of white-collar workers.

According to the lower-class theory, salaried employees are proletarians. Like blue-collar workers, whose social situation they share, they are forced to sell their labor-power on the labor market, their economic life is precariously dependent on the business cycle, their interests conflict with those of the employers, and any improvement of their wages, working conditions, and economic life prospects depends exclusively on vigorous collective action. Based on elements of Marxist class theory, this conception identifies white-collar workers not as an estate but as part of the working class. Since the last third of the nineteenth century, the economic situation of many white-collar workers had indeed approached the working conditions of manual labor. Achieving independence had become more rare, economic insecurity had increased, the functions to be performed at work had been increasingly specialized and soon were mechanized as well. The distance between the average employee and the entrepreneur was growing even as the employee's working conditions and life prospects came increasingly to resemble those of blue-collar workers.

After the revolution of 1918 the lower-class theory seemed to find strong support in the adoption of trade union practices by white-collar associations. Did this trade unionization signify the final liquidation of occupational politics and the acknowledgement of the class situation, that is, of the basic socioeconomic conflicts between salaried employees and the entrepreneurs? The middle-class conception of the white-collar worker as a private civil servant appeared to fade. A degree of organizational similarity even developed in all blue- and white-collar workers' unions, regardless of their political orientation. Although all of these trends might be seen as attesting to the growing insight of salaried employees into their own proletarianization, it must yet be emphasized that these new proletarians, despite their unionization, did not renounce their privileges in social prestige vis-à-vis the old manual-labor proletariat. Disregarding a relatively small, radical minority, unionization did not signify a turn by salaried employees to anticapitalistic efforts and socialist aims.

First, in this connection, trade union efforts to increase wages and improve working conditions do not result in the socialization of the means of production and are not necessarily linked to the socialist demand to bring it about. On the contrary, before World War I the socialist idea had already been crowded out among the workers by the practical daily work of the trade unions. The pledge to socialism became a kind of rhetorical tribute functionaries paid to the reformist movement in order to remind Social Democratic workers of the political and moral dignity withheld from them by the state. Such reminders did not imply an obligation to promote social revolution, but increased solidarity in the struggle for social progress and Social Democratic seats in the Reichstag. Thus, even the old proletariat did not fight foremost for the realization of socialism but for raising the standard of living. It is possible to view this phenomenon as an aspect of the embourgeoisement of the old proletariat and then to ask why white-collar workers, in pursuing their interests, should have been less middle-class-oriented than blue-collar workers.

But the decisive problem for the lower-class theory was the undeniable fact that a large majority of the so-called new proletariat, despite its unionization, became politically active neither along with nor next to the old proletariat, but in fact emphasized their differences over their similarities. Despite their trade-union activities, the majority of the white-collar workers continued to insist on their social superiority over blue-collar workers. They also detested and maligned the general political values which the majority of blue-collar workers in the Weimar Republic held dear, including democracy, parliamentarianism, reconciliation, and the desire to reach an understanding with the victorious powers following World War I. Like their views on social policy, the unionization of the middle-class associations did not at all mean they had abandoned their middle-class conceits. Instead, of the three types of unions that white-collar workers could have joined during the Weimar years only the "middle-class" organizations *gained* in size and importance. Toward the end of the Weimar Republic they emphasized the middle-class self-understanding of white-collar workers even more sharply than they had at its beginning. For example, in 1931 a programmatic publication of the GdA, which was politically more moderate than the DHV, stated that "the commercial clerk, the technician, the foreman, and the office employee in the past were miles removed from political thought and feeling. . . . War, revolution, and the postwar period have been unable to change anything in this innate attitude of the white-collar workers. On the contrary, today's salaried employee feels himself more strongly than ever to be a member of the 'new middle class.'"[14]

The lower-class theory explained the orientation of the white collar workers' middle-class associations as the result of their "false consciousness." But how did it explain false consciousness? The evidence used by its adherents to demonstrate that nothing must exist in practice that did not exist in theory was deplorably scanty. False consciousness was usually presented as a symptom of a general retrogression. Different tempos in the development of the relation of production and of the conceptions which human beings form of them created the possibility of "inadequate," historically obsolete thinking. Also, the tradition of a non-proletarian, middle-class past remained alive among the salaried employees, and thus prevented their recognition of the current social situation. It was only a matter of time, however, before sociological enlightenment would illumine this situation darkened by wishes, memories, habits, and resentments.

In the most concise ideological critique, which was published prior to 1933, the history of white-collar workers was divided into three phases.[15] After attributing an ideal-typical ideology to each phase, each type of white-collar workers' association was located in its appropriate phase according to the ideology which best fit it. As a result of this procedure, all non-socialist associations could be viewed as living under the spell of the past. Only the free trade union Afa-Bund had reached the historical and ideological crest of the present. It alone offered the "true," correct consciousness, because only its conception of white-collar workers as "new proletarians" corresponded to the most recent economic situation. The result was the following scheme:

Social position	Corresponding ideology	Today's organization
Phase 1: assistant to employer	Not *yet* employer.	Vela
Phase 2: new middle class	*Not* worker but *new* class between "the" classes.	DHV, GdA
Phase 3: salaried employee	*Not* worker, but part of the proletariat.	Afa-Bund

This ideological critique, which summarizes what the lower-class theory has to offer with respect to the phenomenon of rank and esteem, does not excel in precision. Whether the notion that past traditions haunt the present can be reconciled with the categories of the class theory is at least questionable and in any case should be suggested only if it can be demonstrated that specific institutions and particular current social conditions sustain a consciousness that was based upon and corresponded to earlier conditions of production.[16] Without such a demonstration, the relationship between base and superstructure, or reality and consciousness, is destroyed.

Middle-class conceptions also derived the social consciousness of white-collar workers from their traditions,[17] which they valued positively, as opposed to the lower-class theory's negative valuation. Tradition was regarded not as a source of error but as an especially valuable testimony to social rank and esteem. The precision of this derivation again left much to be desired, but because the middle-class conceptions were not based on the methodological presupposition that consciousness corresponded to reality, their shortcomings may be more easily forgiven.

The proponents of the lower-class theory moved away from tradition with the speed of those who felt themselves to be in possession of the rational truth. Once they were engaged in a conflict with "ideologues" who derived the rank of the white-collar workers from traditions, they could no longer defend the rank of salaried employees against attacks that originated in the camp of manual workers. They did declare that the salaried employee, though a proletarian, was no blue-collar worker, but they never focused on the difference. When C. Nörpel,[18] a spokesman for manual labor, attacked the privileges of white-collar workers in his fight for collective labor legislation, their representatives could only parry with arguments closely akin to middle-class notions. Thus, when Nörpel declared that no fundamental difference existed between the labor of workers and that of salaried employees, and that the latter were only legally privileged, the representatives of the proletarian white-collar workers replied that the salaried employees performed "after all . . . special functions. . . . If a struggle against the existing law pertaining to salaried employees . . . had anything to do with socialism, then socialism would be tantamount to the equalization of all workers on the lowest level. Socialism is the precise opposite. . . . It is correct, isn't it, that socialism can be created only if the highly qualified strata of labor, i.e., the salaried employees, can also be counted on to support it?"[19] Regardless of whether this rejoinder was true or false, it was in any case not supported by the conception of salaried employees as proletarians. Instead, it relied on a modified class theory which presented the proletariat as hierarchically stratified. The principles of this modification, however, were not closely considered. Such as effort would have involved an analysis of social rank, its significance, and its content, and this in turn would have forced a revision of the Marxist theory of true and false consciousness. In other words, in their reply to Nörpel's argument, the proletarian white-collar workers appeared suddenly as highly qualified workers. This made sense with regard to the relatively conservative foremen, but not to the average socialist member of the ZdA and the Butab, that is, the proletarian commercial and technical employees.

Notes

1. Thus, the DHV pointed out in its polemics against Vela, the association of executive employees: "It is sensible for salaried employees who advance to executive positions to remain in the associations which they joined at the beginning of their professional careers." (*Rechenschaftsbericht* (Hamburg, 1928), p, 269). J. Silbermann, a functionary of the VwA, did not classify the "other managers" of the census, including the directors, as "independents" but as salaried employees. (*Die Angestellten als Stand* (Berlin, 1932), p. 20).

2. P. Bröcker, *Die Arbeitnehmerbewegung* (Hamburg, 1919), p. 98; M. Rössiger, *Der Angestellte von 1930* (Berlin, 1928), p. 15.

3. Cf. F. Croner, "Der Begriff der Angestellten in der neueren Rechtssprechung," (*Ass,* vol. 60, (1928), p. 188. The concept of the salaried employees according to the 1911 insurance law for salaried employees does not coincide with that of the 1929 law on shop councils; cf. E. Lederer and J. Marschak, "Der neue Mittelstand," (Tubingen, 1926), pp. 120–41, note 2.

4. DHV. ed. *Die Gehaltslage der Kaufmannsgehilfen,* (Hamburg, 1931), p. 9.

5. Concerning the DHV view of technical employees, cf. also O. Thiel,

Die Sozialpolitik der Kaufmannsgehilfen, (Hamburg, 1926) p. 4. "The GdA organizes not only male and female salaried employees of every kind but also certain groups of higher workers, male and female, whom we cannot recognize as salaried employees." Technical employees reversed the bias: "Unfortunately, it is often forgotten that the production of goods precedes their distribution." Butab, ed., *Der Techniker im Tarifvertrag,* p. 8.

6. W. D. von Witzleben, "Der Tarifvertrag für die Angestellten der Berliner Metallindustrie," (Berlin, 1926), p. 27.

7. I. Silbermann, *Die Angestellten als Stand,* (Berlin, 1932), p. 5.

8. Departing from its usual stress on professional consciousness, the DHV reproached the bank clerks—i.e., white-collar workers with a truly pronounced professional pride—that their attitude was outdated: "The old social isolation of the bank clerks from the majority of other commercial clerks has favored this attitude. But this attitude is especially misplaced in banking, because there the enormous number of dismissals during the past years, which has forced tens of thousands of bank clerks into other enterprises, has clearly demonstrated that they can prevail only as members of the big family of commercial clerks," *Rechenschaftsbericht des DHV für 1928,* (Hamburg), p. 88.

9. W. Sombart, "Beruf," *Hwb der Soziologie,* in A. Vier Kandt (ed.), p. 31.

10. H. Schäfer, "Die leitenden Angestellten: Ein neuer sozialer Typus," *Bergwerks Zeitung,* 11 November 1928.

11. The following information on the number of job applications submitted by unemployed executives taken from *Rechenschaftsbericht der Vela 1929,* (Hamburg), pp. 246–47, may complement the picture: 1–50 applications were submitted by 186 unemployed executives; 50–100 by 111; 100–200 by 87; 200–300 by 43; 300–600 by 44; 600–1000 by 19; and 1000–1500 by 13. Twenty-one persons said they had sent "hundreds" or "innumerable" applications. In 12 cases no reply was received; in 117 cases less than 10 percent of the written applications were answered, in 89 cases 10–20 percent, in 56 cases 20–30 percent. The remainder received replies more frequently.

12. A. Zimmermann, *Der Deutschnationale Handlungsgehilfen-Verband,* (Hamburg, n.d), p. 95.

13. According to the report of the factory inspector; cf. the statistic in GdH (ed.), *Die kommende Angestelltengeneration,* (Berlin, 1933), pp. 11–18.

14. *Der GdA-Führer, 1931,* p. 120. Cf. also J. Jahn, "Das Sozialbewusstsein der Angestellten," (Der Kaufmann in wirtschaft und Recht, 1930), pp. 246–47.

15. F. Croner, "Die Angestellten seit der Währungsstabilisierung" (Ass vol. 60 (1928), pp, 103–46. For a recent, much more detailed Marxist analysis of white-collar workers, cf. U. Kadritzke, *Angestellte: Die geduldigen Arbeiter* (Frankfurt, 1975). The book combines a praiseworthy presentation of copious data with the demand that the reader translate the author's views, which are hidden in a doctrinaire jargon, into intelligible German. They defy translation into English. For example, Kadritzke writes about insurance for salaried employees:

"Die spezifische, durchaus schon taktisch konzipierte 'Borniertheit' der Bourgeoisie konstituiert in der Gründung einer besonderen, die rechtliche Exklusivstellung ergänzenden Angestelltenversicherung ein Moment der 'Angestelltenmentalität,' das, obgleich seine objektive gesellschaftliche Basis schon zu schwinden beginnt, die Formen der folgenden Klassenauseinandersetzungen doch *folgenreich bestimmen kann*" (p. 226).

16. C. Dreyfuss in *Beruf und Ideologie der Angestellten* (Munich, 1933), recognized this fact, which constitutes the methodological merit of his book. Dreyfuss endeavored to prove in detail that the entrepreneurs created ever anew the *illusion* of prestige through the carefully calculated creation of an artificial hierarchy in the firm. Although this explanation does not suffice to explain the phenomenon of social esteem, it is more productive than the Marxian assumption of "false consciousness."

17. Cf. J. Jahn, *Das Sozialbewusstsein der Angestellten* (Der Kaufman in Wirtschaft Recht, 1930).

18. C. Nörpel, "Grenzen des Arbeitsrechts" *Der Arbeit*, vol. 8 (1932). Cf. also in the same journal the discussion following this article.

19. Afa-Bund, ed., *Protokoll des 4. Afa-Gewerkschaftskongresses*, (Berlin, 1931), p. 151.

4 The Growth of the New Middle Class*

Anthony Giddens

There is a now famous short passage in the "fourth volume" of *Capital, Theories of Surplus Value,* in which Marx criticizes Ricardo for having neglected "the constantly growing number of the middle classes, those who stand between the workman on the one hand and the capitalist and landlord on the other." These middle classes, Marx declares, "are a burden weighing heavily on the working base and increase the social security and power of the upper ten thousand."[1] The statement is an enigmatic one, in spite of some recent attempts to make it appear otherwise,[2] because it does not accord with the main weight of Marx's theoretical thinking, either on class in general, or the "middle class" in particular. It must be attributed to the remarkable prescience of a man whose insights not infrequently broke the bounds of the theoretical formulations whereby he sought to discipline them. That it describes a fundamental aspect of modern social reality is unquestionable; and the same is true of the more characteristic Marxian conception that the tendency of capitalist development is to diminish the proportional significance in the class structure of those whom he normally designated as the "petty bourgeoisie." I shall henceforth refer to this grouping, however, as the "old middle class," using the term "middle class" without qualification to refer to propertyless non-manual, or "white-collar," workers.

The decline of the old middle class, while a definite and identifiable phenomenon in the capitalist societies since the nineteenth century, has not proceeded in quite the radical fashion which Marx probably, and later Marxists certainly, expected. Not only are there, even today, important differences between the contemporary societies in terms of the

* Reprinted from Anthony Giddens, *The Class Structure of Advanced Societies* (New York: Harper Collins, 1975).

relative size of the old middle class, but its decay has taken the form of a slowly declining curve, rather than a progressive approach to zero. Bernstein and Lederer, two of the first self-proclaimed Marxists to attempt systematically to confront the problems posed for orthodox Marxist theory by the burgeoning of the white-collar sector, were almost as perturbed by the stubborn persistence of the old middle class as by the growth of the new. But, however important the old middle class may remain in certain countries, there can be no doubt that the phenomenon of overwhelming consequence since the turn of the century is the massive relative enlargement of the white-collar sector.[3]

In spite of general agreement upon the decline of the old middle class, statistical comparisons between different countries are extremely difficult to make. Modern economists have not been greatly interested in very small enterprises, and the relevant statistical materials are extremely patchy and incomplete. The figures do, however, suggest a general pattern which applies, although with quite wide discrepancies, to most of the capitalist societies: a pattern of a steady relative diminution of small businesses (including within this category small farms, manufacturing and retailing enterprises) from the closing decades of the nineteenth century up to the early years of the 1930s; whence the decline continues, but at a considerably reduced gradient. Compared with larger enterprises, however, small businesses typically manifest a very high rate of turnover.[4]

There are also problems in making comparisons between different societies in the overall growth of white-collar labor, but the general trends are so striking that these can be overlooked for present purposes. The relative advance of the white-collar sector has proceeded furthest in the United States, which has recently been hailed as the first "middle-class society."[5] Whether or not this is so, in the sense of manual workers being outnumbered by white-collar workers, depends upon the criteria used to make the relevant discriminations between occupational categories. Thus one recent estimate (1969) places them at parity, each comprising 48 per cent of the total labour force; if, however, only the male labour force is considered, manual workers outnumber non-manual employees by 54 to 41 per cent. Certainly, in terms of the proportion of white-collar workers in the labor force as a whole, few other capitalist countries come near to matching the United States. Figures for Britain for 1959 show 29 percent of the total labor force as non-manual workers, a rise of only 1 percent over 1951, and 7 percent more than 1921. In Japan, in 1963 white-collar workers numbered 27 percent of the non-agricultural labour force, an advance from 24.5 percent in 1944.[6] It has been commonly assumed that the differences between the United States and countries such as Britain and Japan are simply a matter of "lag," indicative of the lower level of technical development of these countries—and that therefore in this case it is the United States that shows to the other societies "the image of their own future." But there are some indications that this may be a mistaken, or at least an oversimplified, conclusion. For there seems to have occurred a levelling off of the relative growth of the white-collar sector in the United States over the past decade; and a similar phenomenon seems also to have occurred in other societies, but at the considerably lower ratios of non-manual workers that characterize these societies compared with the United States. An illustrative case is that of Britain, quoted above; another is that of France, where the ratio has barely changed over the last dozen years.[7]

But, of course, it is misleading in itself to treat white-collar labor as an undifferentiated category, and the overall expansion of the white-collar sector in capitalist societies conceals differential rates of growth in various occupational subcategories. Whereas the relatively early enlargement of the white-collar sector mainly concerned the growth of clerical and sales occupations, in neocapitalism those occupations usually grouped by census statisticians as "professional and technical" labor show the highest recent rates of development—although these nowhere comprise any more than a fairly small minority of white-collar workers as a whole.

THE CONDITIONS OF MIDDLE-CLASS STRUCTURATION

The differentiation between the market capacities conferred by educational and technical qualifications, as compared with manual skills or pure labor-power, in capitalist societies has everywhere taken the form not only of quite clear-cut divergences in income, but also in other modes of economic reward. In terms of income alone, while there have been certain important internal changes within the general category of white-collar labor as a whole, there has been an overall stability in the differential between the mean incomes of non-manual versus manual workers—that is to say, if real income distributions at the turn of the century are compared with those of today, since there have been substantial fluctuations in interim periods. Thus in both Britain and United States the differential between non-manual and manual workers was reduced during World War I, and again during the subsequent war, and has since re-established itself.

The significant changes which have occurred, now well-documented, concern, first, a relative diminution of the income of clerical workers within the white-collar sector, and, secondly, the development of some degree of "overlap" at the margins between non-manual and manual labour.[8] But out of these changes in the gross income statistics an enormous mythology has been built, in much of the technical literature on class as well as in the lay press. The apparent merging in the economic returns accruing to manual compared with non-manual labour looks very different if the facts of the matter are inspected more closely. In the first place, the traditional superiority of the white-collar worker in terms of job security has by no means disappeared: in general terms, non-manual workers continue to enjoy a greater measure of security, even there is some cause to suppose that certain categories of manual workers will increasingly enjoy more favorable contractual conditions in the future. Secondly, typical patterns of overall career earnings are quite different in the two categories. It is not only the oft-quoted fact of the range of promotion opportunities which are potentially open to white-collar workers, but are largely denied to manual workers, which is at issue here. Even leaving this aside, the latter characteristically experience a "declining curve" of earnings which the former, often having guaranteed annual increments, usually do not encounter. Thus Fogarty shows that, in Britain, unskilled manual workers reach peak income at an average age of 30, and hence drop some 15–20 percent to retirement age; skilled workers tend to reach their peak earnings some ten years later, and subsequently drop about 10–15 percent.[9] In addition, the length of the working week of manual workers is longer than that of non-manual employees: in 1966 in Britain the former averaged 44 hours a week, as compared with 38 hours for white-collar workers.[10] Thirdly, a considerably larger proportion of those in non-manual occupations are in receipt of fringe benefits of various kinds, such as pension and sick-pay schemes: in most countries these workers also gain disproportionately from tax remissions as result of participation in such schemes.[11]

While there are variations in these phenomena between different societies, particularly if we consider the case of Japan, these do not alter the overall picture. If we consider the totality of economic returns available to manual and non-manual workers, the idea that any kind of overall "merging" of the two groupings is taking place may be unequivocally rejected. The overlap is confined to segments of skilled manual occupations on the one hand, and of clerical and sales occupations on the other. But the major characteristic of these latter occupations is that they are everywhere increasingly monopolized by women—a fact of great importance in considering the nature of the boundary between the working and middle classes. Thus in Britain, which appears typical in this respect, the proportion of women in white-collar occupations rose from 30 to 45 percent between 1911 and 1961; but they are almost wholly clustered in clerical and sales occupations—those which Lockwood has referred to, perhaps somewhat archaically now, as "white-bloused" occupations. In fact, it has recently been claimed, *à propos* of clerical labour, that "In the future, the few men remaining in clerical jobs will be 'juniors' working their way up and the routine male clerk, as a career grade, will become extinct."[12]

In enquiring into the factors linking these differences in

market capacity to class structuration, we are fortunate to possess a number of fairly detailed cross-national studies of social mobility which, whatever the methodological difficulties involved, allow us to reach some quite definite conclusions as regards the mediate structuration of the class relationships differentiating middle and working classes. In the capitalist societies, since the end of the nineteenth century, there has typically been a substantial amount of upward intergenerational mobility across the non-manual/manual line; but this is primarily to be explained in terms of the relative expansion of the white-collar sector. The thesis originally promoted by Lipset and Bendix, however—that rates of intergenerational mobility from manual to non-manual labor tend to be basically similar in the advanced societies—is evidently oversimplified, if not entirely misguided. Thus, as S. M. Miller showed, there are significant differences, even if the state socialist societies are excluded, between countries in terms of the *patterning* of mobility chances. Some societies have low rates of upward and downward intergenerational mobility across the non-manual/manual line; some show considerably higher rates of both upward mobility, while others have yet different combinations of these rates. One of the significant findings of social mobility investigations is that virtually all movement, whether upward or downward, inter- or intragenerational, across the non-manual/manual division, is "short-range": that is to say, takes place in such a way as to minimize achieved differences in market capacity.[13] Thus there is some sense in speaking, as Parkin does, of the operation of a sort of "buffer zone" between the two class groupings: most mobility takes place in and out of this zone, which acts to cushion any tendency towards the collapse of mobility differentials separating the two. Those social mobility investigations which include time-series cohort studies indicate that there has not been much change in rates of mobility between manual and non-manual labour over the period since World War I.

Taken overall, the findings of these studies show quite conclusively the importance of mediate structuration as a major source of class differentiation between non-manual and manual labour in the capitalist societies. But this can only be analytically separated from the various bases of proximate structuration, which in fact help to explain the origins of observed variations in mobility chances. Primary among these is the division of labor characteristic of the productive enterprise, and the paratechnical relations associated with it; and this is obviously linked to, but again has to be analytically distinguished from, the system of authority relationships that pertain within the enterprise.

It is perfectly clear that, since the first origins of the modern large-scale factory, there has come into being a generic disparity between white- and blue-collar labor – suggested by those very terms themselves, as well as by the terminology of "non-manual" and "manual" work—in terms of task attributes in the division of labour. As Lockwood has stressed, the clerical worker, with a relatively weak market capacity, has typically shared conditions of labor which have far more in common with higher-level managerial workers than with the workers on the shop-floor. Clerical employees work in the "office," which is normally materially separated from the shop-floor and often is elevated above it, such that the office workers may physically "look down upon" the workers. Whereas the nature of manual work-tasks frequently involves strenuous and exhausting labour in conditions which soil the hands and clothing, the clerk normally works in a relatively clean environment, at a task which simply involves the manipulation of symbolic materials. Even clerical workers, quite apart from higher-level management, may have little or no direct contact with manual workers, since the foreman is normally the principal channel of communication between office and factory floor. In Lockwood's words: "The converse of the working cooperation of clerks and management is the social isolation of the office worker from the manual worker. The completeness of the separation of these two groups of workers is perhaps the most outstanding feature of industrial organization."[14] Obviously the degree to which this is so varies, both in relation to size of enterprise and to the particular industrial sector involved; but the general principle holds good, and also applies to the case of Japanese industry, where the organization of the enterprise is in some other respects quite different from that typical of Western societies; although in Japan the separation of white-collar from manual labor in the enterprise has been historically reinforced by the status discrimination between *shokuin* and *koin.*

In his analysis, however, Lockwood assimilates these aspects of the paratechnical relations of modern factory organization with the authority relationships of the enterprise. But while these factors may be closely associated within the characteristic form of productive organization in capitalist societies, and even in the advanced societies in general, it is important to draw a general distinction between them. For, at the cost of some degree of oversimplification, it can be said that, while any substantial modification of a system of paratechnical relations necessarily involves alteration to pre-existing techniques of production, change in the authority system does not inevitably entail modification in technique— a fact which becomes of major importance in assessing certain possibilities of "industrial democracy" in both capitalist and state socialist societies. The authority structure of the enterprise should be regarded neither as an inseparable part of the paratechnical relations of modern industrial production, nor, in Dahrendorf's view, as constituting a "class system" *sui generis,* but as one factor promoting the structuration of class relationships. From this latter aspect, we may accept Lockwood's designation of authority as a significant element contributing to a general class differentiation between white- and blue-collar labor. In all capitalist societies, the authority structure of the industrial enterprise is basically hierarchical within management; but manual workers confront management as a grouping subject to directive commands, without themselves being part of a command hierarchy. As Lockwood indicates, even clerical workers participate in such a hierarchy, and correspondingly tend to be regarded by the workers, and to regard themselves, as "belonging to management": clerks, in Croner's term, participate in the delegation of authority, while even those blue-collar workers with the most favorable market capacity, skilled manual workers, do not.[15]

There has been much debate recently over how far what I have called class structuration is in some sense "primarily" influenced by relationships established within the enterprise, or alternatively how far it is conditioned first and foremost by factors extrinsic to the productive organization itself. Even the protagonists in the debate, however, have to admit that there is no question of any simple determinism involved, one way or the other, and for my purposes here it is sufficient to stress that there are necessarily definite *inter*connections between intrinsic and extrinsic factors, which in a more detailed discussion could fairly easily be spelled out more precisely. The most important of these factors in promoting a general differentiation between white- and blue-collar workers are the distributive groupings formed by neighborhood "clustering," and certain types of status group formation. The tendency toward neighborhood clustering undoubtedly varies substantially, both in relation to differences in size and density of urban areas, and to differences in the overall social and political structures of the capitalist societies. Thus the existence of a large underclass, as in the United States, partially cuts across any very clear contrast between "middle-class neighborhoods" and "working-class neighborhoods," although it by no means obviates it altogether. Moreover, neighborhood class segregation can be counteracted, in so far as national or local bodies intervene in the "free market in housing" by neighborhood planning. But the strength of the tendency towards neighborhood separation is undeniable, especially in the "old-established" capitalist societies like Britain, and is supported by the fact that the greater job security that is characteristic of white-collar labor generally makes for a wider availability of house loans and mortgages.[16]

Obviously neighborhood class segregation is never complete, and there are differences between neighborhoods within the major class categories: as represented, for example, by the existence of so-called rough and respectable working-class, neighborhoods, in which there is an evident recognition (at least on the part of the "respectable") of a definite status discrimination between types of housing area. But this complicates rather than undermines the predominant line of demarcation, concentrated most strongly upon the white/blue-collar division. Neighborhood differentiation undoubtedly has an important effect upon the "visibility" of class relationships. When people are asked to draw "phenomenal maps" of city neighborhoods, these show large blank areas which represent neighborhoods of which they have little knowledge—and among which there is normally a pronounced skewing in class terms.

Differences in neighborhood organization are directly bound up with the exploitative connotations of class relationships, apart from those pertaining to the economic sphere itself—particularly insofar as these differences influence the distribution of educational chances. The mechanisms which govern the process whereby "vicious circles" of underprivilege are set up in this respect are by now well understood. Working-class families are larger in average size than those of the middle class, and the amount of direct parental contact is lower—a phenomenon which, insofar as it influences the verbal facility of children, may have lasting effects upon intellectual abilities. Parental attitudes to education among the working class, moreover, often tend to be unfavorable. As regards schools, poor equipment and poor facilities in the underprivileged areas are associated with badly qualified teaching staff and an educational environment in which problems of control assume precedence over intellectual development as such.

A number of fairly recent, and well-known, studies in European countries have demonstrated that class awareness, rather than class consciousness, is the typical cognitive perspective of the middle class.[17] The "image of society," as Willener calls it, of the white-collar worker involves a hierarchical perception of occupational levels distinguished by differences of income and status—an evident generalization from the hierarchical system of authority in which the non-manual worker is located. Movement up or down this hierarchy is perceived to be decided by the initiative and energy shown by any particular individual. Consistent with this "individualism" is a general willingness to accept "deferred gratification" as a necessary investment to secure anticipated future rewards. Such an "image of society" does not inevitably preclude the possibility of subjective class identification, but it very definitely inhibits the formation of certain levels of "class consciousness." Conflict and struggle play a part in this imagery, but primarily in terms of the striving of the individual to secure a social position which accords with his talents and zeal, not as any sort of class confrontation.

The connections which can be presumed to exist between

such class awareness and the sources of proximate structuration of the middle class indicated above, are easy to see. But it is equally easy to generalize too readily from the European experience, in two respects: in treating what is again essentially an abstract, or "ideal-typical," presentation of the class awareness of the white-collar worker as if it applied *en bloc* to the middle class in the different European countries; and in failing to look closely enough at non-European societies where these patterns are less clear-cut. The first point is important with regard to evaluating recent interpretations of changes which some observers believe are occurring at the lower levels of the white-collar sector, and which in a certain sense are "proletarianizing" clerical labor. As in the debate over separation of ownership and control, there is a manifest danger that the extant reality will be contrasted with what is in fact an ideal-typical conception of the past, thus making it appear that much more striking transformations have occurred than have actually taken place. The parochialism of simply taking European examples is readily demonstrated by considering the case of Japan, where the "individualism" of the white-collar worker in the West is tempered with a strong dose of "collectivism" in outlook. The Japanese *sararyman* in a large company, while normally having to achieve entrance to the company through intensely competitive examinations, tends to accept an "image of society" which emphasizes the significance of group loyalty rather than individualistic achievement.[18]

SOURCES OF DIFFERENTIATION WITHIN THE MIDDLE CLASS

We may distinguish two major sources of differentiation within the middle class as a whole: that having its origin in differences in market capacity, and that deriving from variations in the division of labor. The most significant type of difference in market capacity is undoubtedly between the capacity to offer marketable technical knowledge, recognized and specialized symbolic skills, and the offering of general symbolic competence. The marketability of specialized symbolic skills has normally been protected or enhanced by the systematic enforcement of controlled "closure" of occupational entry, a particular characteristic of professional occupations. The growth of professional occupations has been particularly marked in neo-capitalist society. In the United States, for example, the proportion of professional workers in the male labor force almost trebled between 1950 and 1970, and a similar trend can be observed in other societies, even if the total proportion of professionals in the labor force does not approach that of the United States (about 15 percent). While the professions obviously share certain elements in common with other occupational associations, notably the trade unions, which attempt to impose control over the distribution of market capacities, in other respects they are quite distinct from these. The professional association functions not only as a medium of occupational control, but seeks also to establish ethical prerogatives governing general "standards of conduct."[19]

Although there certainly are controversial problems of sociological analysis posed by the existence of the professions, professionalization does not offer major difficulties for class theory. The same cannot be said, however, of other sources of differentiation within the middle class, which have caused many authors to doubt altogether the applicability of any such generic term as the "middle class." The term appears to have a definite usefulness in relation to white-collar workers within organizations, where these workers are part of a definite "office," and consequently of a bureaucratic hierarchy of authority. But what of workers whose tasks are not primarily "manual," but who are not so clearly involved in any such clearly identifiable hierarchy, and who, while they may often be connected with the professions, are not of them? As C. Wright Mills puts it: "The old professions of medicine and law are still at the top of the professional world, but now all around them are men and women of new skills. There are a dozen kinds of social engineers and mechanical technicians, a multitude of Girl Fridays, laboratory assistants, registered and unregistered nurses, draftsmen, statisticians, social workers. In the salesrooms, which sometimes seem to coincide with the new society as a whole, are the stationary salesgirls in the department store, the mobile salesmen of insurance, the absentee salesmen—the ad-men helping others sell from a distance."[20] What, if anything, do such a bewildering variety of occupations share in common with each other, let alone with the white-collar worker? Adopting Renner's concept, and modifying it for his own purposes, Dahrendorf has argued that the common element is to be found in the fact that white-collar workers constitute a "service class" which "provides a bridge between rulers and ruled."[21] But this is hardly convincing. What it seems to represent is an attempt to find some place for a concept of a "middle class" within Dahrendorf's more general endeavour to link class theory to a dichotomous authority scheme, and hence shares the flaws inherent in that general conception. But more especially, it fails to deal adequately with the problem of the heterogeneity of "services" offered by those in the diversity of occupations mentioned by Mills: it is not particularly enlightening to learn that what a draftsman shares with a social worker is that each is part of a "bridge between rulers and ruled."

The primary defect in the conception of the "service class," in this latter connection, is that *it does not distinguish adequately between class and the division of labor*; or, expressed another way, it does not distinguish between two aspects of the division of labor—differentiation of occupations in respect of divergences in market capacity on the one hand, and in respect of divergences in paratechnical relations on the other. The second, as I have stressed, should be regarded as one major component of class structuration on the basis of market capacity: if it can be a source of the homogenization of class relationships, so can it also be a source of *differentiation* in class structuration, even where similar market capacities are involved. The same is true of authority systems, which Dahrendorf seeks to make the essential axis of class structure itself. Thus a draftsman and a social worker may have a broadly similar market capacity, in relation to the economic returns their skills may earn them when offered for sale on the market, but their position in the division of labor, in the sense in which I have used the term, may be quite different; and both may differ from the clerical worker in the large organization in respect of not belonging so clearly to a specific "level" in a hierarchy of authority.

WHITE-COLLAR UNIONIZATION

If the relative expansion of the white-collar sector has been a fundamental stumbling-block to Marxist theory, this is in large part because of the fact that non-manual workers have been "falsely class conscious." This phrase can refer to at least two sets of distinguishable phenomena: the general predominance of "class awareness" amongst white-collar workers; and the apparent greater reluctance of white-collar workers to associate in occupational unions compared with manual workers (together with a reluctance, when they do form unions, to affiliate themselves too closely with those of blue-collar workers).

Rates of white-collar unionism actually differ quite considerably cross-nationally, as does the degree of separation of white-collar from manual unions. It does appear to be almost universally the case that the level of unionization of white-collar workers, in any given country, is lower than that among blue-collar workers: Japan, however, is one society which may be regarded as a probable exception to this. According to one estimate, of the 9.3 million workers who were union members in Japan in 1963, at least 35 per cent were in white-collar occupations—a higher proportion than that represented by the white-collar sector in the labor force as a whole. Japan also differs from Western countries in other aspects of unionization. In general, among the latter countries, it seems to be the case that white-collar unions have taken the lead from manual unions with respect to levels of unionization. Those countries where blue-collar labor is highly organized, such as Sweden, also tend to have relatively high rates of white-collar unionization; other societies, such as Britain, show lower levels of both white- and blue-collar unionization. Even where there has been a fair degree of "mixed" union membership, that is to say, with non-manual and manual workers belonging to the same unions, it has normally been the blue-collar membership which has played the most active dominating role. But in the Japanese labor movement these roles have been reversed, with the white-collar elements playing a more stable part, while union membership has taken its strongest hold in those sectors of the economy in which the white-collar sector has expanded most rapidly since the war. In contrast with Western societies, union "mixing" is the rule rather than the exception in Japan, something which is undoubtedly closely bound up with the fact that it is the enterprise, rather than the occupation, which is usually most prominent in the consciousness of both white-collar and blue-collar workers.[22] As a mass phenomenon, white-collar unionization in Japan dates primarily from the period after the war, with the membership concentrated in "enterprise-wide" unions; although about 20 per cent of the total union membership is in solely white-collar unions, these are for the most part in sectors where only non-manual workers are employed. Within the enterprise unions, half the union leadership is drawn from white-collar groupings, and there have been only a small number of instances where white-collar workers have broken away from these unions to form their own associations.[23] While there are tensions within contemporary union organization in Japan, tensions which spring in substantial degree from divisions between manual and non-manual factions, there is no indication of any pronounced tendency towards the development of a major separatist white-collar union movement.

France is one of the few Western countries in which there is something of a history of a close integration of non-manual and manual workers within the labor movement. It is perhaps significant that, as Crozier has pointed out, the French term *employés*, while normally applied to non-manual workers, can be used to refer to all workers within an enterprise; there is no generic term corresponding to *Angestellte*, or to "white-collar worker" (or the less commonly used "black-coated worker"). The early sales and clerical unions, the *Chambre syndicale fédérale des employés*, founded in the latter part of the nineteenth century, were radical in orientation, and the *Chambre* took part in the founding of the central union organization (CGT) in 1895.[24] In subsequent periods, white-collar unions have played a part in several periods of open industrial conflict, such as the general strikes of 1919 and 1936.[25] Since the war, white-collar unions, like the manual unions, have been divided along ideological lines, according to whether they affiliate themselves with Communist, Socialist or Christian organizations, with the latter two being most important. In most of the other capitalist societies, however, there is a quite marked degree of separation, and often of antagonism, between white-collar unions, even where they are nominally attached to the same federations. Britain is a case in point. The white-collar unions in Britain, on the whole, have looked to the manual unions as their model and, with the exception of the National Association of Local Government Officers (until 1964), have generally sought affiliation with the Trades Union Congress. But they have also for the most part carefully maintained their separate identity, and have remained conscious of the task of protecting their specific interests.

Why are rates of unionization, in terms of union membership, generally lower among white-collar than among manual workers? As regards those groupings of white-collar workers who enjoy relatively privileged forms of market capacity, there would seem to be no particular difficulty in providing an answer to this question, since their economic interests, their place in the hierarchy of the enterprise, and their class awareness, all clearly act to distance them from involvement with unionization or with collective action. But strongly developed, and occasionally militant unions, as opposed to professional associations, are not completely unknown among those with privileged market capacity (for example, airline pilots), even if they are relatively rare. An analysis of the factors influencing the level of unionization in those occupations whose market capacities are closest to those of manual workers (of whom clerical workers may be regarded as the most instructive case) should also shed light upon these other instances.

It is now well established that, in recent years, a series of changes have affected the economic position of the clerical grouping compared with the higher levels of the working class. The most important of these changes are: a relative decline in the income and other economic advantages of clerical workers vis-à-vis the more affluent groupings in manual work; and a transformation of the nature of the tasks, and therefore of the paratechnical relations, formerly characteristic of clerical work in the division of labor. It is clear that various long-term factors have weakened the economic differentials between clerical workers and the more "affluent" sections of the working class. The arrival of near-universal literacy has diminished the market capacity of general symbolic competence; the very expansion of the white-collar sector itself has reduced the "scarcity factor" involved in access to routine non-manual occupations. It is not only in terms of income, however, that clerical employees have seen their economic circumstances lessened compared with blue-collar workers: in most countries, the other forms of economic differential which in the past tended to separate manual and non-manual labor have to some extent diminished. The very appropriateness of the designation "clerical" becomes questionable in the light of the introduction of mechanical means of carrying out tasks previously involving the "pen pushing" of the clerk. The influence of each of these sets of phenomena upon pre-existing class relationships has frequently been exaggerated, not only in terms of their statistical significance, but also because of the effects of the "feminization" of clerical labour. But it is impossible to decry either the reality of these changes, or their connection to rising rates of unionism, and they provide a clear indication of some of the conditions governing the unionization of white-collar labor in general—conditions which may be treated in terms of the variable factors of class structuration.

It is evident, in the first place, that there is little or no tendency to unionization where superior market capacity is associated with the possibility of promotion chances up an administrative hierarchy, and is further supported by a form of class awareness stressing "individualism," cognitively and evaluatively. Chances of career mobility are undoubtedly particularly important here. Historically, one of the characteristics separating the clerk from the manual worker has been the fact that the former has nominally, and to some degree actually, enjoyed promotion possibilities which were not open to the latter. Insofar as the position of clerical workers is subject to a career "block," such that opportunities of career mobility are only open to those with specialized academic qualifications, there is likely to be a strong stimulus to unionization and to collective action. The existence of career "blocks" (so-called balkanization), undoubtedly is the major factor influencing unionization among those of superior market capacity. Occupations such as school teaching, where high rates of unionization are common, even though the level of income and economic advantages are quite considerable, are characteristically those in which, once the given occupational position is reached, the chances of further career mobility are limited. Thus, in Britain, for instance, school teachers reach a ceiling income at a relatively early age: and the possibilities of promotion to a headmastership are, statistically speaking, very slim indeed.[26]

In all capitalist societies there are wide disparities between different industries in rates of unionization of white-collar labor, which are clearly influenced by divergences in the characteristic form of paratechnical relations. White-collar workers are less often concentrated in large, homogeneous productive establishments than manual workers—certainly one factor tending to promote a high level of unionization. Administrative centralization, however, particularly if it is associated with a developed technical rationalization of working conditions, tends to stimulate white-collar unionization: thus the civil service normally shows very high rates of union membership in the lower grades. In France, for example, 40 per cent of civil servants are union members, compared with an average of only something like 15 percent in the private sector; in Japan, the figure is fully 90 percent. The mechanization of certain clerical tasks has been widely interpreted as a process of the "proletarianization" of the lower levels of white-collar labor, and hence as the principal factor underlying rising union membership; but in fact comparative studies of variations in white-collar unionization indicate that the centralization and rationalization of administration is more important in promoting a high rate of unionization.[27] The reasons for the relatively low level of unionization of white-collar workers are obviously not completely distinct from the factors influencing the relationships between non-manual and manual unions. Apart from the case of Japan, it seems to be very generally true, as mentioned previously, that direct contact with blue-collar unions has often provided an impetus to white-collar unionization: thus with the exception of the civil service, union membership tends to be higher among clerical workers in industries where they are in immediate contact with strongly unionized manual workers, such as mining, engineering or transportation.

PROLETARIANS OR NOT? THE THEORY OF TH "NEW WORKING CLASS"

I have already stressed that it is mistaken, or at the very least misleading, to speak of a class as an "actor," especially in the way in which, for example, such writers as Lukács and and Touraine are prone to do. A class is not even a "group"; the concept, as I have defined it, refers to a cluster of forms of structuration based upon commonly shared levels of market capacity. This applies with particular force to the position of the middle class within the contemporary capitalist societies, since middle-class individuals normally lack a clear conception of class identity and, even when unionized, characteristically do not embrace any form of conflict consciousness.

Since the turn of the century, when the rate of relative increase in the white-collar sector first became apparent, the idea has been advanced—particularly, of course, by Marxist authors—that this "new middle class" will become split into two: because it is not really a class at all, since its position, and the outlook and attitudes of its members, cannot be interpreted in terms of property relations. Hence, so the argument runs, the majority of white-collar workers will become "proletarianized," as befits their condition of propertylessness, while a small minority will move into the dominant class. Today, some seventy years later, the facts continue to belie such expectations. In the contemporary societies, there are two connected sets of processes which are commonly pointed to in order to support modern variants of the notion expressed by the cumbersome term "proletarianization." One is the post-war growth in the white-collar unions, and the other is the influence of mechanization. Each of these expresses significant changes occurring at certain levels in the class structure. But these changes do not involve any major process of interpenetration of middle and working classes. As regards the white-collar unions, the evidence indicates that the process of their growth, which in any case in most instances is not an increase in "union density," but an increase which simply keeps pace with the expansion of the non-manual sector as such,[28] does not in and of itself carry any particular consequences for the labor movement as a whole. In other words, this growth tends to be accommodated within the existing pattern, whatever this may be in a particular society. Where there are marked divergences and conflicts between manual and non-manual unions, these persist, or may even become accentuated; where there is a higher degree of mutual penetration, the rise in white-collar unionism does not significantly alter such a situation.

The impact of mechanization is perhaps more difficult to assess. Certainly it is a phenomenon which dates back a long way, although recent years have seen the introduction of new forms of computerized techniques into office work. While many discussions of the conditions of white-collar labor ignore the distinction, there is just as much need to differentiate "mechanization" from "automation" in the office as in the factory—although in neither case does the latter form of technology, relating only to a minor segment of the labor force, have the significance which some (including Marx, and more recently Marcuse) have wished to claim for it. It is misleading to suppose, as Marxist authors commonly do, that the effect of the mechanization of office work, the beginnings of which can be traced to the last two decades of the nineteenth century, has been progressively to eliminate the differences between office and shop-floor. Mechanization, as involved in factory labor, tends to define the total character of the labor task, often reducing the role of the worker to "machine-minding." But this has generally not been the case with mechanization in the office, where typewriters, adding machines, dictating machines, etc., appear as adjuncts to clerical labour, rather than transforming it altogether. Women, who comprise a category within the labor force which is systematically discriminated against in terms of level of income and career opportunities, largely monopolize those occupations which are wholly routinized (e.g., typist, stenographer). For other clerical workers, the judgment offered by a recent researcher aptly summarizes the position: "what these machines really replaced was a great deal of laborious manual effort in checking data and routine arithmetical calculations ... some understanding of the business continued to be the desirable qualification of the clerical worker, whether his work was done by manual or mechanical means."[29]

The recent trend towards automating office tasks, by the

use of computers in white-collar occupations, does tend to effect a more total reorganization of office work. But research upon the influence of the adoption of computerized methods upon paratechnical relations indicates that, far from serving to promote the "proletarianization" of clerical employees, these normally have the consequence of producing a diminished demand for routine workers, increasing the need for more highly educated and qualified personnel. Thus a study by the US Bureau of Labor Statistics, of twenty offices which introduced large-scale computers, showed that about two-thirds of the office employees stayed at the same job level as prior to computerization, a third were upgraded to higher-level positions, while no more than 1 per cent were downgraded to more routine jobs. Comparable figures appear in most other studies. As regards those directly involved in the running of office computers—computer operators, programmers, etc.—research indicates that the level of educational qualifications, and the period of training involved, are substantially greater than is demanded of other employees in non-supervisory positions.[30]

We continued to hear the judgment delivered by orthodox Marxist authors that, as it has recently been expressed, "salaried workers . . . find themselves carefully *separated* from the rest of the proletariat by the artifice of the bourgeoisie, not by scientific analysis [*sic*]. The fact that they wear a white shirt and are paid at the end of the month is hardly sufficient to place in question their *objective* membership of the working class, even if their *subjective* consciousness remains confused."[31] It is surely time to abandon such naïvetés; and they have indeed been abandoned by some of the more original Marxist writers, and others influenced by them, who have sought to replace the traditional idea of "proletarianization" with a conception of a "new working class," led by technically qualified workers whose conditions of labor would seem at first sight to separate them quite decisively from the bulk of manual workers.

There are in fact several theories of the "new working class." Here I shall consider only that conception of the "new working class" which is linked to the idea that sections of what used to be called the "new middle class," together with certain groupings of manual workers, are moving towards forming what Garaudy, following Gramsci, refers to as an "historic bloc," which has a revolutionary potential in neo-capitalism. Unlike the other theories of the "new working class," this has been mainly worked out by Marxist writers, particularly in France, and received a major stimulus from the events of May 1968 in that country. In contrast to the more traditional Marxist approach, this theory does not attempt to explain away the conduct and values of white-collar workers as "false class consciousness," or to neglect the general significance of the expansion of the non-manual sector in the capitalist societies, but rather looks for a novel basis for incorporating segments of white-collar labor within the "working class," defined in a particular way. This is found in the crucial importance of scientific and technical ideas to neo-capitalism: the production and dissemination of scientific knowledge becomes the primary "force of production" in neo-capitalist society. Engineers, scientists, technicians of all sorts thus occupy a pivotal place in the socioeconomic order. But rather than affiliating themselves with other groupings in the "middle class," these workers constitute a new vanguard of the working class—not because they are "proletarianized" in the conventional sense of the term, as regards income and economic rewards; but because they experience, in acute form, a "contradiction" between their need for autonomous control over their work task (the production of knowledge) and the bureaucratic exigencies of the organization to which they are subject. As Touraine expresses the notion:

> We are not thinking here of the new "proletarians," of white-collar workers who must carry out tasks as repetitive, monotonous and constraining as those of workers on the assembly-line, but rather of relatively high-grade categories: technical workers, designers, higher level white-collar employees, technical assistants, who do not take part in the bureaucratic game, but who are more directly exposed to its consequences than workers of the traditional type.[32]

The necessarily autonomous process of the creation of ("universally valid") technical knowledge clashes with the subordination of such knowledge to the economic aims of the productive enterprise.[33]

Whatever its deficiencies, the theory appears to fit the contemporary trend in the white-collar sector within the capitalist societies, which in some degree has been towards the specific growth of technically specialized occupations. However, it is open to a number of objections. In the first place, one of the premises upon which it rests, the supposition that, in neo-capitalism, knowledge has supplanted technology as the principal productive force, is highly questionable. Even if this were acceptable in the form in which it is put forward, there would be some reason to doubt the overall claims which have been made for the theory, because it tends to exaggerate considerably the degree to which "scientific and technical" workers have penetrated even those industries making use of highly advanced techniques.[34] More importantly, however, the sense in which the "new working class" is a "class" is ill-defined and ambiguous. Sometimes the term is used, in ways akin to Garaudy's notion of the new "historical bloc," to refer to an integration of the bulk of the (manual) working class with the "knowledge producers"; sometimes to designate a merging of the latter with those segments of the working class who, because their tasks are becoming automated, become "controllers" of machinery rather than "operatives" subject to the dictates of the machine; and sometimes to describe only the new technically qualified experts themselves. But in none of these cases is it clear what the rationale is for calling the grouping in question a "class"—and, like most previous approaches in class theory, it tends to conflate the two aspects of the division of labor which I have distinguished: scientific knowledge as a basis of market capacity, and as a basis of position in a system of paratechnical relations.

Finally, it should be pointed out that the theory is at variance with reality, if it is to be advanced as a generic interpretation of the rise of a new proto-revolutionary force in neo-capitalist society. In the United States, which boasts the largest proportion of workers who should comprise the "new working class," there is no sign of the revolutionary potentialities anticipated by the progenitors of the theory. It is not accidental, in point of fact, that the doctrine of the "new working class" should have been primarily developed by French authors: for, in a certain sense, it could be held that the "historic bloc" has been seen in action in the happenings of May 1968. But the reasons for this might lie less in the factors specified in the theory, and generalized to neo-capitalism as a whole, than to other characteristics of the structure of French society which, given the long-standing affiliation of white- and blue-collar workers in the union movement, might explain the incidence of both working-class and middle-class radicalism in that country.

Notes

1. *Theories of Surplus Value*, vol. 2 (London 1969), p. 573.
2. cf. Martin Nicolaus, "Proletariat and middle class in Marx: Hegelian choreography and the capitalist dialectic," *Studies on the Left*, 7 1967. The author's analysis of Marx's problems with the "middle class" turns upon what I consider to be a mistaken separation between Marx's concern with "the market" in his early writings and with the theory of surplus value in his later works.
3. The attention given to what Lederer and Marschak called "Der neue Mittelstand" in Germany in the 1920s and early 1930s obviously relates to the internal problems of Social Democracy and the rise of Nazism. It might be pointed out that the "official" theory of the right-wing, anti-semitic *Deutschnationale Handlungsgehilfen-Verband* emphasized the significance of the participation of the white-collar worker in the delegation of entrepreneurial authority, and the existence of promotion opportunities, as distinguishing him from the manual worker. For the basic sociological works of the period see Emil Lederer and J. Marschak, "Der neue Mittelstand," *Grundriss der Sozialökonomik*, vol. 9 (I), 1926; and Lederer, *Die Privatangestellten in der modernen Wirtschaftsentwicklung* (Tübingen 1912).
4. For some cross-national comparisons, see Bert F. Hoselitz, *The Role of Small Industry in the Process of Economic Growth* (The Hauge 1968).
5. *Vide* Joseph Bensman and Arthur J. Vidich, *The New American Society* (Chicago 1971), for an exposition of the latest in a long line of putative "revolutions" stretching from Burnham onwards: the "revolution of the middle class."
6. Figures for the USA calculated by Gavin Mackenzie from US census data; the additional 4 per cent and 5 per cent represent farm-workers. Other data are taken from Guy Routh, *Occupation and Pay in Great Britain, 1906–60* (Cambridge 1965); and Solomon B. Levine, "Unionisation of white-collar employees in Japan," in Adolf Sturmthal, *White-collar Trade Unions* (Urbana 1966).
7. Michel Crozier, *The World of the Office Worker* (Chicago, 1971), pp. 11–12; and "White-collar unions—the case of France," in Sturmthal, op. cit., pp. 91–2.

8. cf. Routh, op. cit.; Robert K. Burns, "The comparative economic position of manual and white-collar employees," *The Journal of Business*, 27, 1954; US Department of Labor, *Blue-Collar/White-Collar Pay Trends. Monthly Labor Review*, June 1971; and Crozier, *The World of the Office Worker*, pp. 12–15. For an assessment of how far progressive income tax affects these income profiles, see Frank Parkin, *Class Inequality and Political Order* (London, 1971), pp. 119–21.

9. M. P. Fogarty, "The white-collar pay structure in Britain," *Economic Journal*, 69 1959. Hamilton points out that statistics concerning skilled manual workers often include foremen, whose wages are normally markedly higher than those of skilled workers as such; foremen are more appropriately regarded as supervisory, non-manual workers: Richard Hamilton, "The income difference between skilled and white-collar workers," *British Journal of Sociology*, 14, 1963. As regards the "declining curve" of income, however, Mackenzie indicates that this probably holds for a certain proportion of clerical workers, as well as manual workers: See Gavin Mackenzie, "The economic dimensions of embourgeoisement," *British Journal of Sociology*, 18 1967, p. 32; this article critically examines the preceding work by Hamilton.

10. George Sayers Bain, *The Growth of White-Collar Unionism* (Oxford 1970), p. 59.

11. A survey in Britain in 1961 showed that, whereas 86 per cent of white-collar workers were involved in sick pay schemes, only 33 per cent of manual workers were so covered: HMSO, *Sick Pay Schemes* (London 1964). See also The Industrial Society, *Status and Benefits in Industry* (London 1966); aspects of this work are criticized in Bain, op. cit., p. 64.

12. Enid Mumford and Olive Banks, *The Computer and the Clerk* (London 1967), p. 21.

13. S. M. Miller, "Comparative social mobility," *Current Sociology*, 1, 1960. Blau and Duncan show that, in the American social structure at least, the first job has a basic influence on achieved mobility: while the gross amount of mobility experienced by those starting their careers in white-collar occupations may be about the same as that of those starting in manual jobs, the former tend to experience much greater *net* mobility, even judged in relation to parental occupation (Peter M. Blau and O. D. Duncan, *The American Occupational Structure* New York 1967).

14. David Lockwood, *The Blackcoated Worker* (London, 1958), p. 81.

15. Fritz Croner, *Die Angestellten in der modernen Gesellschaft* (Cologne 1962), pp. 34ff.

16. An interesting example of an attempt to reduce class differentiation in housing in Britain is given in Leo Kuper, *Living in Towns* (London 1953). While recognizing the existence of class segregation in neighbourhood organization in Japan, Dore stresses in his study of a Tokyo ward that, as he puts it: " 'Japanese-ness,' as opposed to 'Western-ness,' is still a criterion of some importance for dividing men from their fellows and one which does not necessarily follow

economic status lines" (R. P. Dore, *City LIfe in Japan*, London 1958, pp. 12–13).

17. The leading works are: Alfred Willener, *Images de la société et classes sociales* (Berne 1957); Heinrich Popitz *et al.*, *Das Gesellshaftsbild des Arbeiters* (Tübingen 1957). See also Dahrendorf, *Class and Class Conflict* (Stanford, 1959), pp. 280–9; John Goldthorpe *et al.*, *The Affluent Worker in the Class Structure* (Cambridge 1969), pp. 116–56; Hansjürgen Daheim, "Die Vorstellungen vom Mittelstand," *Kölner Zeitschrift für Soziologie und Sozialpsychologie* 12, 1960; Siegfried Braun and Jochen Fuhrmann, *Angestelltenmentalität* (Neuwied 1970). This latter work, however, questions some of the traditional views.

18. cf. Ezra F. Vogel, *Japan's New Middle Class* (Berkeley 1963), pp. 142–62; and Chie Nakane, *Japanese Society* (London 1970), pp. 115ff.

19. Terence J. Johnson, *Professions and Power* (London 1972), pp. 54ff.

20. C. Wright Mills, *White Collar* (New York 1951), p. x.

21. Dahrendorf, "Recent changes in the class structure of European societies," in *Class and Class Conflict in Industrial Society*, op. cit., pp. 248–9.

22. According to Taira, 87 per cent of Japanese unions are of the enterprise type, and about 80 per cent of organized labour belongs to them. Koji Taira, *Economic Development and the Labor Market in Japan* (New York 1970), p. 168.

23. Solomon B. Levine, "Unionisation of white-collar employees in Japan," in Sturmthal, *White-Collar Trade Union*, op. cit., p. 238. On the development of enterprise unionism, see also Levine, *Industrial Relations in Postwar Japan* (Urbana 1958).

24. cf. Édouard Dolléans, *Histoire du mouvement ouvrier*, (Paris 1953), vol. 2, pp. 13–56.

25. According to Crozier: "it is from this period (1919–20) that we can date the deep allegiance of the French white-collar world to the workers' cause. To be sure, this unity would remain extremely vague and would accommodate itself to much opposition. Officially, however, it could never again be brought into question. The Catholic unions, which until then remained dubious, had at last shown that at the decisive moment they took sides with the strikers. Even the white-collar employees in banks, those last bastions of bourgeois respectability, had followed" (*The World of the Office Worker*, p. 46).

26. cf. Asher Tropp, *The School Teachers* (London 1957).

27. cf. Lockwood, *The Blackcoated Worker*, op. cit., pp. 89ff.

28. For figures on Britain, see Bain, *The Growth of White-Collar Unionism*, op. cit., pp. 38–9.

29. Jon M. Shepard, *Automation and Alienation* (Cambridge, Mass. 1971), p. 43. cf. also Dorothy Wedderburn, "Annäherung von Angestellten— und Arbeiterätigkeiten?," and subsequent contributions in Günter Friedrichs, *Computer und Angestellte*, vol. 2 (Frankfurt 1971).

30. US Department of Labor, *Adjustments to the Introduction of Office Automation*, Bulletin no. 1276 (Washington 1960). Other contributions to a now very large literature include Leonard Rico, *The Advance against Paperwork* (Ann Arbor 1967); H. A. Rhee, *Office Automation in*

Social Perspective (Oxford 1968); Enid Mumford and Olive Banks, *The Computer and the Clerk*, op. cit.; W. H. Scott, *Office Automation* (OECD 1965).

31. Maurice Bouvier-Ajam and Gilbert Mury, *Les classes sociales en France*, vol. 1 (Paris 1963), p. 63.
32. Alain Touraine, *La société post-industrielle* (Paris 1969), pp. 82–3.
33. Serge Mallet, *La nouvelle classe ouvrière* (Paris 1963); Pierre Belleville, *Une nouvelle classe ouvrière* (Paris 1963). See also Mallet, "La nouvelle classe ouvrière en France," in *Les classes sociales dans le monde d'aujourd'hui*, op. cit.
34. cf. Stanley Aronowitz, "Does the United States have a new working class?," in George Fischer, *The Revival of American Socialism* (New York, 1971), p. 203.

Part II

The Status Sphere and the Psychology of Classes

5 The Status Sphere*
Hans H. Gerth and C. Wright Mills

Prestige involves at least two persons: one to claim it and another to *honor* the claim. The bases upon which various people raise prestige claims, and the reasons others honor these claims, include property and descent, occupation and education, income and power—in fact, almost anything that may invidiously distinguish one person from another. In the status system of a society these claims are organized as rules and expectations governing those who successfully claim prestige, from whom, in what ways, and upon what basis. The level of self-esteem enjoyed by given individuals is more or less set by this status system.

There are, thus, six items to which we must pay attention. From the claimant's side: (1) the status claim, (2) the way in which this claim is raised or expressed, (3) the basis upon which the claim is raised. And correspondingly from the bestower's side: (4) the status bestowal or deference given, (5) the way in which these deferences are given, (6) the basis of the bestowal, which may or may not be the same as the basis upon which the claim is raised. An extraordinary range of social phenomena are pointed to by these terms.

Claims for prestige are expressed in all those mannerisms, conventions, and ways of consumption that make up the styles of life characterizing people on various status levels. The "things that are done" and the "things that just aren't done" are the status conventions of different strata. Members of higher status groups may dress in distinct ways, follow "fashions" in varying tempi and regularities, eat and drink at special times and exclusive places in select society. In varying degrees, they value the elegant appearance and specific modes of address, have dinner together, and are glad to see their sons and daughters intermarry. From the point of

* Reprinted from Hans H. Gerth and C. Wright Mills, *Character and Social Structure: The Psychology of Social Institutions* (New York: Harcourt Brace Jovanovich, Inc., 1953).

view of status, the funeral, as a ritual procession, is an indication of prestige, as are the tombstone, the greeting card, the seating plan at dinner or the opera. "Society" in American cities, debutante systems, the management of philanthropic activities, the social register and the *Almanach de Gotha*—noble titles and heraldic emblems—reflect and often control the status activities of upper circles, where exclusiveness, distance, coldness and condescending benevolence towards outsiders often prevail.

Head roles in any institution may be the basis of status claims, and any order may become the social area in which these claims are realized. We can conceive of a society in which status rests upon economic class position and in which the economic order is dominant in such a way that status claims based on economic class are successfully raised in every order. But we can also imagine a society in which status is anchored in the military order, so that the person's role in that order determines his chance successfully to realize status claims in all, or at least in most, of the other orders. Thus the military role may be a prerequisite to honorific status in other publicly significant roles.

Of course, men usually enact roles in several orders and hence their general position rests on the combinations of roles they enact.

Claims for prestige and the bestowal of prestige are often based on birth into given types of kinship institutions. The black child, irrespective of individual "achievement," will not receive the deference which the white child may successfully claim. The immigrant, especially a member of a recent mass immigration, will not be as likely to receive the deference given to the "Old American," immigrant groups and families who are generally stratified according to how long they and their forebears have been in America. Among the native-born white of native parentage, certain "Old Families" receive more deference than do other families. In each case—race, nationality, and family—prestige is based on, or at least limited by, descent, which is perhaps most obviously a basis of prestige at the top and the bottom of the social ladder. European royalty and rigidly excluded racial minorities represent the zenith and nadir of status by birth.

Upper-class position typically carries great prestige, all the more so if the source of money is property. Yet, even if the possession of wealth in modern industrial societies leads to increased prestige, rich men who are fresh from lower-class levels may experience difficulty in "buying their way" into upper-status circles. In the southern states, in fact, impoverished descendants of once high-level old families receive more deference from more people than do wealthy men who lack appropriate grandparents. The kinship may thus overshadow the economic order. The facts of the *nouveau riche* (high class without high prestige) and of the broken-down aristocrat (high prestige without high class) refute the complete identification of upper-prestige and upper-class position, even though, in the course of time, the broken-down aristocrat becomes simply broken-down, and the son of the *nouveau riche* becomes a man of "clean, old wealth."

The possession of wealth also allows the purchase of an environment which in due course will lead to the development of these "intrinsic" qualities in individuals and in families that are required for higher prestige. When we say that American prestige has been fluid, one thing we mean is that high economic-class position has led rather quickly to high prestige, and that kinship descent has not been of equal importance to economic position. A feudal aristocracy, based on old property and long descent, has not existed here. Veblen's theory[1] was focused primarily upon the post-Civil War period in the United States and the expressions of prestige claims raised in lavish consumption by the *nouveau riche* of railroads, steel, and pork. In a democratic society equipped with mass media we are not surprised to find that many images of upper-status types are diffused. It is also well known that in contrast with feudal elites the American upper classes have not shied away from publicity. Society columns and obituary pages chronicle the activities and connections of conspicuous members of the high-status groups.

The prestige of the middle strata in America is based on many other principles than descent and property. The shift to a society of employees has made *occupation* and the *educational* sphere crucially important. Insofar as occupation determines the level of income, and different styles of life require different income levels, occupation limits the style of life. In a more direct way, different occupations require different levels and types of education, and education also limits the style of life and thus the status successfully claimed.

Some occupations are reserved for members of upper-status levels, others are "beneath their honor." In some societies, in fact, having no work to do brings the highest prestige; prestige being an aspect of the property-owning class, the women with high class husbands becoming specialists in the display of expensive idleness. But only when those who do not need to work have more income than those who must, is idleness likely to yield prestige. When work is necessary but not available, "leisure" means unemployment, which may bring disgrace. And income from property does not always entail more prestige than income from work; the amount and the ways the income is used may be more important than its source. Thus the small *rentier* does not enjoy an esteem equal to that of a highly-paid doctor. Status attaches to the *terms* for income, to its source and timing of payment. Socially the same number of dollars may mean different things when they are received as "rent" or "interest," as "royalties" or "fees," as "stipends" or "salaries," as "wages" or as insurance benefits." Men striving for status may prefer smaller salaries to higher wages, meager royalties to substantial profits, an honorific stipend to a large bonus.

Among the employed those occupations which pay more, and which presumably involve more mental activities and entail the power to supervise others, seem to place people on higher prestige levels. But sheer power does not always lend prestige: the political boss renounces public prestige—except among his machine members—for power; constitutional monarchs, on the other hand, retain and possibly gain public prestige but lose political power. In offices and factories, skilled foremen and office supervisors expect and typically receive an esteem which lifts them above unskilled workers and typists. But the policeman's power to direct street masses does not bring prestige, except among badly frightened drivers and little boys.

The type of education, as well as the amount, is an important basis of prestige; "finishing" schools and "prep" schools turn out ladies and gentlemen fit to represent their class by styles of life which, in some circles, guarantee deference. In other circles the amount of intellectual skill acquired through education is a key point for estimation. Yet skill alone is not as uniform a basis for prestige as is skill connected with highly esteemed occupations.

All the variables which underpin status—descent, skill (on the basis of education and/or experience), biological age, seniority (of residence, of membership in associations), sex, beauty, wealth, and authority—may be quite variously combined and usually in typical ways. These combinations may be and often are quite intricate. For example, the cross-tabulation of descent, wealth, and skill alone logically yields the following types: where wealth and high birth is combined with skill we may find, for example, the experienced statesmanship of a Churchill; but where there is wealth and high birth but no skill, perhaps a publicized heir or heiress, or an hereditary successor to throne. The self-made man of the nineteenth century in the United States had wealth and skill but low birth; the uneducated black woman who suddenly wins the sweepstakes, has wealth, but low birth and no skill.

Sir Walter Scott, a heavily indebted nobleman who did well as a writer, had no wealth but both high birth and high skill. And famous artists, such as Beethoven, or famous scholars such as Albert Einstein, did not have wealth or high birth, but excelled in skill. The Russian refugee nobleman who became a waiter in a Paris hotel lacked both wealth and skill although he had high birth. Finally, the Jewish Luftmensch,[2] the hobo, the tramp, or the black farmhand probably have no wealth, no birth status, and no skill.

Such a panorama may serve to indicate the manner in which one raises questions and classifies observations about the status sphere of given social structures.

We cannot take for granted that to claim prestige is automatically to receive it. Status conduct is not so harmonious. The status claimant may in the eyes of others "overstate" his "true" worth or may be considered "conceited." If he understates it, he may be considered "diffident" or "humble." The conceited status claimant may of course receive the deference he claims, but it is likely to be "spurious deference" for "spurious claims." His conceit in fact, is often strengthened by flattery, sometimes to the point of megalomania, as with despots in a context of priestly or courtier byzantinism or organized mass adulation.

In cases of mistaken judgment people may give genuine deference on the basis of spurious or pretended claims; there are the false Messiahs, the false prophets, the false princes, and the professional charlatans.[3]

Spurious deference for misconstrued claims may be illustrated by referring to the mock coronation of Christ as "the King of the Jews" with the crown of thorns. Genuine respect for genuine claims needs no particular elaboration.

False humility is often transparent as a technique for eliciting deference. We call it "fishing." The bid for good will, with which speakers often open their talks, is often no more than thinly veiled flattery of the audience. Once upon a time kings were flattered; today more often "the people" are. To be sure, such flattery of the people goes hand in hand with open disdain for the European "masses" or the American "suckers." Hitler proved highly successful in allocating to German Gentiles the rhetorical certificate of presumably high birth and ancestral background by calling them each and every one "Nordics."

Thus the extent to which claims for prestige are honored, and by whom they are honored, varies widely. Some of those from whom an individual claims prestige may honor his claims, others may not; some deferences that are given may express genuine feelings of esteem; others may be expedient strategies for ulterior ends. A society may, in fact, contain many hierarchies of prestige, each with its own typical bases and areas of bestowal; or one hierarchy in which everyone uniformly "knows his place" and is always in it. It is in the latter that prestige groups are most likely to be uniform and continuous.

Imagine a society in which everyone's prestige is clearly set and stable; every man's claims for prestige are balanced by the deference he receives, and both his expression of claims and the ways these claims are honored by others are set forth in understood stereotypes. Moreover, the bases of the claims coincide with the reasons they are honored; those who claim prestige on the specific basis of property or birth are honored because of their property or birth. So the exact volume and types of deference expected between any two individuals are always known, expected, and given; and each individual's level and type of self-esteem are steady features of his inner life.

Now imagine the opposite society, in which prestige is highly unstable and ambivalent: the individual's claims are not usually honored by others. The ways in which claims are expressed are not understood or acknowledged by those from whom deference is expected, and when others do bestow prestige, they do so unclearly. One man claims prestige on the basis of his income, but even if he is given prestige it is not because of his income but rather, for example, because of his education and appearance. All the controlling devices by which the volume and type of deference might be directed are out of joint or simply do not exist. So the prestige system is no system but a maze of misunderstanding, of sudden frustration and sudden indulgence, and the individual, as his self-esteem fluctuates, is under strain and full of anxiety.

American society in the middle of the twentieth century does not fit either of these projections absolutely, but it seems fairly clear that it is closer to the unstable and ambivalent model. This is not to say that there is no prestige system in the United States; given occupational groupings, even though caught in status ambivalence, do enjoy typical levels of prestige. It is to say, however, that the enjoyment of prestige is often disturbed and uneasy, that the bases of prestige, the expressions of prestige claims, and the ways these claims are honored are now subject to great strain, a strain which often throws ambitious men and women into a virtual status panic.

As with income, so with prestige: white-collar groups in the United States are differentiated socially, perhaps more decisively than wage workers and entrepreneurs. Wage earners certainly do form an income pyramid and a prestige gradation, as do entrepreneurs and *rentiers*; but the new middle class, in terms of income and prestige, is a superimposed pyramid, reaching from almost the bottom of the first to almost the top of the second.

People in white-collar occupations claim higher prestige than wage workers, and, as a general rule, can cash in their claims with wage-workers as well as with the anonymous public.

This fact has been seized upon, with much justification, as the defining characteristic of the white-collar strata, and although there are definite indications in the United States of a decline in their prestige, still, on a nationwide basis, the majority of even the lower white-collar employees—office workers and salespeople—enjoy a middle prestige place.

The historical bases of the white-collar employees' prestige, apart from superior income, have included (1) the similarity of their place and type of work to those of the old middle classes which has permitted them to borrow prestige. (2) As their relations with entrepreneurs and with esteemed customers have become more impersonal, they have borrowed prestige from the management and the firm itself, and in exclusive stores, from wealthy patrons. (3) The stylization of their appearance, in particular the fact that most white-collar jobs have permitted the wearing of street clothes on the job, has also figured in their prestige claims, as have (4) the skills required in most white-collar jobs, and in many of them the variety of operations performed and the degree of autonomy exercised in deciding work procedures. Furthermore, (5) the time taken to learn these skills and (6) the way in which they have been acquired by formal education and by close contact with the higher-ups in charge has been important. (7) White-collar employees have "monopolized" high school education—even in 1940 they had completed twelve grades to the eight grades for wage workers and entrepreneurs. They have also (8) enjoyed status by descent: in terms of race—in the early 1950s black white-collar employees existed only in isolated instances—and, more importantly, in terms of origin—in 1930 only about 9 percent of white-collar workers, but 16 percent of free enterprises and 21 percent of wage workers were foreign born. Finally, as an underlying fact, the limited size of the white-collar group, compared with wage workers, has led to successful claims to greater prestige.

Status may be said to "overlay" class structures. Each has its peculiarities and its relative autonomy, yet the first is dependent upon the second as a conditioning and limiting factor. One of the great perspectives of social thinking has been the formulation of the transition from feudalism to capitalism in terms of the shift from "status" to "contract," or from "feudal estates" to "class society." One of the aspects noted in this formulation is that, since the great middle-class revolutions, legally privileged and underprivileged estates of feudalism and absolutism have been leveled down, for "equality before the law" meant doing away with legal status barriers. This of course does not mean doing away with status groups, nor with all grounds upon which status distinctions rest. But it does mean that status dimensions are more closely tied to the economic order and that class dynamics are automatically transformed into status dynamics.

The leading groups devoted to military, political, juridical, and religious pursuits stand out in all societies. So among top status groups are found warriors, priests, kings, lords, and gentlemen. To these have been added the "merchant princes" and "oil kings" as well as "lumber kings," "railroad czars"—in short, as Franklin D. Roosevelt called them, "the economic royalists." A variety of status groups may emerge on the basis of one class. Upper-class youths may thus be divided into "the smart set" and "the steady conservative set." The smart set may "sow their wild oats," take up eccentric faddish behavior, and seemingly break with the old ways of their steady parents, who may smilingly remember their own "crazy days," and rely on their wellborn children to "find their way" back. The steady set may remain sober in mind and body, take early to correct family routine, and play a quiet game of cards with a moderate drink. Among working classes, one set of men may devote themselves to labor union activities and possibly to politics; they may accordingly feel different from and superior to workers who are nothing but sports fans and movie addicts. When Jewish traditions and cosmopolitan milieu combine, a special group as, for example, the Garment Workers Unions of the Eastern United States may create cultural activities of all sorts which bring special and general public prestige. But regardless of status proliferation, any basic change in class position usually does exert its restrictive or its facilitating influence. If mass unemployment during a world depression reduces income levels, heightens feelings of insecurity, intensifies competition for jobs, reduces family savings and earnings—then status differentiation among the lower classes is minimized, there is no money for educational pursuits and mass luxuries, for leisure-time hobbies, and membership in many organizations.

Industrialization and applied science have increased man's mastery of nature to a previously undreamt extent, but they have also made mankind interdependent, and dependent upon the functioning of the world economy as a sort of "second nature." Accordingly, concern with economic life has become public and the control of strategic economic institutions has given rise to public distinction. Captains of industry have thus attained high prestige positions. The Kaiser was behind the times when he mocked Mr. Lipton as a "tea merchant" who did not quite qualify for royal friendship. On the other hand, he did seek to "ennoble" Alfred Krupp, the cannon king of the Ruhr, and it was possibly a sign of the times that Krupp felt a noble title could add nothing to the prestige of his name, based on his steel plant and its output.

Power over the political and military, the economic and the religious community brings prestige to those who legitimately make or pronounce the key decisions, or to those to whom the key decisions are ascribed by the community. Such power is today exercised at the tops of large-scale, far-flung, and steeply graded organizations of government, army, church, and business. All the staff members of such organizations are likely to enjoy prestige, whatever prestige the world at large gives to the respective organizations. When the state is highly sentimentalized—usually because the church has been closely allied to state power and the prince once stood at the head of the church—a religious halo is bestowed upon "the state" and upon all who serve it. And when the ecclesiastic structure is the one stable and ancient organization in a history of changing state constitutions, then ecclesiastic prestige may overshadow that of the state, and a cardinal or "prince of the church," holding life-long tenure of office, may rank higher than an ephemeral president of a republic. Big power carries in its train big prestige. Powerful nation-states in the long run get greater prestige for their members than do small states. Thus the American passport secures for its bearer greater respect in the world than the Hungarian passport.

And yet this statement must be qualified, for prestige based purely on power may in fact rest on "fear" rather than on sympathetic respect. Power as such may be sought as an end by many men, but most men sooner or later will ask, power for what? They will not accept power as an ultimate end, and whenever power is "naked" it is likely to be questioned as "abusive." In order to be respected, power must be disguised as estimable ends; it must be thought to serve the alleged ends of justice and freedom and other aspirations. It must be sanctioned and implemented by *credenda* and *miranda* in order to be admired.[4] Only then will it exercise its "spell" over man. Such a spell may be elaborated by specialists, and when the elaborated values are widely shared we may speak of "cultural prestige." Power and cultural prestige combined fascinate man and secure the glory of power, or "majesty."

Notes

1. See Thorstein Veblen, *The Theory of the Leisure Class* (New York: Viking, 1924).
2. A man without an occupation, formerly found among Eastern European Jews.
3. On professional charlatans, see Grete de Francesco, *The Power of the Charlatan* (New Haven: Yale Univ. Press, 1939).
4. See Hans H. Gerth and C. Wright Mills, *The Psychology of Social Institutions* (New York: Harcourt Brace Jovanovich, 1953), ch. XIV. The Sociology of Leadership. Cf. C. E. Merriam, *Political Power* (Glencoe, Ill.: Free Press, 1950), Chapter IV.

6 The Foundations of Social Rank and Respect*

Hans Speier

In order to understand more precisely the claims to rank and social respect advanced by the white-collar workers, it must be emphasized at the outset that Weimar Germany was a capitalist society overlaid with peculiarly German features. In this society a plurality of social valuations based on noble birth, wealth, state office (both civilian and military), education, religious denomination, and "race" competed with one another. Corresponding to these social valuations were different conceptions of domination, different ideals of the order of social ranks, different social distinctions and stigmas, and different styles of life.

These numerous valuations—the ethical foundations of the social order of ranks—were alien to one another. For example, the social respect which the civil servant claimed and enjoyed by virtue of his participation in the power of the state contradicted the valuations reflected in the social rank of the industrialist, inasmuch as the latter's prestige was based on wealth and economic success. The entrepreneur enjoyed respect because he owned capital. The respect of the civil servant was tied not to his wealth but to his service, although the higher civil servant received a relatively high salary. A lower civil servant was generally more highly regarded than a manual worker drawing equal pay, and among civil servants of equal pay the political civil servant (the so-called *Hoheitsbeamte*) was esteemed more highly than the economic civil servant (the so-called *Betriebsbeamte*) who worked for the state-owned railroad or a comparable enterprise.

Similar differences in rank existed within hierarchies formed on the basis of other valuations. Just as in the ancien régime

---

* Reprinted from Hans Speier, *German White Collar Workers and the Rise of Hitler* (New Haven: Yale University Press, 1985).

the French *noblesse d'épée* (nobility of birth) were more highly regarded than the *noblesse de robe* (nobility of office), so in Germany old nobility and old wealth were more distinguished than the newer aristocracy and *nouveaux riches*. In the army social distinction was determined not only by military rank but also by the reputation of a particular regiment, which was manifested in, among other things, the percentage of noblemen among its officers. At the time of Wilhelm II, it was ironically said in aristocratic circles that "we have seven regiments of curassiers; the eighth is located in Cologne," where the sons of bourgeois magnates and industrialists did their service.[1] As regards social prestige acquired through education, the differing values placed on humanistic or natural science studies were sometimes reflected in distinctions of rank; beyond this, finer distinctions related to faculty and specialization. Generally, the social ranks of the officer and the educated person are not the same in all societies. Both the military officer and the university professor enjoyed higher respect in the German empire and in the Weimar Republic than, say, in the United States. The same held true of the civil servant and the salaried employee.

The social limits of the different valuations are never definitely drawn. Members of aspiring strata assert that the valuations upon which their claims for rank and honor are based are morally superior to those of the ruling strata. The aspirants try either to devaluate and destroy the alien honor or to participate in it by virtue of intermarriage or individual ascent. The menaced strata in their turn may attempt either to limit the social field of their own valuation more strictly or to yield and broaden it. Thus, toward the end of the eighteenth century the German nobility began "to study with middle-class seriousness." They put—in the words of the non-noble A. L. Schlözer[2]—"a one in front of their birthzero, maintaining thereby anew their old superiority over the middle class," that is, a nobleman's worth equaled zero, but through studying he could raise it to ten. He did so by following the principle of valuation that championed education over noble birth. Thereafter, especially in nineteenth-century Germany, the principles of valuation favoring wealth and education became closely allied. Similarly, before World War I more and more middle-class elements entered the officer corps, at first in those parts of the army where horseback riding was not of paramount importance and newer technical requirements had to be met (engineers, foot artillery).

A comparative historical investigation of social rank and honor would show that a social order comprising the whole nation exists only if either (1) a valuation has monopolistic status, that is, it is generally recognized and its representatives are at the same time its rulers, or (2) a recognized rank order of valuations exists, so that a particular kind of rank and honor predominates, as it did under the feudal aristocracy in old Prussia. Only if one of these conditions exists will the people be sufficiently integrated to form a stable social order.[3]

For its part, the industrial labor force was ostracized for many years in Germany prior to World War I and was feared by the ruling classes because of its organizational success. The workers were not fully citizens, just as, in general, the idea and nature of responsible citizenship were both unpopular and unknown among the middle and upper classes in prewar Germany because of the authoritarian character of the state. Friedrich Engels still held the opinion that universal military service would weaken and eventually cause the class-based state to collapse because it incorporated young proletarians into the army, but his expectation was not fulfilled. Rather, school and military service contributed to the dissemination of notions that exalted disciplinary order. This fact benefited the trade unions and big economic enterprises, was romanticized in the life of voluntary associations, and later tempted adventurous intellectuals to assert a close connection between Prussianism and socialism. Prior to World War I some segments of the population regarded socialist workers as "scoundrels without a fatherland"—an evil phrase that became popular. The error of this opinion was revealed in 1914 as the international slogans of the German labor movement faded and Social Democratic functionaries and workers fought and died for the nation, which in peacetime had denied them political membership.

Despite the dictated peace of Brest–Litovsk, which ended the war with Russia, German military leaders lost the war. This notwithstanding, they advised the emperor to abdicate his political power, which they had already de facto wrested from him. The collapse was born of the military inferiority of the Reich, of political hubris, and of the social short-sightedness of the ruling classes. But this did not prevent those guilty of the defeat from circulating the legend of "the stab in the back," a myth designed to hold the republican caretakers of a bankrupt Germany responsible for its defeat and misery.

In the aftermath of the war the political and trade union representatives of the workers gained power and prestige, which frightened the middle class. Those strata which traditionally had been superior to the workers appeared to suffer losses of economic security, political influence, and social respect even as the workers—at least politically and socially—were ascending the social ladder. The result was doubly unbearable for descending groups. To their absolute deterioration was added the relative decline of their positions.[4]

Salaried employees were also drawn into the whirlpool of this social development. While a minority of organized white-collar workers became more class-conscious, the majority not only defended both their special legal privileges vis-à-vis blue-collar workers and the representation of their interests against the entrepreneurs, but also placed an especially high value on their rank and prestige in order to demonstrate continued social superiority over manual workers.

The German middle strata were neither rich nor aristocratic, their education left something to be desired, and, except for police, postal employees, streetcar conductors, firemen, and the like, they did not wear uniforms. They could share the social standards and rank of nobility, wealth, education, and civil or military state service only in one of four ways that were to some degree open to all underclasses:

1. through occasional individual ascent to the ranks of the highly regarded and socially privileged;
2. passively, through preference extended by members of the upper classes who after the model of a patron-client relationship grant certain social advantages or privileges over still lower strata;
3. actively, through admiration and emulation of higher styles of consumption if only in trivial substitutes and inexpensive ways—as was true, for example, of the eighteenth-century

middle-class pattern of buying inexpensive silhouettes instead of more costly portraits painted for aristocrats in oil on canvas; and

4. through ostentatious disrespect—partly condescending and partly hostile—for those strata which, according to the traditional conception of upper-class standards and styles, did not deserve respect.

Of these four avenues of protecting and increasing social rank and prestige, the first two became increasingly blocked as the capitalist system was entrenched. Ascent to economic independence became even more rare. The claim of a private civil servant (*Privatbeamter*) to be close in social standing to civil servants turned out to be illusory as the life of the white-collar worker became less secure. Neither the state nor entrepreneurial circles sought to assuage the class struggle by maintaining or enlarging middle-class privileges pertaining to social insurance and labor law. Instead, white-collar workers had to defend their privileges politically and with the help of their unions against the interests of the entrepreneurs. The economic and social interests of the salaried employees sometimes coincided with those of manual workers, but the white-collar workers highly valued a style of life which distinguished them from blue-collar workers, even if such a distinction was not supported by an inequality of income. Similarly, the majority of salaried employees did not welcome the workers' increase in power after the revolution, even though they also benefited from the government's recognition of trade unions. In general, most salaried employees continued to cherish a belief in their social, political, and moral superiority over the manual workers.

Not only did many white-collar workers retain their anti-proletarian attitudes and values despite their own proletarianization, they also maintained some positive commitment to middle-class traditions. Otherwise, those psychologists would have been right who, like Hendrik de Man, discovered in the attitudes of middle-class employees nothing but the resentment of an "office slave" who, in the rationalized enterprise, mourned the passing of the velvety sofa and the family journal of his parents. Resentment might have played a role occasionally but it was not fed merely by nostalgic memories.

The legal privileges of white-collar workers were partly responsible for distinguishing their political attitudes from those of manual laborers, as were some features of their working conditions that precluded their reception of socialist ideas. At least one such feature, that of "hidden class membership," is discussed in some detail in Chapter 7. Hidden class membership prevailed not among those employees who worked in a smaller enterprise and were therefore traditionally middle-class-oriented, if only by contact with the old middle class, but rather among their colleagues who worked in the larger enterprises. According to the lower-class theory, the salaried employees' working conditions should have made it more difficult for them to preserve their anti-proletarian inclinations. However, their hidden class membership provides an institutional explanation for their "middle-class" attitudes.

An attempt will also be made to determine more precisely the foundations of the white-collar workers' social rank and respect. Some portions of the salaried-employee stratum claimed and were granted their social rank and respect on grounds that are listed here in summary form:

1. Due to delegated participation in the respect of those who dominated the enterprise, (a) as assistants of the small entrepreneur, and (b) as functionaries of the capitalist.
2. Due to education, (a) by appreciating and acquiring products of culture, which the worker allegedly neglected, or (b) by participation in knowledge offered by natural science and in technology.
3. Due to stressing nationalistic convictions, (a) by devotion to pre-republican values of the state and the military, as expressed above all in service and discipline, or (b) by devotion to anti-republican values as "warriors in civilian clothes."

These foundations of social rank and respect are not independent of one another in reality. The social rank of white-collar workers can be traced to all three (and in addition to legal privileges). However, for sociological purposes they require analytic separation. Reality also favors such a separation, inasmuch as different white-collar groups based their claims to rank and esteem on different principles of respectability. Thus, principle 1.a pertained exclusively to (small-town) employees working in small enterprises, while principle 1.b was of greatest importance to employees in middle-sized enterprises. All employees may have gained in respect due to a liberal education (2.a), but since the spread of modern, specialized scientific education is an urban phenomenon, principle 2.b primarily helped white-collar workers in large cities. The claim to respect based on nationalist convictions and attitudes (3.a) was apparently widespread among all middle-class groups, whereas 3.b pertained mostly to ideologues, functionaries, and members of the DHV.

Notes

1. H. Speier, "Das Proletariat und seine Kritiker," *Die Neue Rundschau*, vol. 43 (1932), p. 295.
2. A. L. Schlözer, *Theorie der Statistik*, (Göttingen, 1804), p. 134. On the transvaluation of social esteem, cf. also H. Speier, "Militarism in the Eighteenth Century," *Social Order and the Risks of War*, esp. the sections "Society vs the State" and "The Devaluation of Courage," (New York, 1952), pp. 241–52.
3. Cf. M. Weber's definition of social order, in *Economy and Society* (New York, Bedminster, 1968), pp. 926–7.
4. On the concept of "relative deprivation," now often used in American sociology, see H. Speier, "Social Stratification," in M. Ascoli and F. Lehmann, eds., *Political and Economic Democracy* (New York, 1937), pp. 264–5.

7 Bureaucracy and Masked Class Membership*

Hans Speier

The hierarchy within the enterprise, in which white-collar workers in middle- and large-sized enterprises are placed, is not adequately reflected in titled positions like president, vice-president, treasurer, section chief, and so forth.[1] It reaches much further down into the enterprise than the system of titles would suggest. In the private firm, as distinct from governmental bureaucracy, only the upper ranks are distinguished by titles. Neither is organizational refinement accurately reflected in salary differences. These merely approximate the hierarchy but do not coincide with it. Not all typists, draftsmen, or auxiliary bookkeepers receiving equal pay are also of equal rank. In contrast, the power to give orders, which spreads downward from top management in ever smaller allotments, is a more precise index of hierarchical position. The hierarchy of persons and the distribution of power to give orders may be represented by pyramids that resemble one another, except that the second stands on its head: the greatest concentration of power is at the top of the hierarchy. More power to give orders is therefore an indication of greater proximity to top management. Not only is the degree of delegated power to give orders an index of hierarchical position, it is also the most important principle of hierarchical stratification; it flows from the domination of the enterprise. Frequently but not necessarily connected to the power to give orders is responsibility.[2]

Another possibility for attaining higher rank, one associated neither with the power to give orders nor with responsibility, is the organizationally conditioned relationship to persons with power to give orders. For example, the private secretary, because of her "confidential position," is superior

---

* Reprinted from Hans Speier, *German White Collar Workers and the Rise of Hitler* (New Haven: Yale University Press, 1985).

151

not only to the typists, but frequently also to higher employees. It is also possible for a "private" relationship with persons wielding the power to give orders to enhance one's rank within the hierarchy. To be sure, this private relationship—with a friend, comrade in the same regiment, a member of the same lodge or student corps, or partner in a love affair—must be known in the enterprise in order to result in further distinction.

The capacity to enhance rank must also be attributed to education. For example, among employees of equal rank the "doctor" (Ph.D.) is distinguished, as is the working student who eats at the boss's table in the office dining room. In Anglo-Saxon countries enhancement of rank owing to education is somewhat less effective, if only because non-medical academic degrees do not entitle the holder to be addressed as "Doctor" (*Herr Doktor*).

Even efficiency can be a distinguishing factor among employees of equal rank. The best draftsman is a bit ahead of other draftsmen receiving the same pay; the fastest typist rises in prestige above equally paid typists. Possibly, this advantage may be traced to the assumption that the most efficient employees possess better chances of promotion and of resisting economic adversity.

Finally, experience in the enterprise or length of service can enhance hierarchical rank. The apprentice in his third year is superior to the first-year apprentice, and if higher age carries no stigma—which it often does in times of crisis—the eldest in any given rank enjoys certain advantages.

Examined closely, all these foundations of distinction can be reduced to participation in the power or prestige of those who dominate the enterprise.[3] The authority to give orders, responsibility, a special relationship with a superior (whether it originates within the enterprise or is of a private character), and length of service—all these constitute the means by which an individual can participate in the power and prestige of management. The same holds indirectly true of education, inasmuch as its acquisition depends, as a rule, on the prerequisite of an advantaged social origin, that is, on social proximity to the rulers of the enterprise. Finally, efficiency can also entitle one to ascent within the hierarchy, either actually or according to widely held expectations.

The captains of enterprise determine the specific content of respectability, inasmuch as their publicly recognized leadership, which is proclaimed by ideologues, also serves to legitimate the respect of subordinate persons. In principle, the same observations also hold true of societies with nationalized economies, in which leadership over a specific enterprise is executed by persons who owe their office to the decision of political power holders. In this case, respect, and the efforts of subordinates to gain it, are permeated by military, precapitalist, or anti-capitalist valuations, depending on how claims to legitimacy by the ruling class are publicly justified. Although rights of co-determination given to the lower ranks can reduce abuses of the authority to give orders, they cannot abolish either the indispensable hierarchical relations within the enterprise or the differences in social respect to which those relations give rise.

If it were possible to flatten out the hierarchy completely, and thus to abolish the institution to which respect and power are owed, the social respect of the white-collar workers would disappear. More precisely, since the social respect of salaried employees may also rest on other foundations, the social respect that is "produced" within the enterprise would disappear. Nowhere, of course, is the hierarchy completely flattened out, not even in giant enterprises,[4] but its effects have been modified by the depersonalization of control. Furthermore, because of the increasing size of the enterprise and the growing refinement of its hierarchy, those who occupy the lowest levels have increased in greater numbers than those at the top. As a result, an egalitarian situation has been created at the lowest levels of the hierarchy. The mass character of white-collar workers at the lowest levels enfeebles the hierarchical principle. Quite rightly, the dependence of "the" white-collar workers has always been demonstrated with reference to these employees holding the lowest hierarchical positions. Because they no longer participate in the power and respect that accrues to higher positions in the hierarchy, lower-level white-collar workers recognize more readily the proletarian features of their situation than do other salaried workers, among whom those features are less pronounced. The visible equality of their powerlessness and the absence of prestige privileges condemn them to be the inevitable victims of the hierarchy.

The hierarchy within larger enterprises must now be considered in another perspective. Not only does it serve as a foundation of white-collar prestige by allowing employees to participate in the power and respect of management, it also aids in masking their class affiliation.

In the large enterprise the capitalist is but a shadowy figure. As a person, he is invisible. The employee never meets him, but instead meets many people to whom functions of the capitalist have been delegated. Most, if not all, of these functionaries are employees. In the small and, to some degree, the medium-sized enterprise, employee and employer meet as persons. As the enterprise grows in size, however, the class affiliation of the superior is increasingly hidden.

The social appearance of any individual employee is determined by the observer's vantage within the hierarchy. Thus, depending on the observer's own position, an employee may appear as a superior with authority to dispose, manage, give orders or control, or as a subordinate who follows orders, or more simply, as a giver or taker of work. Simple reference to the hierarchical stratification of the functionaries inadequately comprehends this phenomenon, for the decisive fact is that a single person possesses both proletarian and capitalist qualities. The correspondent who is subordinate to and receives directives from the chief of his section also transmits them to the secretary who takes his dictation. For her he is the boss (and she frequently calls him that). She, in turn, may function as a superior to the messenger, as, for example, when she orders him to have the typed letters signed or to discreetly fetch her a glass of water from the fountain. The employee who calculates the cost of filling an order reports to the chief of the bureau of calculations. In large enterprises, especially in cases of mass production, it is possible to separate out the mere arithmetic aspects of the work and have them done (with the help of machines) by less qualified persons. In relation to them the calculator functions as superior, especially when mistakes are discovered. He does not supervise the manager and the foremen, but they are nevertheless "forced to respect him, because he can—and even must—look into their cards."[5]

The last illustration indicates that the phenomenon of hidden class membership is ubiquitous. It pertains not only to employees who have authority, however limited, to give orders to subordinate employees, but also to persons who work in other bureaus on the same level of the hierarchy and who perform one-sided or mutual-control functions within the organization. Thus, a study suggests: "The bureau of calculations always fights the engineer in charge of time studies, because he gives the impression that the bureau's employees are weak in arithmetic."[6] Indeed, even subordinate employees can perform functions of employers in relation to "superior" employees. The girl who wraps the merchandise in the department store "controls" the work of the salesgirl; typists paid according to piecework or receiving premiums "pressure" their superiors, the correspondents, toward rational distribution and circumspect preparation of work, thereby increasing the "higher" performance that is not paid by piecework. These subordinate personnel perform as if on behalf of the invisible capitalist.

It is not at the hand of the capitalist, therefore, that many employees directly experience exploitation. Rather, it is at the hand of one another. The messenger boy is exploited by the typist who rushes him; the typist is exploited by the correspondent, who determines, within limits, her immediate workload; the correspondent is exploited by his section chief, to whom he reports; the manual worker is exploited by the foreman; workers and foremen, among others, are exploited by employees in the bureau of calculation and in the office controlling production deadlines; these are exploited by their immediate supervisors, and so on. In short, the experience of the employee points not to capitalists and class enemies, but to other employees who act like capitalists even though they do not own the means of production. Taken at its extreme, this situation seems to prove B. Traven's anarchistic contention that the worker's greatest enemy is the worker. This, however, would be going too far, for workers are enemies only where they compete with other workers.

The phenomenon of hidden class membership produces the fetish of the superior and engenders moral confusion. The fetish of the superior is fundamentally important not only in the large enterprise but in modern society at large: the less comprehensible the total fabric of social life, the

more difficult it becomes to locate the individual who is
responsible for mishaps. Accountability in fact becomes
anonymous because everyone can rightly claim to have performed only his or her required function. Every superior
follows the instructions of his superior. Even the president
of a large corporation depends upon a board of trustees or
upon bankers who grant him loans, and even they are not
"free." The lack of freedom that almost everyone seems to
bewail is very real and, apparently, very difficult to endure.
Life pulsates between people, not between people and institutions. For this reason, human actions and reactions are
characterized by an irremediable immediacy. They may be
theoretically "false" to some intellectuals, but they are quite
real to the people involved. Thus, workers who had beaten
up a white-collar employee declared that "the gentleman is
a matter of indifference to us, we only wanted to hit the
directorate." Similarly, the poor person typically directs his
envy not at the millionaire, who is mythical to him, but at
the neighbor who is only a little less poor but whose relative affluence he can see. The rage of a laid-off employee
can often find no concrete object other than the hapless
employee who works overtime at the unemployment office,
is not highly paid, and certainly does not represent the capitalists. Animosity against the means test is directly expressed
against the person who administers the test, even though
he is not responsible for this requirement. Finally, hatred
against the state has always been directed foremost against
policemen, who represent the power of the state to its subjects.

According to Marx, the struggle of workers against individual capitalists (as, for example, in the uprising of the
Silesian weavers) is the product of an early, inchoate stage
of capitalism, in which labor lacks both mass character and
insight into the "real" structure of the system. Marx was
theoretically correct in arguing that the dependence of wage
earners upon the capitalist cannot be suspended by the
destruction of machinery and by action against individual
entrepreneurs. But even though the real structural relationship
between capitalist and wage earner is abstract and nebulous, the workers' need to find some specific individuals
responsible for their situation remains strong enough to
continually disturb the circles of abstraction.[8]

The phenomenon of hidden class membership demonstrates the inadequacy of any sociological approach that simply regards salaried employees as proletarians, for such a categorization fails to comprehend their situation in the large enterprise. Consider the correspondent in the large enterprise. His colleague in a small enterprise works without assistants and under the direct supervision of the entrepreneur. He is more difficult to replace than the correspondent who is only one among many in the large establishment, for his experience in the enterprise carries more weight. Disregarding the different resiliencies of small and large enterprises during an economic crisis, the more independent correspondent in the small establishment is clearly less proletarianized than his colleague in the large firm, no matter how their wages compare. Although the correspondent in the large enterprise is objectively more dependent than his small-firm counterpart—because of the division of labor—he possesses the authority of a superior in relation to the typist and other assistants, whereas his colleague does not. Moreover, he wields this authority despite his greater dependence and despite the narrower range of his work. Considering his greater authority, then, the correspondent in the larger enterprise is less a member of the proletariat than his colleague in the small firm who completely lacks the employer's authority. This example merely points to the social consequence of the division of labor, which has made possible the increase of white-collar workers in relation to the total workforce.

The phenomenon of hidden class membership has a neutralizing effect upon social conflicts. The industrial employee not only encounters the phenomenon, he personifies it. He is continuously entangled in a living contradiction: as employee he must pursue his employer's interests or else risk failure as an employee. This inevitable dilemma is created in the middle-sized enterprise as capitalist power is delegated to the salaried employee. In the big enterprise the same tendency prevails, but the division of labor is more elaborate and the delegation of managerial functions is restricted to ever more modest quantities of power and respect. Salaried employees in these large enterprises are left with nothing to value apart from internal order. Inasmuch as they contribute to the orderly functioning of the establishment, they are perhaps inclined as good Germans to idealize the discipline to which they are subjected.

To some degree, blue- and white-collar workers are equally exposed to the hidden class membership of the superior. Like the salaried employees, manual workers never meet the capitalist, and they encounter in the superior a "false" social quality. That is, they fail to see the foreman, the section boss and his assistant, the time checker, as the employees they are. They do see themselves "correctly," however. In the shop the manual workers are mostly in touch with other workers, with people whose social quality is unambiguous and cannot be distorted because they have little authority to give orders to others. If the manual laborer does encounter the phenomenon of hidden class membership, it is usually in salaried employees rather than in other manual workers. Moreover, the authority exercised by these employees is frequently associated with some legal privileges. This connection is significant in furthering solidarity among manual laborers and in impeding their solidarity with white-collar workers.

Salaried employees in large enterprises encounter false class membership far more often than do manual workers, for they more frequently meet people whose social character changes with the level of the hierarchy from which it is observed. They are also more likely to encounter colleagues whose social position is subject to false assessment, because an uncommon capacity for objectivity is required to look beyond their social position and recognize the character of their labor, their replaceability, and the insecurity of their lives.

Only certain strata within the enterprise are so situated that they can easily look through the veils of hidden class membership. This is especially true of the very lowest strata, who lack even the least significant capitalistic functions. Thus, alert, observant messenger boys, who are in contact with many salaried employees of different rank, are often able to offer insights that are astonishingly free of distortion and that can contribute to a concrete sociology of the enterprise.

Only the lowest ranks of white-collar workers are, like manual workers, exposed to the phenomenon of hidden class membership without embodying it themselves. For various reasons, however, even they do not fully avail themselves of the chance to be free of illusions. At least three of these reasons deserve mention.

A large number of these unqualified employees consists of women who leave employment earlier than men and who therefore think more optimistically of the future if they think of it at all. Their attitudes and opinions are influenced not only by work experiences but also by their anticipated gender experiences (marriage, child-rearing). It is perhaps possible to trace the sober, trade unionist orientation of technical personnel, as well as their coolness toward the middle-class ideal of compromise, to the fact that even the lowest positions are held by men rather than women. Of course, the more radical orientation of the technical employees must be attributed to other causes as well.

In retail trade the salesperson's illusion of freedom—that is, his or her representation of the enterprise in contacts with customers—reduces the psychological impact of economic insecurity.

In the giant enterprises of industry, however, the discipline governing personnel is even more exacting than it is in commerce. It reaches down to the last anonymous employee who services the office machines, and it is unmitigated by personal contact with "undisciplined" people who do not belong to the office—that is, with customers. The lowly worker can choose either to criticize the discipline to which he is subjected or else to endow it with an ideology. He usually does the latter, for otherwise, instead of participating as a co-worker in the order which has seized him, he falls victim to loneliness.

Notes

1. Regarding the hierarchy in the office cf. G. Briefs, "Betriebssoziologie," in A. Vierkandt (ed.), *Hwb der Soziologie*, (Stuttgart, 1931), pp. 441ff.; C. H. A. Geck, *Die sozialen Arbeitsverhältnisse im Wandel der Zeit* (Berlin, 1931), p. 51; C. Dreyfuss, *Beruf und Ideologie der Angestellten* (Munich, 1933), pp. 11ff.; J. Silbermann, *Die Angestellten als Stand* (Berlin, 1932), pp. 12ff.

2. To offer an extreme example from a large firm known to me in 1932, a subordinate correspondent consoled a typist who had complained about the routine character of her work as follows: "You can advance." "How?" "If you prove to be efficient, you will be permitted to type the opening of replies on your own initiative rather than by dictation." This meant that she would be permitted to type on her own: "Gentlemen, we acknowledge with thanks the receipt of your letter dated . . ."

3. It is well known that the differences in rank among executive employees are reflected in income, size and furnishings of the office, use of a company car, and the like. In addition, of special importance are ease and frequency of access to persons of higher rank and greater power. A modern, grotesque example taken from the higher American bureaucracy of the White House—not different in principle from the bureaucracy in private business—is given by T. H. White in his book about President Nixon's administration. White writes that familiarity with "the political topography" makes it possible "to judge the importance of people" by the location of their office. Then he tells the following anecdote about Daniel P. Moynihan, later U.S. Ambassador to the United Nations and, still later, U.S. Senator from New York: "In his rivalry with Arthur Burns in the first year of the Nixon administration, Moynihan opted for a tiny office in the basement of the White House West Wing, next to Kissinger's, while Burns opted for a large suite of offices for himself and staff across the street in the Executive Office Building. Moynihan, whose wisdom is at once profound and practical, had made the better choice—'Why, it meant I could piss standing next to Haldeman in the same toilet,' he said one day, explaining the strategic geography of the White House," (T. H. White, *Breach of Faith* (New York, 1975), pp. 113–14).

4. Also not in the large firms of retail trade. Cf. the instructive functional analysis of a department store with about 700 employees by H. Schröer, *Die betriebliche Ausbildung des Verkaufspersonals im Einzelhandel,* (Stuttgart, 1933), pp. 14ff.; cf. also F. Nordsieck, *Die schaubildliche Erfassung und Untersuchung der Organization* (Stuttgart, 1932), p. 80; and F. Nordsieck, "Die Arbeitsaufgaben und ihre Verteilung," *Hb des Einzelhandels,* (Stuttgart, 1932).

5. E. Kannwitz, "Aus dem Berufsleben eines technischen Vorkalkulators." *Jugend and Berut,* March 1931.

6. F. Giese, *Methoden der Wirtschaftspsychologie der werksleiter,* no. 5, (1928), p. 276.

7. Reported by C. Höfchen, in H. Potthoff, ed. *Die sozialen Probleme des Betriebs* (Berlin, 1925), p. 290.

8. This basic fact can also be found in international affairs. A highly renowned British statesman, asked about the possibilities of securing peace, proposed on the wireless that diplomats be the first sent to the front if war broke out.

8 Economic Class, Status and Personality*
Joseph Bensman and Arthur J. Vidich

Throughout the recent literature on class, attention has been paid only infrequently to the specific relationships between status and social and economic class, despite the fact that this discussion has covered a wide range of historical periods and almost all points in the social structure.

Here we wish to discuss in a relatively abstract and general way the central themes of economic analysis that appear to underlie most theories of social class. By making these themes explicit we hope to set the framework for a subsequent analysis of changes in social and economic class in American society, especially as they relate to class life-styles and social status, the cultures of various classes, personality in relationship to class, politics in relationship to class, and to overall changes in the "class system" as a separate entity. In order to do this we must first specify the basic economic dimensions of class. We have chosen to focus on:

1. The business cycle as a measure of economic opportunity, noting particularly how the movements of the cycle are related to the political and social psychology of classes.
2. The business cycle in relation to the underlying historical–secular trend. Here we wish to note how the cyclic movement and the long-term trend relate to changes in classes and class systems.

This analysis does not offer a new theory. Rather, we wish to state for present purposes what is implied by several older theorists such as Schumpeter, Veblen, Selig Perlman, and Mannheim, and certain contemporaries such as Gerth and

---

* Reprinted from Joseph Bensman and Arthur J. Vidich, *The New American Society* (Chicago: Quadrangle Books, 1971).

161

Mills who have worked in this tradition. From this statement we hope, in later chapters, to draw a portrait of established and emerging status and class structures in the United States.

NONECONOMIC MEANINGS OF BUSINESS CYCLES

Any measure of the business cycle, no matter how it is determined or specifically calculated, can be viewed also as a measure of existing income opportunity in society as a whole. Upward movements of the cycle are characterized by investment and expansion. Corresponding with rises in investment and expansion is a range of economic opportunities more or less directly connected to the rise. These opportunities exist in the form of

1. Possibilities for employment in previously nonexistent jobs.
2. Greater income for existing jobs.
3. Overtime employment at existing jobs.
4. Greater availability of existing jobs.
5. Greater possibility for mobility from job to job.
6. Enhanced income possibilities through capital investment and technological change.
7. Greater possibilities for the expansion of businesses.
8. Increased chances for the accumulation of capital.
9. Chances for greater return on invested capital.
10. Profits from the sales of inventories due to rises in prices.

In a downward movement of the economy these forms of opportunity are reversed and become so many losses in opportunity. The lack of, or availability of, opportunity in these terms is a description of the movement of the whole of society rather than a description of the opportunity chances of particular individuals, and in this sense is an economic statement rather than a statement about class.

The description of the business cycle as a series of different types of income opportunity and loss of opportunity is only one way of viewing the noneconomic meanings of economic movements. In a complex money economy, one man's opportunity can be another man's loss. When it is understood that a major correlate of business upturn is an increase in prices and price levels, the operation of the business cycle can be viewed not simply as a set of increased or decreased opportunities but also as a set of increased or decreased costs to members of the society. Moreover, the movement of business is not a unitary phenomenon affecting all groups and individuals equally. The effects of both the upward and downward movement on different groups and individuals depend on their relationship to the direction of change. There are, of course, leads and lags in price and cost levels that arise out of "premature" and "delayed" price rises, inventory conditions, time spreads between production and sale, the incurring and liquidating of debts, and similar phenomena. The cumulative effect of such factors prevents a direct and equal reflection of economic trends in the income distribution and the relative class position of individuals.

The relationship of groups and individuals to these somewhat irregular changes in income opportunities and costs can nevertheless be stated in a clear enough manner to enable us to see their economic and social consequences. The position of an individual or a group in the economic structure can be defined by the relations of that individual or group to changes in the average net income of the total economy or, conversely, to changes in average net costs of the total economy. The average net income of the individual or group may rise or fall in phase with changes in average net income, and at faster or slower rates. This can be expressed in the ratio of the percentage change in average net *group* income to the percentage change in average net *total* income. This we label the *income elasticity* of a group in a market relationship. The same may be done for the relationship of a group to changes in total average costs. This ratio is the *cost elasticity* of a group. The consequences of these changes on a particular group become apparent when it is realized that *changes in income elasticity do not necessarily coincide with changes in cost elasticity.* For this reason, various individuals and groups are differently affected by changes in the opportunity and cost structure of the total economy. For some groups, income opportunities may expand faster than costs, whereas for others, costs may rise faster than income. Put simply, an aged person with a fixed income has no income elasticity, and a nonunionized producer who has no inventory carryovers has enormous cost elasticity.

The relationship among costs, prices, and time in an upward movement of the economy lead to three different situations.

1. A rise in income at a faster rate than a rise in costs results in an accumulation of "unearned" increment due to the increasing difference between income and costs.
2. The reverse is a cost rise at a more rapid rate than an income rise, a situation that leads to an accumulation of losses.
3. Income and costs can rise at equal rates and in an upward movement sustain a fixed relationship to each other.

The same relationships are possible in a downward movement of the economy wherein the relationships between costs and income are simply reversed. Thus there may be gainers and losers in both inflationary and deflationary periods, depending on the relationship of their income and cost elasticity.

The three situations described for the upward and downward movements actually describe three general cases wherein, theoretically, the social effect resulting from the movement will be the same whether the movement is upward or downward. Movement in either direction will place individuals and groups in one of the following three situations:

1. The movement of the business cycle is favorable to the economic position of a specific group. This group moves upward at a faster rate than the average upward movement or moves downward at a slower rate than the average downward movement. In either case the class or individual experiences an above-average success. In subsequent discussion we will refer to these groups as *ascendant* groups.
2. The movement of the cycle is unfavorable to a specific group. This group moves upward at a slower rate than the average or moves downward at a faster rate. Such groups will be referred to as *descendant* groups.

3. The individual or group in question remains unaffected because the cost–income ratio remains the same in spite of the movement of the cycle. This group moves in phase with the total average movement of prices and costs. These groups will be referred to as the economically *unaffected.*

Each of the above situations is a theoretically possible relationship between an individual or group and cyclical movement in the economy as a whole. In each of these typical economic situations there develop correlative social and psychological attitudes that reflect the economic position of the individual or group in the movement as a whole.

The business cycle is so important to the underlying dynamic of personality that its movements can be directly related to the individual's conception of himself, of others, of the future, and of the world. The relationships between economic movement and personality will be especially marked for those individuals who are prone to construct a definition of who and what they are by comparing themselves with others to whom they are socially related and whose response they consider socially significant. This whole matter can be put in another terminology: because of differences in income and cost elasticity, business cycles affect individuals and groups differently, and therefore their social relationships, self-definition, expectations of the future, and world views are continuously altered by inflationary and deflationary economic movements. The invidious comparison of oneself with others and with one's previous status provides a psychological framework for defining oneself.

THE BUSINESS CYCLE AND THE PSYCHOLOGY OF CLASSES

These economic and psychological relationships can be illustrated with examples for each of the typical situations. To the extent that we deal with typical situations, our examples are deliberately heightened for illustrative purposes. Whether the examples are markedly accurate depends on the rapidity of changes in the class's comparative economic position and the length of time covered during the upward or downward movement. Short-term economic advantages and disadvantages for a given group are more likely to cause only immediate buoyancy or depression in the group without affecting its overall ideology; long-term movements will shape the personality and political psychology of classes.

While short-term economic gains and losses are less likely to produce stabilized norms for a class, sharp gains or losses in individual cases often produce highly dramatic consequences. Major losses like those of the 1929 depression may result in idiosyncratic suicides. Major unanticipated gains may result in *la folie du succès*, and wild spending sprees resulting in economic irrationalities and the appearance of joyous narcissism. Apart from such dramatic examples, wide fluctuations in gains and losses in the short run can result in feelings of elation or depression, illusions of persecution or godly selection, feelings of real or imagined rejection by former peers or ridicule by former inferiors. Thus what appear to be symptoms of individual pathology are social and economic in origin.

Short-term fluctuations especially, however normal, are likely to be important for another reason: they accentuate and dramatize the long-term trend. Thus a group that has been losing ground slowly and undramatically over a long period of time may suddenly perceive the erosion of its economic position only during a downturn of the business cycle. Or, it may discover its overall decline only when it fails to make a recovery proportionate to that of the whole economy during a subsequent recovery. Thus the expansion and contraction of business levels may serve to heighten the awareness of individuals and classes of their relative positions, not only in respect to the short term but also in respect to the long-term trend. Unstylized short-run responses are likely to be replaced in the long run by stylized ideological responses which become a stable part of the personality and life-plan of a class.

TYPES OF RELATIONSHIPS TO ECONOMIC MOVEMENTS

Type I: Ascent in Relation to the Average Movement of the Economy

The individual whose income opportunity expands at a faster rate than the general price level (whether advancing or declining) experiences "unearned" increments of success. That is, the price movement itself, apart from his direct efforts, is working in his favor. Because of his unexpected success, this individual is likely to be optimistic, aggressive, self-assured, and oriented to a future that he envisages as holding possibilities for ever greater success. This is the classical psychology of the *parvenu* who, because he is favorably situated in relation to the economic drift, sees himself—usually unconsciously—as fulfilled and justified by his actions. "Making it" with the upward movement means not looking to the past, or redefining the past to make it more attractive.

Illustrations of this type are Henry Ford, Sr ("History is bunk"), the Texas oil barons, insurance executives, advertising, radio and TV executives, and, until recently, the missile and computer industries including inventors, manufacturers, scientists, and technicians. For these groups the projection of the present into the future leads to an expectation of ultimate self-fulfillment. This future-mindedness deemphasizes qualities such as introspection, self-awareness, or disinterested intellectual pursuit. Such successful groups will be committed to the established scheme of society, which they will identify with their own success. They will characteristically be without resentment, except for a resentment they may hold against those groups that had achieved and sustained a predominance over them and had previously denied them social recognition. Thus, for example, the Texas oil barons can resent the Wall Street financiers and Eastern upper-class socialites and yet be quite untouched by any other feeling of resentment. Within their psychological purview, there is no one else available for them to compete with. Ascendant groups will tend to be uncritical and affirmative.

Ascendant groups are also likely to assert the functional value of their current economic activity. According to type, this means pointing out, for example, the decisive role of oil in comparison with coal (its importance to the national income, welfare, defense, and so forth); the indispensability of advertising for the continued successful operation of the total economy, the humanitarian and welfare functions of insurance and the functional necessity of upper-level management in all expanding bureaucracies. In their institutional and self-legitimations, ascendant groups hold that the price and salary mechanism is a true measure of social utility, and that all other yardsticks for measuring it—such as intelligence, pietistic selflessness, or humanitarianism—disguise the operation of true social value. In the last analysis, they would say, "Preachers as well as professors have to be paid by somebody." Life and all its codes are committed to the current direction of the movement that accounts for their above-average success. The entire world is pulled into their buoyant psychological vortex.

Where ascendancy rests upon large but short-run gains, the immediate response is likely to be unstylized, vulgar, conspicuous consumption and a ritualistic pursuit of pleasure. Frequently such "unexpected" short-run gains are likely to surprise the individual himself. He finds it hard to believe in his own good fortune. If it persists, he is likely to discover objective bases for his success, and the emotional quality surrounding it will be transformed from one of being surprised at his own good luck to accepting success as if it were earned. Should the advantage accrue from a downward price movement, the person may rediscover or reconstruct the virtues of those habits of mind—lack of venturesomeness, parsimoniousness, cost-consciousness, high liquidity preference—that are rewarded by a declining market. In this case the group or individual in question feels vindicated for upholding time-honored virtues. Such a hoarding mentality was rewarded in the early years of the depression in the 1930s, when cautiousness with cash paid off. Only since the early 1990s have these virtues been once again rewarded—a cause of deep resentment among groups deriving their income from nonexpanding sections of the economy.

Type 2: Descent in Relation to the Average Movement of the Economy

In some cases the income opportunities of individuals or groups expand at a slower rate than the general movement of prices and wages. This would be the case of the worker whose wages do not automatically escalate with price rises. Some persons, such as the pensioner or the unorganized worker with a relatively inelastic income, many experience relative or absolute decline in income due to an inflationary movement. Groups whose income expands at a slower rate than the general price movement find themselves in an invidious position with respect to both their previous economic status and to those who have not experienced a similar decline. These persons' response to their descendance is determined by the social and economic level they occupied before the movement that resulted in their decline.

Compared with other groups, their economic and psychological starting point in the earlier period could have been favorable or unfavorable. The *starting point* of a descending group is crucial, so much so that it affects its entire subsequent response. Two typical starting points and responses are as follows.

First groups that earlier were in *favored* economic positions, but now find themselves displaced by other ascendant groups, tend, in the short run, to develop a psychology of status defensiveness. In an effort to defend their status, despite the erosion of its economic underpinnings, they tend to justify themselves on grounds other than economic function or wealth. Like Warner's upper upper class in Yankee City, such a group asserts its heredity, the dignity and source of its income rather than its absolute size, or any of the higher functional values whose carriers they can claim to be. They discover the superiority of their morality, breeding, blood, taste, dress, and other consumption styles. They assert the superior value of such social functions as political qualifications and personal leadership rather than economic skills and activities. The classic example of this type is the English landed aristocracy, which historically moved from lordly and manorial roles to political ones in phase with the encroachment of industrial predominance.[1] In post-Civil-

War America, the southern landed aristocracy followed a similar path, attempting to uphold its way of life well into the twentieth century to the point where it was sustained only by a compulsive enactment of hollow social rituals, as described in the works of Tennessee Williams. In contemporary times this drama of social "face-saving" is enacted wherever landed wealth is losing predominance to industrial and commercial wealth.

An identical psychological situation occurs in periods of prolonged inflation. The rapid devaluation of currency brings to the foreground a range of social types who, at least for the period of inflation, win out in the competition. Germany in the 1920s, as described by Erich Maria Remarque in *The Black Obelisk*[2] is a case in point.

The social and time perspective of descending groups is toward the past and its hallowed traditions. The relevance of the current social drift is denied by the psychological device of refusing to recognize the movement of time and social change. Because their commitment is to the past, groups like this are resentful of anyone who denies the past, particularly the *parvenu*, the "vulgar mob," the social climber, and all other ascendant types and groups. Because of these dynamics, descendant groups attempt to attach themselves to archaic styles of consumption that cannot easily be emulated. They use or display heirlooms, antiques, or other consumption items not easily available on the market or unattainable by cash purchases: they make much of the old school emblem, the white shoe, peculiarities of linguistic usage, and other quaint or archaic prestige symbols. If the economic pressures are persistent and failure looms, these defensive tactics eventually lead them to withdraw into small social enclaves that deny admission to newcomers, with the result that they become more and more removed from the main feeling and tone of the society as a whole. In their final defense they give others the impression of being quaint relies of the past, if not odd. On the plane of social action they will attempts to use political methods[3] to prevent ascendant economic groups from achieving the full social and economic return from their economic rise. In sum, they make major claims to prestige on the basis of past performance and noneconomic functions.

If one focuses on the very short-run effects rather than on the long-run trends, one finds that the descendent group tends to develop a psychology of grumbling and dissatisfaction, and postpones expenditure on durable goods. Individuals within the group, generally speaking, experience idiosyncratic "personal" moods of depression. This is likely to be the case for certain groups during periods of temporary recession, as in 1949, 1954, 1970 and 1990; or for any fixed-income groups in an inflationary war economy without wage and price controls. The idiosyncratic nature of such moods is most pronounced when economic misfortune affects only an individual or a relatively small group.

The pattern of resentment elected by this group always centers on one common device; namely, any group that threatens its particular area of ascendancy will be resented. The resentful groups as well as the objects of resentment can exist at different levels in the social structure, and the objects selected can be composed of quite disparate groups whose minimum qualification for selection is their measure of social visibility. Thus a white-collar group in the United States may resent highly paid industrial workers in a manner similar to the ways that a landowning group in the nineteenth century resented manufacturers. Only moderately successful children of Italian and Irish immigrants resent strongly even the physical mobility of blacks and Puerto Ricans into their environs, and blacks, whatever their sense of injustice about their own position, have been intolerant of Puerto Ricans and of Jews who have been more mobile than themselves in their own environment. Jews in Europe and America, after leaving the ghettos and scaling the pyramids of society, have been the object of resentment by successively higher social classes in phase with their own ascent. One can define social mobility by locating the class groups that resent others' ascendancy.

The second kind of descendent group is that in an economically *unfavored* position before an upward phase of the economy. Such persons find themselves further disadvantaged, and their psychological responses are quite different from those who began in a favored position. Their decline is a decline from nadir, and so is experienced in a quite different way from a decline that allows more favorable memories of the past.

Because of their unfavorable memories of the past they are less likely to be committed to it. In a psychological sense they have no past because they do not care to remember it. For a different reason they are as fully uncommitted to the present as the descending group described above, whose commitments were totally to the past. This is because relative to their previous situation they have nothing to lose. Theirs, then, is a psychology of noncommitment to both present and past, of resenting and rejecting the total framework of society. When such groups act (the Townsendites in the 1930s and some radical movements in the United States, and, in general, communists who lack an economically secure past), it is to seek political solutions for economic problems and to make broad attacks on the framework of constituted society. Even when not politically radical, their fundamental psyche is one of resentment. Their perception, intelligence, and attention are directed to discovering flaws and weaknesses in the character and morality of the system and in the individuals who symbolize it. Profane and irreverent attitudes toward society's most cherished and hallowed institutions and symbols can be held without compunction.

In some cases the rejection of the present constitutes a total rejection of the dominant materialistic system and all its sustaining values. Such total forms of rejection can lead to the construction of imaginary alternative worlds, which may take the form of projected utopias or a projected religious ordering of the world. Forms of total rejection can involve images of future other worlds, hopes for divine intervention or miraculous universal revelations, or, finally, hopes for a total apocalypse. Only this imagined future is real and alive. The sublimation of current resentments thus may have the respectability of the religious: religion absorbs and disguises what would otherwise be a radical dissatisfaction and a potential threat to the equanimity of the established scheme of society.[4] This psychology need not be limited to absolutely marginal groups. It can also be characteristic of relatively marginal groups such as intellectuals and various segments of the middle class.[5]

The marginality of middle-class youth is structural in character, in the sense that youth increasingly have been kept off the labor market until well past the teenage stage. What with graduate education, scholarships, and remittances, many have not appeared on the labor scene until well into their thirties. This structural marginality results in a lack of commitment to the economic institutions and to an increased anxiety about accepting these commitments. Anxieties about failure and an inability to compete increase as one approaches the age when it appears that he must begin to compete. Entry into the labor market at the higher ages undoubtedly increases the anxiety. The result may be forms of rebellion based on fears of deprivations that the youth have not yet even experienced.

The absolutely marginal groups need not seek their solution in apocalypse or otherworldliness. The range of secular institutions and activities that permit the expression of resentment or vicarious feelings of superiority is broad, as one would expect in a secular society. The mass media, with its parade of villains, bestiality, and sadism, serves the purpose for those who do not find the "religious" way. The orgy the public display of the nude, the provocative Hollywood starlet and so forth, allow each according to his needs to sublimate his hostility, resentment and masochism in a vicarious playing of his sexual role in relation to the particular object in view. A major form of secular escape is drug abuse, ranging from the quasi-religiously defined usage associated with Zen to the withdrawal and retreat from the world associated with other drugs. Intensive escape from routine is associated with amphetamines and other "uppers." According to this theory, these forms of secular escape become all the more socially necessary and all the more intensely displayed and employed during expansive phases of business, when the failure of the unsuccessful is accentuated. It is a truly modern phenomenon that responses to movements of the economy can be expressed by the ingestion of modern and not so modern chemicals.

Type 3: Economically Unaffected Groups

The situation for economically unaffected groups is one in which income position roughly corresponds to the movement of the total economy. This group's response to the economic movement is not easily predictable. This is because much of the response will be determined not only by the group's position before the latest business movement but also by the movement of other socially visible groups whose movement does not parallel its own. In other words, this group's own position, while remaining stationary relative to the movement of business, is drastically altered in comparison with other groups that move out of phase with the general movement. The group's response is conditioned by its relative lack of movement. An apt illustration of this is the case of almost any white-collar group whose income has kept pace with price rises since 1950 but which has experienced a decline relative to the enormous advance of skilled workmen who moved from no employment to high-wage full employment during the same time.

This category of the economically unaffected contains several possibilities:

First, if the individual or group was relatively well favored in the previous phase and continues to be relatively well favored in the present, while the group nearest to it in the previous phase achieves greater gains in the present one, it will tend to respond in the same way as the descendant groups mentioned earlier. The response will be the same in spite of the fact that the group's position will not be directly affected by its own relationship to the economy. The similar response in this case is evoked by the invidious comparison the group makes between itself and socially visible and competitive groups. Members of this group differ from those of a descendant group in that they are less likely to be deeply emotionally involved in their comparative failure, since their loss is relative and not absolute. It is easier for them to sustain favorable self-images and perhaps even to retain high expectations. Their specific experiences will mainly define the structure of their resentments.

Second, a group that, while remaining in a largely unchanged position relative to the total movement of prices and opportunity, sees other groups that were previously higher descending to its own position, presents an entirely new possibility. The stationary group may achieve some degree of vindication for prior defeats, and may have opportunities to express resentments that were previously unexpressed, as did professors and intellectuals vis-à-vis businessmen in the 1930s. It may also see in the descending group opportunities for establishing social contacts that would not have been feasible in the past; the economically ascendant group now finds itself in the position of being able to associate with groups that were previously above it. For example, any portrait of the postbellum American south (as described by Faulkner, among others) shows this reversal of roles. For the descendent group, however, social meetings on the downward slope tend to make the descent a little more unbearable; the result is to stimulate defensive action of a political and social nature by the descendent group.

Type 4: Psychologically Unaffected Groups

There are, finally, groups that may experience no shifts in psychological tone and attitude, even in the face of extreme changes in the business cycle. These groups do not fall into clear-cut categories, but if classified along economic lines there are three of them.

First, market-oriented groups that are protected from the vicissitudes of the business cycle by virtue of their capital and income sources are not psychologically affected by a relative decline in their position. That is, their access to wealth is so steady that a relative decline does not affect their image of their present or future expectations. An example would be the hoarder with vast cash reserves or highly mobile noncurrency investments (jewels, valued works of art, and so forth).[6] Perhaps the best example, however, is that of the leading wealthy families with highly diversified investment portfolios.

Second, groups that are partially or completely protected from the fluctuations of the market because of the public or semipublic nature of their sources of income are similarly psychologically unaffected. One example would be groups whose investments are in large portfolios of government bonds, or in industries that are publicly subsidized in phase with price movements, such as utilities or atomic weapons. During the Cold War another example would have been such bureaucratic groups as the armed services, the intelligence corps and groups in advanced weapons research, testing, and manufacturing, whose work serves higher military purposes not subject to price-cost fluctuations. The market affects these groups only insofar as state income is drastically altered by business movements. As a rule, the average military man (excluding perhaps the top military leaders) has anxieties only about the appropriation and does not concern himself with business conditions. The conception of self, future, and world is apt to be given by participation in the totally encompassing and psychologically monopolistic institution. In such total institutions, the rest of the world is conceived of as the "outside."

Finally, there are the economically submarginal groups who are unaffected psychologically by market fluctuations because they do not participate at any time in the market system. The subsistence farmer in the market economy who does not orient himself to the market is unaffected by movements of business. He subsists at all price levels.[7] The most obvious examples, perhaps, are individuals more or less permanently incarcerated in mental institutions and prisons, a not insubstantial portion of the population. But this is not the only case of being completely removed from economic participation. Bums, hoboes, tramps, transients, scavengers, gypsies, the habitués of Skid Row, and like newer dropouts, provided they do not graduate out of the ranks in periods of prosperity, can all be immunized from business fluctuations. Since they are not economically committed to society in any of its phases, there is little possibility for induced resentment[8] and little expectation of anything but immediate survival and gratification in terms of values and standards outside the framework of the dominant social order.

SECULAR TRENDS, CHANGES IN CLASS STRUCTURE, AND ALTERATIONS IN WORLD VIEWS

While the analysis given above may explain the successes and failures of groups in relation to the total economy and to other groups during short- and long-run economic movements, it does not explain the social consequences of secular trends that span long periods of time.

Beyond a single cycle of inflation and deflation, one can see class history as a series of responses to such cycles. The effects of a succession of cycles we call a short-term trend. When social history is viewed from the perspective of the short-term trend, we can see another set of implications from business movements. The secular trend may continuously work against a group, which thereby suffers an historic decline, irrespective of temporary gains and losses. If such a group loses continuously for a long enough period of time it may in time virtually drop out of existence, as happened with the old southern aristocracy. Another possibility is that a group will recoup losses suffered in a previous phase; for such a group the intermediate phases are a kind of equilibrium wherein gains and losses occur only to a minor extent. As an example of such differential effects, we can note that small business, which lost ground in the 1930s, regained it in the 1950s; but in the long run it appears to be placed in a more and more defensive position in comparison with big business. The same has been true of the family-sized farm which has been largely displaced by corporate industrialized agriculture. On the other hand top businessmen and managerial executives in both of these phases did not lose their power, influence, or prestige.[9]

Over even longer periods of time, other factors operate that are independent of any particular phase of the business cycle and that radically reconstitute both the economic and the social structure in ways that are impossible to predict in advance. The long-range secular trend, while it is related in its consequences to the consequences of business cycles, leads to more basic changes in the organization of the economy and its technological structure.

The significant factors in the long-range secular trend are (1) changes in the rate of accumulation of capital, and (2) changes in the dominant forms of capital in the society.

Rate Changes in Capital Accumulation

The rate of capital accumulation affects the structure of the entire class system and sets the larger framework of economic opportunity.

If accumulation increases at an increasing rate, society is likely to be expansive at almost all levels. This is the classic image of the frontier society in a state of accelerating expansion. In this situation the invidious "comparison with others" is less likely to prevail as a basic psychological dimension of social life, because all groups share in the expanding opportunities. Opportunity is a continuously growing pie with larger and larger slices for each man. So long as the size of his slice increases, the individual's attention is directed inward to his success as it relates to his own past; he does not develop a sharp consciousness of external competition. In the United States in the nineteenth century, for example, immigrants who came with nothing willingly accepted what they got because it was more than they had had. They compared their life in America with their life in the "old country," and so long as they were "getting ahead" in America they did not resent those longer-term Americans who had already achieved success. The immigrant is the pure case, but the same psychology applied to the westward movement of "Yankee" Americans who entered on the ground floor of that economic expansion. Slavery and, to a large extent, segregation and discrimination until recently prevented black Americans from sharing in such opportunity. In a long-term period of economic expansion, when opportunity is broadly available, defensive, invidious comparison is not likely to be found.

In a capital expansive age, the dominant tone of society is likely to be optimistic, future-oriented, and self-confident. The image of the future appears so golden that the past is rarely noticed. Tensions between classes tend to be reduced the success of one person does not appear to be contingent on another's loss. A general emphasis is placed upon individual opportunity, individualism, individual initiative and entrepreneurship rather than on collective class corporatism. The system of mobility is more likely to be an open class system and technical competence and achieved status are likely to be rewarded. In the United States this was the age of Horatio Alger and the Great American Dream.

If capital accumulation occurs at a decreasing rate, on the other hand, this is experienced by individuals as a shrinkage of opportunity. From the point of view of "society," individual assertiveness and aggressiveness decline in value. Society tends to focus less on individuals and more on classes and groups. The psychological tone of society as a whole is apt to be a defensive one in which past accomplishments and historical heroes are favorably reassessed. The traditions of the past are accentuated and glorified. Paralleling a return to the past is an accentuation of class conflict; class comes to be recognized as a social phenomenon and is experienced as a psychological milieu. The class conflict, however, may occur at a legal rather than at a revolutionary level; or the personal tensions arising from the visibility of class differences may be wholly internalized and expressed in idiosyncrasies of individual behavior, including neuroses and psychoses. For many members of society, adaptations and adjustments between the values of the earlier age—emphasizing equality, individualism, and status achievement—and the newer values of group identity and collective corporatism will have to be made. Individuals, or more probably generations, that are psychologically caught between the two periods will often experience identity crises. David Riesman in his book *The Lonely Crowd*[10] and William H. Whyte in his book *The Organization Man*[11] together depicted the identity crises and corporate aspects of mid-twentieth-century American history. Individualism as an ideology is being replaced only with difficulty by group, corporate or status categories of identification. Contemporary class psychology is most closely related to this stage.

A third possibility arises where capital accumulation does *not* occur.[12] In this case all major accumulation has taken place and the plant is merely sustained. In the history of Western capitalistic countries, this would be the stage following previous ones of increasing rates of accumulation and increasing accumulation at decreasing rates. When no accumulation takes place, opportunity ends in all but the traditionally established spheres, and a psychology of defending established gains and privileges sets in. In this case society is likely to take on a caste character, where opportunity is rigidly allocated on the basis of ritual, legal, and religious sanctions. Status rather than class becomes a dominant organizing principle. Class conflict is minimal, and individuals exist not as legal entities but only as members of a corporate class. Psychologically there is a loss of self in the external rhythm and ritual of prescribed codes of behavior that are intolerant of both individualism and of sensitive awareness of pasts and futures. The transition to this state, when it occurs to the individual during a decisively important stretch of the secularization process, is apt to be fraught with internal crises and upheaval. Britain would be an example of a country where the rate of capital accumulation has fallen sharply and where much of social policy is an attempt to maintain international standards and advantages, despite the lower rate of accumulation.[13]

The underdeveloped world, now undergoing the initial stages of accumulation, experiences the frontier psychology at least in those of the traditional strata who are given access to participation in the new opportunities. But any application of this model to the underdeveloped world must be done with great caution, since accumulation in these cases is frequently only a secondary effect of primary accumulation in the world's metropolitan centers.

Changes in the Form of Capital

Long-term changes in the rate of capital accumulation primarily affect the rigidity and flexibility of the class system; or, to state the matter differently, the measure for the secular trend would be a measure for class flexibility or inflexibility. The content of the class system itself is still another matter. The content of the class system—which groups and individuals come to predominate and which lose ground—is determined by the shifts in the kinds of capital wealth, emerging technologies and forms of institutional organization that become the basis of society. Capital can be based on land, mining, plant, inventory, contracts, brand names, reputation and so forth. Different forms of capital and technology gain ascendance in different periods, just as different forms of capital are accumulated at different rates. Class predominance in the overall structure of society, then, is a function of the ascendance of forms of capital and differences in the rates of accumulation of the different forms.

Each form of capital, wealth or organization is accompanied by different sets of skills, education, personality characteristics and occupations. The growth of a given form of capital, wealth, or organization thus results in a reconstitution of the characteristics, of the labor force as well as the educational system, personality formation, and class institutions. Thus changes in the form of capital result in premiums being placed on individuals who possess the skills and characteristics appropriate to the expanding sector. Conversely, previously favored groups are devalued by such forms of social change. When this phenomenon occurs, the individual responds in the way described earlier in this chapter.

Seen in these terms, the decline of feudalism, for example, can be stated simply as a decrease in the relative importance of land as a form of capital and an increase in the relative rate of growth of commercial and later, industrial capital. The decline of feudalism came about because the expansion of a particular form of capital brought with it new classes—new economic actors who collected around the new possibilities, techniques, and opportunities. In due course social, economic and political interests arose to defend and further the legal establishment of what had been only socially recognized economic interests and positions.

The success of a class or an economic group, while based upon economic and political power, has consequences for more than the economic and political organization of a society. When a predominant class has distinctive ideologies, skills, and personality traits, its success results in the legitimation of these personal and cultural characteristics. They become incorporated in the predominant personality models of society and become the object of emulation, education, and reward in many sectors of the society. Thus every change in the structure of the class system results in a change in the distribution of personalities within the society. Weber's classic studies on China and India stress precisely this point. The dominance of the political bureaucrat in the former Soviet Union and the business bureaucrat in the West are earlier examples. The "scientific" businessman, the Ph.D. in mathematics or physics who enters the missile-hardware or electronics business, or the computer-minded organization man, are current examples.

Such transformations of capital form land and commercial bases to industrial and scientific bases at the present time in the underdeveloped world constitute a major revision and reorganization of the class structure of underdeveloped societies. The process is not necessarily a repetition of the earlier shift from feudalism to capitalism as experienced in the Western world, since the major sources of investment for economic development are external to the underdeveloped world.

Industries whose form of capital accumulates at a slower rate, or not at all, provide little opportunity to the ambitious and competent. At the same time slowly accumulating forms of capital fail to attract the best personnel in society. The vested interests, irrevocably committed to a form of capital or technology that declines or that has a relatively slower rate of growth, find their past superiority increasingly threatened by individuals attached to newer and faster-growing industries. The "establishment" is apt to seek government intervention to protect its income and status position; thus, for example, mineral-resources industries such as copper and petroleum have sought government support to prevent the decline of their capital investment. A still better example is the railroad industry, which has been threatened since the 1920s by more-highly mobile and direct forms of transportation such as trucks and aircraft—that is, forms of capital that bring a much higher return per unit invested. Again, in such cases, attempts are made to dip into the public treasury to protect earlier capital investments. The military and economic indispensability of the firm to society as a whole justifies claims for such subsidies. When a sufficient number of defensive groups arise—usually in a stage of decreasing rates of accumulation—competition for protective legislation and fiscal favors can become intense. This is approximately the case in the United States at the present time in connection with steel, petroleum, automobiles, airframes coal and computer technology. Increasingly, political rather than market decisions determine the distribution of gains and advantages. Thus political brokers and officials may be in a position to make crucial societal decisions. When this occurs in a bureaucratic environment, phenomena such as influence peddling, lobbying, bribery, blackmail, payoffs, and other such activities are apt to become the basis of honorable professions, without which the economic decisions in the bureaucratic marketplace would be hard to make. Conflicts for hegemony between such groups determine the subsequent structure of society, and in a basic sense determine the relationships between social class and economic opportunity.

In the bureaucratic state, military and foreign policy require huge governmental investment and expenditure in the building of industries or in the transferring of investments and expenditures from previously favored industries to other industries. Thus missile-building and the military hardware industry, as well as electronic and specialized scientific, instrument, chemical and biotechnology industries, may expand at previously unanticipated rates, producing new subclasses and new prestige, power, and income for those classes. At the same time, relative loss of government subsidies may devalue the past claims and standing of all other groups relative to the new groups, and especially those groups whose skills, abilities, and position were due to subsidies that have been cut or replaced by those of the new groups. Government policy, always important in the past, now increasingly affects the total character of the class system within American society.

Notes

1. A substantial portion of the English landed aristocracy, as pointed out by Barrington Moore in *Social Origins of Dictatorship and Democracy, Lord and Peasant in the Making of the Modern World* (Harmondsworth: Penguin, 1968) were able to survive because they shifted the basis of their investment from land to trade and later to industry. In doing so, however, much of their character as a landed aristocracy was lost.
2. (New York: Harcourt Brace & World, 1957).
3. The Protestant upper classes have thus attempted to exclude newer immigrant groups from political and economic leadership as long as possible a process documented by E. Digby Baltzel in *The Protestant Establishment* (New York: The Free Press, 1964).
4. This is the classic psychology of the slave, the disfranchised, and the marginal, particularly in epochs of institutional intractability. The original and essentially slave morality of Christianity has asserted itself repeatedly. Jehovah's Witnesses have been known to cheer enthusiastically for a prediction of the imminent apocalypse and total

destruction of the world. Similar psychological phenomena have been widely noted in lower-class American blacks and Puerto Ricans.

5. The rate of production of intellectuals in the United States in the postwar years appears to be greater than the ability of bureaucratic expansion to absorb it. The expansion of advertising, the mass media, and "researching" during these years has provided major areas of intellectual opportunity. Thus the marginality of intellectuals has until recently been more a product of secular trends than of cyclical movements.

6. The small-time hoarder is a different case. In an inflationary phase he sees his hoard (his life work) evaporate and bitterness results. In a deflationary phase his hoard expands in value and he beats his chest with pride and self-satisfaction.

7. The pure type, of course, is possible only in squatting and marginal rural areas, where land taxes are very low or where poaching is possible. To the extent that such groups orient themselves to cash income, no matter how peripherally, marginally or sporadically, they will be affected if only minimally by the availability of opportunity in inflationary and deflationary periods, for example the competition for manual, unskilled and menial positions increases sharply during depressions.

8. Although all sorts of idiosyncratic resentment may persist throughout and despite all economic movements.

9. The defensive psychology of businessmen in the 1930s is best described in Robert and Helen Lynd, *Middletown in Transition* (New York: Harcourt Brace & World, 1937), which presents a description of businessmen's attitudes toward self and world at the point where their conception of the universe has been drastically challenged by the failure of the market.

10. *A Study of the Changing American Character* (New Haven: Yale University Press, 1950).

11. William H. Whyle, *The Organization Man* (New York: Simon and Shuster, 1956).

12. The failure of a society to maintain past levels of expansion can have a variety of causes. In some cases external and internal exploitation can both cause past capital to be disinvested (that is, used up without replacement) or expropriated and exported. In other cases the effect of a depression can demoralize the capital-accumulating classes, so that their economic approach is to hoard or preserve past wealth rather than accumulate new wealth. In underdeveloped countries a combination of political instability and economic immaturity causes the new elites either to deposit profits from capital investments in foreign banks or to dissipate wealth in extravagant living. Economic inefficiency can cause the simple erosion of capital. This is especially true after a revolution, when a new political elite begins to exercise investment functions according to political criteria.

Finally, a successful business class, after having accumulated capital, can shift its economic interest from industrial investment and expansion to investments in real estate, foreign investment, trade, banking, and shipping, neglecting in doing so the internal industry of the country. At the same time the scions of Protestant buccaneers become gentlemen who restrict their economic activity and become interested in politics, the arts, culture, sports, or gentleman farming. This latter process does not impede capital accumulation if the resources diverted to such activities are not too great, or if a new class of business buccaneers who stimulate investment replaces the old investors.

13. This is not to say that the British economy has ceased to expand or that it is at a zero rate of investment as it was in 1930. Moreover, in the case of Britain the decline in the rate of expansion was, at least until 1945, partly compensated for by the opportunity offered by the empire. For France, on the other hand, such factors as a stable population and an early retirement age acted to offset the effects on opportunity caused by the decline in the rate of expansion.

Part III

The New Middle Classes in the United States

9 The New Middle Class, I*
C. Wright Mills

In the early nineteenth century, although there are no exact figures, probably four-fifths of the occupied population were self-employed enterprisers; by 1870, only about one-third, and in 1940, only about one-fifth, were still in this old middle class. Many of the remaining four-fifths of the people who now earn a living do so by working for the 2 or 3 percent of the population who now own 40 or 50 percent of the private property in the United States. Among these workers are the members of the new middle class, white-collar people on salary. For them, as for wage workers, America has become a nation of employees for whom independent property is out of range. Labor markets, not control of property, determine their chances to receive income, exercise power, enjoy prestige, learn and use skills.

OCCUPATIONAL CHANGE

Of the three broad strata composing modern society, only the new middle class has steadily grown in proportion to the whole (Table 9.1). In 1870 there were three-quarters of a million middle-class employees; by 1940, there were over twelve and a half million. In that period the old middle class increased 135 percent; wage workers, 255 percent; new middle class, 1600 percent.

The employees comprising the new middle class do not make up one single compact stratum. They have not emerged on a single horizontal level, but have been shuffled out simultaneously on the several levels of modern society; they now form, as it were, a new pyramid within the old pyramid of society at large, rather than a horizontal layer. The great bulk of the new middle class are of the lower middle-income

* Reprinted from C. Wright Mills, *White Collar: The American Middle Classes* (New York: Oxford University Press, 1951).

Table 9.1   The labor force, 1870–1940 (in percent)

	1870	1940
Old middle class	33	20
New middle class	6	25
Wage-workers	61	55
Total	100	100

brackets, but regardless of how social stature is measured, types of white-collar men and women range from almost the top to almost the bottom of modern society (Table 9.2).

The managerial stratum, subject to minor variations during these decades, has dropped slightly, from 14 to 10 percent; the salaried professionals, displaying the same minor ups and downs, have dropped from 30 percent to 25 percent of the new middle class. The major shifts in overall composition have been in the relative decline of the sales group, occurring most sharply around 1900, from 44 percent to 25 percent of the total new middle class; and the steady rise of the office workers, from 12 percent to 40 percent. Today the three largest occupational groups in the white-collar stratum are schoolteachers, salespeople in and out of stores, and assorted office workers. These three form the white-collar mass.

Table 9.2   Composition of the new middle class, 1870–1940 (in percent)

	1870	1940
Managers	14	10
Salaried professionals	30	25
Salespeople	44	25
Office workers	12	40
Total	100	100

White-collar occupations now engage well over half the members of the American middle class as a whole. Between 1870 and 1940, white-collar workers rose from 15 to 56 percent of the middle brackets, while the old middle class declined from 85 percent to 44 percent (Table 9.3).

Negatively, the transformation of the middle class is a shift from property to no-property; positively, it is a shift from property to a new axis of stratification, occupation. The nature and well-being of the old middle class can best be sought in the condition of entrepreneurial property; of the new middle class, in the economics and sociology of occupations. The numerical decline of the older, independent sectors of the middle class is an incident in the centralization of property; the numerical rise of the newer salaried employees is due to the industrial mechanics by which the occupations composing the new middle class have arisen.

Table 9.3   Composition of the old and new middle classes, 1870–1940 (in percent)

	1870	1940
Old middle class	85	44
Farmers	62	23
Businessmen	21	19
Free professionals	2	2
New middle class	15	56
Managers	2	6
Salaried professionals	4	14
Salespeople	7	14
Office workers	2	22
Total middle classes	100	100

INDUSTRIAL MECHANICS

In modern society, occupations are specific functions within a social division of labor, as well as skills sold for income on a labor market. Contemporary divisions of labor involve a hitherto unknown specialization of skill: from arranging abstract symbols, at $1000 an hour, to working a shovel, for $1000 a year. The major shifts in occupations since the Civil War have assumed this industrial trend: as a proportion of the labor force, fewer individuals manipulate *things*, more handle *people* and *symbols*.

This shift in needed skills is another way of describing

the rise of the white-collar workers, for their characteristic skills involve the handling of paper and money and people. They are expert at dealing with people transiently and impersonally; they are masters of the commercial, professional, and technical relationship. The one thing they do not do is live by making things; rather, they live off the social machineries that organize and coordinate the people who do make things. White-collar people help turn what someone else has made into profit for still another; some of them are closer to the means of production, supervising the work of actual manufacture and recording what is done. They are the people who keep track; they man the paper routines involved in distributing what is produced. They provide technical and personal services, and they teach others the skills which they themselves practice, as well as all other skills transmitted by teaching.

As the proportion of workers needed for the extraction and production of things declines, the proportion needed for servicing, distributing, and co-ordinating rises. In 1870, over three-fourths, and in 1940, slightly less than one-half of the total employed were engaged in producing things (Table 9.4).

Table 9.4   Structure of employment, 1870–1940 (in percent)

	1870	*1940*
Producing	77	46
Servicing	13	20
Distributing	7	23
Co-ordinating	3	11
Total employed	100	100

By 1940, the proportion of white-collar workers of those employed in industries primarily involved in the production of things was 11 percent; in service industries, 32 percent; in distribution, 44 percent; and in co-ordination, 60 percent. The white-collar industries themselves have grown, and within each industry the white-collar occupations have grown. Three trends lie behind white-collar jobs being the most rapidly growing of modern occupations: the increasing pro-

ductivity of machinery used in manufacturing; the magnifica-
tion of distribution; and the increasing scale of co-ordination.

The immense productivity of mass-production technique
and the increased application of technological rationality
are the first open secrets of modern occupational change:
fewer men turn out more things in less time. In the middle
of the nineteenth century, as J. F. Dewhurst and his associates have calculated, some 17.6 billion horsepower hours
were expended in American industry, only 6 percent on
mechanical energy; by the middle of the twentieth century
410.4 billion horsepower hours will be expended, 94 percent on mechanical energy. This industrial revolution seems
to be permanent, seems to go on through war and boom
and slump; thus "a decline in production results in a more
than proportional decline in employment; and an increase
in production results in a less than proportional increase
in employment."

Technology has thus narrowed the stratum of workers
needed for given volumes of output; it has also altered the
types and proportions of skill needed in the production
process. Know-how, once an attribute of the mass of workers,
is now in the machine and the engineering elite who design
it. Machines displace unskilled workmen, make craft skills
unnecessary, push up front the automatic motions of the
machine-operative. Workers comprising the new lower class
are predominantly semi-skilled: their proportion in the urban
wage worker stratum has risen from 31 percent in 1910 to
41 percent in 1940.

The manpower economies brought about by machinery
and the large-scale rationalization of labor forces, so apparent in production and extraction, have not, as yet, been
applied so extensively in distribution—transportation, communication, finance and trade. Yet without an elaboration
of these means of distribution, the wide-flung operations of
multi-plant producers could not be integrated nor their
products distributed. Therefore, the proportion of people
engaged in distribution has enormously increased so that
today about one-fourth of the labor force is so engaged.
Distribution has expanded more than production because
of the lag in technological application in this field, and
because of the persistence of individual and small-scale

entrepreneurial units at the same time that the market has been enlarged and the need to market has been deepened.

Behind this expansion of the distributive occupations lies the central problem of modern capitalism: to whom can the available goods be sold? As volume swells, the intensified search for markets draws more workers into the distributive occupations of trade, promotion, advertising. As far-flung and intricate markets come into being, and as the need to find and create even more markets becomes urgent, "middle men" who move, store, finance, promote, and sell goods are knit into a vast network of enterprises and occupations.

The physical aspect of distribution involves wide and fast transportation networks; the co-ordination of marketing involves communication; the search for markets and the selling of goods involves trade, including wholesale and retail outlets as well as financial agencies for commodity and capital markets. Each of these activities engage more people, but the manual jobs among them do not increase as fast as the white-collar tasks.

Transportation, which grew rapidly after the Civil War, began to decline with respect to the numbers of people involved before 1930; but this decline took place among wage-workers; the proportion of white-collar workers employed in transportation continued to rise. By 1940, some 23 percent of the people in transportation were white-collar employees. As a new industrial segment of the U.S. economy, the communication industry has never been run by large numbers of free enterprisers; at the outset it needed large numbers of technical and other white-collar workers. By 1940, some 77 percent of its people were in new middle-class occupations.

Trade is now the third largest segment of the occupational structure, exceeded only by farming and manufacturing. A few years after the Civil War less than 5 out of every 100 workers were engaged in trade; by 1940 almost 12 out of every 100 workers were so employed. But, while 70 percent of those in wholesaling and retailing were free enterprisers in 1870, and less than 3 percent were white collar, by 1940, of the people engaged in retail trade 27 percent were free enterprisers; 41 percent white-collar employees.

Newer methods of merchandising, such as credit financing, have resulted in an even greater percentage increase in the "financial" than in the "commercial" agents of distribution. Branch banking has lowered the status of many banking employees to the clerical level, and reduced the number of executive positions. By 1940, of all employees in finance and real estate 70 percent were white-collar workers of the new middle class.

The organizational reason for the expansion of the white-collar occupations is the rise of big business and big government, and the consequent trend of modern social structure, the steady growth of bureaucracy. In every branch of the economy, as firms merge and corporations become dominant, free entrepreneurs become employees, and the calculations of accountant, statistician, bookkeeper, and clerk in these corporations replace the free "movement of prices" as the co-ordinating agent of the economic system. The rise of thousands of big and little bureaucracies and the elaborate specialization of the system as a whole create the need for many men and women to plan, co-ordinate, and administer new routines for others. In moving from smaller to larger and more elaborate units of economic activity, increased proportions of employees are drawn into co-ordinating and managing. Managerial and professional employees and office workers of varied sorts—floorwalkers, foremen, office managers—are needed; people to whom subordinates report, and who in turn report to superiors, are links in chains of power and obedience, co-ordinating and supervising other occupational experiences, functions, and skills. And all over the economy, the proportion of clerks of all sorts has increased: from 1 or 2 percent in 1870 to 10 or 11 percent of all gainful workers in 1940.

As the worlds of business undergo these changes, the increased tasks of government on all fronts draw still more people into occupations that regulate and service property and men. In response to the largeness and predatory complications of business, the crises of slump, the nationalization of the rural economy and small-town markets, the flood of immigrants, the urgencies of war and the march of technology disrupting social life, government increases its co-ordinating and regulating tasks. Public regulations, social services, and business taxes require more people to make mass records and to integrate people, firms, and goods, both within government and in the various segments of business and private life. All branches of government have grown, although the most startling increases are found in the executive branch of the Federal Government, where the needs for co-ordinating the economy have been most prevalent.

As marketable activities, occupations change (1) with shifts in the skills required, as technology and rationalization are unevenly applied across the economy; (2) with the enlargement and intensification of marketing operations in both the commodity and capital markets; and (3) with shifts in the organization of the division of work, as expanded organizations require co-ordination, management, and recording. The mechanics involved within and between these three trends have led to the numerical expansion of white-collar employees.

There are other less obvious ways in which the occupational structure is shaped: high agricultural tariffs, for example, delay the decline of farming as an occupation; were Argentine beef allowed to enter duty-free, the number of meat producers here might diminish. City ordinances and zoning laws abolish peddlers and affect the types of construction workers that prevail. Most states have bureaus of standards which limit entrance into professions and semi-professions; at the same time members of these occupations form associations in the attempt to control entrance into "their" market. More successful than most trade unions, such professional associations as the American Medical Association have managed for several decades to level off the proportion of physicians and surgeons. Every phase of the slump–war–boom cycle influences the numerical importance of various occupations; for instance, the movement back and forth between "construction worker" and small "contractor" is geared to slumps and booms in building.

The pressures from these loosely organized parts of the occupational world draw conscious managerial agencies into the picture. The effects of attempts to manage occupational change, directly and indirectly, are not yet great, except of course during wars, when government freezes men in their jobs or offers incentives and compulsions to remain in old occupations or shift to new ones. Yet, increasingly the class levels and occupational composition of the nation are managed; the occupational structure of the United States is being slowly reshaped as a gigantic corporate group. It is subject not only to the pulling of autonomous markets and the pushing of technology but to an "allocation of personnel" from central points of control. Occupational change thus becomes more conscious, at least to those who are coming to be in charge of it.

WHITE-COLLAR PYRAMIDS

Occupations, in terms of which we circumscribe the new middle class, involve several ways of ranking people. As specific activities, they entail various types and levels of *skill*, and their exercise fulfils certain *functions* within an industrial division of labor. These are the skills and functions we have been examining statistically. As sources of income, occupations are connected with *class* position; and since they normally carry an expected quota of prestige, on and off the job, they are relevant to *status* position. They also involve certain degrees of *power* over other people, directly in terms of the job, and indirectly in other social areas. Occupations are thus tied to class, status, and power as well as to skill and function; to understand the occupations composing the new middle class, we must consider them in terms of each of these dimensions.

"Class situation" in its simplest objective sense has to do with the amount and source of income. Today, occupation rather than property is the source of income for most of those who receive any direct income: the possibilities of selling their services in the labor market, rather than of profitably buying and selling their property and its yields, now determine the life-chances of most of the middle class. All things money can buy and many that men dream about are theirs by virtue of occupational income. In new middle-class occupations men work for someone else on someone else's property. This is the clue to many differences between the old and new middle classes, as well as to the contrast between the older world of the small propertied entrepreneur and the occupational structure of the new society. If the old middle class once fought big property structures in the name of small, free properties, the new middle class, like the wage workers in latter-day capitalism, has been, from the beginning, dependent upon large properties for job security.

Wage workers in the factory and on the farm are on the propertyless bottom of the occupational structure, depending upon the equipment owned by others, earning wages for the time they spend at work. In terms of property, the white-collar people are *not* "in between Capital and Labor"; they are in exactly the same property-class position as the wage workers. They have no direct financial tie to the means of production, no prime claim upon the proceeds from property. Like factory workers—and day laborers, for that matter— they work for those who do own such means of livelihood.

Yet if bookkeepers and coal miners, insurance agents and farm laborers, doctors in a clinic and crane operators in an open pit have this condition in common, certainly their class situations are not the same. To understand their class positions, we must go beyond the common fact of source of income and consider as well the amount of income.

In 1890, the average income of white-collar occupational groups was about double that of wage workers. Before World War I, salaries were not as adversely affected by slumps as wages were; on the contrary, they rather steadily advanced. Since World War I, however, salaries have been reacting to turns in the economic cycles more and more like wages, although still to a lesser extent. If wars help wages more because of the greater flexibility of wages, slumps help salaries because of their greater inflexibility. Yet after each war era, salaries have never regained their previous advantage over wages. Each phase of the cycle, as well as the progressive rise of all income groups, has resulted in a narrowing of the income gap between wage workers and white-collar employees.

In the middle 'thirties the three urban strata—entrepreneurs, white-collar, and wage workers, formed a distinct scale with respect to median family income: the white-collar employees had a median income of $1896; the entrepreneurs, $1464; the urban wage workers, $1175. Although the median income of white-collar workers was higher than that of the entrepreneurs, larger proportions of the entrepreneurs received both high-level and low-level incomes. The distribution of their income was spread more than that of white-collar workers.

The wartime boom in incomes, in fact, spread the incomes of all occupational groups, but not evenly. The spread occurred mainly among urban entrepreneurs. As an income level, the old middle class in the city is becoming less an evenly graded income group, and more a collection of different strata, with a large proportion of lumpen-bourgeoisie who receive very low incomes, and a small, prosperous bourgeoisie with very high incomes.

In the late 'forties (1948, median family income) the income of all white-collar workers was $4000, that of all urban wage workers, $3300. These averages, however, should not obscure the overlap of specific groups within each stratum: the lower white-collar people—sales employees and office workers—earned almost the same as skilled workers and foremen,[1] but more than semi-skilled urban wage workers.

In terms of property, white-collar people are in the same position as wage workers; in terms of occupational income, they are "somewhere in the middle." Once they were considerably above the wage workers, they have become less so; in the middle of the century they still have an edge but the overall rise in incomes is making the new middle class a more homogeneous income group.

As with income, so with prestige: white-collar groups are differentiated socially, perhaps more decisively than wage workers and entrepreneurs. Wage earners certainly do form an income pyramid and a prestige gradation, as do entrepreneurs and rentiers; but the new middle class, in terms of income and prestige, is a superimposed pyramid, reaching from almost the bottom of the first to almost the top of the second.

People in white-collar occupations claim higher prestige than wage workers, and, as a general rule, can cash in their claims with wage workers as well as with the anonymous public. This fact has been seized upon, with much justification, as the defining characteristic of the white-collar strata, and although there are definite indications in the United States of a decline in their prestige, still, on a nation-wide basis, the majority of even the lower white-collar employees—office workers and salespeople—enjoy a middling prestige.

The historical bases of the white-collar employees' prestige, apart from superior income, have included the similarity of their place and type of work to those of the old middle-classes which has permitted them to borrow prestige. As their relations with entrepreneur and with esteemed customer have become more impersonal, they have borrowed prestige from the firm itself. The stylization of their appearance, in particular the fact that most white-collar jobs have permitted the wearing of street clothes on the job, has also figured in their prestige claims, as have the skills required in most white-collar jobs, and in many of them the variety of operations performed and the degree of autonomy exercised in deciding work procedures. Furthermore, the time taken to learn these skills and the way in which they have been acquired by formal education and by close contact with the higher-ups in charge has been important. White-collar employees have monopolized high school education—even in 1940 they had completed 12 grades to the 8 grades for wage workers and entrepreneurs. They have also enjoyed status by descent: in terms of race, black white-collar employees exist only in isolated instances—and, more importantly, in terms of nativity, in 1930 only about 9 percent of white-collar workers, but 16 percent of free enterprisers and 21 percent of wage workers, were foreign born. Finally, as an underlying fact, the limited size of the white-collar group, compared with wage workers, has led to successful claims to greater prestige.

The power position of groups and of individuals typically depends upon factors of class, status, and occupation, often in intricate interrelation. Given occupations involve specific powers over other people in the actual course of work; but also outside the job area, by virtue of their relations to institutions of property as well as the typical income they afford, occupations lend power. Some white-collar occupations require the direct exercise of supervision over other white-collar and wage workers, and many more are closely attached to this managerial cadre. White-collar employees are the assistants of authority; the power they exercise is a derived power, but they do exercise it.

Moreover, within the white-collar pyramids there is a characteristic pattern of authority involving age and sex. The white-collar ranks contain a good many women: some 41 percent of all white-collar employees, compared with 10 percent of free enterprisers, and 21 percent of wage workers, are women.[2] As with sex, so with age: free enterprisers average (median) about 45 years of age, white-collar and wage workers, about 34; but among free enterprisers and wage workers, men are about 2 or 3 years older than women; among white-collar workers, there is a 6- or 7-year difference. In the white-collar pyramids, authority is roughly graded by age and sex: younger women tend to be subordinated to older men.

The occupational groups forming the white-collar pyramids, different as they may be from one another, have certain common characteristics, which are central to the character of the new middle class as a general pyramid overlapping the entrepreneurs and wage workers. White-collar people cannot be adequately defined along any one possible dimension of stratification—skill, function, class, status, or power. They are generally in the middle ranges of each of these dimensions and of every descriptive attribute. Their position is more definable in terms of their relative differences from other strata than in any absolute terms.

On all points of definition, it must be remembered that white-collar people are not one compact horizontal stratum. They do not fulfil one central, positive *function* that can define them, although in general their functions are similar to those of the old middle class. They deal with symbols and with other people, co-ordinating, recording, and distributing: but they fulfil these functions as dependent employees, and the skills they thus employ are sometimes similar in form and required mentality to those of many wage workers.

In terms of property, they are equal to wage workers and different from the old middle class. Originating as propertyless dependents, they have no serious expectations of propertied independence. In terms of income, their class position is, on the average, somewhat higher than that of wage workers. The overlap is large and the trend has been definitely toward less difference, but even today the differences are significant.

Perhaps of more psychological importance is the fact that

white-collar groups have successfully claimed more prestige than wage workers and still generally continue to do so. The bases of their prestige may not be solid today, and certainly they show no signs of being permanent; but, however vague and fragile, they continue to mark off white-collar people from wage workers.

Members of white-collar occupations exercise a derived authority in the course of their work; moreover, compared with older hierarchies, the white-collar pyramids are youthful and feminine bureaucracies, within which youth, education, and American birth are emphasized at the wide base, where millions of office workers most clearly typify these differences between the new middle class and other occupational groups. White-collar masses, in turn, are managed by people who are more like the old middle class, having many of the social characteristics, if not the independence, of free enterprisers.

Notes

1. It is impossible to isolate the salaried foremen from the skilled urban wage workers in these figures. If we could do so, the income of lower white-collar workers would be closer to that of semi-skilled workers.

2. According to our calculations, the proportions of women, 1940, in these groups are: farmers, 2.9%; businessmen, 20%; free professionals, 5.9%; managers, 7.1%; salaried professionals, 51.7%; salespeople, 27.5%; office workers, 51%; skilled workers, 3.2%; semi-skilled and unskilled, 29.8%; rural workers, 9.1%.

10 The New Middle Class, II*

C. Wright Mills

Ever since the new middle class began numerically to displace the old, its political role has been an object of query and debate. The political question has been closely linked with another—that of the position of new middle-class occupations in modern stratification.

This linkage of politics and stratification was all the more to be expected inasmuch as the white-collar worker as a sociological creature was first discovered by Marxian theoreticians in search of recruits for the proletarian movement. They expected that society would be polarized into class-conscious proletariat and bourgeoisie, that in their general decline the in-between layers would choose one side or the other—or at least keep out of the way of the major protagonists. Neither of these expectations, however, had been realized when socialist theoreticians and party bureaucrats began at the opening of the present century to tinker with the classic perspective.

In trying to line up the new population into those who could and those who could not be relied upon to support their struggle, party statisticians ran squarely into the numerical upsurge of the white-collar salariat. The rise of these groups as a problem for Marxists signalled a shift from the simple property versus no-property dichotomy to differentiations within the no-property groups. It focused attention upon occupational structure. Moreover, in examining white-collar groups, along with the persistent small entrepreneurs of farm and city, they came upon the further fact that although the new middle class was propertyless, and the smaller entrepreneurs often suffered economic downgrading,

* Reprinted from C. Wright Mills, *White Collar: The American Middle Classes* (New York: Oxford University Press, 1951).

members of these strata did not readily take to the socialist ideology. Their political attachments did not coincide with their economic position, and certainly not with their imminently expected position. They represented a numerical upthrust of falsely conscious people, and they were an obstacle to the scheduled course of the revolution.

THEORIES AND DIFFICULTIES

To relate in detail all the theories that followed upon these discoveries and speculations would be more monotonous than fruitful; the range of theory had been fairly well laid out by the middle 'twenties, and nothing really new has since been added. Various writers have come upon further detail, some of it crucial, or have variously combined the major positions, some of which have had stronger support than others. But the political directions that can be inferred from the existence of the new middle class may be sorted out into four major possibilities.

First, the new middle class, in whole or in some crucial segment, will continue to grow in numbers and in power; in due course it will develop into a politically independent class. Displacing other classes in performance of the pivotal functions required to run modern society, it is slated to be the next ruling class. The accent will be upon the new middle class; the next epoch will be theirs.

Second, the new middle classes will continue to grow in numbers and power, and although they will not become a force that will rise to independent power, they will be a major force for stability in the general balance of the different classes. As important elements in the class balance, they will make for the continuance of liberal capitalist society. Their spread checks the creeping proletarianization; they act as a buffer between labor and capital. Taking over certain functions of the old middle class, but having connections with the wage workers, they will be able to co-operate with them too; thus they bridge class contrasts and mitigate class conflicts. They are the balance wheel of class interests, the stabilizers, the social harmonizers. They are intermediaries of the new social solidarity that will put an end to class bickering. That is why they are catered to by any camp or movement that is on its way to electoral power, or, for that matter, attempted revolution.

Third, members of the new middle class, by their social character and political outlook, are really bourgeoisie and they will remain that. This is particularly apparent in the tendency of these groups to become status groups rather than mere economic classes. They will form, as in Nazi Germany, prime human materials for conservative, for reactionary, and even for fascist, movements. They are natural allies and shock troops of the larger capitalist drive.

Fourth, the new middle class will follow the classic Marxian scheme: in due course, it will become homogeneous in all important respects with the proletariat and will come over to their socialist policy. In the meantime, it represents—for various reasons, which will be washed away in crises and decline—a case of delayed reaction. For in historical reality, the "new middle class" is merely a peculiar sort of new proletariat, having the same basic interests. With the intensification of the class struggle between the real classes of capitalist society, it will be swept into the proletarian ranks. A thin, upper layer may go over to the bourgeoisie, but it will not count in numbers or in power.

These various arguments are difficult to compare, first of all because they do not all include the same occupations under the catchphrase "new middle class." When we consider the vague boundary lines of the white-collar world, we can easily understand why such an occupational salad invites so many conflicting theories and why general images of it are likely to differ. There is no one accepted word for them; white collar, salaried employee, new middle class are used interchangeably. During the historical span covered by different theories, the occupational groups composing these strata have changed; and at given times, different theorists in pursuit of bolstering data have spotlighted one or the other groups comprising the total. So contrasting images of the political role of the white-collar people can readily exist side by side (and perhaps even both be correct). Those, for instance, who believe that as the vanguard stratum of modern society they are slated to be the next ruling class do not think of them as ten-cent store clerks, insurance agents, and stenographers, but rather as higher technicians and staff engineers, as salaried managers of business cartels and big officials of the Federal Government. On the other hand, those who hold that they are being proletarianized do focus upon the mass of clerklings and sales people, while those who see their role as in-between mediators are most likely to include both upper and lower ranges. We have split the stratum as a whole into at least four sub-strata or pyramids, and we must pay attention to this split as we try to place white-collar people in our political expectations.

Most of the work that has been done on the new middle class and its political role involves more general theories of the course of capitalist development. That is why it is difficult to sort out in a simple and yet systematic way what given writers really think of the white-collar people. Their views are based not on an examination of this stratum as much as on, first, the political program they happen to be following; second, the doctrinal position, as regards the political line-up of classes, they have previously accepted; and third, their judgment in regard to the main course of twentieth-century industrial society.

Proletarian purists would disavow white-collar people; United Fronters would link at least segments of them with workers in a fight over specific issues, while carefully preserving organizational and, above all, doctrinal independence; People's Fronters would cater to them by modifying wage worker ideology and program in order to unite the two; liberals of "Populist" inclination, in a sort of dogmatic pluralism, would call upon them along with small businessmen, small farmers, and all grades of wage workers to coalesce. And each camp, if it prevailed long enough for its intellectuals to get into production, would evolve theories about the character of the white-collar people and the role they are capable of playing.

As for political doctrines, the very definition of the white-collar problem has usually assumed as given a more or less rigid framework of fated classes. The belief that in any future struggle between big business and labor, the weight of the white-collar workers will be decisive assumes that there is going to be a future struggle, in the open, between business and labor. The question of whether they will be either proletariat or bourgeoisie, thus in either case giving up whatever identity they may already have, or go their independent way, assumes that there are these other sides and that their struggle will, in fact if not in consciousness, make up the real political arena. Yet, at the same time, the theories to which the rise of the new middle class has given birth distinguish various, independent sectors of the proletariat and of the bourgeoisie, suggesting that the unit of analysis has been overformalized. The problem of the new middle class must now be raised in a context that does not merely assume homogeneous blocs of classes.

The political argument over white-collar workers has gone on at an international scale. Although modern nations do have many trends in common—among them certainly the statistical increase of the white-collar workers—they also have unique features. In posing the question of the political role of white-collar people in the United States, we must learn all we can from discussions of them in other countries, the Weimar Republic especially, but in doing so, we must take everything hypothetically and test it against U.S. facts and trends.

The time span of various theories and expectations, as we have noted, has in most of the arguments not been closely specified. Those who hold the view that white-collar workers are really only an odd sort of proletariat and will, in due course, begin to behave accordingly, or the view that the new middle class is slated to be the next ruling class have worked with flexible and often conflicting schedules.

What has been at issue in these theories is the objective position of the new middle classes within and between the various strata of modern society, and the political content and direction of their mentality. Questions concerning either of these issues can be stated in such a way as to allow, and in fact demand, observational answers only if adequate conceptions of stratification and of political mentality are clearly set forth.

MENTALITIES

It is frequently asserted, in theories of the white-collar people, that there are no classes in the United States because "psychology is of the essence of classes" or, as Alfred Bingham has put it, that "class groupings are always nebulous, and in the last analysis only the vague thing called class-consciousness counts." It is said that people in the United States are not aware of themselves as members of classes, do not identify themselves with their appropriate economic level, do not often organize in terms of these brackets or vote along the lines they provide. America, in this reasoning, is a sandheap of "middle-class individuals."

But this is to confuse psychological feelings with other kinds of social and economic reality. Because men are not "class conscious" at all times and in all places does not mean that "there are no classes" or that "in America everybody is middle class." The economic and social facts are one thing; psychological feelings may or may not be associated with them in expected ways. Both are important, and if psychological feelings and political outlooks do not correspond to economic class, we must try to find out why, rather than throw out the economic baby with the psychological bath water, and so fail to understand how either fits into the national tub. No matter what people believe, class structure as an economic arrangement influences their life chances according to their positions in it. If they do not grasp the causes of their conduct this does not mean that the social analyst must ignore or deny them.

If political mentalities are not in line with objectively defined strata, that lack of correspondence is a problem to be explained; in fact, it is the grand problem of the psychology of social strata. The general problem of stratification and political mentality has to do with the extent to which the members of objectively defined strata are homogeneous in their political alertness, outlook, and allegiances, and with the degree to which their political mentality and actions are in line with the interests demanded by the juxtaposition of their objective position and their accepted values.

To understand the occupation, class, and status positions of a set of people is not necessarily to know whether or not they (1) will become class-conscious, feeling that they belong together or that they can best realize their rational interests by combining; (2) will organize themselves, or be open to organization by others, into associations, movements, or political parties; (3) will have "collective attitudes" of any sort, including those toward themselves, their common situation; or (4) will become hostile toward other strata and struggle against them. These social, political, and psychological characteristics may or may not occur on the basis of similar objective situations. In any given case, such possibilities must be explored, and "subjective" attributes must not be used as criteria for class inclusion, but rather, as Max Weber has made clear, stated as probabilities on the basis of objectively defined situations.

Implicit in this way of stating the issues of stratification lies a model of social movements and political dynamics. The important differences among people are differences that shape their biographies and ideas; within any given stratum, of course, individuals differ, but if their stratum has been adequately understood, we can expect certain psychological traits to recur. The probability that people will have a similar mentality and ideology, and that they will join together for action, is increased the more homogeneous they are with respect to class, occupation, and prestige. Other factors do, of course, affect the probability that ideology, organization, and consciousness will occur among those in objectively similar strata. But psychological factors are likely to be associated with *strata*, which consist of people who are characterized by an intersection of the *several* dimensions we have been using: class, occupation, status, and power. The task is to sort out these dimensions of stratification in a systematic way, paying attention to each separately and then to its relation to each of the other dimensions.

The question whether the white-collar workers are a "new middle class," or a "new working class," or what not, is not entirely one of definition, but its empirical solutions is made possible only by clarified definitions. The meaning of the term "proletarianized," around which the major theories have revolved, is by no means clear. In the definitions we have used, however, proletarianization might refer to shifts of middle-class occupations toward wage workers in terms of: income, property, skill, prestige or power, irrespective of whether or not the people involved are aware of these changes. Or, the meaning may be in terms of changes in consciousness, outlook, or organized activity. It would be possible, for example, for a segment of the white-collar people to become virtually identical with wage workers in income, property, and skill, but to resist being like them in prestige claims and to anchor their whole consciousness upon illusory prestige factors. Only by keeping objective position and ideological consciousness separate in analysis can the problem be stated with precision and without unjustifiable assumptions about wage workers, white-collar workers, and the general psychology of social classes.

When the Marxist, Anton Pannekoek for example, refuses to include propertyless people of lower income than skilled workers in the proletariat, he refers to ideological and prestige factors. He does not go on to refer to the same factors as they operate among the "proletariat," because he holds to what can only be called a metaphysical belief that the proletariat is *destined* to win through to a certain consciousness. Those who see white-collar groups as composing an independent "class," *sui generis*, often use prestige or status as their defining criterion rather than economic level. The Marxian assertion, for example L. B. Boudin's, that salaried employees "are in reality just as much a part of the proletariat as the merest day laborer," obviously rests on economic criteria, as is generally recognized when his statement is countered by the assertion that he ignores "important psychological factors."

The Marxist in his expectation assumes, first, that wage workers, or at least large sections of them, do in fact, or will at any moment, have a socialist consciousness of their revolutionary role in modern history. He assumes, secondly, that the middle classes, or large sections of them, are acquiring this consciousness, and in this respect are becoming like the wage workers or like what wage workers are assumed to be. Third, he rests his contention primarily upon the assumption that the economic dimension, especially property, of stratification is the key one, and that it is in this dimension that the middle classes are becoming like wage workers.

But the fact that propertyless employees (both wage workers and salaried employees) have not automatically assumed a socialist posture clearly means that propertylessness is not the only factor, or even the crucial one, determining inner-consciousness or political will.

Neither white-collar people nor wage workers have been or are preoccupied with questions of property. The concentration of property during the last century has been a slow process rather than a sharp break inside the lifespan of one generation; even the sons and daughters of farmers—among whom the most obvious "expropriation" has gone on—have had their attentions focused on the urban lure rather than on urban propertylessness. As jobholders, moreover, salaried employees have generally, with the rest of the population, experienced a secular rise in standards of living: propertylessness has certainly not necessarily coincided with pauperization. So the centralization of property, with consequent expropriation, has not been widely experienced as "agony" or reacted to by proletarianization, in any psychological sense that may be given these terms.

Objectively, we have seen that the structural position of the white-collar mass is becoming more and more similar to that of the wage workers. Both are, of course, propertyless, and their incomes draw closer and closer together. All the factors of their status position, which have enabled white-collar workers to set themselves apart from wage workers, are now subject to definite decline. Increased rationalization is lowering the skill levels and making their work more and more factory-like. As high-school education becomes more universal among wage workers, and the skills required for many white-collar tasks become simpler, it is clear that the white-collar job market will include more wage worker children.

In the course of the next generation, a "social class" between lower white-collar and wage workers will probably be formed, which means, in Weber's terms, that between the two positions there will be a typical job mobility. This will not, of course, involve the professional strata or the higher managerial employees, but it will include the bulk of the workers in salesroom and office. These shifts in the occupational worlds of the propertyless are more important to them than the existing fact of their propertylessness.

ORGANIZATIONS

The assumption that political supremacy follows on from
functional, economic indispensability underlies all those theories that see the new middle class or any of its sections slated
to be the next ruling class. For it is assumed that the class
that is indispensable in fulfilling the major functions of the
social order will be the next in the sequence of ruling classes.
Max Weber in his essay on bureaucracy has made short shrift
of this idea: "The ever-increasing 'indispensability' of the
officialdom, swollen to millions, is no more decisive for this
question [of power] than is the view of some representatives of the proletarian movement that the economic indispensability of the proletarians is decisive for the measure of
their social and political power position. If 'indispensability'
were decisive, then where slave labor prevailed and where
freemen usually abhor work as a dishonor, the 'indispensable' slaves ought to have held the positions of power, for
they were at least as indispensable as officials and proletarians are today. Whether the power . . . as such increases
cannot be decided *a priori* from such reasons."

Yet the assumption that it can runs all through the white-
collar literature. Just as Marx, seeing the parasitical nature
of the capitalist's endeavor, and the real function of work
performed by the workers, predicted the workers' rise to
power, so James Burnham (and before him Harold Lasswell,
and before him John Corbin) assumes that since the new
middle class is the carrier of those skills upon which modern
society more and more depends, it will inevitably, in the
course of time, assume political power. Technical and managerial indispensability is thus confused with the facts of power
struggle, and overrides all other sources of power. The de-
ficiency of such arguments must be realized positively: we
need to develop and to use a more open and flexible model
of the relations of political power and stratification.

Increasingly, class and status situations have been removed
from free market forces and the persistence of tradition,
and have been subject to more formal rules. A government
management of the class structure has become a major means
of alleviating inequalities and insuring the risks of those in
lower-income classes. Not so much free labor markets as

the powers of pressure groups now shape the class positions and privileges of various strata in the United States. Hours and wages, vacations, income security through periods of sickness, accidents, unemployment and old age—these are now subject to many intentional pressures, and, along with tax policies, transfer payments, tariffs, subsidies, price ceilings, wage freezes, et cetera, make up the content of "class fights" in the objective meaning of the phrase.

The "Welfare State" attempts to manage class chances without modifying basic class structure; in its several meanings and types, it favors economic policies designed to redistribute life risks and life chances in favor of those in the more exposed class situations, who have the power or threaten to accumulate the power, to do something about their case.

Labor union, farm bloc, and trade association dominate the political scene of the Welfare State as well as of the permanent war economy; contests within and between these blocs increasingly determine the position of various groups. The state, as a descriptive fact, is at the balanced intersection of such pressures, and increasingly the privileges and securities of various occupational strata depend upon the bold means of organized power.

It is often by these means that the objective position of white-collar and wage worker becomes similar. The greatest difficulty with the Marxist expectation of proletarianization is that many changes pointing that way have not come about by a lowering of the white-collar position, but often more crucially by a raising of the wage worker position.

The salary, as contrasted with the wage, has been a traditional hallmark of white-collar employment. Although still of prestige value to many white-collar positions, the salary must now be taken as a tendency in most white-collar strata rather than a water-tight boundary of the white-collar worlds. The contrast has rested on differences in the time span of payment, and thus in security of tenure, and in the possibilities to plan because of more secure expectations of income over longer periods of time. But, increasingly, companies put salaried workers, whose salary for some time in many places has been reduced for absences, on an hourly basis. And manual workers, represented by unions, are demanding and getting precisely the type of privileges once granted only white-collar people.

All along the line, it is from the side of the wage workers that the contrast in privileges has been most obviously breaking down. It was the mass-production union of steel workers, not salaried employees, that precipitated a national economic debate over the issue of regularized employment; and white-collar people must often now fight for what is sometimes assumed to be their inherited privilege: a union of professionals. The Newspaper Guild, has to insist upon dismissal pay as a clause in its contracts.

Whatever past differences between white-collar and wage workers with respect to income security, sick benefits, paid vacations, and working conditions, the major trend is now for these same advantages to be made available to factory workers. Pensions, especially since World War II, have been a major idea in collective bargaining, and it has been the wage worker that has had bargaining power. Social insurance to cover work injuries and occupational diseases has gradually been replacing the common law of a century ago, which held the employee at personal fault for work injury and the employer's liability had to be proved in court by a damage suit. In so far as such laws exist, they legally shape the class chances of the manual worker up to a par with or above other strata. Both privileges and income level have been increasingly subject to the power pressures of unions and government, and there is every reason to believe that in the future this will be even more the case.

The accumulation of power by any stratum is dependent on a triangle of factors: will and know-how, objective opportunity, and organization. The opportunity is limited by the group's structural position; the will is dependent upon the group's consciousness of its interests and ways of realizing them. And both structural position and consciousness interplay with organizations, which strengthen consciousness and are made politically relevant by structural position.

11 The Transformation of the Black Middle Class*
Arthur S. Evans, Jr[1]

In the mid-20th century only 10 percent of all black workers were employed in middle-class occupations. Today, however, they represent approximately 27 percent of employed blacks (Landry, 1987; 2–3). This significant increase was a consequence of events occurring during the 1960s, such as an expanding economy, the Civil Rights Movement, and the implementation of state and federal laws mandating equal employment opportunity for all American citizens. Since the decade of the 60s, blacks have experienced a greater degree of social mobility than in the past because of the plethora of white collar occupations now available to them. For many white collar workers, employment is a primary source of social identity. Hence, one expects that as job demands gain in importance, individuals will become detached from other primary associations having a basis in family, spirituality, race, and ethnicity. Of particular concern for this paper, the rise of blacks into the ranks of the middle class may function to slowly dissipate racial solidarity and/or social cohesion between themselves and lower-class blacks. In other words, I am suggesting that for the black middle class, the priorities of work and living a middle-class lifestyle may, over time, take precedence over attachment and identification with issues involving race. This paper suggests then, that the identification of the black middle class with the black lower class will decrease as the former continues to occupy white collar positions and to experience upward social mobility. Indeed, this has already occurred to a significant degree, and as a result the black middle class's traditional leadership role in the black community has been altered.

---

* Reprinted from *The International Journal of Politics, Culture and Society*, vol. 6, no. 2 (New York: Human Sciences Press, 1992).

The effects of structural change on middle-class behavior and attitudes have been addressed by Mills (1953). He explained that following the First World War, technology, standardization, and mass communication increased, resulting in white-collar workers replacing independent entrepreneurs (e.g., farmers and businessmen) as the new middle class. Emerging norms and values in the new milieu stressed that workers should conform their attitudes and behaviors to corporate expectations. To the new white-collar workers, the corporate culture represented a significant change from the work environments they were accustomed to in the pre-World War I era. As a consequence, they found themselves disadvantaged and lacking a history and tradition for making adequate adjustments to their new work situation (Mills, 1953). Today's black middle class finds itself in a predicament similar to that described above, because in both cases, past prescriptions for role enactment are/were inadequate for addressing present actualities.

POLITICAL PSYCHOLOGY OF THE BLACK MIDDLE CLASS: CRITIQUES

Study of the black middle class has its origin in the work of E. F. Frazier, a student of acculturation and assimilation processes. A student of race relations, Frazier focused on the consequences of migration and urbanization, and the manner in which these events produced changes in social relations. For example, he saw the black migration in the first half of the 20th century to Northern and Midwest urban areas as leading to significant changes in customs and mores in the black community (1957, 1964). Following Park (1928), he believed that the social organization of a community breaks down when contact and collision occur between new cultures, and that individuals experience a sense of emancipation, releasing energies formerly controlled by custom and tradition (Edwards, 1974, pp. 85–117; Conyers, 1986, pp. 77–93). However, while the individual gains a sense of freedom, he/she is left without the direction and control previously supplied by custom (Park, 1928). Frazier (1957) believed that the black migration to urban centers after World

War I involved more than physical relocation. It also meant a social transformation of the self, breaking with family and community, and adjusting to the new environment. Thus, migration can be problematic, because it makes it difficult for individuals to establish their sense of place and position in the new setting. In addition, migration breaks down the support of tradition and custom, leaving the individual totally responsible for making choices and finding direction. In his book *The Negro Church in America*, Frazier (1964) shows that the newly emergent classes of blacks in the cities were rootless – i.e., he shows how the black proletarian masses experienced social problems of crime, delinquency, broken families and the like after migrating to urban areas. In addition, he (1957) described the social disorganization of the black middle class in his book *Black Bourgeoisie*, where he portrayed them as new to urban life and having distorted values, not rooted in their former rural experience but in the emulation of the urban white middle class. According to Frazier (1957) the black middle class lacked strong entrepreneurial skills but nevertheless persisted in the belief of "making it" in the business world. The black middle class' preoccupation with status and imitation of the white upper class led Frazier to conclude that their life style was undesirable and held little substance.

The migration and urbanization of blacks following World War I resulted in black communities which were capable of supporting a growing black middle class. Unlike their white counterparts, black middle-class people were subjected to *de jure* and *de facto* segregation, which forced them to turn to the black community for occupational sustenance. The chance of being employed in middle class jobs was limited, because within the black community few "respectable" and high paying jobs existed. For example, according to Drake and Cayton (1962, pp. 214–262) only those occupations involving direct, personal contact with black customers (teacher, barber, beautician, minister, mortician, social worker, doctor and lawyer) were open to members of the black middle class. Despite their higher occupational standing in the black community, the black middle class was still regarded by whites as second class citizens. Their special qualities, which were at times admired by the black lower class, were irrelevant for overcoming their disesteemed status among whites. Like all blacks, then, the black middle class could not easily escape discrimination and segregation. To help alleviate this status inconsistency, black middle class persons employed two opposing strategies: some attempted to distance themselves from the black masses, while others tried to establish greater social solidarity with them. A brief description of these strategies follows.

SOCIAL DISTANCE TOWARD THE BLACK MASSES

Some support exists for the argument that middle class blacks have traditionally preferred little social contact with the black lower class. Lemann (1991; pp. 37–50) explains that middle class blacks blamed lower class blacks for their subordinate status, and therefore they avoided contact with them. For example, in Clarksdale, Mississippi the black middle class lived in separate sections within the black community, attended separate churches, sent their children to different schools, and centered their lives around middle class associations such as the Masons and the Knights and Daughters of Tabor. Drake and Cayton (1962) show that in Chicago, during the "Great Migration," the black middle class regarded the poorer black sections of town with horror, as breeding grounds for immorality and locations to be ignored by "respectable" blacks. Likewise, Lane discusses Philadelphia during the same time period:

> The black bourgeoisie, or urban elite was noted over the years for its exaggerated insistence on respectability, even puritanism, and its refusal to identify with the great mass of the black population . . . The social rituals of Philadelphia's black elite are best seen as part of a struggle not to reject the working class but to distinguish themselves . . . (1986, pp. 145).

In those cases where the black middle class initiated contact, it was primarily for the purpose of providing leadership in solving "embarrassing" problems of social disorganization among the black lower class. To address these problems, middle class blacks often used black newspapers and other types of media that provided specific instructions to the lower class on "proper" conduct and dress. Middle class blacks believed that if the black lower class failed to change its actions, their negative attributes would ensure the continuation of white racism and discrimination against all blacks, regardless of class standing (Lemann, 1986, p. 52). Indeed, the Urban League was established on the firmly held belief that lower class blacks needed to be taught the proper ways of acculturation to urban life (Drake and Cayton, 1962). It should be noted that since middle class blacks believed the black lower class was a major impediment to their receiving equal treatment from whites, their motivation for being a watchdog over community morals and behavior stemmed not always from personal benevolence, but rather from a selfish need to garner white respect. Since persistent and unequal treatment represented to the black middle class a negation of their achieved social status, they held a vested interest in steering lower class black behaviors in a "positive" direction (Lane, 1986, pp. 126–40).

The themes developed above were reiterated by Harold Cruse in his work *The Crisis of the Negro Intellectual.* According to Cruse (1967), the black middle class, being politically, socially, and economically marginal, was unwilling and unable to play any commanding role in politics, economics, and culture. He believed that throughout its history the black middle class's role as leader with respect to the black community had been shameful. Indeed, Frazier (1957, 1963) also saw the split between the black middle class and the black urban masses, and the failure of the former to promote leadership for the black masses:

When the opportunity has been present the Negro bourgeoisie has exploited the Negro masses as ruthlessly as have whites. As the intellectual leaders in the Negro community, they have never dared think beyond a narrow opportunistic philosophy that provided a rationalization for its own advantages. Although the Negro bourgeoisie exercise considerable influence on the values of the Negro, they do not occupy a dignified position in the Negro community. The masses regard the Negro bourgeoisie as simply those who have been lucky in getting money which enables them to engage in conspicuous consumption. While this class pretends to represent the best manners or morals of the Negro, the masses regard such claims as hypocrisy (1963, p. 272).

Cruse (1967) also argued that the black bourgeoisie lacked a solid economic base in both the black and white communities. As a result, he explains, the black middle class was cut off from most economic, cultural and organizational ties with the black lower class. He believed that since the black middle class does not control the black market, it cannot develop positive relationships with the black working class either economically, politically, or culturally. As a consequence, social cohesion, necessary for cultivating racial goals and nationalistic sentiments, cannot be achieved among the black population. Cruse (1967) supports his view that the black middle class has historically played an ineffective leadership role in the black community by denouncing them for not publishing books, owning theaters and significantly contributing to black cultural advancement through music and art. He concludes then, that the black middle class is rootless because it has no cultural base. Like Cruse (1967), Neal (1970) suggests that middle class blacks do not feel racial consciousness and/or black group solidarity. For example, he claims that large segments of the black middle class:

> have played a continually regressive non-national role in black affairs. They thrive off the crumbs of integration, and these bourgeois elements have become de-racialized and de-cultured, leaving the black working class without voice or leadership, while serving the negative role of class buffer between the deprived working class and the white ruling class elites. In this respect, such groups have become a social millstone around the necks of the black working class (Neal, 1970, p. 4).

Perhaps the most outspoken contemporary critic of the black middle class is Nathan Hare (1965). According to Hare the black middle class has consistently rejected all identification with the black lower class and its traditions, and through delusions of wealth and power it has sought identification with a white America which rejects it. He further argues that the black middle class rejects being black, but must, at the same time, accept the subordinate place designated for all blacks. Once again, middle class blacks are said to reject group identity, have no sense of group consciousness, and therefore lack a sense of group solidarity.

The writers discussed above have consistently argued that the black middle class, rather than concern itself with the lives of the masses and values necessary for the struggle for equality, has been deficient in its role as leader of the black community. They see the black middle class as following a line of action which mimics the behavior of white Americans. For this reason then, the black middle class is seen as lacking acceptance in the black community, while ironically its members are still rejected as equals by whites. In these writers' views, providing relevant political leadership to uplift the black masses is the responsibility of the black middle class. This expectation has its antecedents in W. E. B. DuBois's (1903, pp. 31–76) notion of the "talented tenth," a privileged stratum which bears the burden and mission of struggle for the redemption of blacks in American society. But in the view of these writers, because the black middle class is marginal, to the black community, it is incapable of fulfilling a meaningful leadership role.

SOCIAL SOLIDARITY WITHIN THE BLACK COMMUNITY

Bayard Rustin (1969) has noted that when describing black middle class behaviors and attitudes, one must be cognizant that the subjects are both middle class and black. For Rustin (1969, p. 237), it makes little sense to require that middle class blacks behave as if class considerations are unimportant, since the social processes fostering upward mobility are integrated into the personality of the individual. While there is little doubt that the process of social mobility has resulted in a certain degree of social distance between middle class blacks and the larger black community, it is also true that the same process has enabled the former a greater opportunity to be of assistance to the latter. Thus, despite the perspective that the black middle class is socially distant, there is a counterargument suggesting they have a strong sense of social cohesion with lower class blacks. For example, Rustin maintains that many racial victories and other achievements would not have occurred without the participation of the black middle class:

> ... it was middle class Negroes who founded the universities, schools, churches and newspapers which have helped unify and uplift all black people. I am also speaking of the political role they have played in the Negro struggle for equality (1969, p. 238).

According to Rustin (ibid., p. 241), in times of cultural and political conflict, historically the leadership for advancing the racial cause was for the most part provided by the middle class. For example, the NAACP (which is predominantly middle class) won the significant court cases that gave an impetus to the protest movement of the 1960s. Prominent leaders in the black community such as Booker T. Washington, W. E. B. DuBois, Martin Luther King, Frederick Douglass, and A. Phillip Randolph, as well as many of the membership of most civil rights organizations, were generally individuals of middle class origin. Even today, black professionals and entrepreneurs are concentrated and over-represented in the black community, and have black clientele (Boyd, 1991, pp. 409–29; Butler and Wilson, 1988; pp. 127–66). Without the presence of these businesses, the black community would be worse off then it currently is. Rustin (1969, p. 240) explains that as a group, the black middle class has held a profound social vision for leadership in the black community. This vision, he said, resulted from having the necessary time and resources for study and reflection on matters concerning the black community – a luxury not afforded members of the black lower class.

Carson (1989: 92) notes that in addition to assisting the black community in its efforts to achieve equality, middle class blacks have established an excellent 200 year record in philanthropy for racial causes. He (1989, p. 94) explains that organized charitable giving helped to develop black schools, black banks, black insurance companies, and other essential services in the black community. His review of black philanthropy indicates that the black community has always relied on and received charitable resources from the black middle class to provide relief for the less fortunate, and to sustain social protest. An example of middle class blacks exerting the power of philanthropic activity is the civil rights movement.

It would not be much of an overstatement, if at all, to suggest that the civil rights movement was perhaps the greatest mobilization of charitable activity of any group to be witnessed to date in America. Between 1957–1968, the various civil rights organizations assembled thousands of individuals into a national protest movement that raised money, collected and disbursed food, and recruited volunteers to participate in boycotts, sit-ins, and marches across the country (Carson, 1989: 96).

Likewise, R. Frazier (1987, 89–90) argues that the black middle class has always orchestrated major initiatives in meeting the needs of other blacks who are not as fortunate. She (1987) points to the programs of civic, professional, fraternal and religious organizations as proof that middle class blacks have made significant contributions to the larger community. Not only do middle class blacks comprise the bulk of the memberships of sororities and fraternities, but they are also over-represented in the NAACP Legal Defense and Education Funds, the Joint Center for Political Studies, Southern Christian Leadership Conference, United Negro College Fund, PUSH, Urban League, and the NAACP. In these organizations topics such as affirmative action, career planning, hunger, pay equity, economic self sufficiency, child care, teen-age pregnancy, drug and alcohol abuse, domestic violence, political participation, health and other issues affecting blacks are discussed and addressed. Lastly, Frazier (1987, 90) demonstrates that politically, the black middle class launched massive voter registration drives via having themselves deputized and setting up booths in shopping malls, church yards, and other sites convenient to the masses. These examples then, show that the black middle class has a tradition of philanthropy and volunteerism. While some may regard these types of activity as a conservative approach to achieving black equality, it is important to point out the inaccuracy of this assumption. As Carson (1989, p. 96) explains, at times in the history of black Americans, these types of activities have been all-inclusive: the centerpiece of liberal, conservative, and nationalistic strategies for black socioeconomic progress.

In addition to providing direct support to the black community, there is evidence that prior to the 60s, the very presence of the black middle class living in inner-city neighborhoods reinforced and perpetuated mainstream values and thereby enhanced the social organization of the black community through a strong sense of norms, behaviors, neighborhood identification, and social cohesion. Wilson (1987, 56) argues that important institutions in the inner-city areas such as churches, recreational facilities, and schools could not have remained viable without significant support from the black middle class. Those in the black middle class, then, have historically served as role models to lower class blacks, as well as social buffers that deflected the full impact of white segregation and discrimination:

> . . . the very presence of these families . . . provides mainstream role models that help keep alive the perception that education is meaningful, that steady employment is a viable alternative to welfare, and family stability is the norm, not the exception (Wilson, 1987: 56).

STRUCTURAL CHANGE AND EMERGENCE OF THE NEW BLACK MIDDLE CLASS

During the 60s, the civil rights movement and a healthy economy stimulated an increase in the number of blacks reaching middle class status. Today, the black middle class represents approximately 27% of the working black population (Landry, 1987: 194–196). In comparison to blacks in the lower class, the black middle class today fares better on all socioeconomic indicators (Wilson, 1987: 110–15), though some still experience racial prejudice and discrimination (Feagin, 1991: 101–116; Willie, 1983; Collins, 1983). Unlike prior generations (e.g., see Frazier, 1957; Muraskin, 1975; Kronus, 1971), many in the black middle class are younger and have parents whose origins are in the lower and/or working classes (Landry, 1987: 86). Between 1970 and 1989, black families with incomes over $50,000 grew to 14%, while the percentage of black families earning less than $10,000 rose to almost 26% (Farley and Allen, 1987: 107). These data indicate that while the middle class is growing, the economic gap between it and lower class blacks is widening. This economic gap could result in greater fragmentation and diversity between blacks as class divisions become more important than racial solidarity.

Prior to the 1960s the black middle class was mostly composed of small entrepreneurs whose economic position was achieved and maintained by drawing resources from the black community (Frazier, 1957; Lane, 1986, 144–86). This intraracial symbiotic relationship changed in the 1960s as a result of the introduction of laws ending *de jure* segregation and discrimination in employment and housing. The most notable gains for the black middle class occurred in professional employment, income of married-couple families, higher education, and home ownership. According to Wilson (1987: 109), the number of blacks in professional, technical managerial, and administrative positions increased by 57% between 1973 and 1982, while the number of whites holding these positions rose only 36% during the same period. The median annual income for black married couple families was $20,586 compared to $26,443 for whites in the same category. When black husbands and wives were employed and were between the ages of 24 and 35, the economic gap between the races was less than $3,000 (Wilson, 1987: 109).

For the most part, many in the black middle class found employment and security in state and local government, aided by the bureaucratic growth generated by the "Great Society Program" of the Johnson administration. According to Brown and Erie (1981: 299–330) the employment of blacks alone in "Great Society" programs and public social welfare programs increased by 850,000 from 1960 to 1976. At the same time, a growing number of the new middle class blacks found employment in national and international job markets which are part of the corporate world and consequently unattached to the concerns of the black community (Davis and Watson, 1982). It should be noted that a high proportion of these jobs went not to lower class blacks, but rather to more advantaged blacks who already had a higher education and income (Lemann, 1991: 180–88). Glenn Loury observes that:

> It is clear from extensive empirical research . . . that the positive impact on blacks which this program has had accrues mainly to those in the higher occupations . . . If one looks at relative earnings of black and white workers by occupation going back to 1950, one finds that the most dramatic earnings gains for blacks have taken place in the professional, technical, and managerial occupations, while the least significant gains have come in the lowest occupations, like laborer and service worker. Thus, a broad array of evidence suggests, at least to this observer, that better placed blacks have simply been able to take more advantage of the opportunities created in the last 20 years than have those mired in the underclass (1984: 13–14).

As a result of structural changes members of today's black middle class, in contrast to lower class blacks, are occupationally established, upwardly mobile, and hold relatively secure positions in the labor market. However, occupational demands and role performances may leave them little time to give support and interest to the black community. One theoretical reason for this expectation is that new middle class members are increasingly moving out of a secondary labor market into a primary one. According to the dual labor market theory, lower status blacks have traditionally worked at menial jobs in the irregular economy, which are dead end, and carry few fringe benefits (Denton, 1985; Bonacich, 1972, 1976). In contrast, jobs held by today's black middle class are more rewarding since these often offer a career, higher pay, and substantial benefits. Such rewards, however may come at a cost because their attainment and retention require that recipients demonstrate commitment and dedication to the organization, occupational roles, and time patterns established by the employing business. Pratt (1981: 317–33) and Hawley (1950) demonstrated that work schedules within the primary labor market tend to preempt time, thereby forcing non-work-related activities to be scheduled in residual times. Inferring from this, one might reasonably expect that employment demands on black middle class workers may regulate their social relations and involvement in the black community. In other words, the type, extent, scope and intensity of social relations between the black middle class and the rest of the black community depend on time conventions and role expectations which are conditions of employment. Thus, social mobility and structural changes may work over time to diminish the black middle class' ability to establish and maintain social relations, social cohesion, and social solidarity with the black masses. If left unchecked, then, their labor force attachments could result in increasing fragmentation and social distance from issues and concerns directly affecting the black community. There are indications that the black middle class and the black masses are beginning to perceive greater social distance between themselves. A national poll, conducted in 1992, of 1,211 black adults showed that 94% of respondents believed that civil rights organizations (primarily established by the black middle class) had lost touch with every day problems such as high dropout rates, unemployment, low self-esteem, teen-age pregnancy and family disintegration. Sixty-four percent of the respondents reported that civil rights groups were doing a poor job, or were ambivalent toward fighting crime, while 55% said that these organizations did a poor job of building social solidarity and social cohesion within the black community (Saunders and Woolfe, 1992: 5).

Another indicator of wider recognition of the social distance between the two groups appeared in a *Newsweek* article about the aftermath of the devastating 1992 Los Angeles riots, in which those who took to the streets were described as " . . . clearly part of a relatively small urban underclass that is now as distinct from the black middle class as it is from the white middle class" (Morganthau, 1992: 28). A companion article stated the riots " . . . made politicians . . . seem like irrelevant bystanders. Leaders of traditional civil-rights organizations looked just as out of touch" (Fineman *et al.*, 1992: 31).

Traditionally, the black middle class provided leadership within the black community by fighting against federally sanctioned discrimination through supporting court cases and corrective legislation. However, today, unlike in the past, overt discrimination is not perceived as a major barrier to black progress because it is not as pervasive (Wilson, 1980;

Sowell, 1990). The problems the black middle class faces today are different and more subtle than those experienced in the past. Problems which threaten the social organization of the black community today are to a large extent internal and beyond the scope of past leadership tactics. For example, school dropouts, teen-age parents, drugs and murder are problems requiring leadership strategies that are different from those used in the past (Farley and Allen, 1987; Edelman, 1987; Haynes, 1987).

THE POLITICAL MEANING OF OCCUPATIONAL DISCIPLINE

The connection between employment and social relations of the black middle class has not been addressed adequately in the literature. Despite this, social scientists agree that one's location and degree of involvement in the labor market have salient implications on social structure and individual perception. Work is much more than merely a means of making money. Work also establishes the framework for daily behavior and patterns of interaction because of the discipline and regularity it imposes. Regular employment provides the bases for temporal and spatial aspects of social life. Not only do those employed in the primary labor market have regular incomes, but they are more likely to have a coherent organization of expectations and goals (Wilson 1991: 1–14). According to Wilson (1991: 11), regular employment tends to be associated with strong labor force attachment, high self efficacy, and different social orientations from the unemployed, who are also more likely to perceive workers as holding "rational plans" as well as "unorthodox beliefs." In turn, these are reinforced or strengthened by the perceptions and attitudes of others in their immediate environment who have similar views (Wilson, 1991: 12). From the aforementioned then, we can infer that employment will have a significant effect on attitudes and perceptions of the black middle class.

One fact frequently overlooked by students of race and ethnic relations is that, for many middle class blacks, significant changes have occurred in the personality because of employment related expectations. For example, Davis and Watson (1982) in their book called *Black Life in Corporate America: Swimming in the Mainstream* show how many individuals in the black middle class are operating in foreign social space with unfamiliar protocol, habits, manners, values, and styles of thinking that until recently were new to them. Davis and Wilson also talk about the adaptation of black culture to white culture and white culture to black. One place that this adaptation can readily be seen is in the integration of the managerial middle class of American society. Without a doubt, anyone who works for any length of time in these roles will be changed. Corporations (in which many middle class blacks work) have found ways to make people into the persons they want them to be. For example, in this type of work setting the work demands a different kind of attention and commitment than in the secondary labor market. More significantly, the job becomes part of the person and necessitates that personal behavioral style fit the demands of the system. Industriousness and intelligence are important but these alone are not the primary qualities needed to do a good job in this setting; rather, the primary qualities flow from a way of looking at work, at people – a way of perceiving the human condition, human nature and human purpose. In addition, work in these settings involves a method of viewing relationships and acquiring the emotional values that come into play in developing one's behavior, perceptions of self, and perceptions of the way that others relate to self (Davis and Watson, 1982: 61).

According to William H. Whyte in his book *The Organizational Man*, in order to fit into this model, one has to assume a new identity by negotiating a truce between the old and the new required selves (1956). He argues that the corporation has its own pragmatic sense of how a person must be to get along. It expects of the individual images that its citizens respond to, either positively or negatively, and its own vocabulary and way of speaking. It has its own methods of resolving conflict, its own motivational techniques, system of reward and punishment, and its own ways of looking at time and judging its use. In addition, its norms define acceptable ways to be assertive. The organization knows how to create conflict and manage that conflict in ways that are beneficial to itself. Hence, in order to do the work, one has to know how to dress "properly," how to negotiate, and how to role-play. One has to know how to control anxiety and stress, how to plan, forecast, and how to minimize the personal effects of bad plans. At the same time one must be able to call attention to one's good work. All organizational people have some problems adapting to these expectations, but blacks may have more difficulty because their cultural experiences are further removed from the corporate or organizational model than are whites. However, once blacks have undergone a process of organizational development there is greater estrangement between themselves, their families, and communities; yet often there is no correspondingly greater comfort level between them and the white managers they work with and for (Davis and Watson, 1982).

Work in the primary labor market, then, suggests that constituents of the black middle class must constantly make difficult choices as they negotiate their way in two different worlds. In one world they are judged by their credentials and capabilities, while in the other racial allegiance is of paramount concern. The former black Chair of the Congressional Budget Committee, William H. Gray, exemplifies this conflict:

> The issue is: I'm Chairman of the Budget Committee, a Democrat. I build consensus. I walk out with a budget. Now, do I vote against my own budget.... That doesn't make a lot of sense ... I'm not here to do the bidding of somebody just because they happen to be black. If I agree with you, I agree with you. I set my policy. I think it's fair policy, but that policy has noting to do with being black. It has to do with the position I have institutionally as Chairman of the Budget Committee (Pianin, 1987: 15).

Poussaint (1987: 76–80) explains that as black middle class people become socialized into their work roles they are more likely to feel no obligation to "less fortunate" blacks, and some are becoming angry and resentful when it is suggested that they give something back to the community. Increasingly, middle class blacks are annoyed that whites tend to perceive them in terms of their racial identity and thus as not significantly different from "underclass" blacks. Such perceptions afford the black middle class no recognition for their social and economic achievements. In addition, the effects of employment in the primary labor market on the black middle class can be seen in conservative attitudes emerging in this group. Many, especially those working in predominantly white settings, object to affirmative action, welfare, and other government programs that have historically benefited blacks. Some middle class blacks worry that the existence of these programs can be taken by others to imply that their social mobility was not attained by virtue of personal initiative or hard work, but rather through advantages handed to them undeservedly by the government. Hence, they are defensive toward these programs and reject them in principle as a way of asserting that their own success is based on merit rather than governmental favoritism.

In general then, work for the black middle class today has meant that a significant rift is beginning to emerge between racial solidarity and class identification. This writer suspects that this social rift will continue to be a significant one, especially as black middle class individuals continually depend upon broad-based coalitions to support their upward mobility in the work place. In other words, as the black middle class is exposed to many of the same experiences, frustrations, and expectations in the work world as its white counterparts, the result will be that the nature of the job as well as social class will be a better predictor of social attitudes and behavior than race.

MOVING ON UP

The entrance of blacks into the white-collar job market, along with federal laws passed to ensure equal employment opportunity and fair housing, have functioned to increase the exodus of middle class blacks from the central cities. This recent migration is significant since it indicates that middle class blacks, when the opportunity arises, will move away from the black lower class in the same manner that whites vacate neighborhoods when middle class black families move in their area. Thus, the migration of more than 6,000,000 middle class blacks from the inner city to suburbia between 1960 and 1990 has important implications for leadership of the black masses in the future. The migration out of the inner city by the black middle class was the result of the civil rights movement, which largely freed them from discriminatory housing restrictions.[2] It is this migration which caused inner city neighborhoods to lose a large number of residents so that today, they appear empty and undesirable.

According to Landry (1987), approximately one-third of all black families earning $25,000 or more live in predominantly white suburban communities. Danziger and Gottschalk (1985: 32) noted that over the last 30 years census tract areas designated as impoverished have become worse off as middle class blacks moved away and the number of poor within them increased. Lemann (1986: 37–53) supports this contention by showing how North Lawndale, in Chicago, lost its middle class black population in the 60s and 70s as more than half its black population moved away. In the same decade the area around Forty-seventh and South Parkway, the old vibrant heart of the South Side Ghetto, lost 38 percent of its black population. The Robert Taylor homes, whose extremely low rents and solid construction for years attracted long waiting lists, are now 20 percent vacant. This isn't only happening in Chicago. The South Bronx lost 37 percent of its population between 1970 and 1980. More than 100,000 black Chicagoans moved to the suburbs in the '70s; 224,000 blacks moved from Washington, D.C. to its suburbs; 124,000 from Atlanta to its suburbs (Lemann, 1986: 53). There's no mystery as to why so many middle class blacks left the ghettos. They wanted to feel safe on the streets, send their children to better schools, and live in more pleasant surroundings; in particular, riots drove many people away. Probably, virtually everyone who could leave did. In addition to the migration of families, many black businesses, churches and other institutions that supported social cohesion in the black community also left. According to Wilson (1987: 143), this migration has resulted in instability in inner-city neighborhoods. As already noted above, in the past, the very presence of the black middle class provided stability to inner-city neighborhoods and reinforced and perpetuated mainstream patterns of norms and behaviors. Their presence also enhanced the social organization of these areas. Thus, the exodus of the black middle class from the inner city removed an important "social buffer" that could deflect the full impact of the kind of prolonged and increasing joblessness that currently plagues inner-city neighborhoods. The very presence of the black middle class in the inner cities enhanced the basic institutions there (churches, schools, stores, recreational facilities) because much of the base of their support came from the more economically stable and secure families. Lastly, the black middle class were mainstream role models that helped to keep alive the perception that education is meaningful, that steady employment is a viable alternative to welfare, and that family stability is the norm, not the exception (Wilson, 1987: 56).

Unlike the black middle class of a generation ago, the black middle class today is not as close socially or geographically to the black masses; consequently, they are less likely to have meaningful and significant relations with them (Wilson, 1987: 143). Indeed, as is true for many white Americans, some in the black middle class feel no responsibility toward blacks left behind (Lacayo, 1989: 68).

CONCLUSIONS

The integration of middle class blacks into the white collar labor market will inevitably result in a loss of their racial attachment to the black masses. While the problems of lower class blacks are urgent and in need of redressing, the black middle class is slowly abdicating its traditional leadership role in the black community as its preoccupation with social class, employment, and the amenities which flow from these, take precedence over race. One reason for this shift in focus is that the nature of the problems addressed by the black community has significantly changed. In the past the black middle class leadership focused primarily on racial issues involving prejudice, discrimination, racism and their political and economic effects. Today, it is no longer clear that the problems besetting the inner city black community are so easily traced to racism. Problems such as drugs, crime, unemployment, etc., are considerably more complex, difficult to address, and harder to solve. Unlike in the past, the problems faced by blacks today derive from multiple sources that are both external and internal to the black community. The complexity and intractability of these problems are as bewildering to middle class blacks as they are to everyone else. Because they don't know quite what to do — and because, as this paper points out, they have other things to do – they sometimes do nothing at all. As middle class blacks continue to partake of the vision of the "American Dream," I expect that their traditional concern for the problems of lower class blacks will be replaced by issues closely affiliated with their new social status. Hence, past concerns of middle class blacks, such as employment, affordable housing, and urban violence will be supplanted with issues such as job promotions, job performance, white picket fences in suburbia, and ensuring that their children attend proper schools. Such issues are personal and of a different nature than the issues of the past (e.g., Civil Rights, discrimination, segregation, and so forth) that required middle class leadership. Since members of the black middle class are increasingly working in the national and global job markets (i.e., national banks, insurance companies, retail firms, industries, universities, and government agencies) I expect that the demands of their work will function to cause greater social distance between themselves and lower class blacks. This expectation is based on the notion that work in the middle class often requires its employees to make significant shifts and adjustments in social and temporal orientation away from racial identification with the larger black community and toward the objectives of the employing organization.

To what degree, then, is the black middle class capable of responding in a leadership role to the problems faced by the black lower class? In the news media, many members of the black middle class are portrayed as being very concerned about "not forgetting where they came from," and making magnanimous efforts to assist their less fortunate brethren. Black churches, fraternity and sorority chapters, and groups such as "100 Black Men" exemplify such efforts. Most middle class black people now have parents or siblings still living in poverty-stricken areas. But this link will dissipate over time, as these relatives die, and especially as the children of today's black middle class families reach adulthood, having lived their entire lives in suburbs. Perhaps in the future middle class blacks may refer to what is now called the underclass as "poor black trash," akin to whites' term for white people whose behavior they disavow.

What could we really say to them now except a murmured 'How you doing Bro,' as we hurried along to catch the train that would take us to another appointment or conference; another step on our frenzied stair of upward mobility? Our eyes would pity them, our palms would open to them, and quickly shut again. And while we hated to talk about it, we knew that we had moved beyond them forever (Puckrein, 1984).

Notes

1. The author thanks Annette Evans and Marsha Shapiro Rose for their advice during the preparation of this manuscript.
2. It should be pointed out, however, that though some members of the black middle class have recently gained an entrance into an integrated housing market, the level of black residential segregation has actually changed very little over the last 30 years. For example, Gross and Massey (1991: 347–360) show that at all levels of education, income, and occupational status, blacks are highly segregated from whites. Blacks earning more than $50,000 per year are more segregated than Latinos earning under $2,500.

References

Bonacich, Edna (1972) "A Theory of Ethnic Antagonism: The Split Labor Market," *American Sociological Review*, vol. 37, pp. 547–59.

Bonacich, Edna (1976) "Advanced Capitalism and Black/White Race Relations in the United States: A Split Labor Market Interpretation," *American Sociological Review*, vol. 41, pp. 34–51.

Boyd, Robert L. (1991) "A Contextual Analysis of Black Self-Employment in Large Metropolitan Areas, 1970–1980," *Social Forces*, vol. 70, pp. 409–29.

Brown, Michael K. and Steven P. Erie (1981) "Blacks and the Legacy of the Great Society: The Economic and Political Impact of Federal Social Policy," *Public Policy*, vol. 29, pp. 299–330.

Butler, John Sibley and Kenneth L. Wilson (1988) "Entrepreneurial Enclaves: An Exposition into the Afro-American Experience," *National Journal of Sociology*, vol. 2, pp. 127–66.

Carson, Emmett D. (1989) "The Evolution of Black Philanthropy: Patterns of Giving and Volunteerism," in Richard Magat (ed.), *Philanthropic Giving: Studies in Varieties and Goals* (New York: Oxford University Press).

Collins, Sheila M. (1983) "The making of the Black Middle Class," *Social Problems*, vol. 30, pp. 369–81.

Conyers, James E. (1986) "Who's Who Among Black Doctorates in Sociology," *Sociological Focus*, vol. 19, pp. 77–93.

Cruse, Harold (1967) *The Crisis of the Negro Intellectual: From Its Origins to the Present* (New York: William Morrow).

Danziger, Stanley and Gottschalk, Paul (1985) "The Poverty of Losing Ground," *Challenge*, vol. 7, no. 2, pp. 30–45.

Davis, George and Gleeg Watson (1982) *Black Life in Corporate America: Swimming In the Mainstream* (Garden City: Doubleday).

Denton, John (1985) "The Underground Economy and Social Stratification," *Sociological Spectrum*, vol. 5, pp. 31–42.

Drake, St. Clair and Horace R. Cayton (1962) *Black Metropolis: A Study of Negro life in a Northern City* (New York: Harper and Row).

DuBois, W. E. B. (1903) "The Talented Tenth," in Booker T. Washington *et al.*, *The Negro Problem: A series of Articles By Representative American Negroes of Today* (New York: James Pott).

Edelman, Marian W. (1987) *Families in Peril: An Agenda for Social Change* (Cambridge: Harvard University Press).

Edwards, G. Franklin (1974) "E. Franklin Frazier," in James Blackwell and Morris Janowitz (eds), *Black Sociologists: Historical and Contemporary Perspectives* (Chicago: University of Chicago Press).

Farley, Reynolds and Walter R. Allen (1987) *The Color Line and the Quality of Life in America* (New York: Russell Sage Foundation).

Feagin, Joe R. (1991) "The Continuing Significance of Race: Antiblack Discrimination in Public Places," *American Sociological Review*, vol. 56, pp. 101–16.

Fineman, Howard *et al.* (1992) "Filling the Political Void," *Newsweek*, vol. 199 (18 May), pp. 31–4.

Frazier, E. Franklin (1957) *Black Bourgeoisie: The Rise of a New Middle Class* (New York: Free Press).

Frazier, E. Franklin (1963) "What Can the American Negro Contribute to the Social Development of Africa?," in Horace Mann Bond (ed.), *Africa as Seen by American Negro Scholars* (New York: American Society of African Culture).

Frazier, E. Franklin (1964) *The Negro Church in America* (New York: Schocken).

Frazier, Regina Jollivett (1987) "Is the Black Middle Class Blowing it?", *Ebony*, vol. 42, pp. 89–90.

Gross, Andrew B. and Douglas S. Massey (1991) "Spatial Assimilation Models: A Micro–Macro Comparison," *Social Science Quarterly*, vol. 72, pp. 347–60.

Hare, Nathan (1965) *The Black Anglo Saxons* (New York: Marzani and Mansell).

Hawley, Amos H. (1950) *Human Ecology* (New York: Ronald Press).

Haynes, Cheryl D. (1987) *Risking the Future: Adolescent Sexuality, Pregnancy, and Childbearing* (Washington: National Academy Press).

Kronus, Sidney (1971) *The Black Middle Class* (Columbus: Charles E. Merrill).

Lacayo, Richard (1989) "Between Two Worlds," *Time*, vol. 133 (13 March), pp. 58–68.

Landry, Bart (1987) *The New Black Middle Class* (Berkeley, Los Angeles: University of California Press).

Lane, Roger (1986) *Roots of Violence in Black Philadelphia* (Cambridge: Harvard University Press).

Lemann, Nicholas (1986) "The Origins of the Under-Class," *The Atlantic*, vol. 257, pp. 35–57.

Lemann, Nicholas (1991) *The Promised Land: The Great Black Migration And How It Changed America* (New York: Alfred A. Knopf).

Loury, Glen C. (1984) "On the Need for Moral Leadership in the Black Community," paper presented at the University of Chicago, sponsored by the Center for the Study of Industrial Societies and the John M. Olin Center, Chicago, 18 April 1984.

Mills, C. Wright (1953) *White Collar: The American Middle Classes* (New York: Oxford University Press).

Morganthau, Tom (1992) "Beyond Black and White," *Newsweek*, vol. 119 (18 May), pp. 28–30.

Muraskin, William A. (1975) *Middle-Class Blacks In A White Society: Prince Hall Freemasonry in America* (Berkeley: University of California Press).

Neal, Larry (1970) "New Sense-The Growth of Black Consciousness in the Sixties," in Floyd Barbour (ed.), *The Black Seventies* (Boston: Porter Sargent Publisher).

Park, Robert E. (1928) "Human Migration and the Marginal Man," *American Journal of Sociology*, vol. 33, pp. 881–93.

Pianin, Eric (1987) "The Congressional Black Caucus May be a Victim of Success," *The Washington Post National Weekly Edition*, 12 October p. 15.

Poussaint, Alvin F. (1987) "The Price of Success," *Ebony*, vol. 42, pp. 76–80.

Pratt, Lois (1981) "Business Temporal Norms and Bereavement Behavior," *American Sociological Review*, vol. 46, pp. 317–42.

Puckrein, Gary (1984) "The New Black Middle Class," *Miami Herald*, 1 April, p. 6E.

Rustin, Bayard (1969) "The Role Of The Negro Middle Class," *The Crisis*, vol. 76, pp. 237–42.

Saunders, Michael and Tao Woolfe (1992) "Poll: Blacks Say Action Groups Out of Touch," *Sun Sentinel*, 1 March, p. 5B.

Sowell, Thomas (1990) *Preferential Policies: An International Perspective* (New York: Morrow).

Whyte, William H. (1956) *The Organizational Man* (New York: Simon and Schuster).

Willie, Charles (1983) *Race, Ethnicity and Socioeconomic Status* (Bayside: General Hall).

Wilson, William J. (1980) *The Declining Significance of Race: Blacks and Changing American Institutions* (Chicago: University of Chicago Press).

Wilson, William J. (1987) *The Truly Disadvantaged: The Inner City, The Underclass, and Public Policy* (Chicago: University of Chicago Press).

Wilson, William J. (1991) "Studying Inner-City Social Dislocations: The Challenge of Public Agenda Research," *American Sociological Review*, vol. 56, pp. 1–14.

12 Changes in the Life-Styles of American Classes*

Joseph Bensman and Arthur J. Vidich

THE CREATION OF LIFE-STYLES

As Max Weber noted in his essay "Class, Status and Power," capital, wealth, and income are not by themselves sufficient as indices for specifying the life-styles of classes. Within given income levels, the way in which income is spent involves elements of choice. Life-styles may thus take a variety of forms within the same income categories, depending upon the character of consumption choices.[1]

In considering the problem of the life-styles of classes in the United States, we have found it useful to refer to Harold Finestone's seminal essay on "cat" culture (1957). In that essay called "Cats, Kicks, and Color," Finestone, using Johan Huizinga's theory of play, pointed out that one of the major characteristics of the black American "cat" culture is its artificiality. The cat literally invented his own language, his own morality, his own dress styles, and his own codes of interpersonal conduct. He used all of these inventions to frame a total way of life for himself. The cat who was denied access to the life-styles of the dominant culture could borrow directly from that culture to construct his own way of life. Reacting to rejection by the dominant culture, the cat insulated himself by developing a unique life-style. At least within his own self-selected group he thus achieved a basis for dignity, self-respect, and status competition.

The artifice of cat culture was maintained by the conscious effort of those involved in it. Black youth in the cat culture

---

* Reprinted from Joseph Bensman and Arthur J. Vidich, *The New American Society* (Chicago: Quadrangle Books, 1971).

deliberately cultivated a style of living and playfully changed and restyled, elaborated and extended it. The cat, even while creating and enacting his life style, knew that it was an artificial convention that could not be lived completely within the embrace of the dominant culture. As Finestone noted, "He has to make place in his scheme of life for police, lockups, jails and penitentiaries, to say nothing of the agonies of withdrawal distress." Always there were occasions when the cat was forced to suspend his play, to look consciously at himself with a sense of irony and satire. When he did so, he faced the fact that there was nothing left in life for him. When his play collapsed, the cat stepped outside himself and became a bemused spectator of his own play without having any other basis for a viable self.

Apart from black youth culture, the Finestone essay, in pointing out the conscious and artificial play of cat culture, permits us once again to raise the general question of the authenticity and spuriousness of life-styles and class "cultures."[2] The existence of artificial life-styles, self-consciously created as if they were works of art, suggests a lack of inevitability in the living patterns that classes adopt. The stages of class experience through which the individual passes in the course of the life cycle do not present an easy succession of life patterns that the individual can accept as "natural" or "authentic." It would rather seem that each stage in the class history of the individual presents a problem of learning new class patterns. The greater the individual's mobility, the greater the amount of flexibility and "learning" necessary for each stage. The greater the mobility, the greater will be the consciousness of adopting new patterns of conduct demanded by each change in status. Instances of rapid mobility are thus psychological equivalents of the experience of black youth in American society. In both instances life-styles are artificial creations or adoptions. The bearer himself is aware of the fact that the style can be donned and discarded at will and, therefore, it can be acted out with some degree of self-irony and self-satire. The irony and satire express a certain degree of discomfort which the individual experiences when behaving in a way that he does not see as "natural," or "authentic," or ordinary.

In our terms, an "authentic" life-style is one that exists as part of the "natural" and "inevitable" environment of the individual. The individual, without reflection, assumes that he has been destined for the way of life that in fact is his. He takes his way of life for granted and acts it out without self-consciousness, defensiveness, or irony.

While there is an abundant literature on the artificial nature of black life-styles and on the adaptive capacities of mobility-minded whites, the same kind of reporting is not available for white middle-, upper-middle-, and upper-class life-styles. One significant exception is Seeley, Sim, and Loosely's *Crestwood Heights* (1956), as it is discussed in *The Eclipse of Community*, (1960), in which Maurice Stein points out the ironic element in the life-style of the upper middle class of Toronto. The subjects of that study displayed a capacity to talk objectively and analytically about themselves and their participation in the community. Thus they could consciously analyze what one had to do in order to "get along" in Crestwood Heights. They worked at behaving appropriately and understood the consequences of alternative lines of conduct. Newcomers to the community displayed a facility for picking up the cues and quickly adjusted themselves to the Crestwood Heights style. In all of this there was a quality of both ironic self-detachment and self-rationalization not dissimilar to the self-rationalization of the bureaucratic personality.

While *Crestwood Heights* most clearly expresses the theme of self-irony, similar themes have been expressed for the metropolitan New York City upper-middle class in A. C. Spectorsky's book *The Exurbanites* (1955), and for the aspiring middle-class Levittown dweller in John Keats's book *The Crack in the Picture Window* (1957). On another plane, the element of ironic self-detachment is the basic theme of Jules Fieffer's cartoons, whose contents appeal precisely to those who are the objects of his satire. We are not dealing here only with intellectual sophisticates and beats, since magazines such as *Playboy, Esquire,* and the *New Yorker*, in their overall tone, make similar appeals to their respective readers. The existence of a market for satire on middle- and upper-middle-class life-styles suggests that the phenomenon of ironic self-detachment is a generalized feature of a number of life-styles in American society.

It is our contention that present American life-styles are predominantly self-conscious creations that permeate almost all aspects of American life, with a few exceptions to be noted. Lacking the sanction of tradition, these patterns are not lived with the comfort that comes from being taken for granted, but rather are known to be artificial. The major traditional life-styles of the nineteenth century are now defunct and have been replaced by new sets of living patterns unique to American history.

THE DECLINE OF OLDER LIFE-STYLES

The literature on class points to the dominance of several distinct traditional life-styles in the United States.

First, the historically dominant life-style tradition is perhaps best defined as Babbittry—the aggressive, social, uncultured, energetic, optimistic way of life of the late frontier. In many respects Babbittry is a secularization of life-styles associated with those of the fundamentalist Protestant "bible belt" as they emerged out of the revival of Methodist and Baptist movements in the early and mid-nineteenth century. This style is stereotyped in the small-town, churchgoing Protestant moralism of the midwest, especially in the Iowa of Grant Wood, who in his paintings, depicts the parsimonious, taciturn upholders of public propriety.

Second, the urban aristocracy of the late nineteenth century best illustrates traditional upper-class life-styles. Brahmin culture on Boston's Beacon Hill (which itself, in its indigenous elements, was a dilution of earlier New England transcendentalism) suggests this style. Gramercy Square intellectualism in New York City was a similar phenomenon. In both these instances there were social, cultural, and intellectual affiliations with European, especially English, elements, reflecting the absence of an American tradition upon which to draw. These European affiliations were frequently with aristocratic and intellectual culture as was the case, for example, with Henry Adams. Such imitation can, of course, be looked upon as a continuation of a process already begun within the European upper classes themselves. Throughout the seventeenth and eighteenth centuries the landed aristocracy of Europe was penetrated by newly wealthy bourgeoisie who adopted this life-style. By the time the Americans began to imitate the Europeans, their model was largely an imitation itself. As Georg Simmel and Huizinga have pointed out, the life-style of the European aristocracy, having been cut off from its historical roots in the Middle Ages, especially in the religious brotherhoods of knights, by the time of the *ancien régime* had become but a shadow of its former self. Such artificial mummification was imitated and continued in the upper-class style of the American south, which emphasized elegance, leisure, *noblesse oblige*, high etiquette, and slavery. The Civil War rent this class asunder, but its style remained as a model for would-be southern belles and aristocrats.

Like those of the European aristocrats before them, American upper-class life-styles underwent a continuous process of dilution. In the nineteenth century the entrance of the robber barons into this class provided an infusion of healthy vulgarity. With newly gained wealth from newly formed industries, they added gaudiness and garrishness to American upper-class culture. These styles were described by Veblen (1953), Edith Wharton, in her many novels, and Gustavus Myers (1937).

There is clear evidence that these upper-class life-styles have declined and all but disappeared. Certainly there are no more southern aristocrats who can be taken seriously. Senator Claghorn, the mint-julep-drinking southern colonel, and Blanche DuBois, the deluded postbellum belle in *A Streetcar Named Desire*, caricature a dead epoch. A few aged dowagers on Beacon Hill represent a living connection to the nineteenth century, but that tradition has been effectively broken by the industrialization of Boston's Route 128. Gramercy Square, now in the jet age, qualifies as an historical monument. The Babbittry of Iowa and Minnesota has given way to the vacation-minded, Cadillac-driving farmer who may still go to church but takes his Bermuda trip more seriously. Whether their economic basis was destroyed or not, that these life-styles have not been able to sustain themselves requires some explanation.

Between 1880 and 1924 hundreds of thousands of immigrants from southern and eastern Europe entered the United

States. They entered the society beneath the Anglo-Saxons and northern Europeans who had come earlier to set the tone of traditional American life-styles. The new immigrants thought the streets of America were paved with gold, and in trying to make their dream come true they absorbed many elements of American culture while bolstering authentic American vulgarity. The sociologists and social philosophers of the 1920s and 1930s, calling this "assimilation," tried to show how the southern and eastern European Catholic and Jewish immigrants were becoming Americanized by absorbing the cultural patterns of American life—patterns that these sociologists were never able to define.[3] In fact, the immigrants absorbed American culture, and enriched it, by over-affirming the American dream.

The end of immigration in the 1920s halted the process by which American cultural patterns were continuously reinforced by the support of new adherents. For the first time in American history, American culture was left with the problem of supporting itself with the cultural resources of a population born and bred within it. Through all of American history, Europe and its immigrants had provided examples, models, and styles that served as tradition for a society without a history. These infusions provided a succession of accretions that supported life-styles not capable of supporting themselves indigenously. It is quite apparent that without new immigrants after 1924, the older styles of American culture have not been able to support themselves. All the historic forms of American life-styles are on the verge of collapse and, especially between 1950 and 1970, have succumbed to a series of new trends. The evidence for these new trends is suggested by the following:

First, a "cultural revolution" has occurred that makes possible the life of the sophisticated consumer of the arts. The "arts explosion" supported by foundation expenditures now has an economic and fiscal basis for careers, markets, and consumers. Consumption of the arts in their old classic and ultramodern forms has become a basic way of life in suburbia, in middle-class urban developments, and in Iowa, where farmers' wives can now purchase "original" oil paintings directly from Sears, Roebuck. It is clear that artistic cultivation, sophistication, and consumption serve as a new basis for status and life-styles in the broad middle sector. No matter how dependent on the Old World cultural tradition America may continue to be, this is a wholly new development and one that has replaced small-town, middle-class, bourgeoisie Babbittry, not to mention the values upheld by the Protestant church.

Second, for the upper class it appears that a new international society dominated by "international aristocrats" has emerged. This is a class composed of multimillionaire international businessmen, Greek shipping magnates, Latin-American aristocrats, Southeast-Asian politicians, Spanish nobility, world political leaders, movie stars, artistic heroes, models, fashion designers, and party girls. Their style of life became immediately recognizable when it was presented as la dolce vita. The movie by that name emphasized the moral and cultural degeneracy of a style that includes jet travel, leisure, international partying, Swiss boarding schools, swimming off yachts in the Mediterranean, and residences and apartments on several continents.

These life-style themes presented in the cultural explosion and in the behavior of the international upper class have become the models for most other life-styles in the United States. As a result, a new set of styles has emerged, replacing the older forms indigenous to the nineteenth century. The older forms now exist only at the fringes of American life, where exposure to society's central tendencies is weak. The surviving nineteenth-century life-styles still practiced in limited ways include the following.

First, the culture of Appalachia (wherever it may be found, if and when it has not degenerated into a roadside culture of neon lights, pinball machines, juke boxes, and Lolitaism), the Swamp Yankee culture of New England, the marginal dirt-farmer culture of upper Wisconsin and Michigan, ghost mining towns in the Far West, and Tennessee hillbillies—all represent survivors of this unhallowed past. Rural poverty programs, their workers and, their literary spokesmen, rediscovered this America in the 1960s and have helped to bring it into the modern world.

Second, there are pockets of black revivalist culture in the south and in the urban north, but frequently they have been contaminated by black bourgeoisie, cat, or poverty cultures, all of which directly or indirectly reflect the middle class. The civil-rights movement and black nationalism have made major inroads into revivalism. Martin Luther King, Jr, as a Protestant, bible-oriented minister, stood as a symbol that bridged the gap between the older religion of passive hymn-singing-supplication-for-redemption-from-a-white-god and the newer passion for civil disobedience and militant activism associated with black nationalism and separatism. The new secular redemption consists either of an admission into a black version of the American way of life or a re-creation of it under black leadership. These movements will put an end to the historic tradition of black revivalism that was part of a once-dominant American tradition connected to slavery. Black nationalism rejects the idea of admission to white society, but so far has offered no ideal of a life other than that of permanent revolt. The idea of negritude, French-African in origin, is a proposed alternative. To the extent that negritude glorifies the African past, it is acceptable only to a minority of militants, most of whom are young; but it has had revolutionary effects upon both black and white styles of dress and grooming.

Third, an authentic American way of life that parallels black revivalism is the old southern redneck culture of the county courthouse and the cotton-and-tobacco-warehouse town, best symbolized by the Ku Klux Klan. Klan redneck culture emerged out of the southern defeat in the Civil War and has survived and maintained its dignity at the expense of the southern black. It appears that the civil-rights movement, the FBI, and the federal government have put this tradition on the defensive; but under the increased pressures of civil-rights and black-nationalist movements, and federal programs, redneck racism has become increasingly politicized and diffused throughout America. Politicized racism, even under such southern politicians as George Wallace and Lester Maddox, has been fairly weak and largely confined to the south until now.

Fourth, in those small towns of the north that have survived the population declines caused by the industrialization of agriculture since World War II, there still exist innumerable Babbittlike businessmen, conventional and philistine in their tastes and ultra-conservative in their politics.

We have described the type in our book *Small Town in Mass Society (1968)*. Metalious' *Peyton Place* (1956) portrays the direction this style takes when it decides to move.

Fifth, the last major residue of tradition is the older generation of immigrants. Traditional cultures are relished and relived by these immigrants acting within their own age and ethnic groups. Thus it is still possible to find the authentic enactment of Jewish traditions in Brooklyn when a group of old *shtetl* cronies meet for a social or ritual evening. To some extent, a different form of *shtetl* culture was propagated by the influx of Hasidic Jews from Poland and Hungary after World War II. As described by Solomon Poll in his book *The Hasidic Community of Williamsburg* (1962), these Jews settled in Brooklyn and in other outlying areas of metropolitan New York City and contributed a new dimension to immigrant culture, at times to the embarrassment of more acculturated Jewish groups. Postwar Puerto-Rican and Latin American groups tended to repeat the pattern in which village and church organizations provided the forms for "old-country" culture and mutual aid in conflict with the attractiveness of their new surroundings. In a manner almost parallel to the description of the Polish peasant given by W. I. Thomas and Florian Znaniecki (1927), these organizations fight to retain their hold over their members in the face of the homogenizing process of American life. Older immigrant groups such as the Slovenes retain their organizations, and when they meet at an annual lodge picnic will act more like Slovenes than "Americans." But the ethnic cultures of the older immigrants exist side by side with the mass consumption of television. In old age, after a lifetime of "hard work and struggle," the immigrant wishes to indulge and enjoy himself, and does so by allowing himself to be embraced by mass culture. The older immigrant exists culturally between a Lawrence Welk–Art Linkletter–Peyton Place syndrome and selected styles and tastes reminiscent of his European past. With the passing of this last generation of foreign-born Americans, many connections to European peasant, ghetto, and rural-poor culture will end.

Needless to say, there remain some groups—the children and grandchildren of immigrants—who have not completely "made it" out of their ethnic cultures and who are not secure in their Americanism. These groups eagerly embrace the visible and obvious symbols of Americanism: they are attentive to mass culture and ardent in their purchase of consumer durables such as automobiles, homes, televisions, and stereos. They voice a strident overaffirmation of Americanism as they see it, patriotism, and a virulent opposition to those who have not yet "made it"—the blacks and the Spanish—and toward those who have but do not appreciate it, namely white, middle-class college youths.

CAUSES FOR THE DISAPPEARANCE OF OLDER LIFE-STYLES

How can we account for the disappearance of the dominant forms of culture and life-styles of the late nineteenth and early twentieth centuries? Four factors seem to be at work.

First, one factor, already noted, was the stopping of immigration in 1924, which ended the mass cultural transfusions off which American culture had been living for more than a hundred years. The culture of the immigrant has always been at odds with that of the dominant society, and it has always been defensive. Because their cultural tradition was defensive, the American-born children of immigrants disidentified with their parents and their immigrant past, which was the process of Americanization. But before 1924 the process was never completely successful. As long as there were continuous waves of new immigrants, acculturation could never be complete. After 1924, however, the psychology of second-generation disidentification proved to be the decisive factor in the break with earlier immigrant cultures.

Second, up to the end of World War II rural American culture, partly immigrant itself, was in a situation similar to that of the immigrant. The culture of the dominant urban society was not directly accessible to the sons and daughters of rural Americans throughout the years of the rapid contraction of rural society (particularly the years 1890 to 1950), when the cities achieved overwhelming dominance in American life. Like immigrant culture, rural culture was not attractive to its youth. The lure of the big city for rural youth has been endlessly documented. After World War II rural youth left their homes for the blandishments of urban and metropolitan life and identified with an urban culture that they knew only as a stereotype learned from exposure to the mass media. Thus, though they had no clear-cut models of life-styles with which they could identify in advance of migration, rural youth forsook their tradition in spite of all its wholesomeness and Babbittry.

Third, before World War II the crucial factor leading to the decline of traditional upper-class life-styles was the end of the opportunity for making new fortunes. America's great established industrial and fiscal families rationalized the processes of reinvestment, expansion, capital growth, and horizontal and vertical monopoly. By retaining control even while decentralizing through the use of professional managers (whose loyalties they obtained by a liberal sharing of profits), the great wealth-holders of the late nineteenth and early twentieth centuries became stabilized. This meant that the second, third, and fourth generations of the stabilized wealthy families became accustomed to their wealth, did not have to spend all their time making money, had time to develop new tastes, and, finally, became conscious of the vulgarity of their rubber-baron ancestors and parents. These wealthy descendants began to seek social and civic respectability, following the usual processes of cleaning money by techniques such as commissioning biographers or historians to etch new portraits that transformed robber barons into industrial statesmen, burying old scandals, gaining college educations at prestigious institutions, establishing universities and colleges, collecting art, setting up philanthropies under the family name, and holding dignified cotillion and debutante ceremonies. They linked themselves through marriage to the European nobility and the earlier respectable, but declining, landed wealth. Newport, Arlington County, Beacon Hill, Upper Park Avenue, Grosse Point, Lake Placid, and similar places have been centers for their activities.

In an effort to find alternative points of identification, later generations continued and intensified the practice of importing models of conduct based upon those of European nobility (the old saga of the American heiress and the Italian duke). While this was an established American upper-class practice, after World War I it took a different form. This was exactly the time when the European nobility had declined and degenerated through the loss of its functions, a process brought about by the democratic or totalitarian movements that replaced remnants of feudal society in England and on the continent. What was then emulated was a style that had no social or economic basis and was, at the time of emulation, inauthentic. But the "aristocratic" model still looked good to newly wealthy Americans. Its slow attrition did not matter, particularly since a new connection had been established between Europe and Hollywood. This link to the Hollywood celebrity added the glamor and excitement of international immorality, a combination that provided a solution for the quest for a meaningful use of economically enforced leisure by the American upper class.

Traditionally, the European nobility have welcomed the infusions of money and support given by American Maecenases, though it should be noted that the Americans have not been unique in patronizing the defunct European nobility. American benefactors have their counterparts in the Orient, the Middle East and, especially, Latin America. Weber, though perhaps not Schumpeter, would have been impressed by the capacity of Europeans to make a highly profitable industry out of their ability simply to act out a style completely lacking an economic, political, or social base. In one of its more obviously commercial forms, this style involved the sale of fake antiques by the titled but impoverished owners of authentic antiques to newly rich and impressed Americans. This process of making capital out of nothing represents the higher artistry of the magician.

Since the development of jet air travel, pursuit of the new international, European-focused upper-class life-style no longer requires residence in any given country. The world becomes the stage for international play, fun, and excitement. Segments of this new class have embraced the new sophistication of the jet-set and discotheque life. They have successively embraced *la dolce vita*, op, pop, camp, the multi-media, drug and counter cultures, and sophisticated Black Panther and white SDS radical movements. This should not be surprising, for historically the upper classes have always produced more than their share of liberated individuals. What is remarkable is the fantastic speed at which these cultural movements have been accepted and abandoned by, among others, upper-class adherents.

Membership in the international set is drawn from all parts of the world. Money, titles, sexual attractiveness, and reputation are the major qualifications for entry. A new upper-class model without a national base has emerged and provides something to emulate in place of the older American upper-class gaudiness and vulgarity.

Fourth, there have been drastic changes in the occupational structure of the Western world, especially in the United States, that have resulted in a new middle class of college-bred administrators, professionals, and managers. The members of this class, emerging especially since World War II and to a large extent based on America's new world position, have achieved a prosperity far beyond their youthful expectations of success. They have experienced a sense of self-esteem in their new positions of responsibility in business, industry, bureaucracy, and academia. But for all its economic success and sense of self-esteem, this class is new to the American scene and lacks an established tradition to fall back upon. It finds itself in the position of having to create a life style that will somehow express its newfound sense of dignity and social self-esteem. At the same time this new life-style has had to organize a leisure created by reduced hours of work. In its quest this class has provided a seminal solution for the problem of defining new life-styles for the rest of American society in the post-World War-II period.

NEW WHITE-COLLAR LIFE-STYLES

In finding themselves inordinately successful and prosperous by their own standards, the members of the higher managerial, administrative, professional, intellectual, and bureaucratic class have been forced to live off a past that did not prepare them for these positions. A large number of the members of this class are descendants of ethnic and rural parents whose cultures they have rejected. Almost all of them are college educated. Though it is difficult to prove, it is likely that their college experience was the source from which their new life-style could be built.

Having rejected its own past, this generation was in a particularly impressionable position with regard to its college experience, so that what it saw and did in college provided it with its first alternative to the rejected ethnic and rural culture. Thus the culture of the American university and the bearers of this culture – the university professors – are of critical importance as models for shaping the new middle-class life-styles.

To the rural and ethnic youth who went to college in the 1930s and 1940s, college culture and the professorial life-style appeared to be the epitome of refinement, sophistication, and gentility. The generation of GI-Bill World War II veterans who went to college from 1945 to 1952 was the largest contingent to be so exposed and impressed. In their experience, campus life involved the use of literature, art, music, theater, and museums as major supports to leisure. These patterns, once seen, became a reservoir of life-style models that the college graduate could take with him when he entered the occupational world, especially during the 1950s when he moved to the suburbs and embraced a way of life for which he had no role models.

Under the stress of having to adopt new leisure models for which his family background left him unprepared, the new suburbanite, and especially his wife, could revert to these college-diffused but skin-deep patterns of cultivated, genteel leisure. Since most of the new suburbanites' neighbors were in the same position, each helped the other in affirming the new suburban patterns, and all were provided encouragement, direction, and assistance by women's, household, and gardening magazines and Sunday supplements.

In all of this the university professor has played a special role. As the bearer of a genteel campus culture, he had the advantage that his interest in art, literature, poetry, music, and drama was part of his professional qualifications for office. It was not that he was cultured per se but that cultural dissemination was his job, and he had an almost exclusive monopoly on conventional culture. The bearers of this campus culture at that time, in the 1920s, 1930s and 1940s, though including some intellectual refugees from Europe, were mainly white, Anglo-Saxon Protestants. And almost every campus had at least one tweedy, pipe-smoking, casual, unhurried, unbusinesslike "eastern" professor who had, if not a family tie, at least a school tie to "eastern culture." Through the image of eastern culture a model of upper-middle-class, cultivated gentility was broadly diffused to several generations of aspiring second-generation ethnic and rural immigrants. For these latter groups, which later became the suburban middle class, the campus experience left an indelible impression that was later reinvoked in the suburban setting. It is for this reason that the upper-middle-class suburb resembles, especially on weekends, a campuslike setting.

After World War II the American university entered a phase of large-scale expansion that required the recruitment of new staff from the ranks of educated second-generation ethnic and rural immigrants. These immigrant sons formed a new stratum of university officials and professors, and in their new roles on the campus adopted a life-style reminiscent of the one they had only observed earlier. In the 1950s and 1960s their enactment of the style validated their own mobility. They were also able to impress the style on their less-cultivated students, who were now exposing themselves to the process of acquiring middle-class gentility.

The university now became the major center for the production of culture and for setting new styles of cultural consumption and leisure. Poets in residence, sports celebrities, writers' conferences, foundation-supported theaters, encounter groups, businessmen's retreats, and avant-garde anti-culture became part of the campus cultural scene. Today the university has a major function in supporting the life-style patterns of a newly ascendant middle class and its youth.

While the campus became a major source of cultural consumption and leisure models, it has not been the only one. Paralleling developments in the university, European and English literature presented a model of upper-middle-class life that was sophisticated, casual, carefree, bland, and slightly immoral. This too was a way of life of genteel cultural consumption. As described by Noel Coward, Evelyn Waugh, and many others, the inhabitants of this world seemed never to work at jobs, taking endless delight in pursuing a lightheaded existence of interpersonal repartee and pleasure based on a moral code that bore no relationship to Babbittry and its Protestant morality.

Later, as it developed, television and its commercial advertisements presented still another variation of "fun" morality. Cigarette ads specialized in romantic scenes in sporting environments—menthol cigarettes and canoes in cool water, suggestively romantic scenes of single women in sports cars at carefree sandy beaches—in all a highly active, social, fun-loving, expensive, smiling, sporty, physically fit, sweet-smelling, and romantic way of life, with no suggestion of seriousness. This model was fabricated by the exurbanite copywriter and TV producer and was in fact a portrayal of their own idealized self-image projected onto a public seeking consumption styles and life patterns to organize their own leisure.

As the cultural revolution moved on, TV and TV commercials found it harder to stay ahead of the trends. Commercials flirted with the new pornography, go-go girls, the sexually liberated woman (Virginia Slims cigarettes), op and psychedelic artwork, camp cartoons, and soul. Television programs have mirrored for their audiences all of the problems of inadequate parents and revolutionary youth, but television producers have found it difficult to develop either moral or ethical criteria for the resolution of these problems. They would like to identify with both youth and parents, radicals and conservatives; but value conflicts run deeply, and television declines to offend. Continuous compromise leaves all issues unresolved.

The themes developed between the late 1930s and the early 1950s on campus, in literary portrayals, and by mass media were the basic raw materials out of which post-World War-II middle-class and suburban life-styles were constructed. If these styles or segments of them had been thoroughly and fully absorbed, they might have provided a basis for an authentic way of life. By authentic we mean no more than an unselfconscious acceptance of one's way of life. Its validation would rest in its self-confident acceptance. But this did not happen. Perhaps the creation of new models had occurred so rapidly that the individuals who seek these styles cannot absorb them in one generation; or perhaps the speed of middle-class success and mobility since World War II offered too many opportunities to don and discard a succession of ways of life. As a result, each *stage* in the life-cycle of the new middle class has posed the problem: how shall I live?

Above all, the emphasis has been upon consciousness of choice. But this consciousness itself reveals the fact that the individual has no past to which he cares to refer as a guide for conduct in his new status. Instead he looks around to see what others are doing, just as others are watching him. Since the new middle class has nothing of its own upon which to draw, models are ultimately absorbed from the other major sources we have mentioned. The result of all this is that the individual emulator is uncomfortable. There is always a slight self-conscious defensiveness in his attitude about himself. He tries to play down his success if it exceeds that of his neighbors. He may retain an interior decorator to style his home and then apologetically mock himself for the luxury of his tastes, acting as if he were detached stranger in his own home. Or, again, he may complain of his children's high styles of taste and their expense, comparing their charmed life with his struggle for success, at the same time taking pride when possible in youth's ability to openly and blatantly enjoy itself in a self-satisfied upper-middle-class style. No wonder Fieffer and Spectorsky, the satirists of this class, are embraced by its members. And no wonder a good deal of humor within such circles consists of self-satire, self-mockery, and invidious comparisons of those who have not sufficiently absorbed the canons of taste appropriate to a given income and life stage, and those whose income is not adequate to maintain an idealized life-style. At such psychological points there is an awareness of the self-conscious manner of the life-style. But this awareness is also an affirmation of the style, because no alternative is available to the individual. In this sense the upper-middle class is in the same psychological situation as Finestone's cats.

PROSPECTS FOR STABILITY IN LIFE-STYLES

It is theoretically possible to imagine that with the passage of time, over a period of several generations, the life-styles from cat to swinger currently evolving may become so accepted that the irony and self-consciousness associated with them will disappear. With time they could become traditional and assume a measure of dignity. While this is conceivable, there are several limitations and restrictions on this process in the United States.

Each new recruit or group (if one sees the process as involving a progression of ethnic and other ascendant groups) entering these forms of status competition tends to absorb the current styles of prestige and competition at a higher and more perfected level than the older and more established groups they are emulating. Thus the Irish upper class has gone beyond the upper-crust Episcopalians and Presbyterians in their acting out of upper-class styles: the Kennedys would be a perfect example. Upper-class Jews, in their efforts to catch up, have exceeded Episcopalian codes of sedateness, social ritual, and dignified public service. On another upper-class level, shipping merchants, opera stars, and cinema celebrities have gone far beyond the upper class in exhibiting upper-class styles of degeneracy and immorality. In upper-middle-class suburbia it is a common joke that the nouveau riche Jewish lady collects New England antiques, wash basins, pine bureaus, and other objects for which she is practically the only market. Yet another example is the university professor who was a Methodist or Baptist, but now, trying to perfect the campus life-style, joins a middle-class Episcopalian church, thereby creating a new Episcopalian manner in the community. Because the emulator is not fully cognizant of what it is he is emulating, he frequently caricatures his models and in so doing creates a new style. But the drama of emulation also affects the emulated, who views with anxiety the too-perfect competition of the emulator. Thus both the emulated and the emulator add new dimensions to existing life-styles. So long as there is mobility, which creates such needs for emulation, it will be difficult to stabilize life-styles and give them the legitimacy of tradition.

A second source of strain derives from within the family structure of the mobile middle classes. Children, particularly in the middle class, easily perceive their parents' mobility patterns because each change of income and each change of residence associated with it call forth demands from parents to behave in new ways more appropriate to their new status level. The parental lecture goes something like this: "This is not Madison [or Brooklyn], it is Concord [or Babylon] and that sort of thing isn't done here." These children are victims of their parents' aspirations for their children to be more successful than themselves in conforming to the new life-styles. They pressure their children to exhibit the preferred life-styles more perfectly than the parents themselves have been able to. John Seeley, Alexander Sim, and Elizabeth Loosely, in their study *Crestwood Heights* (1956), describe the parental anxieties that are expressed in excessive demands on their children for artistic, social, intellectual, or other such performances. When performance falls short, there is ready recourse to reading specialists, tutoring, and psychiatrists. Eric Erikson, in *Childhood and Society* (1950), has not noted this phenomenon in his examination of the early life stages, but we would argue that it is a major factor in shaping the consciousness of middle-class youth to an awareness of the fictions upon which their lives rest. Thus these children are even more aware than their parents of the artificiality, superficiality, and inauthenticity of their parents' and their own way of life.

One result, for at least some middle-class youth, is to resent what they regard as the hypocrisy of their parents and, if their parents insist upon imposing their styles, to seek alternative styles of their own, a search that is supported by elderly radical youth leaders, disc jockeys, psychedelic religious leaders, campus radical professors, exponents of new pop and op, multimedia communications, and perpetually youthful senators, mayors, and governors. Thus the children's resentment may lead directly to middle-class juvenile delinquency or to other forms of rebellion against gentility. In carrying out their rebellion, middle-class youth adopt life-styles that are beat, existentially honest or hippy, politically radical, anti-mobility-minded, rebellious against the bureaucratic world as they experience it in the universities and, finally, emulative of the cat, who in turn is a grotesque emulation of the life-styles of the parents of middle class youth.

It is perhaps too soon to ascertain the outcome of this intergenerational process since the proportion of youth who rebel as opposed to those who choose the parental life-styles are not yet known. And more important, it is not known to what extent such rebellion actually results in the creation of new life-styles. There is always the possibility that the rebellious styles are merely passing stages in the process of socialization to the middle class way of life, as illustrated by the yuppie culture of the 1980s.

Let us assume that there are few alternatives to the newly emerging life-styles whose major themes we have described. If the social pressures in support of these styles take on the forms of a major social movement sanctioned by communications management and supported by the economic and political institutions of the United States, it is possible that these new life-styles will become a permanent part of American culture and that in several generations they may become authentic.

Notes

1. In dealing with "class" and especially the life styles of classes, we are primarily concerned with the distributive behavior of individuals and families who are roughly in the same economic situation. We are not here concerned with behavior that is collectively organized and expressed through such institutions as parties, associations, groups and other collectivities.

2. This is an issue first raised by Edward Sapir in his essay "Culture, Genuine and Spurious," *American Journal of Sociology* vol. XXIX (1924), pp. 401–29, and continued by Melvin Tumin in "Culture, Genuine and Spurious: A Re-evaluation," *American Sociology Review*, vol. X, no. 2 (April 1945). We have dealt with this theme in *Small Town in Mass Society*, chap. 4, "Springdale and the Mass Society" (Princeton University Press, 1958), pp. 80–107 (enlarged 2nd edition, 1968).

3. Some sociologists defined these cultural styles in terms of Anglo-Saxon Protestant and north European criteria. Others developed an image of a "melting pot," which by its very nature was not definable.

References

Erikson, Eric (1950) *Childhood and Society* (New York: W. W. Norton).

Finestone, Harold (1957) "Cats Kicks and Color," *Social Problems*, vol. V, no. 1, p. 3–13.

Keats, John C. (1957) *The Crack in the Picture Window* (Boston: Houghton Miflin).

Metalious, Grace (1956) *Peyton Place* (Austin, Texas: S & S Press).

Myers, Gustavus (1937) *History of the Great American Fortunes* (New York: The Modern Library).

Poll, Solomon (1962) *The Hasidic Community of Williamsburg* (New York: Schocken Books).

Seeley, John, R., Alexander Sim and Elizabeth Loosely (1956) *Crestwood Heights: A Study of the Culture of Suburban Life* (New York: Basic Books).

Spectorsky, A. C. (1955) *The Exurbanites* (Philadelphia: Lippincott).

Stein, Maurice (1960) *The Eclipse of Community: An Interpretation of American Studies* (Princeton University Press).

Thomas, W. I. and F. Znaniecki (1927) *The Polish Peasant in Europe and America* (New York: Knopf).

Veblen, Thorstein (1953) *The Theory of the Leisure Class: An Economic Study of Social Institutions* (New York: Mentor Books).

Vidich, Arthur J. and Joseph Bensman (1968) *Small Town in Mass Society: Class, Politics and Religion in a Rural Community* (Princeton University Press, rev. edn).

Part IV

The New Class System in the United States: Life-Styles and Political Orientations

13 The New Class System and its Life-Styles*

Joseph Bensman and Arthur J. Vidich

If one took the characteristic life-styles now visible in American society and assumed that they were to become the basis for forming the future life-style traditions of the different classes, what would the American class structure look like? Of course, classes do not simply disappear. Even with changes in their economic basis classes remain, though their psychology may be drastically altered. The same is true of life-styles. New life-styles may replace older ones even while the economic basis of both styles remains the same. More likely, however, new life-styles will not completely replace old ones, but will simply become accretions on them. Any innovations in life-styles thus increase the complexity of the class system because older classes and styles coexist with the new ones. Recognizing this, we can foresee not only new classes and styles but also a wide range of different life-styles within each stratum.

THE UPPER CLASSES

The upper classes include the older industrial aristocrats whose wealth was accumulated after the Civil War and sustained up to the depression of the 1930s. The investments of this class were in banking, chemicals, railroads, steel, shipping, petroleum, and automobiles. Some of the familiar names are du Pont, Whitney, Adams, Harriman, Eaton, Rockefeller, Mellon, Duke, Pew, Manville, and Ford. These "groups" have survived a number of economic cycles over a

---

* Reprinted from Joseph Bensman and Arthur J. Vidich, *The New American Society* (Chicago: Quadrangle Books, 1971).

variety of industrial phases and have remained at the top. Now that they are stable in their economic positions, they can afford a certain amount of patrician restraint and *noblesse oblige*. In both business and philanthropic activities they have sufficient confidence in their own social and economic positions to be able to allow paid professionals to manage their wealth. E. Digby Baltzell (1958) has been the major sociological chronicler of their mentality and life-style, and the historian Gabriel Kolko (1962) has most carefully analyzed the mechanisms by which they have protected and maintained their wealth. In modern times no one has analyzed the administrative and legal structures by which the families making up this group are organized, though Robert Brady, in his book *Business as a System of Power* (1943), suggested how this might be done.

This segment of the upper class has a long and continuing tradition of social intercourse with European nobility, eastern Ivy League schools, and the exclusive New York City social and debutante life. Because both their social and economic activities have an international flavor, upper-class individuals tend to be internationally minded, and they occasionally come in contact with and "use" world-minded intellectuals as spokesmen for projects consistent with worldwide business interests.

Since the 1920s new sets of investment opportunities have accounted for additions to this upper class. These opportunities include Texas oil, space industries, electronics, communications, real estate, air transport, and the entire industrial expansion of the West. Names like Hunt, Murchison, Getty, Hughes, Giovanini, Kaiser, and Kennedy are most closely associated with these opportunities. The older industrial aristocracy regards these groups as *nouveau riche* and for this reason the newer wealth has not been admitted into this class nor has it accepted the patrician style. In being excluded the new groups have tried to invent their own styles, which include massive purchases of art, establishing universities and other monuments, subsidizing sons in political and journalistic enterprise, overcompeting in conspicuous philanthropy, and, above all, linking themselves to the international life of the jet and celebrity sets. These styles of living and pleasure go beyond the patrician style. For example, Howard Hughes distinguished himself by his investments in Hollywood starlets (Jane Russell) and Las Vegas real estate, and J. Paul Getty bought an English manorial estate. Grace Kelly married Prince Rainier and upheld a principality, rejuvenated by this transfusion of American beauty, aspiration, and nouveau wealth.

But not all these *nouveaux riches* have been internationally successful. Where this wealth is not internationally minded or not successful enough to become so, it will attempt to join older regional elites from previous periods. In cities like St. Louis, Cleveland, and Milwaukee, post-World-War-II real-estate speculators may hobnob with old German brewery families. Out of such regional elites new national and international elites may emerge, depending upon the future potential of the industrial base off which they live. It is difficult to foresee who from this group will rise to the top, because capital-growth patterns are difficult to predict.

In addition to the older industrial aristocrats and the *nouveaux riches*, there is a type of wealth based on a wholly new kind of economic opportunity in American society. As we have noted before, the federal bureaucracy and the elite managerial class in modern industry are now in a position to command important investment and political decisions. These people have the power to determine the distribution of contracts, and subcontracts, and great expenditures of money. These upper-level bureaucrats and managers, whose positions are based on talent, hold key positions in society and are indispensable to its functioning. It is "natural" that they should receive a disproportionate share of the social wealth. Through processes such as stock options, "kick-backs," "marrying the boss's daughter," "taking over the firm," "salvaging a declining corporation" and so on, the managers can acquire wealth. We have in mind men such as McNamara of Ford, the Defense Department, and the World Bank; Gruenwalt of du Pont, who married the boss's daughter; Litchfield, a professor whose consulting activities gained him control of a corporation and who later became president of a university; Theodore Sorensen, now with a New York law firm; and Leonard Bernstein, Sol Linowitz, Abe Fortas and more recently Steve Ross and Michael R. Milkin. Though these men have not necessarily acquired massive wealth, they have established themselves in positions from which they may build substantial equity. It is difficult to say which of them will accumulate successful "portfolios," but, in the long run, wealth-holding follows the key positions to which they have access.

Insofar as successful bureaucrats and managers aspire to upper-class social status, they are unique in that they constitute a new stratum for recruitment into the upper class. As *potential* recruits, however, they face the problem of whose styles to emulate, and thus they have a choice. The choices available include the styles of the older social aristocracy, the *nouveau riche* style of the oil–electronics–space-industry types, the style of politically ascendant wealthy groups, or that of the socially minded international set. Specific choices will determine specific future fates, and the heir of this generation of successes may or may not emerge at the top, depending on social and fiscal decisions made by the principals during this generation.

Related to the higher managerial and bureaucratic expert is the Ph.D. *nouveau riche*. The former Cal Tech, Columbia, MIT, Harvard, Berkeley, or Chicago academic or scientist–technician turned entrepreneur is a special case of a single idea related to space, electronics, data-control systems, or atomic energy being used to inaugurate an industry. These Ph.D. technicians add a wholly new dimension to potential upper-class life-styles. Because their major life experience was in the university, they have an intellectual and literary bent which historically has not been characteristic of the American upper class. While Ph.D. technicians are bookish and literary, they can also follow the stock market with mathematical precision. They have a talent which is highly remunerative, so they are appreciated even by old-style, upper-class business vulgarians. To the extent that they are admired by their economic superiors, they may be both accepted and emulated by them. Where that is the case, they may influence the future conventions of upper-class life-styles.

All these groups—based on old wealth, massive wealth, vulgar wealth, intellectual wealth, and managerial–bureaucratic wealth—are joined by the international class of movie

stars, sports heroes, artistic heroes, space heroes, and drama-
tized political heroes who through personal effort, skill, and
talent have distinguished themselves in a special line of human
endeavor. They are recognized because they are active, ex-
citing, and proficient. Personal, physical, intellectual, or
technical performance is impressive especially to old-line *rentier*
wealth, which, because it has never been asked to do anything (after the first and second moneymaking generations),
is overly impressed by any achievement. This provides the
link between the old-line wealth and the celebrity.

It seems likely that two dominant themes will be added
to the styles of the traditional American upper class. One is
the expansiveness of the Texas tycoon, whether oil businessman or political manipulator: in either case he steps out in
a big way unselfconsciously, confident that his manner will
produce results because it had done so in the past in Texas.
The gall of the Texan will continue to help shape in the
future, as it has in the past, the leadership style of the United
States on the world scene.

The other theme is provided by the Ph.D. intellectual–
entrepreneur of space, science, and data-processing, who in
his narrow instrumental rationality thinks of himself as an
educated man. He is literate, reads and writes books, and
thinks the problems of the world can be solved by his methods
without knowing that once upon a time St. Simon, Comte
and Marx had similar visions. In the meantime, he has brought
intellectuality to the life-style of the American upper classes.
The new technically-based industries and Washington, with
its big federal budgets, provide the basis for this emergent
class. In its major outlines this class parallels emergent
managerial, technical, and bureaucratic upper-class patterns
that appear to be characteristic of modern Russia.

A major innovation in the United States, though not in
Europe, has appeared among both new members of
the upper class and the scions of the older upper class. This
is upper-class radicalism. Not only is it appropriate for the
upper class to engage in the degenerate sexuality described
by Robert Graves in his Claudian novels, by Choderlos de
Laclos in *Les Liaisons Dangereuses* and by Federico Fellini in
"La Dolce Vita" but also in the use of drugs, as illustrated
in De Quincey's *Anatomy of Melancholia*. Various forms of

gambling and alcoholism are not new to the upper class, but "radical chic" in politics is. It involves an identification with the political movements of the lowest classes through social affairs which become prestigious events designed to raise political funds for the downtrodden, the oppressed, and revolutionaries. To be sure, not all of this new politics comes from the old upper classes. Increasingly it is a means by which artistic social climbers demonstrate their liberalism, their modness—not madness—and their in-ness. Frequently they are so "in" that they are ahead of all others who by definition must be out. Of course, "radical politics," whether it represents new or old wealth, provides an ideology for personal liberation beyond politics. It may be sexual, personal, or cultural. It seeks to escape from the bonds of classes, but is usually enacted in the form of a class-based arrogance which justifies itself in the right of the individual to such stylized behavior.[1] The best description of this in European society is in Dostoevsky's *The Possessed* or Turgenev's *Fathers and Sons.* Such behavior can be found in the old upper class in all societies, and at times in new classes where the acquisition of wealth is so great in a short time that the group has not had time to learn to be degenerate in more sophisticated ways.

The new "radical chic" includes, then, the sons and daughters of America's wealthiest families, some of whom financed the Students for a Democratic Society (SDS), the Weathermen, and the Columbia and Harvard riots. It also includes radical "think tanks" and journalistic ventures which have had the misfortune of being economically successful, though it is hard to determine whether this was an intention or a result. As the new upper-class political style emerges, it becomes apparent that the new styles can be profitable and appropriate to all classes. One of the great virtues of commercial capitalism is that its market mentality and its permissiveness permit profit-making from all forms of self-destruction, whether political, narcotic, or alcoholic. Herbert Marcuse argued that the promiscuity of such permissiveness is actually a permissive repression. We would disagree, arguing that such permissiveness represents the destruction of the older repressive culture and is really the new culture.

THE UPPER-MIDDLE CLASS

The upper-middle class historically has been the responsible backbone of the community because of its civic participation and its support of cultural affairs. All large and medium-sized cities can point to the older and distinguished residential suburbs (Westchester, Shaker Heights, West Hartford, The Main Line, Brookline, Scarsdale, Harrison, The North Shore) which date to the 1920s and earlier. In some cities this upper-middle class may be regarded as the upper crust, but this is true only from a local perspective. When this local upper crust in compared with the national and international upper class, it is clearly only an urban and regional upper-middle class with an economic base in upper-middle management—proprietors and executives in retailing and distribution, the more successful of the fee professionals, and so on. Since the Second World War, however, this older upper-middle class has been joined by newcomers who have deviated from the older suburban style. The new segments of the upper-middle class located in the greatly expanded suburbia and exurbia have added new dimensions to upper-middle-class life-styles.

In the more sophisticated and advanced regional, suburban, and university centers, upper-class styles have penetrated the class system. With the development of mass media and mass communications, patterns of emulation have been diffused culturally and geographically throughout the society. The density of the new culture is determined by previous class position, social and cultural mobility and sensitivity, and access to the mass media. Radical chic now an emerging style, will compete with and be partially absorbed by the following styles, some of which are themselves relatively new and unstabilized.

First, the style of the country gentleman includes the image of the serious-minded sportsman or the nautical devotee, or some combination of these. During leisure hours the advocate of this style retreats into his chosen pleasure and invests substantial portions of his earnings to maintain it. The country gentleman emphasizes the estate-like quality of his residence with elaborate gardens, swimming pools, and other yard facilities. The nautical gentleman builds his life around a boat, nautical dress styles, and involvement in cup races. This sporting life is combined with fashionable, elaborate entertainment and membership in country or golf clubs which incorporate all members of the family into their activities. This outdoor, healthy, casual, and sophisticated approach carries with it only a minimum emphasis on culture, urban sophistication, and avant-gardism. Fresh air and sun are preferred to books and intellectually taxing activities, and so these groups are less likely to orient themselves toward the city in their recreational patterns.

Second, the style of the culture-vulture intellectual, as opposed to that of the country gentleman, emphasizes cultural consumption and quasi-avant-garde cultural sophistication. Books, talk, theater, music and museum-going are standard fare. This group has been in the vanguard of the cultural revolution in recent times. It has embraced the avant-garde arts, the emphasis on movies as an art form, the theater of the absurd, multimedia experiments, new forms of music, pop and op art, and the new pornography. The publishing industry, book and record clubs, music groups. Broadway and off-Broadway theater, and dance have all depended on the cultural demand created by this segment of the upper-middle class. Authentic cultural producers frequently resent this group because they have destroyed the exclusivity of the arts. This group lives in suburbs but are close to the city, in luxury apartments bordering the city; or in the city itself, in upper-middle-class apartments if the children have gone to college or have not yet been born. Here we find studied bohemianism and the cocktail-party circuit attended by artists or intellectuals in temporary captivity. Among this group are many people who, though they graduated from the university, have psychologically never left it. A high percentage of them, especially around the larger cities, are Jews.

Third the cultured academic may not be a professor, but he aspires to be both cultural and gentlemanly in a pastoral environment that finds the university setting to be the ideal place of residence. Thus businessmen, upper-level managers, and professionals have chosen to live in the vicinity of places like Cambridge, MIT, Princeton, Ann Arbor, UCLA, Berkeley, and almost any other major university environment. Princeton, New Jersey is populated by upper-echelon Wall

Street professionals who own reconstructed early-model luxury cars, attempt to participate in university-connected cultural events, maintain old school ties, and, in general, tone down their affluence in order to leave the impression of established, secure, genteel solidity. The Ph.D. nouveau riche contributes substantially to this style, for it offers a convenient compromise between an intellectual past and newly acquired economic success.

Fourth, the fun-lover specializes in active social participation—sports, indoor and outdoor parties, dancing, discotheque, world travel, hunting safaris, flying, and skiing. This group in its focus on "fun" most obviously models itself on the jet set and is primarily concerned with movement, gaiety, and remaining eternally young. Though it may occasionally evidence a mild interest in culture, it does not take culture seriously because it does not wish to sit in any one place for too long.

A special, primarily occupational variant of this active group are the young men who specialize in being on the move and who convey the impression of being "in"—influential in science, technology and administration. The type is exemplified in the world-traveling junior executive, the dashing astronaut, or the youthful college president. They appear to be in a hurry to get somewhere to solve some complex problem which is partially secret and very important, and their manner is always slightly boastful. Although they are likely to be quite a distance from the men at the very top, their life consists in advancing their contacts. Occasionally the right contact may pay off. These men, who are highly elastic to opportunity, represent the middle ranks of government and large-scale business.

Lastly there is the old-upper-middle-class vulgarian who believes in conspicuous consumption. In the postwar period he is unable to crystallize a pattern of consumption because there is no single style he can understand. For the most part these are people who own their own businesses and who, not without diligence and hard work, have risen far beyond their expectations. They are ready to enjoy the benefits of their business success, but lack both a model to imitate and the sophistication to create their own style. They are left holding a bundle of money, without knowing exactly what to do with it. Thus the plethora of Thunderbirds Cadillacs and Lincolns among middle-aged and older Iowa farmers, merchants and small-town bankers, who, also in the winter months take a two-week Caribbean cruise. The urban businessman in construction, retailing, or insurance, who invests in conspicuous consumption, is another example. For the most part, the necessity for hard work isolates this group from the life-styles that would validate their small business successes.

THE LOWER-MIDDLE CLASS

The lower-middle class follows the themes indicated for the upper-middle class, but it does so from a different historical base. Going to church, taking pride in property, being neat and orderly, and showing a capacity for moral indignation against corruption are the chief elements of the lower-middle-class legacy. These traditional lower-middle-class virtues are in conflict with modern upper-middle-class and university-bred sophistication, and are declining under the pressure of the new patterns.

This conflict in class values can be seen clearly in the older lower-middle-class and middle-class religious groups, for example, the Baptists, Methodists, Congregationalists, and the Church of the Latter Day Saints. The older generation which has lived through the moral epoch and into the modern epoch still wishes to uphold the older, bible-loving Christian virtues. Yet in their older age and retirement they also wish to loosen up a bit and enjoy themselves—so perhaps some drinking may be condoned, and perhaps even a trip to a wicked place like Las Vegas, a night on the town, a sexy movie, or a lascivious thought. The older moralists have relaxed their morality on the grounds of a deserved self-indulgence.

But they differ from the upper-middle classes because they have not yet absorbed the newer life-styles. This lack of acceptance of the new tone of the classes above them expresses itself in attitudes of resentment and moral indignation against the immorality of society. The older moralists point to the political and economic corruption of establishment leaders and to the degeneracy of the international celebrity set.

Though they may still be actively religious in the old sense and, in their view, pursuing the way of Jesus, their moral indignation has largely been secularized. Now it is expressed in political protests and reform movements such as pro-Americanism or antipornography, or organizations espousing such virtues as integrity, honesty, public service, citizenship and opposition to corruption. Their resentments focus upon Blacks and college radicals, whom they believe to be not only lacking in traditional American virtues but expect to be rewarded for these vices. This group was once called the silent majority; it includes some southern Baptists, who are at once exponents of the old virtues and examples of the fall from grace into secular corruption. No doubt this is one of the reasons why they played their roles as anti-heroes so successfully. The combination of middle-class fraud and Puritan righteous indignation is, of course, one of the basic elements of the American tradition.

The younger generation in the lower-middle-class presents a different problem. Although those in small towns and medium-sized cities may have been exposed to the morality and religiosity of their parents, they have been more thoroughly exposed to upper-middle-class patterns in youth magazines, television, and the cinema. Unlike their parents, this group will have had direct exposure to the new sophistication at the state university or city college, which is their instrument of mobility. The conflicts expressed by these youth are different from those of their parents.

The residues of virtue and morality they carry with them are at odds with the secular world they live in. Their parents, in their view, have submitted to the system and show no concern for the world. The children point to flaws and weaknesses at all levels of society and see bureaucracy robbing them of their freedom and dignity. Like that of their parents, their moral indignation has been secularized, but in their case it is expressed as disgust with their parents, their elders, and with dehumanized bureaucracy. At present these youth often express themselves in protest, reform, peace, youth, religious revival, rock-festival revival, existentialist, or radical activities to save the world. If they are not liberated, they may join the hard-hats and express their resentment by attacking those who have succeeded in "liberating" themselves. In the lives of these young people, "liberation" can produce total reversals and inversions of social character in short periods of time.

For the youth of the lower-middle class, especially those who go to college, the culturally stylized life of the upper-middle class always represents an example if not an option. Their desire to go to college is itself an affirmation of a desire to ascend; but going to college delays the real issues of life for four years, and so for these years it is still possible to protest, reject, and remain morally uprighteous. The protest, criticism, and political activities of these youth are alternatives to the styles of life and morality displayed by the upper-middle class. As these youth end their college careers, get married, have children, acquire mortgages, and hold down jobs, they may be forced to shed protest politics, civil rights and reform movements. It would appear that the protests of these youth groups represent the last measure of rebellion against their own cooptation into the upper-middle class. Much of politics on the campus, then, is not politics in the usual sense at all, but only a expression for or against cooptation into the affluent middle class.

To carry the point one step further, once coopted the issue of cooptation and depoliticization is not wholly resolved. The education of the middle class often leads to unexpected success within the establishment. The larges of the corporate, publishing, and banking worlds as well as of universities and philanthropic institutions may lead to impressive incomes which the individual may find reprehensible in terms of his earlier rebellion. He must find a way to live with both his older radical idealism and his new success.

The resolution of this problem seems to lie in the pursuit of culture in such a way that radical ideals can be expressed without threatening the job. Thus a substantial radical political literature exists and a great number of morally, religiously, and sexually irreverent books and periodicals are published. Radical idealism and politics easily become intellectualized. Politics can become a cultural activity, like listening to fine music or the various varieties of hard rock. In this way political intellectualism and cultural aspiration operate in the same direction. Culture becomes the opiate of the aspiring educated classes.

THE WORKING CLASSES

The working classes are in the most difficult position of all in American society. They do not have access to a university education, nor do they receive any training in the higher cultural forms. They are therefore cut off from the mainstream of the new culture. When they are exposed to the new culture it is primarily through the mass media or casual personal contacts. Thus they are not able to emulate the new styles accurately, and when they try, their efforts result in caricatures. Only in small communities and in rural areas are members of the working classes coopted into middle-class activities. In those marginal areas the working classes may exhibit some of the middle-class styles, but this is only at the small-town level. For the most part the working-class style always falls short of providing an independent basis for a working-class life-style. Some authors have talked about a working-class or lower-class subculture as if it were independent from the rest of society and its classes. These authors have failed to notice that the poverty of lower-class culture is a result of its failure to be sufficiently emulative *because* it is outside the mainstream of society, and not because it has created something on its own.

To the extent that the working classes are aware of new life-styles of which they are not a part, they are desperately conscious of their personal educational disadvantages. They resent the educated unless they are their own children. They become aware of the error of not having finished high school or of not having gone to college. Thousands of degree-giving institutes, including adult and evening education courses in universities, cater to this specific desperation.

Their awareness of their own educational deficiencies accentuates their desire to educate their children, some of whom will go to a city college or a state university. Those who are successful will enter the middle class and thus affirm the American dream. The continuous expansion of the higher educational institutions in providing for an avenue of mobility keeps alive the older American equalitarian and success ethic. The working classes, though they are unsuccessful themselves, can feel vindicated if their children get an education.

Life for the working classes is not wholly dismal. They are offered a broad fare of engaging and distracting involvements: the mass media (football, baseball and basketball games, space shots, sit-coms and so on); fishing, hunting, and camping; unlimited home improvements by the do-it-yourself method; and Catholic religiosity, Protestant self-satisfaction, beer and compulsiveness as outlets that allow them to make their compromise with life in an increasingly middle-class world to which they feel they do not belong. They can strive to belong, and even though their children do not go to college, they can get jobs and help in the acquisition of the American symbols of success: automobiles, garden tractors, houses, modern furniture, outboard motors, video equipment, camping trailers, and a million other objects from American industry.

All of this is possible because for skilled and semiskilled white union members, life in America has not been at all bad. America has not suffered a major depression since World War II, and the recessions have been of short duration. Wage raises have remained reasonably in line with the rising cost of living, and there have been opportunities for overtime, moonlighting and jobs for wives and unmarried children. Since most of these opportunities are, for the older generation, greater than they had expected in their depression-bound youth, they have some grounds for satisfaction. The new chances for consumption have given them a stake in American society. As union members they remain loyal insofar as the unions serve as bargaining agents; otherwise they are not much interested in labor's traditional causes. Their stake in society, protected by seniority and virtual job monopolies, makes them hostile to the aspirations of less-favored groups who seek economic and social equality. Organized workers, favored by the relatively benign labor legislation and economic policies of the Kennedy and Johnson administrations, have become increasingly conservative. They have developed vested interests, and resist those below who would challenge their new prosperity and their claims to having made it in America. Some of them become adherents of racist arguments.

THE SUBWORKING CLASSES

Subworking classes are committed to almost nothing except immediate pleasure. The original members of this class (hoboes, tramps, and bums) have been joined by cats, hippies, opouts, copouts, dropouts, surf bums, communards, and other economically marginal groups. Narcotics, alcohol, sex, or some other inarticulate activity short of suicide is used to absorb time, attention, and energy. Oddly, this style is itself an emulation of the jet-set and upper-middle-class fun and immorality ethic which in part derives from a kind of emulation of this same subworking-class style of life. Radical chic culture appears to be the common ground for these two extremes, allowing the upper and lower classes to have fun together *en passant.* Earlier forms of radical chic were the weekend meeting of the Vassar coed and the black "cat", or the NYU Bronx bagel and the Tomcat, who could exploit each other in the name of civil rights. But such relationships can exist only in a make-believe world. The upper-discotheque and Ivy League girl can maintain the fiction (temporarily) much more easily than the cat or other outcast who after the weekend must go on living without a future. Of course, if she wishes, the Ivy League girl (or boy) can also drop out.

The major problem of pursuing such a life-style is the need to accept the total inaccessibility of success as defined in the society at large, and the accompanying feeling of failure. No matter how much contact these subclasses have with the "slumming" coed, the well-intentioned civil-rights worker, the northern white liberal, the Jewish college radical, the well-meaning Protestant minister or Catholic priest, they have almost no way out of their situation. No matter how extensive the poverty programs, this class is stalemated. This is why violence and aggressiveness in such groups are erratic, unpredictable, and imperfectly contained. Violence is always possible, especially when triggered by community-action programs and the emulation of peaceful civil-rights demonstrations.

Protest movements, civil-rights programs, and community action solutions are not simple attempts to deal with this uncontained aggression. Their meaning differs for two different groups of the subworking class.

First, there is the traditional-minded subworking class which depends upon religion and religious ecstasy to provide a controlled release for emotion and resentment. The Southern black and the Harlem store-front minister are prime examples. Historically, since the time of the Romans, Christianity has served this function more efficiently than most have been willing to recognize. Religion in its Protestant variation has accomplished a similar function for the black in America, though lately the Catholics have seen that they too have an audience. Both the Protestant and the Catholic churches now offer themselves as a point of attachment for those members of the subworking class who would like to avoid descending to the very bottom of the social heap.

Yet religion, whether Catholic or Protestant, in its very nature a symbolic activity, is never wholly successful in pacifying the people. Martin Luther King Jr., up to 1966, seems to have swayed the mass with his message of Christian non-violence and to have prevented more civil violence than otherwise would have occurred. His assassination may have removed a major brake on potentially violent civil and political action among both organized and unorganized blacks. But extreme deprivation, provocation, or social contagion can always evoke hostility and aggression as a response to long-term, institutionally-based deprivation. Nowadays among the subworking class, even the religious are not wholly predictable.

Second, the older Christian ethic attempted to justify slavery and to reconcile the slave to his lot. It also justified and reconciled lower-class positions by emphasizing that the social world reflects God's will. The new wrinkle in this ethic is the secular politicizing of the subworking class, particularly urban blacks and Puerto Ricans. These new nationalist and protest groups have begun to accept the implications of direct action. Through movements of black nationalism, riots, urban guerilla warfare, and other forms of group assertion, their actions stand opposed to the religious forms of sublimation that until recently have controlled them.

The major issue for these secularized and politically prodded subworking classes is whether they can develop a leadership with the political skills and abilities to organize and sustain the process of politicization. This remains to be seen.

If the process follows the classic American pattern, responsible black leadership will be coopted as it has been in the past, leaving the masses of blacks to their own devices. At best this means having to produce a continuous succession of new leaders, each of whom after five or ten years of struggle decides he too must think of himself and the needs of his family. All other ethnic groups in the American past have been bought off in this way, so it is not unreasonable to assume that blacks and Puerto Ricans can suffer or enjoy a similar fate. If this happens, the aggressiveness and violence of the subworking-class movement will be turned against itself, with intermittent periods of crisis and disorder, particularly in the cities. On the other hand, if a measure of leadership stability can be achieved, a major new political force will have entered the scene of American politics, and no one can predict what the consequences might be. All in all, these pressures from below offer both creative and destructive possibilities for American society.

LIFE-STYLES IN THE HISTORICAL PROCESS

If the above analysis is correct, it is obvious that throughout American history there has been no life-style capable of sustaining and reinforcing itself from the resources provided by its bearer's children. The great traditional life-styles have been sustained primarily by immigrants from foreign shores, by internal immigrants mainly from rural areas, and by ascendant groups. All of these "immigrants," as strangers who lack confidence in their own past, have emulated upper classes and by so doing have given the emulated style a new vitality until their own children or grandchildren abandoned it. Why has this been so?

Throughout American history, and more recently in Europe as well, the rate of economic and political change has been so great that new patterns have been imposed on whole populations before those populations have had an opportunity to absorb and consolidate older life-styles. An instability of life-style appears in any period of fundamental institutional change, the case of Europe in its emergence from feudalism to capitalism being a prime example: Veblen, in his *Imperial Germany and the Industrial Revolution,* made this a central point in his analysis of Germany and Japan. If the United States, as a world model, fails to stabilize any single set of styles, there will likely be no permanent replacements in Europe and in the underdeveloped world for the traditional life-styles now being forgotten and destroyed.

In much of our analysis there has been little evidence of total innovation in the creation of new life-styles. In almost all cases where there has been some creation, it arises out of imperfect or overperfect emulation. Aspiring classes emulate the stereotyped life-styles of distant and not directly observed groups, and thus introduce the possibility of distortion. Only selected elements of a total life-style are emulated, enhanced, caricatured, and elaborated in the process of stereotyping. In this way meanings are introduced which were only minimally present. For example, the cultural patterns of the English urban middle classes are emphasized and exaggerated by aspirants who emulate that style: selected aspects of the original style take on a quality of completeness and totality they never had. In just this way the culture of the English upper classes has been fractionated into four dimensions of emulation by Americans. As we have described them, these are the gentlemanly style, the search for culture, the fun and immorality theme, and the diversions of the late aristocracy. Each of these dimensions has been the object of emulation by a different group in American society, and each of these groups in turn polarizes the given style and creates a total way of life from it.

When the life-style being emulated is distant, there is also the possibility that only a given historical stage of a life-style may become the object of emulation. Thus an American elite will emulate the life-style of European aristocracies at the exact point when that life-style might collapse if it were not for emulation. Neither group has a basis for its style, except for the fact that the style is validated by emulation. In this mirroring process the parties to the emulation validate each other, where otherwise the style would die.

This same process of emulation, accentuation, and distortion also takes place domestically. In periods of cultural revolution, the amount of distortion in the emulating process is almost unimaginable; but this distortion results in intense innovation and creativity. The rate of change over the last thirty years accounts for what otherwise appear to be discontinuities in cultural traditions and life-styles. It is for this reason that a book like *Catch-22* becomes understandable. For example, lower-class blacks, when attempting to emulate nonblack styles, caricature selective aspects of middle-class culture, both broadening them and investing them with a comic playfulness which in other situations is a "put-on." In so doing they suggest new and unanticipated possibilities for the middle-class fun morality, which in turn is emulated by the very groups who may have been the original source of that emulation. These circulating patterns of emulation add new and unanticipated dimensions to a life-style, revitalize it, and change its characteristics.

The only limit to this ebb and flow of emulation is the social and psychological needs of these groups who do the emulating. These needs, as we have tried to indicate, are based on the collapse of older life-styles and the ability of newer ones to give expression to the changes in the life position of the people involved. In the evolution of society, there would seem to be no end to this process.

Note

1. See Renato Poggioli, *The Theory of the Avant-Garde* (Cambridge, Mass.: Harvard University Press, 1968). Poggioli makes this point with respect to the avant-garde in the arts. Some of his illustrations suggest that by the nineteenth century prestigious modernism includes experimentation with many contemporary forms of drugs: "And from the more or less conscious sense of that relationship there originated among romantic avant-garde artists the illusory hope of being able to attain aesthetic ecstasy, a mystic state of grace, by means of certain physiological and psychological stimulants: opium in the cases of DeQuincey, Coleridge, Novalis, and Nerval; alcohol in the case of Poe; hashish in Baudelaire's case; absinthe in Verlaine's and Rimbaud's—in short, those drugs which give easy access to the 'artificial paradises' found in other heavens than that of art" (pp. 194–195).

To complete the comparisons between classes, we would add that drugs are instrumental to the overworked and underfed lower classes in that they provide a release from pain, especially from hunger. For the upper class, their "pain" is the emptiness of existence; their stylized vices serve to fill such emptiness.

References

Baltzell, E. Digby (1958) *Philadelphia Gentleman: The Making of a National Upper Class* (Glencoe, Ill.: The Free Press).

Brady, Robert (1943) *Business as a System of Power* (New York: Colombia University Press).

Kolko, Gabriel (1962) *Wealth and Power in America* (New York: Frederick A Praeger).

Veblen, Thorstein (1915) *Imperial Germany and the Industrial Revolution* (New York: Macmillan).

14 Liberalism and the New Middle Classes*

Arthur J. Vidich and Joseph Bensman

Almost all dimensions of the middle-class life-style have under-gone revision. In sexual codes, there has been an increasing liberation from the Puritanism of the American Protestant past. In part, this is due to the decline of the ideologically supported image of hell and damnation under the increasing influence of secularism and science; even the last holdouts, the Baptist and Methodist churches, have moderated their earlier positions on sexual codes. Also, one cannot discount the impact of the notion of sexual freedom based upon Freudian psychology and upon cultural relativism, which have exposed several generations to the sexual life of savages and the inner fantasies and secret behavior of prudish Victorians. The idea of sexual liberation and sophistication is also a result, in part, of exposure to European models of sophistication especially as conveyed earlier by the Waughs, Huxley and Noel Coward, and later by French, Italian and Swedish images of *La dolce vita*. Finally, one cannot discount the importance of the simple fact of increased leisure time in permitting greater exploration and development in this area.

Religiously, this new middle class has abandoned all that the Bible-belt once stood for and has transformed the earlier forms of ethnic catholicism into modern forms of American "church-going" and sometimes social action directed by priestly leadership which itself sometimes expresses the new middle-class values by demanding a break with age-old celibacy rules. Fundamentalism is regarded as gauche and all middle-class churches of whatever faith place a high premium on tone, style, architectural sophistication and intellectualized religion.

* Reprinted from Arthur J. Vidich and Joseph Bensman, *Small Town in Mass Society: Class, Power and Religion in a Rural Community*, 2nd edn (Princeton: Princeton University Press, 1968).

Politically the new middle classes are infinitely more liberal than were the middle classes of the pre-1930s. However, these new liberals are not always active in national politics and are interested in local politics in quite special ways. They do not vote according to the older traditional patterns of Republican and Democratic bloc voting at any level—urban, state or regional.

If they are sons of farmers or businessmen in the north and the east, members of these classes are more likely to vote Democrat than did their parents. If they are sons of immigrants who lived in urban Democratic ghettos, they are more likely to vote Republican in the suburbs. If they moved to the far west, there is no predictable pattern between how they vote and how their parents voted. If they are in southern cities, they begin to find it easier to vote Republican.

In short, the new middle classes are developing a perspective of their own that focuses on an interest in a liberal, cultured, sophisticated way of life that is often independent of the traditional identification between voting and position in the economic structure.

The impact of the new classes on politics has made itself felt strongly with respect to political style. The older frontier style of politics involved personal warmth, "cornball" localism, vulgarity, and lowbrow anti-intellectualism. In the past, highly sophisticated, intellectual, cultivated and broadminded political leaders have had to pretend they were rustic boobs in order to retain their popularity with local constituencies. In urban politics, the ethnic politician was forced to retain his accent and his hyphenated Americanism, and he was forced to prove that he had not outgrown his ghetto roots. Neither of these older American styles appeal to the new middle classes.

The new middle classes have become devotees of literate, articulate, cultured, sophisticated and vital "patrician-like" politicians. Representatives of the style most congenial to them are people like Adlai Stevenson, Averell Harriman, John and Robert Kennedy, John Lindsay, Nelson Rockefeller, Eugene McCarthy and Charles Percy. These men are cast not as "lords" of the masses as was the case with F.D.R. but rather as the distillations of new-middle-class aspirations and styles. The middle classes and their particular expectations

have become sufficiently recognizable to call forth a leadership style willing to cater to it. Of course this has not become a dominant style, but rather one that exists in
proportion to the quantitative importance of the middle class.
Recent examples of successful political leaders who show
that the older styles continue to exist along with the newer
one are presidents Johnson, Truman and Eisenhower, and
mayors La Guardia, Wagner and Daley. For the new middle
classes these older styles are regarded as uncouth, crude
and at times vulgar. Thus, for example, much if not most
of the reaction against Johnson in the new middle classes
stemmed from his populist, Texan-frontier, uncultivated style.
By the same token much of his support was based upon the
consonance of his populist style with the personal styles of
his constituencies. Eastern sophisticated middle-class-style
"liberalism," wherever it is expressed in urban America, is at
odds with the older layers of frontier populism in the smaller
towns and in the segments of urban populations which,
though they live in cities, are still populist in mentality. A
large part of politics in the United States is a reflection of
one or the other of these orientations to political styles.
The "educated" middle class would like to conceal its politics of identification with symbols by finding *issues* that express its identification, but just as for the populists, issues
are frequently less important to them than political symbols
that allow them to identify with an image of dignified, educated, reasonableness which is all the more compelling if it
is linked to "Ivy-collegianism."

In local politics, especially in the suburbs, the new middle
classes have been intensely interested in municipal services,
in education and school affairs, in the P.T.A. and, as a sum-
mation of all this, in the school budget. For them the idea
of quality education has had the highest value and they have
shown little respect for traditional tax rates.

In their attitudes of irreverence toward the tax rate, which
in America has been a sacred cow, the new middle classes
have made a major break with the tradition of local politics
in the United States. In middle-class communities the major
and most emotional political issue is the size of the school
budget. This issue is probably the major political issue in
American society insofar as it involves more participation,

more activity and more personal involvement than any other issue, including foreign policy. For the middle classes the school issue is much more important, but because this issue is fought at a local level and because it is a *local* issue for thousands of different and decentralized jurisdictions, it is rarely seen as so central an issue as the more obvious political protests against national policy. Because of its local particularity, the impact on the public consciousness of this issue is hardly perceived. A mass demonstration at the Pentagon has the quality of a national drama, but such dramas occur at infrequent intervals. The new middle classes live with the school issue through the lives of their children and this is a process that commands their attention on a daily and weekly basis. While the new middle classes may be capable of extreme expressions of moral indignation against national political policies, their material commitments are to the education of their children. It is perhaps unfair to reduce middle-class politics to the issue of parental interests in children without offering more demonstrably conclusive evidence. When President Johnson proposed in 1966 that the draft be conducted on a lottery basis, all candidates irrespective of class having an equal chance of being selected, it was the middle classes that appeared to have the greatest objections to this procedure. The issue of the lottery-draft was quietly dropped, but it served as a reminder to the middle classes that their sons have been protected (by attending the university) from the risks of war. When presented with an issue either of education or the draft that affects its children, the middle classes respond not in terms of higher moral values but in terms of self-interest.

In describing these new middle classes as we have above, we have described in somewhat more detail the same middle classes whose emergence in Springdale we recorded in our study, *Small Town in Mass Society* (1968). When we first noticed this class in Springdale, we were not fully aware of what we had encountered though we realized that it was a unique feature of the life of Springdale. Our awareness of what we saw at that time was heightened by the work of other sociologists and social analysts who, in their work, were responding to aspects of the same phenomenon. In the late 1940s and early 1950s a number of different observers responded to the same reality and each saw his discovery in terms of the problem that concerned him.

When we studied Springdale we saw this new middle class in the process of expressing these new life-styles in a small town. At that time this class was unable to impose its "style" on the organizational and political life of the town. The middle class we observed was aggressive and defensive, never sure that it belonged in Springdale but unable to leave it because it had no other place to go. What we saw at that time was the avant-garde of that class, but it was so weak as to be hardly noticeable. However, in retrospect the weakness of that middle class was a simple function of the fact that Springdale was removed from the urban centers of the United States. It rather represented earlier stages of American history which remained viable to the residents of the town because they were more committed to the past than to the future. Springdale represented an earlier stage in American society and was not in the mainstream of American history except for a tiny middle class that had then begun to appear in the town. At that time Springdale had just barely begun to register what was a dominant fact of American life.

THE MIDDLE-CLASS REVOLUTION IN AMERICAN SOCIETY

From our experience in Springdale as it was amplified by the works of other students of the middle class, it became clear that a revolution in American social structure and life-styles had taken place. In comparing our own work with that of Mills, Seeley, Whyte and Riesman, it is clear that the middle-class revolution has occurred at unequal rates in different communities. A community like Springdale at the time we studied it was further removed from the middle-class revolution than other communities like the new suburbs of New York, Cleveland, Milwaukee, St. Louis and so on. The rate of penetration of the new-middle-classes style varies according to place and size of town. With time, the middle-class revolution has spread and penetrated into more and more communities, eventually touching even the most remote hamlets. By now the new middle classes and their styles have been felt in all communities in the country irrespective of size. However, this revolution has not been felt at equal rates and equal levels of intensity in all communities. The differences in rates and intensities account for many of the different types of communities that now exist in the United States. In general terms we would specify four types of communities in which the middle-class revolution has expressed itself.

The Small Rural Town

Springdale at the time we studied it represented a traditional American community in which the middle-class revolution was working itself out. The new middle classes were *not* influential in a political sense, but were influential in their participation in social organizations and in their "way of life" which transmitted new styles to the community. They were in the process of revolutionizing the traditional habits of the town. The more remote a town from the centers of influence, the more removed it will be from the middle-class revolution. No doubt there are communities in *all* parts of the country which still manage to resist the dominance of the new middle-classes' life and intellectual styles. However, it would appear that the small town in the long run will be absorbed into the middle-class culture. Springdale at the time we studied it was already a backwash. Those communities that are still like it now represent the last link in America to the nineteenth century and its values.

The University Town

In those American university towns which do not have industries, the new middle classes are personified by college professors, college administrators and other professionals who are attracted to the town as a place of residence because of the cultural tone given to the town by the university. Frequently the university town is dominated by a middle-class life-style which is an academic variant of the new-middle-class life-style in general. This life-style exhibits an emphasis on cultural consumption of the performing arts as provided by university sponsored music, drama and art shows *and* an active political interest which reveals a parochial and sometimes self-righteous liberalism. In national affairs segments of this group have been leaders in civil rights and peace politics, and other more substantial segments of this same community have been politically involved as experts, consultants and propagandists for the White House and government agencies with respect to foreign, military and domestic policies. In local politics the university middle class has a greater unity of interest which focuses on schools and public services and in its support of these activities has broken from the traditional virtues of parsimony in government and the low-tax ideology characteristic of small businessmen in small communities. These unique features are given a special emphasis to the extent that the university middle classes are self-conscious of their alienation from the ethos of their surrounding region; they stand out and are resented by other segments of the new middle classes. They wear their liberalism as a badge, but they cannot take their way of life for granted.

In some university towns, academicians acting as an interest group have succeeded in gaining control of the machinery of local government. They have done this either directly by taking control of a local party apparatus, by making political alliances with other like-minded groups or by serving as "technical consultants" in solving the specialized problems of government such as municipal finance, assessment policy, zoning and so on. Wherever this shift in political control has occurred, it has had revolutionary effects on the political life of the communities involved, for it has resulted in the defeat of business leaders who traditionally have controlled local government in smaller communities. In larger and medium-sized cities where the university is only one of a number of interest groups, university members have had occasion to make alliances with ethnic and labor leaders and have shared and traded power with them. This has occurred quite frequently in traditionally Republican communities which have now become intermittently Democrat.

The size of the town in which a university is located is the critical factor in determining the capacity of professorial liberalism to place its stamp on the public political life of the community.

The Suburban Community

A similar revolution in middle-class styles has taken place in the suburbs of the great metropolises of America. The people who live in these bedroom communities are the managerial, professional, technical and administrative staffs of the great private and governmental agencies whose offices are located in the central city. In fact the growth of the suburbs and the new middle classes has been proportionate to the growth in size of large-scale enterprises since the end of World War II. Hence, the commuter has become a major factor in American life. Large-scale commuting has also introduced new features into the living styles of the middle classes. For regardless of the respectability they are constrained to demonstrate while at their work site, in their home communities they are "free" to develop life-styles that play on a variety of themes and variations. The local themes around which these life-styles have been built are as follows.

First, the pursuit of socially organized high culture and leisure activities which are focused around a church or temple. Though the activities are not religious in character, the church provides the setting and legitimating tone for forms of sophistication that would have been alien to the ethnic church or to earlier Protestantism.

Second, the organization of life around sports and a social life centered in the country club. Golf, dancing, fishing, tennis, bridge, boating, travel, swimming are organized into a way of life that emphasizes physical fitness, activity, fresh air and sunshine.

Third, the development of refined interests and tastes in cultural activities which are organized in associations, groups, leagues and clubs devoted to the pursuit of art, drama, music and other cultural projects. Activity takes the form of attending concerts, lectures, exhibitions, classes, holding memberships in book and art clubs and participating as performers, artists, promoters, organizers and supporters of the arts.

Fourth, the pursuit of a life of gaiety and wit, modern living and the fun morality. Life is active, informal, sophisticated and broadly tolerant of modern moral and ethical codes. In this group cultural tastes run to folk dancing and singing, the cocktail and costume party and the discothèque.

These styles mix in different ways in different suburbs, but in some cases whole suburbs will be known for a single, predominant style. However, in spite of such differences in emphasis, these communities exhibit characteristic traits. A large amount of formal and informal group activity focuses on the schools, the P.T.A. and class mothers and on debate, discussion, opposition and support of the school budget. Specific issues arise which are part of the school budget: special courses, teacher salary schedules, technical facilities and so on. Local political groups are organized and exist for one school-board election because the issues involved do not parallel any other political issues. After the election such groups disband only to be re-organized frequently along different lines for the next election. During the phase of overt school politics in these communities a substantial portion of the community's attention will be absorbed by the school conflict. Newspaper advertisements are published in support of or opposition to the budget or the bond issue. These are written, financed and published by voluntary committees which also print and distribute handbills, petitions and bulk mailings. Letters to the editor comprise a serious form of public debate. Public meetings, rump caucuses and especially the meetings of the school board are scenes of oral debates, personal animus and expressions of political passions. For short periods of time before and during the election of school-board members and/or the vote on the budget or bond issue, these debates become the central focus of the public life of much of suburbia. Talk continues for a short while after the election. In some cases permanent personal animosities develop which lead to avoidance relationships that are retained for a long time. If a defeat is particularly humiliating, the loser may consider leaving the community. If the issue is particularly intense and lines are sharply drawn, the children in school may be drawn into the conflict and their relationships with teachers and administrators may be affected. If teachers become involved, their involvement can affect their job status in the school. Short of sex, school issues touch most deeply the passions of suburbia.

Second in importance to school-oriented politics are civic

improvement groups which have an interest in reforming and modernizing the community; critical issues include street lighting, sanitation, sidewalk paving, stop signs, safety at intersections, architectural uniformity, preservation of historical monuments, library improvement, zoning and community planning. In more recent times the suburbs have been confronted with the suburbanite black who wishes to join the suburban community. This is a newer issue which has been added to the others and at times has involved as much passion for the whites as the school question.

The groups which make up suburbia react differently to the issues mentioned above. The newer middle classes and the recent arrivals in the suburbs are likely to support all issues aimed at improving the community. They care less about the tax rate and display a willingness to have the best services, the best facilities and a cultured environment. On the other hand, the older groups who lived in the suburbs before the influx of the newer middle classes are more apt to oppose the innovations. For them it may or may not be a question of taxes. If the older residents are locals who lived in what was previously a small town that became a suburb during the expansion since World War II, taxes are likely to be the issue because these older groups do not have urban sources of income; their income is apt to be derived locally, from industry or from small business, and is less apt to reflect recent inflationary trends. If the older residents are suburbanites from an earlier period, for example, prior to World War II, they are apt to be derived from different ethnic stock and are apt to to be more secure and established in their style of life. Their sources of income are not only urban derived but they include some rentiers. In this case taxes are not the issue. The issue is rather one of resenting the newer ethnic and arriviste aspirants whose exuberance and hunger for culture is alien to community tradition. They also resent the boisterousness, the energy and the ceaseless activity of the new arrivals who appear to be pushing their way into organizations and institutions which were regarded as being securely held. The older strata of suburbanites had been accustomed to running the community and resent the new challengers. The new middle classes represent a style that upsets their stable ways of life.

Conflicts such as these are typical of the suburban way of life and its culture. How these conflicts are resolved is not predictable. Some suburbs, for example the working-class suburbs, were created from scratch and do not exhibit these characteristics. Other suburbs are still dominated by the older middle classes and exhibit a quality of stability and tradition that may be the envy of the newer suburbs as well as a model for emulation. These older suburbs can only survive in their accustomed style if their inhabitants sustain their urban sources of income, but inevitably because of age and death they will be replaced by representatives of the newer styles. In some suburbs, the newer middle classes have been completely successful in imposing their style on the suburb and have taken over the political as well as the social institutions in the community. In still other cases, the issue still hangs in balance with no clear and decisive resolution in favor of either the new or the old. In such cases opposing factions sometimes win and sometimes lose. What appears to be a victory may be only a temporary one because the losers had not sufficiently mobilized their forces at the time of their defeat. The suburban political drama takes a very large variety of forms.

The decisive factor in determining victory or defeat for the new middle classes in the suburbs appears to be based on the percentage of the total population that they constitute. When the new middle classes are a sizable minority, they color the whole life of the town but they do not occupy the major institutional positions. When they are a small minority, they live out their life-styles in social enclaves and barely impose their tone on the town, dominating nothing. When their number grows to a size sufficient to give them a feeling that they are unjustly unrecognized and deprived by official institutions, they are apt to make a bid to control the community. No one has yet measured what proportion is necessary for the new middle classes to achieve dominance. However, at some point in the continuing conflict between older tradition and new middle-class aspirations a struggle for the control of the public life of the town ensues. When the new middle classes become dominant, they succeed in imposing their style on other segments of the community. For the past twenty years the new middle classes have for the most part succeeded in asserting their style in hundreds of American suburbs.

The New Urban Middle Class

The same kinds of life-styles and public issues characteristic of the suburbs occur in greatly magnified forms within the metropolis. Certain sectors of the city become the residential centers of the new urban middle classes—silk-stocking districts. These are areas in which high-rent housing and housing developments are concentrated. In New York City, for example, this would include Peter Cooper and Stuyvesant Town, the old (west) Greenwich Village and Washington Square, the upper west side, the east sixties, Brooklyn Heights and Park Slope. In each of these areas, a major proportion of the population are college-educated professionals, managers, technically trained bureaucrats and employed intellectuals. Being closer to the heart of things, they regard themselves as more sophisticated, avant-garde and au courant than are their suburban counterparts who have opted for home ownership and a nonurban environment for their children. In fact, many suburbanites had resided in these urban middle-class enclaves prior to their children having reached school age at which point they moved to the suburbs to avoid the complexities and expense of urban family living.

Within the new urban, middle-class enclaves all of the variations in suburban life-styles are exhibited as in suburbia, except that they are expressed with greater intensity, variety, and modern sophistication. For example, the urban "swinger" and later the yuppie have a style that can be expressed more completely if the devotee lives in Manhattan than if he attempts the style while living in the suburbs. To some extent the residential location of the urban segment of the middle class is determined by the age of children. The urban middle class is most apt to be quite young (with preschool children) or middle-aged (with college-enrolled children). The suburbanites tend to have school-age children younger than college age. Other observers have noted that there is considerable physical mobility between the suburbs and the preferred cliff-dwelling areas of the metropolis. Place of residence is thus not the critical factor in defining the new middle classes.

However, members of the new urban middle class have introduced one major innovation into the middle-class lifestyle. A substantial number of them have entered politics as ideological and/or party activists. In their case, however, they have abandoned the ethnic and bossism political style to which their immigrant parents were frequently committed. Instead they have entered reform politics and have helped to create an image of reform politics as cultured, clean and civilized. Thus reform politics has been responsible for creating a new type of urban political hero whose image is based on cleanness as opposed to bossist corruption. Robert Wagner, the Yale man who was mayor of New York City and was dubbed an old-time boss by the reformers, was followed by John Lindsay, another Yale man, who "came up smelling clean." In New York City the reform political club membership almost coincides with the membership of the alumni associations of City College of New York, Fordham and New York universities. The politics of the urban middle classes are liberal and focus on political honesty, integrity, antibossism and a commitment to high municipal expenditures for improvements of a cultural, educational and humanitarian nature. Under reform leadership the City supports "happenings," park improvements, cultural events and tries to make it a "fun city" as opposed to La Guardia who limited his style to honest, efficient administration and to chasing fire engines and reading comics over the radio during a newspaper strike (which would now be regarded as "campy" by part of the less political urban middle classes). The political problem of the urban middle classes is that as soon as a reform politician is elected to office he is forced to make compromises with the older ethnic bosses and populist politicians in the national, state or city administrations. As soon as he makes these compromises the reform middle class becomes disenchanted and begins to look for new reform candidates, and the original reform candidate is likely to lose the support of his idealistic and liberal constituency. If the elected reform politician does not make these compromises, he finds it almost impossible to function as an urban politician in gaining support for his programs and his district.

For the urban middle classes, narrow class interest in the traditional ethnic and lower-class sense of the term is of less interest than are liberal and cultured orientations and the ideology of political purity. Political life for the politically oriented segments of the urban middle classes is thus a continuous succession of defeats which are never accepted as final defeats because there is always the hope that reform will ultimately win. In the meantime, this middle class can sustain a sense of high-mindedness, reform and purity while not substantially altering the total pattern of urban politics. Our analysis, of course, does not by itself help us to comprehend the older ghetto or the newer race politics of the metropolis. In part, however, the new radical and racial leadership is drawn from disaffected, college-trained, minority youth. On the urban political scene the middle classes have not and are not likely to become sufficiently powerful to dominate urban politics.

THE FUTURE OF THE MIDDLE CLASSES AND THEIR LIFE-STYLES

In the previous discussion we have attempted to define the new life-styles of the new middle classes. We have indicated the nature of these life-styles at their most typical centers. We have further indicated that these life-styles have become diffused throughout our nation's population and are triumphing over older styles as their bearers become a larger proportion of the population of an area. Due to changes in the educational and occupational structure of our society, which make America a more and more middle-class society, we can expect these life-styles to permeate all areas of our society. In the short or long run even the life-styles of the rural community will be affected. We would, of course, expect them to penetrate middle-sized communities, depending, again, on the proximity to centers of diffusion. We noted that even in Springdale the new middle classes had already made a significant impact as early as 1955. At the other extreme, while the urban middle classes have emerged as a distinctive phenomenon and have made an impact on urban society, it is less clear what their chances for future predominance are.

Insofar as urban areas are centers for diffusion of these life-styles they have an importance that goes far beyond their dominance in an immediate urban location. Knowing the centers from which diffusion takes place and the rates of diffusion are important in predicting the future. In general the east- and west-coast metropolises are the centers from which the diffusion takes place. In some respects the west coast has been more inventive and more modern in its cultural development than the east. This claim to cultural leadership by the west is one that is resented by the cultural and other leaders of the east coast (a few years ago this contest was fought in terms of population statistics, but now that California clearly has a larger population than New York the basis upon which superiority is to be judged has shifted to other grounds). While the east- and west-coast metropolises advance their claims against each other, the metropolises in the midwest, particularly Chicago, strive hard to advance their own claims. However, they appear to be trying to advance their own claims primarily by self-consciously trying not to be impressed by either coast. So far Chicago and the middle western urban metropolises have not been able to challenge the inventiveness and cultural sophistication of either of the coasts. Their claims have for the most part been unheard except by themselves.

However, within each of these dominant geographic areas, these giant metropolises have been the center for the development of new cultural and life-style themes, particularly in their suburban, exurban, bohemian and silk-stocking neighborhoods. The concentration in depth of these life-styles varies by region and by city size. In New York, Boston, San Francisco and Los Angeles, the avant-garde middle class reaches its highest expression of "modernity" and sophistication. Places like Chicago are still once removed from the "creative centers." St. Louis, Dallas, Milwaukee, Cleveland, New Orleans and other cities somewhat more distant from the center exhibit a striving, aggressive, somewhat provincial pretentiousness that rings hollow in the face of the "truly authentic" east- and west-coast culture. The rural community and the small town which are most intellectually and culturally distant from the urban centers are farthest removed no matter how physically proximate they may be to the center of urban culture.

The university town regardless of its size is always a sub-center for these new styles because the university citizenry has direct access to them insofar as the styles themselves are products of the university. The university thus becomes a transmission belt to the rest of the immediate vicinity surrounding it irrespective of the density of population in the region. While the east and west coasts set styles at a national level, each university town plays a similar role for a more restricted audience.

However, all areas including rural ones are not far removed from the centers of cultural innovation. The mass media, especially television, film and magazines, disseminate these new life-styles almost instantaneously to all sectors of society, including the deep south, the Maine mountains, the Ozark Hills and rural Appalachia. Under the mass-media system, no area is more remote than another. However, the success of this cultural transmission depends a great deal on the receptivity of the population in the middle-sized cities and in the rural areas to this new cultural exposure and the new life-styles.

There are two groups that are most receptive and hence most critical as points of penetration for the introduction of the new life-styles in the rural areas.

First, the college-educated new middle classes in the 25 to 45 age group who live in tension with the populist culture of their communities. This group feels restricted and hemmed in by traditional small-town values which it escapes from by identifying with external sophisticated styles. This group orients itself to the nearby university and the higher culture as it is transmitted by the mass media.

Second, teen-age youth, especially the children of middle-class parents, who are dissatisfied with the provinciality and narrowness of small-town life look to the mass media for styles of rebellion against what they regard to be the complacency, hypocrisy and dullness of their elders, particularly their parents. Thus it is these young people who are the first in their communities to become aware of the new styles and to adopt them as a form of self-assertion; consequently, they are responsible for introducing them into the town and to their elders. The parents sometimes adopt the styles directly from their children: the mini-skirt would be a case in point as would be the introduction of longer hair styles and beards for men. When these young people go to college they discover more personal and authentic forms and sources of rebellion and more accessible targets in the form of the university administration, the bureaucracy and repressive professors.

To the extent that the remotest areas are thus penetrated we can predict that the revolution from populist, frontier culture is in the process of being disseminated throughout the nation, even in the south, the west and the "upstate" and "downstate" regions of all parts of the country. No doubt such communities are less penetrated than those with multiple forms of access, but the penetration is quite deep and is likely to continue. It may take twenty-five to fifty years before such penetration is completed. But the fact of the penetration, its intensity and its quality pose a number of problems.

The depopulation of the rural community is by no means complete. The intensification of large-scale capital investment in agriculture will continue to drive owners of what were formerly known as family-sized farms out of farming. Many of these farmers and particularly their children will seek work and opportunity in the city. But in "rural" areas, employed managers and technicians, many with university training, will become increasingly numerous and important not only in agriculture, but as officials in local branches of national and regional businesses which are increasingly being located in formerly rural areas. So too as Federal agencies penetrate more deeply and intensively, rural employment will include government officials, hospital technicians and nurses, military personnel, inspectors and investigators, and specialized educational and welfare personnel. Through these personnel channels, the residues of university training and culture will incessantly permeate the rural community with the urban middle-class styles.

Rural youth will continue as in the past to leave the rural community as the city and the university become more compelling magnets. While in the past the rural community has had an over-aged population because of the youthful migration, this tendency is now being corrected by the development of specialized communities for the aged which, with the help of Federal aid, depopulate the rural community of some of its aged residents. The desirability of Florida, California and the south-west as places for retirement communities has corrected somewhat the age distribution in small towns. This population redistribution will help to weaken the commitment of the rural town to its past traditions and will make it more accessible to modern forms of culture.

After all these changes have taken place, what remains is the probability of a continuous and enduring battle between the proponents of populist culture and the bearers of the new urban life-styles, for wherever the latter group reaches sufficient size it challenges the older, traditional group for leadership. In the threat to its leadership the older group sees that it not only faces the loss of community leadership and higher real-estate taxes but also the defeat of its entire way of life. This way of life though on the decline has long historical roots. It is identified with grass-roots democracy, with Americanism and with all the virtues of the American past. For those committed to the past and its values, this decline will be hard to digest.

The danger for the United States is that the hostility, defensiveness, and counteraggressiveness engendered by the immanence of defeat, will become the basis for a backlash against the full sweep forward of American history as it develops in the present and the future. Populism gone sour could become the source of an antidemocratic, quasi-totalitarian reaction which in spite of its origins in an earlier democratic ideology could turn against the new cultural styles evolving in our society. There is thus the risk that in resisting these new life-styles populist democracy may become the basis for new social movements which could subvert the foundations of the present by holding to romanticized images of the past. An organized nativistic movement based partly on a xenophobic isolationism could shelter under its cover not only defensive populists but a variety of other groups whose resentments are less crystallized but which could find a focus in some form of nativism.

We have indicated that the new life-styles are not based on un-American ideas but rather have evolved out of fundamental organizational, economic, educational, and demographic changes in American society. These changes represent fundamental and perhaps irreversible trends in the very structure of American society. Whether one likes the direction of these trends or not, they cannot be wished away, abolished by law or reversed by going back to the past without doing violence to the emergent society. The older populist classes will have to learn to accept defeat gracefully. The newer middle classes, for their part, will have to learn to accept success without exacting vengeance for real or imaginary defeats which occurred in the period prior to its victory. A direct confrontation based on these opposing orientations will have to be avoided if the United States hopes to cope with its other problems.

Reference

Vidich, Arthur J. and Joseph Bensman, *Small Town in Mass Society: Class, Power and Religion in a Rural Community* (Princeton University Press, 1968, rev. edn).

15 The New Conservatism: Political Ideology and Class Structure in America*

Michael W. Hughey

As no one can fail to be aware, in the last several years American society has experienced a powerful groundswell of what are generally identified as conservative ideas. It is only the improved political fortunes of these ideas that is genuinely new, however. Excepting only minor modifications, the ideas themselves have been around for at least two centuries and, indeed, are thoroughly familiar to anyone having even a cursory acquaintance with American history. Economically, they center around the principles of classical liberalism, emphasizing fiscal austerity, free enterprise, business competition, a minimum of government intervention in the marketplace, and an identification of the public good with the welfare of business. Socially, they include commitments to the integrity of the traditional family and its sexual division of labors, to military strength and preparedness, to church and religion, and to essentially Protestant standards of morality, decency, and propriety.

Widespread public support for these conservative ideas did not suddenly emerge full-blown during the 1980 Presidential campaign, despite a general impression to the contrary which is no doubt partly sustained by the tendency of the news media to focus on the specific event, the news item. The first political expression of the resurgence of some of these ideas can probably be traced back to the Goldwater campaign of 1964, in which Ronald Reagan played a minor role, and can be clearly seen in Richard Nixon's election to

---

* Reprinted from *Social Research*, vol. 49, no. 3 (Autumn 1982).

the presidency in 1968. Their political fortunes have continued to grow haltingly since then, becoming more self-conscious and adding new layers, new emphases, and new groups of supporters along the way. Still, the general impression is certainly understandable, for in the late 1970s and early 1980s the new conservatism seemed to explode onto the political stage, culminating dramatically in the decisive election of Ronald Reagan, in his proclamation of a mandate, and in the policies of his administration.

No ideology or set of ideas—including that of the new conservatism—is intrinsically persuasive by the compelling force of its own contents. No ideology, value, or morality is automatically acceptable as right, good, true, or even convincing. In order to be acceptable, any set of ideas must respond in some way to the ideal and/or material needs and interests of the groups which adopt them and which then serve as their social carriers. It is only through these carrying groups that an idea may achieve some social effects. Accordingly, in order to attain dominance in a society, an idea or ideology must appeal to those groups which have the power—be it derived from popular support, coercive ability, respected expertise, or some other means—to translate convictions into policies.[1]

Thus considered, in order to understand the political resurgence of the new conservative ideas, it is necessary to investigate not only specific people and events, but also to explore the social history of these ideas and their contemporary carriers with reference to the social and structural changes in American society which have thrust them into renewed prominence. In this vein, the discussion which follows will be addressed to several questions: To which particular groups and on which particular grounds do the new conservative ideas appeal? What groups serve to carry these ideas and why? Perhaps more to the point since we are considering an apparently sudden change in political climate, what has happened to give these ideas greater appeal at this particular time; why is now their moment? Finally, what changing social circumstances and what corresponding changes in the ideal and material needs and interests of particular social groups have resulted in their current adoption of various of the ideological tenets of the new conservatism?

The general theme of the argument may be disclosed in advance. Support for the new conservatism is not all of one piece. Rather, it is derived from an odd patchwork of groups, some of which are more accustomed to being on opposite sides of most political issues. Generally, I intend to suggest that the new conservatism finds its primary sources of support among three distinct strata, which differ substantially in terms of the foundations of their class positions, their social situations with respect to historic structural developments in American society, and their social character. Furthermore, these three strata, as well as different groups within them, are attracted to different specific features of the new conservatism on the basis of very different needs and interests. Historically considered, it is an unprecedented and odd-bedfellows sort of political alliance that accounts for the current dominance of the conservative ideology. This alliance does not, of course, exhaust the bases of support presently enjoyed by conservative ideas, but it does seem to point to their most important and broadest sources.

AMERICAN GOTHIC: TRADITION AND ITS BEARERS

The primary ideological source as well as substantial political support of the new conservatism can be traced to what C. Wright Mills called the old middle classes, which have comprised the largest and in most respects the most important stratum in American history.[2] In the early nineteenth century, according to Mills's estimate, approximately 80 percent of the labor force fell somewhere into this petit bourgeois stratum. Since then, such overwhelming numerical presence has been consistently eroded as the world inhabited by the old middle classes was abandoned, for reasons to be discussed, by historical developments in the late-nineteenth and twentieth centuries.

Consisting primarily of real-estate speculators, independent farmers, and Main Street businessmen, the old middle classes thoroughly dominated American small towns and rural areas until well into the twentieth century, and in some areas continue to do so today. The class standing of members of this stratum was grounded in their possession of some sort of productive property—a farm, retail business, small manufacturing plant, etc.—which they worked and managed themselves, usually with the help of the entire family. It was, then, a stratum of independent, self-employed enterprisers, of middle-class capitalist entrepreneurs looking out for the "main chance" to seize their own portion of the American dream.

Historically, the prerogative of defining, establishing, and embodying the primary social standards of respectability, of correct behavior, and of success and failure always falls to the socially dominant stratum. As that stratum throughout most of American history, the old middle classes were able through various means to embed their own values, ideals, conceptions, and understandings into virtually every major American institution, thus shaping both the conception and operation of those institutions. That is to say, by virtue of their economic and political domination of local areas throughout the country, the old middle classes defined the standards and values of small-town life and, by extension, of American life generally. Their values became American values, their virtues American virtues.

Most of the old-middle-class values, standards, and morals— including honesty, diligence, industriousness, self-sacrifice, civic-mindedness, piety and self-control—were derived from their Protestant heritage,[3] but they did not depend exclusively on religion for the nourishment and support of these values. Indeed, the old-middle-class ethos was embedded in and fostered by virtually all the institutions they controlled. Family, public schools, and the church itself, for instance, constituted an institutional triumvirate for the transmission of their values across generations, all sharing in and reinforcing one another's responsibility for instilling into children the requisite virtues. Family integrity and parental authority were considered almost sacred, schools were charged with teaching morality and national pride as well as the three Rs, and the church provided both ethical guidance and a reminder that hell was reserved for those who failed their moral lessons.

While, as Max Weber made so clear, the economic contents of "traditional" old-middle-class values also owed a substantial ideological debt to the Protestant ethic,[4] they also developed in ways entirely consistent with the secular rounds

of old-middle-class life. As small entrepreneurs, they cultivated their lands and managed their businesses always with
an eye to expansion and "getting ahead," and would brook
no interference with or limitations on their hopes and possibilities for doing so. For them, unrestrained economic opportunity was sustained at once as a fact of economic life, a
challenge to the ambitious, and a fervently held ideological
commitment. Competition provided the specific mechanism
by which opportunity was pursued, but it was not a morally
neutral or impersonal mechanism. Rather competition was
a test through which individual character was both developed and rewarded. Success, as in some of the older, more
strictly religious equations, was the reward of virtue. Competition, then, has served the old middle classes both as a
secular theodicy of fortune and as a guarantee of individualism and personal freedom.

Politically, the old-middle-class values have always included
a strong and sometimes fervent component of patriotism,
though with significant exceptions in the antebellum South.[5]
Historically, the basis for their national loyalty and patriotic
sentiment has been derived from their strong identification
with the political values and conceptions which, due primarily to their own social dominance, were the dominant
principles of American politics, embedded in American political institutions. Seizing especially on the political rhetoric
of Andrew Jackson, who championed their cause against economic restrictions and monopolistic privileges in the 1820s
and 1830s, the old, small-town business classes were able to
appropriate the political symbolism of American democracy
and adapt it to their own needs, interests, and purposes.
Ultimately, on this basis, local entrepreneurs were able to
establish themselves as defenders of freedom and equality,
the very backbone of American democracy. Of course, to
the Main Street businessman or independent farmer, equality
had as much or more to do with equality of opportunity as
with a concern for political guarantees of basic civil rights.
Their concern, above all, was for the freedom to compete
and profit and the liberty to get ahead. For them, in fact,
the most important responsibility of government was to preserve and protect these economic rights and freedoms at
home and, not infrequently, to extend them abroad. In any

event, by linking laissez-faire and free enterprise with political rights and privileges, the small-town old-middle-class stratum was able to fuse its own economic ideology with national patriotism. It is this linkage between economic and political ideologies that finds expression in the familiar McCarthy-style condemnations of communism as un-American, in equations of democracy with free enterprise, and in remarks like that of Calvin Coolidge, who forthrightly declared that "The business of America is business." It is this linkage also which identifies free enterprise with Americanism and with the American Legion type of righteous militarism, which aspires to make the world safe for democracy and business alike.

Old-middle-class values would continue to be dominant in American society so long as the old middle classes themselves could maintain their local dominance and control of American institutions. The history of the old-middle-class stratum has not, however, been one of uniform success. They have in fact found themselves increasingly on the defensive since the mid- 1800s. For the past century, this has been a stratum in decline.

Beginning in the decades following the Civil War, continuing through the middle 1900s, and accelerating rapidly following World War II, a seemingly inexorable structural revolution has worked to fundamentally transform American society,[6] with unfortunate consequences for the old middle classes. Perhaps most significant, beginning with the Captains of Industry—the ultimate creations of the competitive system—American society has experienced a persistent tendency toward economic centralization, with more and more of industrial and agricultural properties being concentrated in the hands of fewer and fewer owners. In 1976, for instance, the 500 largest corporations controlled fully 72 percent of all manufacturing assets in America, and the proportion of the labor force engaged in agricultural production, 75 percent in 1820, had shrunk to less than 5 percent. As a result of these developments, the old middle classes—a stratum of small-property holders—have witnessed a gradual expropriation of their properties and thus of the very basis of their class positions.

Not only did their class positions suffer, but the old middle classes were also able to exercise less and less influence in many areas once subject to their control. As another consequence of economic centralization, for instance, absentee ownership became increasingly common, resulting in a situation where many decisions of crucial importance to their towns and communities were made not on Main Street but in the board rooms of large corporations.[7] Political power, including party politics as well as political administration, was also subject to centralization, shifting from small towns to the cities and, as the federal government gradually usurped more and more authority, from state to national levels. Finally, even within many small towns, especially in the Northeast and in some regions of the Midwest, local political power was appropriated by immigrant groups. Each of these changes brought a further diminution of old-middle-class power. And as the stratum declined both economically and politically, it suffered losses not only in its historical dominance of American institutions but also in its ability to define the values on the basis of which those institutions would operate.

Of course, the old middle classes did not just suddenly slip into social oblivion, never to be heard from again. Indeed, despite their decline at all levels—numerical, economic, and political—a sizable remnant of the old middle classes continues to survive in rural areas and small towns, especially in the South, Midwest, and Southwest, which, after the 1880s, had become a second area of settlement for Iowans, Nebraskans, and other Midwesterners. By and large, the economic fates of these survivors continue to be dependent on local markets and, as a result, they tend to be marginal to the larger corporate economy. Still, the old middle classes do survive.

They have not survived unscathed, however. Particularly, their slow decline in the face of emergent structural developments has been sufficient to engender a fundamental change in the old-middle-class social psychology, which has grown less optimistic and self-assured and more defensive and self-protective. The very fact that their fall from social dominance has been gradual, continuing now for more than a century, means that they have had ample opportunities to recognize their own decline and to try and prevent further erosion and even to reverse the process. In the past, they have tended to respond aggressively to their declining situation. The old middle classes have always possessed a self-righteous certainty—itself a product of their Protestant heritage—that theirs is the right way of life, that their values are morally correct, and that in some respects they are God's chosen people, His American elect, with a divine mission to fulfill. On those occasions, then, when they have perceived their values to be directly threatened by some identifiable enemy, they have responded with the crusading zeal of the wounded self-righteous and have vigorously reasserted their values in the political arena. In this sense, the Temperance Movement and Prohibition, Know-Nothingism and various other expressions of American nativism, Populism, to some extent Progressivism, the Ku Klux Klan (a regional example), the Scopes "Monkey Trial," and various other incidents of fundamentalist resurgence all serve to chronicle the indignant response of the old middle classes to their own decline. Similarly, as "supply-siders" long before the term was invented, they strenuously opposed New Deal legislation and Keynesianism, fearing they would erode the autonomy of the independent businessman, destroy free enterprise, and place America's economic fortunes in the hands of Eastern financiers and unscrupulous monopolists. Fearing also that another war would bring to fruition the federal "octopus" already inherent in New Deal domestic programs and that it would unleash class and racial conflict, urban squalor, and communist uprisings, many members of the old middle classes were strongly committed to isolationism. Through such organizations as the America First Committee and with no less a spokesman than renowned aviator Charles Lindbergh, they strenuously opposed foreign entanglements in anticipation of World War II and resisted efforts to organize American business as preparation for fighting it, ultimately accepting intervention only when they had no choice.[8] In some of these cases, the old middle classes emerged victorious, but the victories were only temporary for the drift of history was against them. The new American society that was emerging left very little room for the champions of the old.

For the last forty years or so, the old middle classes have been relatively quiet, at least considered against the frequency and intensity of their outbursts in earlier decades, some of

which have just been listed. This should not be taken, however, as an indication that the old middle classes have finally
surrendered to their collective fate, or that their remaining
members are too few to make political waves. Rather, since
around the time of World War II, their attention has been
largely absorbed by other circumstances which have tended
to crowd out old-middle-class recognition of their own decline.

World War II itself provided one major diversion, absorbing virtually all groups into the collective solidarity of the
war effort. Given their ingrained patriotism, the old middle
classes were particularly involved once the nation was committed to combat, and ultimately derived feelings of pride
and superiority both from the war's outcome and from the
fact that America emerged from it as the world's dominant
nation, both militarily and economically. In their eyes, America
had finally assumed its rightful place in world affairs, that
of world leadership.

Following the war, recognition that their way of life was
declining, which might otherwise have been channeled into
political discontent, was further obscured by a collective fear
and hatred of communism. The Cold War (especially as fought
by McCarthy), though it identified an enemy antithetical to
the old-middle-class way of life, nonetheless diverted attention from their decline and fastened it instead on what turned
out to be a relatively insignificant red herring. So preoccupied were they with the supposed menace of communism
that they did not recognize the more immediate threats to
their way of life, or even that it was threatened by sources other
than communism.

Such recognition was further, and finally, blunted by the
unprecedented prosperity ushered in by the postwar years.
With the economic pie growing larger and with virtually all
groups receiving larger slices, to most groups, including the
old middle classes, there seemed little ground for discontent. This was especially true for those segments of the old
middle classes who, with the considerable benefit of the same
New-Deal and Keynesian policies they had once strenuously
opposed, had achieved a measure of success in the interim.
Many of these monied members of the old middle classes
were now retiring to cities in the Sun Belt states, and especially to California, where they invested in real estate and

joined with the regional bearers of their ideology, particularly its economic contents. During the same period, this pattern was paralleled in the movement of an aging generation of Jewish immigrants who, on the basis of their business success, were retiring to Florida and investing in the expanding real-estate markets of that state. These successful Jewish businessmen must be regarded as a unique branch of the monied middle classes, one whose roots are neither Protestant nor Midwestern but whose class positions, like those of the much larger stratum of Midwestern middle classes, rest on private enterprise. The similarities in status between these two monied middle-class groups, despite their differences, establish the basis for a political alliance between them, which we shall return to shortly. It is enough to note for now, however, that for these groups as well as virtually all others, in the postwar years all seemed right with America.

All told, then, the postwar years were a rather remarkable period in American history. Not only did wartime solidarity, Cold War paranoia, and generalized prosperity tend to forestall any potential dissatisfaction by the old middle classes with their continuing and even accelerating decline, but they rather effectively blunted any serious internal discontent at all. The postwar years produced, to a considerable degree, an ideological hegemony or "end of ideology"[9] which the old middle classes took to mean a continuation of their own.

But the illusion could not last, as the 1960s amply demonstrated. That tumultuous decade irreparably shattered the ideological hegemony of the postwar years and stunned the old middle classes into an awareness not only that some American institutions were no longer faithful to their values but that these values were in fact under assault from several different fronts. One of these fronts, it seemed, was manned by black Americans who, in pressing their claims for entry into American life, rejected the former unity as a mask for their own continued exclusion. The old middle classes and those sympathetic to their values both rejected the frequently violent and disorderly techniques used by blacks to make their claims and were ideologically offended by the contents of those claims. Especially in seeking affirmative action in various areas, it seemed to the old middle classes that blacks

were demanding government subsidization and preferential
treatment for their efforts to attain the same social and economic elevation that all other groups had attained by individual efforts alone. To them blacks were thought to be
unwilling to "work their way up," and appeared to be demanding governmental guarantees of their ability to get ahead;
they wanted handouts and a "fixed" competition. And to
the consternation of the old middle classes, the government
seemed to concede to the blacks' demands. On another front,
the old middle classes also witnessed an assault on their
values by white middle-class student activists who, in their
view, were spoiled, slovenly and unclean, traitorous, unwilling to work, ungrateful for their educational opportunities,
sexually immoral, irreverent, irreligious, and frequently sympathetic to communism. They were, in short, wholly lacking in Protestant virtues, and their activities led the old middle
classes, already steeped in anti-intellectualism,[10] to a deeper
suspicion of the universities and university professors. Clearly,
from their point of view, what was happening in America
was wrong.

Despite their growing dismay and disillusionment, the old
middle classes in the 1960s and early 1970s were not well
prepared for a defense of their beleaguered values. Not having
had to exercise them for several decades, they had apparently grown apathetic and rather accustomed to their increasingly peripheral role in American society, and in any
case lacked a prominent national spokesman for their values.
Still, their discontent was growing. In the middle 1960s, it
found expression only as an unorganized and inarticulate
feeling that something was wrong, that American society was
losing sight of its own and their own basic values, both moral
and economic. Barry Goldwater attempted to give voice to
these values in 1964 but could not overcome the many factors working against him.[11] Four years later, however, Richard
Nixon also recognized the important but relatively silent
political voice of the old middle classes and became the
first national politician to fully capitalize on it. To the lower
segments of the old middle classes—those who had not attained success but who, remaining in the South and Midwest, had continued to experience a decline of their own
values and way of life—Nixon's earlier political career of-

fered assurance that he was not "soft" on communism and his "law and order" campaign rhetoric held a thinly disguised promise to end race riots and student disorders. The old Broadway question which was repeatedly raised in the Nixon White House—Will it play in Peoria?—indicates both Nixon's awareness of this portion of his constituency and his effort to keep it satisfied. He was generally able to do so by providing these groups with spending for law enforcement and medical research. While frequently sharing some of these concerns, monied segments of the old middle classes—those who had attained economic success since the New Deal—also embraced Nixon as an alternative to what they regarded as the spendthrift policies of Johnson's Great Society, which seemed to them not only to bestow massive gifts on the undeserving but in its "war on poverty" to put the wrong generals—the poor themselves—in charge of the battle. Nixon was one of them, they thought, as evidenced by the fact that his closest friends included members of their own class, such as Bebe Rebozo, Robert Abplanalp, and J. Williard Marriott. Nixon even provided a personal link between the two major strongholds of this group—California and Florida—by maintaining mini-White Houses in San Clemente and Key Biscayne, thus allowing both to enjoy a connection to the Presidency. Despite their support of Nixon, however, neither the upper nor lower segments of the old middle classes were, at this time, politically vocal or expressive. To be sure, of course, they were not completely mute. Their belligerence, for instance, was given voice through Spiro Agnew, though his "foreign ancestry" and fall from grace prevented his full legitimation as their spokesman. Nonetheless, for the most part both segments of the old middle classes remained politically quiescent, and together comprised a significant portion of Nixon's aptly named "silent majority."

They have since grown rather noisy. Indeed, ultimately, even though racial disturbances and student activism were soon quieted, the old middle classes could not be satisfied, for the decline of their values and way of life had become suddenly visible. Since the 1960s, old-middle-class dissatisfaction has grown and intensified with their increasing awareness that most American institutions have abandoned their values. The new conservatism has been the ideological vehicle of their growing discontent. It is not, however, a vehicle which serves identical needs and interests among its passengers. Indeed, even within the old-middle-class stratum, the same two groups whose silent, inchoate support of Nixon rested on overlapping yet different grounds have developed their respective positions politically and now embrace fundamentally different tenets of the new conservatism, one being primarily concerned with its moral content, the other with its economic message. Each merits separate treatment.

Neoconservatism as Resurgent Righteousness

Historically, the primary basis of old-middle-class acquiescence and attribution of legitimacy to American institutions has been an identification of this stratum with the values and ideals which they made socially dominant and which they perceived to have been embodied in American society. For the lower segments of the old middle classes, this sort of identification has continued to be especially important, for they have failed to develop other—that is, economic—grounds of acquiescence. Since the 1960s, as these groups have been made increasingly and painfully aware, their once-dominant values have not been much reflected in the operation of American institutions. Concretely, from their perspective, the family has been weakened and its integrity undermined by the collective assaults of sexual permissiveness and promiscuity, changing sex roles, gay rights, widely available birth-control and abortion facilities, rising divorce rates, pornography, and feminist ideology. Even the moral sanctity of the home itself is often difficult to preserve against television portrayals of immoral life-styles and activities and, for some, against radio offerings of rock 'n' roll music. For many of the old middle classes, if the family is a haven in a heartless world, it is a haven besieged and in need of defense. From their perspective, of course, they are entirely correct: the "proper" family structure, as they see it, has certainly been weakened and in part by the targets they identify. Family issues may well constitute the central focus of their current conservatism.

But family issues are not, of course, the only source of old-middle-class concern. The educational system also, which once provided firm support for their values and morals, has abandoned traditional values and instead embraced "secular humanism," a catch-all phrase for objectivity and value relativism. They appear particularly disturbed that prayers are no longer allowed in public schools and that evolutionary science is preferred over Genesis.[12] Moreover, as ethnic studies, revisionist viewpoints, and criticism of war entered into the standard curriculum—particularly in the subject of American history, which traditionally has stressed a supremely moral past and ever-more-promissory future—the old middle classes could no longer recognize their own country in the textbooks brought home by their children. It is even possible to view the "new math" as a source of alienation and disturbance for the old middle classes; with its emphasis on decimal and metric systems, it is a "foreign" calculus unfamiliar to the storekeeper. In addition, the old middle classes are concerned that military dominance, from which they derived feelings of pride and superiority, has "slipped" while the communist war machine has continued to make gains. Also, Big Business, in their view, often appears corrupt, self-serving, and unwilling to compete fairly, while government, lacking leadership before Reagan was elected President, has seemed unwilling or unable to do anything about it all. In this sense, as their reaction to the abandonment of their values by American institutions, the new conservatism expresses a crisis of legitimacy experienced by the old middle classes.

All of these ever-increasing old-middle-class concerns have found expression in national politics. Betrayed or abandoned by Nixon and uninspired by Ford, many of the old middle classes embraced the bucolic roots and born-again populism of Jimmy Carter. But as President, Carter also failed to live up to their expectations. At the very time when their increasing anxieties required aggressive, righteous leadership on behalf of the old values, Carter appeared weak and indecisive. Basically, they felt they had elected the wrong Protestant. On the domestic front, Carter talked of sacrifice and offered them civil religion, an abstract, secularized, and intellectually sublimated version of Christian brotherhood and good will.[13] The politically engaged old middle classes, however, demanded a very specific sort of moral revival—nothing less than a realignment of American institutions with their own values. In foreign affairs, Carter's policy was also grounded in his own Protestant heritage, emphasizing international brotherhood, peace on earth, and good will. He offered the United States as an exemplary model for the upliftment of the rest of the world, especially with respect to human rights, and was morally reproachful of those nations indisposed to treat their citizens with Christian decency. In the eyes of the old middle classes, Carter's style resulted in both the loss of the Panama Canal and in the humiliation of America by Iran. Neither was pardonable. He gave them Wilsonian humility when what they wanted was the bully aggressiveness and hairy-chested virility of Teddy Roosevelt. On both domestic and foreign issues, a campaigning Ronald Reagan finally promised them what they wanted.

In the unique set of circumstances that had prevailed in the postwar decades, the values carried by the old middle classes could be largely taken for granted. In the absence of a direct threat, they required neither studied defense nor frequent articulation but for the most part could be simply assumed. Politics affords few such luxuries, however, and simple faith is a frequent casualty of social change. The many changes which have taken hold in America since the 1960s, correctly interpreted by the old middle classes as threats to their way of life, have caused their values to be elevated to a level of conscious awareness. Once they began to be consciously articulated, considered and defended against the forces that would undermine them, these values were increasingly politicized and have finally found expression in a conservative movement that would halt and reverse what their carriers perceive to be the immoral direction of American social change.[14]

In their efforts to do so, they have found in religion a vehicle, catalyst, and frequent voice for their political commitments. Considered historically, of course, this linkage between old-middle-class politics and religion occasions no surprise, for religion has provided both inspiration and a constant source of support for most old-middle-class values and ideals. It is for this reason, in fact, that the contemporary elevation of old-middle-class values to a level of conscious awareness has also stimulated reaffirmations of traditional religiosity. This is especially true of Protestantism and, with respect to such issues as abortion, of Catholicism as well. This simultaneous resurgence of old-middle-class political aggressiveness and religiosity, and the historical connections between the two, further accounts for the current fusions of religious energy and righteous indignation with political conservatism, as expressed in the Moral Majority and similar organizations, in antiabortion and anti-ERA campaigns, and in various other religiopolitical crusades to recapture the lost dominance of the old-middle-class moral values.

To be sure, this combination of righteous activism and conservative politics is by no means unique in American history. As mentioned earlier, the old middle classes have reacted before to their own decline and that of their values, so that in some respects the current expression of old-middle-class conservatism can be viewed as but the most recent upsurge of American nativism. And yet there seems to be something fundamentally different in the present case. Each previous expression of nativism focused on a specific threat—alcohol, evolution, immigrants, political corruption, etc.—which seemed to dominate anxieties and public attention. The current expression of nativism also targets specific evils, of course, but none of them dominates and all seem submerged in a more general and pervasive discontent. That is to say, it reacts not against particular features of modernism, as in the past, but against the whole of modernism as such. If this interpretation is correct, it means that the old middle classes may have finally awakened to the fact that their concerns derive not from the threat of a few identifiable enemies but from the drift of history itself.

It does seem, in fact, that their intention is to reverse the course of recent history and to reclaim by political means the world they have lost. Thus, for instance, old-middle-class groups would outlaw abortion, censor reading materials and television programs, reinstate school prayers, place "creation science" at least on a par with evolutionism, return America to unquestioned military dominance, shore up paternal authority and family integrity, reduce or eliminate support for welfare cheaters and the other unworthy poor, and so on. Each step would restore their standards and values to a dominant position in some sphere of American life.

And yet, the world the old middle classes would resurrect is in large measure one which never existed, for the Holy Commonwealth was never completed in America; it was never as right and good and pure as they imagine. In many respects, theirs is a politics of nostalgia, one which envisions an erstwhile Golden Age through the rose-colored mists of time and distance. And even, moreover, if their vision were accurate, the world of the old middle classes could still not be recaptured, for many developments of the past century cannot likely be reversed. Thus, for instance, large-scale industry, bureaucracy, and government are here to stay. The thorough penetration of large-scale institutions and cultural directives into small towns and rural areas, strongholds of the old middle classes, cannot be undone; they are no longer locally autonomous but have been incorporated into larger markets and political arenas. Like it or not, the old middle classes are now part of a larger social fabric and will remain so. But in resisting that fate, their efforts to change the weave have resulted in new patterns and new cross-stitchings in the American political cloth.

Main Street West: New Bottles for Old Wine

The moralist segments of the old middle classes are of course not alone among the supporters of the new conservative ideology. Were that the case, their ideas almost certainly would not have experienced so strong a resurgence and would not currently dominate American politics. Frankly stated, the carriers of these moral values have probably declined to the point where they no longer possess the necessary political resources of both voting strength and financial means to have generated such an ideological rejuvination by their efforts alone. It is decisive therefore, that other groups have joined with these moralist segments of the old middle classes in supporting the new conservative ideas, though they do so for different reasons and place emphasis on different features of those ideas.

One such group may be referred to as the monied middle classes. Direct descendents of Main Street and heirs to the old-middle-class ideology, particularly its economic contents, they nonetheless do not belong to the Main Street middle-class stratum. Indeed, on the basis of a very different social history and group experience, they have constructed a self-conception and world view quite unlike those of their old-middle-class ancestors and have adapted their inherited ideas accordingly. Specifically, though these monied middle classes have not much modified the contents of old-middle-class economic ideas, they have invested those ideas with new meaning and promise, renewed their vitality, given them a new annunciation freed from the dead weight of the past, and reoriented them in a different direction. More than any other group, these successful middle classes have made the contemporary conservatism, and especially its economic contents, respectable.

American social and economic development has been far from uniform. Indeed, the same structural changes which over the past century have placed the old middle classes, their values, and way of life increasingly on the defensive have penetrated into the countryside in different areas at different times and at different rates of speed and intensity. Generally, they were established first in the Northeast and, following the expansion of the nation itself, were extended southward and westward from there. And always there have been those individuals—either adventurers unable to tolerate being fenced in or common folk seeking the main chance in a less-restricted field—who have moved west ahead of these penetrating structural developments. So many Americans have taken Horace Greeley's advice, and continue to do so, that the most dynamic demographic movement in American history has been that of westward expansion.

In the 1930s, westward expansion was given renewed impetus by catastrophe. Even prior to that decade, largely in response to an energetic booster campaign undertaken in the late 1880s by the aggressive publisher of the *Los Angeles Times*,[15] thousands had moved annually to California, seeking their fortunes by numerous routes. In the thirties, however, as the Depression took its calamitous toll and the Dust Bowl years transformed the once-fertile Midwest into an arid moonscape, a rapidly increasing number of failed farmers, sharecroppers, ruined businessmen, and others fled the Midwest in desperation. Indeed, so dramatically did the number of arrivals in California swell that the state even sought legal measures to turn them back. But its efforts were unsuccessful. Loading all their possessions into and onto the tops of their cars, whole families of "Okies" and "Arkies," whose plight was treated in Steinbeck's *Grapes of Wrath*, made their way to California and sought out whatever opportunity or menial job they could find. And as they moved, they took with them their own old-middle-class economic ethos, acquired on the small farms and Main Streets of hundreds of Midwestern towns.

But California did not represent, nor was it to become, yet another stagnant small town whose Main Street would suffer the same fate as those in other parts of the country. In the popular mind, the West generally and California specifically have long enjoyed a unique reputation. For several generations of Americans, California has been the Promised Land, a place where dreams became reality and hopes were fulfilled. This reputation probably emerged, or in any case was enormously enhanced, by the great gold rush of 1848.[16] With a little luck in what was essentially a hunting and gathering enterprise, one could strike it rich and ascend from rags to riches overnight. Though certainly important, however, the gold rush did not make the only contribution to California's reputation as the Promised Land, for one could also "get rich quick," or relatively quickly, by more conventional avenues. Generally, because post-Civil War structural developments reached it last, California has been the last frontier of entrepreneurship in America. Even as the range of opportunities were progressively narrowed in the East, South, and Midwest, California and neighboring states in the Southwest continued to provide room in which enterprising businessmen could take risks, compete, and get ahead. Whoever wished upon a star in California, to paraphrase one of that state's successful entrepreneurs, would see their dreams come true. To aspiring businessmen, Disney's song promised that the main chance could still be found.

Many found it. Particularly as the Depression drew to a close, numerous fortunes were made in expanding petroleum industries, agricultural production, the growing Hollywood-based motion-picture industry, and real-estate speculation, especially in agricultural lands and in growing cities like Los Angeles where land speculation was linked to manipulation of water rights. Many others found more modest success, but success nonetheless, in restaurants, gasoline stations, small retail shops, poultry ranches, and other small enterprises. While some did strike it rich suddenly and spectacularly in accordance with California legend, the good fortune of most of these enterprising businessmen was the product of that traditional American formula which combined the existence of opportunity with an application of the Protestant and old-middle-class economic virtues of hard work and competitiveness, which they had brought with them from the Midwest to California. It was a product also of the same New Deal legislation they had once resisted as a matter of ideological principle. It was the government, after all, under New Deal programs, which built the dams that made the manipulation of water rights and thus land speculation so profitable. It was the government also which made low-cost guaranteed loans available to adventurous businessmen and which established price supports for oil and for agricultural products. Nonetheless, as a rule these successful enterprisers did not recognize that they were major beneficiaries of government intervention into the economy; they recognized only their success, not the New Deal as a contributing cause of it. They were, as a result, able to regard themselves as classic entrepreneurs and to view their success as the product of nothing more than their own hard work, initiative, diligence, and competitive virtues. To this generation of California businessmen, the lesson could not have been more clear: entrepreneurial capitalism still worked, and the American dream of success through self-reliance was still alive, still possible. In their own experience, they felt, it had been a dream fulfilled.

In the postwar years, this stratum of successful Western businessmen experienced a rapid expansion as large numbers of Midwestern enterprisers, who had attained success through a similar combination of hard work, initiative, and unacknowledged New Deal programs, began moving to retirement communities in the sunnier climate of California and the Sun Belt states. Once there, they joined with the regional bearers of their economic ideology on Main Street West and thus increased the regional political and economic strength of the stratum as a whole. Indeed, largely as a result of this merger, the Western states have become the primary power base for the monied-middle-class stratum and for the economic ideology which it carries. Of course, support for that ideology can also be found on avenues other than Main Street West, as can other members of the monied middle classes. Successful Jewish immigrant businessmen, for instance, who have already been mentioned, began moving in the postwar years to retirement communities in Florida, thus creating in that state a concentration of monied middle classes second only to California. A more specialized Jewish segment of these middle classes can be located among those Jewish intellectuals who, shedding their youthful radicalism along the way, have found success in academia and, more recently, in right-wing foundations; these intellectuals have been instrumental as of late in formulating the ideological defense and justification of neoconservatism. Finally, of course, there are those successful Southern and Midwestern businessmen who stayed home following their retirement, or who have not yet retired, and who are frequently members of the local or even regional elite. Despite such scattered support, however, it is on Main Street West that the monied middle classes established their greatest stronghold.

In the 1970s and early 1980s, the monied middle classes, led by those in the Western states, emerged as a significant political force. Their political spokesman is Ronald Reagan, who in some ways personifies their social experience. Born in 1911 in Tampico, Illinois, Reagan moved to California in 1937 where, though never a major star, he attained some fame and fortune as a Hollywood actor and later as president of the Screen Actors' Guild. With the monied middle classes of his adopted region he shares an economic world view, the product of a shared old-middle-class ideological heritage filtered through the experience of success. As a result, when Reagan made his initial foray into the political arena, speaking in support of Goldwater at the 1964 Republican National Convention, residents of Main Street West were immediately attracted by what they saw and heard. They have since been among Reagan's strongest supporters. They were instrumental, for instance, in financing his campaign for governor of California, and were rewarded with considerable influence in his administration. Reagan's election to the Presidency in 1980, again with their abundant financial backing, represents a leap by the Western wing of the monied middle classes from regional power to national influence. This is true not simply because members of this group were offered high-level government positions—for example, James Watt, William French Smith, and Kitchen Cabinet members Justin Dart, Holmes Tuttle, Earle Jorgensen, and others— but because, again, Reagan is himself a representative of this stratum, sharing in its ideals and values. By and large, it is the world view which he and they share which finds expression in Reagan's policies, especially those having to do with economic and social policy.

Both the world view and the economic policies derived from it reflect the experience of the Western business classes. They are, for the most part, successful, self-made business-men who recognized opportunity and, at personal financial risk, took advantage of it through competition. As self-made Westerners, moreover, these new men of power tend to re-gard the decay and decadence of "old" cities and institu-tions in the Northeast with disdain and look condescendingly at the economic difficulties several of these cities now face, particularly New York. Their own conception of how all levels of the economy should operate in many ways mirrors the conditions of their own success, at least as they perceive those conditions, for again they generally do not acknowl-edge the contributions of Keynesianism and New Deal pro-grams. As expressed in Reagan's national economic policies, this conception includes an emphasis on the "supply side" or productive sector as well as commitments to free enter-prise, competition, and a modified laissez-faire. Concretely, this has resulted in policies designed to increase entrepre-neurial opportunities and investments. Thus, for instance, cutting business income taxes and accelerating depreciation allowances would allow the businessman to keep more earn-ings for investment purposes—a strategy which reveals the entrepreneurial world view of its proponents in its assump-tion that untaxed earnings would be reinvested to increase production rather than in horizontal mergers, consumption, or other unproductive possibilities. Other policies are de-signed to relax economic restrictions and to increase both productivity and competition by reducing government regulations on business activities. Those who succeed in the renewed competition and who make productive contributions to the economy would be rewarded for their efforts by other policies—for instance, those which reduce capital-gains, gift, and estate taxes, thus allowing more money to be retained by the businessman or his family. Finally, in the entrepreneurial world view, the unproductive should not be rewarded for their idleness but should be compelled to seek productive work. This would be accomplished by reducing welfare benefits, food-stamp programs, unemployment benefits, and the like. These and other of Reagan's policies are derived from the world view of a self-considered entrepreneurial stratum and, if fully instituted, would establish at the national level some of the regional economic circumstances under which they believe their own success to have been attained.

This prospect has been greeted with an ambivalent mix of general support and guarded caution by the corporate leaders of American Big Business. If fully instituted, Reagan's economic proposals would resubject them to an irrational, unpredictable, competitive market which they, by virtue of size, resources, political influence, and careful planning, have been generally able to supersede.[17] Risk and competition, the very foundations of economic life for the entrepreneur, hold little appeal for the bureaucratic managers of mature corporations. Rather, they tend to be far more interested in a stable, predictable, rationalized economy in which investment decisions can be made with minimal risk and rising profits can be safely ensured. In accord with that interest, corporate managers also tend to be ambivalent with respect to Reagan's proposals, which again reflect an entrepreneurial ideology, to drastically curtail the government's role in the market and to move closer to a laissez-faire economy. Corporate managers support corporate tax breaks and profitable deregulations but on the whole have grown rather comfortable with government intervention into the private sector. They would, for instance, retain various price supports, guaranteed-loan programs, lucrative government contracts, numerous forms of subsidies to business and the like. Despite their caution, however, corporate leaders are very concerned over the weighty economic problems of high inflation, soaring interest rates, and large national deficits which have emerged in the 1970s, and they seem to feel that major steps will be necessary to solve them. At least in part, Reagan's willingness to take such steps may well account for their initial support of his policies. In the end, however, being less responsive to the optimism of Reagan's entrepreneurial ideology, corporate leaders will evaluate his policies and their support of them by the criterion of business expediency. They are not primarily ideologues but managers, and their support is much less dogmatic than pragmatic. As a result, they will back Reaganomics only insofar as they believe its policies will be successful. As of late, they have grown increasingly wary, particularly in light of the record national deficits contained in Reagan's proposed budgets.

Not surprisingly, the old-middle-class stratum of small Main Street businessmen do tend to be ideologically committed to Reaganomics. It reflects, after all, the very same entrepreneurial ideology for which they have served as traditional carriers and which they passed on to their more successful Western heirs. Indeed, well before Reagan himself achieved any political prominence, the rhetoric of Reaganomics was, and continues to be, celebrated daily in Chambers of Commerce and Rotary Clubs all across the country. And yet, even though the contents of their economic ideologies are identical, there is nonetheless a fundamental difference between the ideology of Main Street and that of Main Street West, a difference which is derived from the very different historical experiences of these two groups.

With individual exceptions, of course, the old-middle-class small-business stratum has known only continuous decline over the last century and, as indicated by a substantial increase in small-business bankruptcies, that decline has rapidly accelerated in recent years. In an immediate and specific sense, Main Street businessmen see in Reagan's economic proposals a possibility of economic survival, particularly in his promise to reduce taxes on their earnings and to lower the interest rates on loans needed to continue operating. In Reaganomics they see the possibility of holding their own in an economy which provides them with fewer and fewer opportunities to do so. But Reaganomics also appeals to this stratum on a more general level. As a result of the structural changes which have worked consistently to undermine their class positions, the old middle classes adhere anxiously and defensively to the economic components of their traditional ideology just as they do to its moral contents. Reaganomics, in echoing their economic faith, appeals to that defensiveness and anxiety by assuring the old middle classes that they and their way of life continue to be important in America and by promising that their economic ideals will again be reflected in the operation of America's economic institutions. By and large, as defeated men and women unable to fully comprehend their own defeat, they cling to their economic faith as one of the last refuges of a decaying way of life. Reaganomics offers them a thin straw of hope which they clutch in near desperation and self-justifying approval, but it is a hope borne of despair and directed to the past. It is a hope of turning back, of returning America to a nostalgic era in which they ruled the economy. As such, it is a hope based on self-deception, for there is no turning back. The old Main Street middle classes embrace the economic principles of the new conservatism as genuine reactionaries who sense the possibility of their own resurrection.

By contrast, the residents of Main Street West have known no decline but only prosperity for themselves and their region. Still flushed with success, their collective psyche and world outlook are not defensive but buoyant and optimistic. The difference is a telling one. Even though the contents of their economic ideology is shared almost completely with the Main-Street middle classes, in filtering that ideology through their own prosperous experience the monied middle classes combine it with a constructive, progressive faith and ground it in a confidence born of success. Theirs is an ideology full of hope, but a hope which arises not from the despair of a declining stratum but from the optimism of an ascending one. In part at least, the optimism of this stratum is reflected in Reagan's personal style of exuding confidence in his economic policies and in his uncompromising faith that they will work. More importantly, their optimism also finds expression in the direction of their ideological orientation, for despite the fact that the economic ideas of the monied middle classes are identified as conservative, they are presented more as a vision of the future than as a return to the past. Main Street West is in fact inhabited by radicals who would replace much of the political and economic framework of contemporary American society with what they regard as the regional conditions of their own success. In this sense, Reaganomics, which embodies their economic principles, is not a defensive retreat into the past but rather a proposal to redeem the nation by extending the California pattern. Progressive in intent, Reaganomics in their view would deliver the nation from the misguided policies of recent history and would at least point it in the direction of the good society.

THE FALL AND RISE (?) OF MODERN LIBERALISM

Even combining the voting strength of the old middle classes and the financial strength of Main Street West, it is unlikely that, by their efforts alone, the new conservatism could have been elevated to its current position of national prominence. Indeed, even though the congruence of their ideological interests has existed at least since the Western enterprisers reached maturity as a stratum—approximately two to three decades—it is only in the late 1970s and early 1980s that their shared ideas have achieved political dominance. For this ideological resurrection to have occurred, it is decisive that they have been joined by numerous supporters from what, given recent political history, is a rather unexpected source. These new supporters, moreover, owing to differences in their social history and in the foundations of their class positions, are attracted to features of the new conservatism on grounds very different from those of the two carrying groups already discussed.

The same structural changes which since the Civil War have worked consistently to undermine the class positions and way of life of the old middle classes have at the same time created the foundations for a new middle-class stratum with a very different way of life. Industrial expansion, economic and political centralization, and the growth of enormous bureaucratic organizations in virtually every area of American life have created a need for a new category of workers. The class positions of these new middle classes are based not on small property holdings but on occupation, and their income is derived not from independent business activity but from a regular salary. Included in this stratum, then, are the white-collar workers and managers of bureaucratic organizations in business, government, and elsewhere and, for present purposes at least, the unionized workers who provide the labor power for industrial corporations. By 1940 in Mills's estimate, the new middle classes comprised 25 percent of the labor force. Today, they are unquestionably the largest single stratum in American society.

A prominent feature of the new conservatism and of Reagan's domestic policies, which was presented under the campaign rubric of states' rights and which has been proposed as a policy under the label of New Federalism, is in significant respects a repudiation of an important yet almost invisible new-middle-class political role which has been gaining importance since at least the New Deal and which came into its own during and following World War II. During this period, political bureaucrats in Washington—a segment of the new middle classes—have increasingly appropriated much control of social, economic, and other programs, administering these programs at the national level, which is of course the natural habitat of these political bureaucrats since they are themselves products of political centralization and large-scale bureaucratic administration. The programs they manage, moreover, are frequently administered in accordance with their own vested interests as employees in maintaining and expanding welfare-state agencies and services and in accordance with their own class interests— for instance, in aiding suburban expansion by subsidizing construction of highways, schools, water and sewage facilities, and the like.

In a sense, Reagan's policies represent a class struggle of sorts between the old middle classes and their allies on one side and the new-middle-class political bureaucrats on the other. Essentially, his policy of New Federalism would have as one effect to expropriate from the expropriators and would return administrative control of various social and economic programs to the state and local levels, which tend to be much more responsive to old-middle-class pressures and whose legislatures are typically more conservative than the federal Congress. Most state and local governments, though also subject to some centralizing tendencies, have not developed the sort of entrenched, new-middle-class bureaucracy which has emerged in Washington. As a result, in most cases policies originating at these government levels have been more easily controlled by old-middle-class interests and more imbued with old-middle-class standards than has been the case with Washington. In some sense, then, Reagan's domestic policies would return more control of major social and economic programs to Main Street, which can then influence the administration of them in accordance with its own standards and interests. As an additional feature of the New Federalism, shifting control of social programs back to state and local levels would also entail a shift in accountability for the administration of those programs. Almost certainly by Machiavellian design—for Republicans have not forgotten the protest marches of the 1960s—some of the heat would be taken off Washington and redistributed among state capitals. In this sense, state governors have reason to be cautious in their response to the New Federalism proposal.

Ironically, in this class struggle Reagan has gained a significant source of support from some segments of the new middle classes themselves. Unlike the old middle classes, the new middle classes have never developed any consistent political standards which can provide a basis for political positions and to which politicians can direct their appeals. Nor have the new middle classes ever developed even a vague sense of class consciousness, of having interests in common. At the end of his book chronicling their social ascent, C. Wright Mills observed that the new middle classes are politically homeless. "They hesitate," he argued, "confused and vascillating in their opinions, unfocused and discontinuous in their actions." They are political "rearguarders" with a tendency to "follow the panicky ways of prestige." Most important, since they lack political standards and a consistent public position, their political direction is usually determined by their private positions. Essentially, Mills wrote in an observation no less true today than thirty years ago, "on the political marketplace of American society, the new middle classes are up for sale." Apparently, for many segments of the new middle classes, Ronald

Reagan is currently the highest bidder.

For the old middle classes, as argued earlier, acquiescence to and legitimation of American institutions has been based primarily on a strong identification with the values which they, as the socially dominant stratum, were able to imbed into those institutions. Confronted with the contemporary abandonment of their values, the old middle classes now seek to resurrect them through a conservative political movement. Some members of the new middle classes undoubtedly share this concern. Values and morals are slow to die, and despite their different economic situation, many of the new middle classes have also inherited a moral legacy from America's past. They too can challenge modernism on moral grounds, even while accommodating themselves to it on virtually every other. Nonetheless, for the new middle classes generally, the decline of old-middle-class values does not appear to be experienced as a problem. Not sharing the same intense commitment to the threatened traditional values and, indeed, lacking any secure values and traditions at all, the new middle classes have not generally shared in the old-middle-class reaction to their decline. They have in fact tended to oppose old-middle-class moral concerns by generally favoring the Equal Rights Amendment, the availability of birth-control and abortion facilities, the exclusion of religious worship from public schools, and so on. In any case, the moralistic features of the new conservatism do not appear to be a primary source of attraction to the new middle classes.

Owing to their own social history and experience, the new middle classes have developed entirely different substantive grounds for acquiescing to and bestowing legitimacy upon American institutions and their operations. The new middle classes are products of a spectacular process of economic growth and expansion which has been transforming American society since the Civil War and which was vastly accelerated following World War II. Coming to maturity during the latter period, the current generation of new middle classes have seen their own rising careers parallel the expansion of American political and economic fortunes in the postwar years, a time when the American Empire was at its peak. As a stratum they have known only constant improvement and uninterrupted economic growth. They have, as a result, grown accustomed to a rising standard of living sufficient to sustain their chosen styles of life with their attendant standards of consumption. For those with managerial positions, this standard of living, indeed the whole foundation of their class positions, has depended upon a salary, regular employment, and the possibility of continuous promotions and raises. For industrial workers, it has depended on regular work, few layoffs, increasing wage-and-benefit packages, and the possibility of overtime work. Both groups, in order to maintain their living standards and chosen life-styles, have further depended more heavily than they have realized upon government subsidies for housing, educational opportunity for themselves and their children, pensions, highways, and numerous other social services. All of these, and ultimately the very livelihood of the new middle classes, are in turn dependent upon a certain level of economic growth. It may well be the case, then, that the price of their acquiescence and cooptation is the continued expansion and performance of the economy on which their way of life is based.

The necessary levels of growth and expansion have, of course, become more difficult to manage during the past decade as higher energy costs, rising inflation, more intense foreign competition, and higher national deficits have all taken their economic toll. At an individual level, the combined effect of these developments is experienced as a reduction in real income, making it more difficult for members of the new middle classes to maintain their chosen ways of life and consumption standards. As a result, the new middle classes have grown increasingly class- and status-defensive throughout the 1970s as economic decline began to make itself felt. Significantly also, as American economic performance has failed to satisfy their needs, interests, and expectations, it has also become less capable of purchasing their quiet cooptation and of ensuring their acquiescence. As one apparent expression of their growing dissatisfaction, many began to support proposed changes in established political and economic formulas, of some of which they have themselves been the primary if largely unwitting beneficiaries. Specifically, as they began to experience economic losses which threatened their ways of life, many of the new middle classes have become increasingly supportive of policies which would allow them to offset these losses to uncontrollable economic circumstances by recouping them through politically manageable property- and income-tax cuts. The first concrete political expression of this tendency probably took shape in what the media dubbed "tax revolt fever," as numerous members of the new middle classes joined in the effort to pass Proposition 13 in California, Proposition 2½ in Massachusetts, and numerous state-income-tax indexing schemes. At the national level, Ronald Reagan was the first major politician to appeal to new-middle-class economic insecurities—as well as to old-middle-class moral dissatisfaction—by promising a 30-percent income-tax cut over three years; his political success would not likely have been possible without considerable new-middle-class support.

The immediate brunt of tax cuts is of course absorbed by the lower classes in the form of reductions in food stamps, school-lunch programs, welfare and AFDC benefits, and other social programs. It is almost paradoxical, given their political inclinations over the last three decades, that this has presented no problem for large segments of the new middle classes. Apparently, the Keynesian-based welfare-state liberalism to which this stratum owes its class positions and with which it has been generally sympathetic does not seem to have developed into a deeply held political philosophy. Indeed, joining such other groups as the old middle classes, both Jewish and Western-Protestant monied middle classes and even some black enterprisers and intellectuals who have "arrived," some segments of the new middle classes appear to have developed an almost nativist distrust and resentment of the new lower classes—blacks and Hispanics—whose needs and claims interfere with their ways of life. If their general reaction to recent economic difficulties may be taken as an indication, the liberalism of the new middle classes does not run deep enough to threaten their purses and can in any case be readily abandoned if it does.

But if segments of the new middle classes will sacrifice the poor and their own liberalism to bolster their personal economic fortunes, they are not likely to silently endure threats to their own ways of life as a result of more extensive tax cuts. As the effects of tax cuts are extended, the new middle classes are beginning to discover that they are themselves the primary beneficiaries of a number of threatened government services and that having government on their backs is in many cases not an altogether uncomfortable burden. It is no accident, for instance, that Reagan's proposed reductions in Social Security benefits—a government-subsidized pension plan for the middle classes—met with widespread opposition and produced his only major defeat during his first year in office. The new middle classes are also likely to react against other government cuts—for instance, reductions in or cancellations of low-cost government loans for purchasing or constructing homes. And they are especially likely to rebel against deep cuts to public education; since their own career positions depend on education, it is a new-middle-class sacred cow that will be extremely expensive to feed without government subsidization. Conceivably, then, as reductions in government services become more extensive, the neoconservative economic policies could well produce a "liberal backlash" as the same new-middle-class groups who once found those policies appealing move back under the wing of the welfare state. To be sure, for most this backlash would not likely be grounded in a genuine commitment to and sincere belief in liberal political philosophy. Rather, it would be a political movement expressing the economic self-interest of the new middle classes and would take the form of a commitment to welfare-state liberalism. Liberalism, in this case, would be the vehicle of self-interest rather than the end of political action. But the effect would nonetheless be the same: the new conservatism would have lost an important and perhaps even decisive source of support to an even higher bid.

Since fiscal austerity and low taxes are time-honored tenets of Main Street economic thought, at least for now the new middle classes have found themselves in unusual agreement with the old middle classes and their Western heirs over economic policies. In this limited instance at least, the agents of tradition and modernism are united in their support of neoconservatism. Even so, however, while the old and new middle classes have joined together as partners in discontent, the foundations of their commitments to the new conservatism are fundamentally different, one being primarily ideological, with moral and economic emphases, the other resting mainly on economic self-interest. Whether this coalition of different segments of the middle classes will endure and even give rise to new alliances and new issues is of course at this point largely a matter of speculation. Undoubtedly, however, it is only by virtue of this mixed bag of allied constituencies who are attracted to different tenets of the new conservatism for very different reasons that its current dominance has been made possible at all.

Notes

1. These comments on ideas and their social carriers represent the condensed themes of Max Weber's sociology of knowledge, derived primarily from his various empirical and theoretical works on world religions. Benjamin Nelson used the term "structures of consciousness" to refer to complexes of ideas and their carriers. This essay is refracted through Nelson's work, especially his ambitious attempt to construct a "comparative, historical, differential sociology in civilizational context" (see his "Civilizational Complexes and Intercivilizational Encounters," *Sociological Analysis* 34 [1973] and "Max Weber, Ernst Troeltsch and Georg Jellinek as Comparative Historical Sociologists," *Sociological Analysis* 36 [1975]) and his interpretation of Weber's Protestant-ethic argument (see especially *The Idea of Usury* [Chicago: University of Chicago Press, 1969]; "Weber's Protestant Ethic: Its Origins, Wanderings, and Foreseeable Futures," in Charles Y. Glock and Phillip E. Hammond, eds., *Beyond the Classics?* [New York: Harper & Row, 1973]; and "Max Weber's 'Author's Introduction (1920)': A Master Clue to His Main Aims," *Sociological Inquiry* 44 [1974].

2. C. Wright Mills, *White Collar* (New York: Oxford University Press, 1951).

3. The "structures of consciousness" of the old middle classes, to make a more limited use of Nelson's term than he intended, were and are largely Protestant. Nelson always insisted that the Protestant ethic had not died but had continued to survive at various levels of American society. If indeed it does live, I would contend, it lives among the old middle classes—not only in terms of its economic ethos but also in terms of its less-recognized and less-understood social ethos, which has been secularized and transvalued into essentially civic virtues.

4. Max Weber, *The Protestant Ethic and the Spirit of Capitalism* (New York: Scribner, 1958); "The Protestant Sects and the Spirit of Capitalism," in Hans Gerth and C. Wright Mills, eds., *From Max Weber* (New York: Oxford University Press, 1946).

5. The antebellum South offers a special case with respect to patriotic

values, for it included groups who were "unpatriotic" by virtue of their slaveholding interests. These groups included not only the wealthy slaveowners who sought a slave empire outside the United States—e.g., in Texas—but also small farmers with few slaves and yeoman farmers whose regional vision of the main chance entailed their acquisition in the future. Ultimately, of course, as the pain of defeat diminished, the Southern middle classes also began to embrace patriotic values, no doubt in part as a claim for re-entry into the mainstream of American political and economic life.

6. Intellectual efforts to comprehend the various dimensions of this transformation have been numerous. See, for instance, Daniel Bell, *The Coming of Post-Industrial Society* (New York: Basic Books, 1973); Paul A. Baran and Paul M. Sweezy, *Monopoly Capital* (New York: Monthly Review Press, 1966); Joseph Bensman and Arthur J. Vidich, *The New American Society* (New York: Quadrangle, 1971); and John Kenneth Galbraith, *The New Industrial State*, 3rd ed. (Boston: Houghton Mifflin, 1978).

7. See, for instance, Thorstein Veblen, *Absentee Ownership* (New York: Viking Press, 1923); W. Lloyd Warner, *The Social System of the Modern Factory* (New Haven: Yale University Press, 1947); and Arthur J. Vidich and Joseph Bensman, *Small Town in Mass Society* (Princeton: Princeton University Press, 1968).

8. For an excellent social history of modern isolationism and its ideological appeal to and sources of support among the old middle classes, see Justus D. Doenecke, *Not to the Swift: The Old Isolationists in the Cold War Era* (Lewisburg, Penn.: Bucknell University Press, 1979).

9. See Daniel Bell, *The End of Ideology* (New York: Free Press, 1962); Seymour Martin Lipset, *Political Man* (New York: Doubleday, 1959); and Chaim Waxman, ed., *The End of Ideology Debate* (New York: Simon & Schuster, 1969).

10. Richard Hofstadter, *Anti-Intellectualism in American Life* (New York: Vintage, 1962).

11. These include a whispering campaign that he was Jewish, his exaggerated emphasis on foreign policy, his own candidness, and his militaristic orientation. In contrast to Goldwater, it was his supporter Ronald Reagan who, in exuding Midwestern values even in Hollywood Babylon, displayed the winning style.

12. In the case of evolutionism, their target is particularly well chosen. Those touting evolution of the species propose to usurp a service formerly monopolized by religion—that of providing us with a myth of origins. It should come as no surprise that those committed to the religious version should act defensively.

13. The concept of an American civil religion was formulated and developed by Robert N. Bellah, particularly in "Civil Religion in America," *Daedalus*, Winter 1967, and in *The Broken Covenant* (New York: Seabury Press, 1975). President Carter, it seems, was much impressed by Bellah's work and even invited him to the much-acclaimed Camp David meeting in July 1979 to consult on the condition of American society generally and energy policy specifically. If the language

and tone of Carter's subsequent address (*New York Times*, July 16, 1979) to the nation may be taken as an indication, Bellah was apparently one of the more influential Camp David consultants. In his speech, Carter spoke of a "crisis of confidence . . . that strikes at the very heart and soul and spirit of our national will" and which is manifest "in the growing doubt about the meaning of our own lives and in the loss of unity and purpose of our nation." In order to recapture our original confidence and spirit, Carter continued, "we simply must have faith in each other and in the nation's future." And especially, we must forsake the path of self-interestedness and take up "the path of common purpose and the restoration of American values," for only this latter path can lead to "true freedom for our nation and ourselves." These themes, though expressed differently, are almost exactly those of Bellah's *Broken Covenant*. For an account of American civil religion which treats it as an intellectualized version of old-middle-class civic morality, see my *Civil Religion and Moral Order* (Westport, Conn.: Greenwood Press, 1983).

14. For a theoretical elaboration of conservatism as tradition made self-conscious, see Karl Mannheim, "Conservative Thought," in Kurt H. Wolff, ed., *From Karl Mannheim* (New York: Oxford University Press, 1971).

15. See David Halberstam, *The Powers That Be* (New York: Knopf, 1979), p. 107. Halberstam's book contains an excellent account of the efforts of the Chandler family dynasty to build and exploit Southern California. In his words: "They [the Chandlers] did not so much foster the growth of Southern California as, more simply, invent it" (p. 94).

16. In Europe, California's reputation after 1848 was that of the new colossus and place where history was being made. Even Marx was fundamentally affected by it, seeing in California all the conditions needed for revolutionary fulfillment of the historical dialectic. For a discussion of the significance of California for Marx, see Stanford M. Lyman, *The Seven Deadly Sins: Society and Evil* (New York: St. Martin's Press, 1978), pp. 253–259.

17. This argument has been developed and elaborated in the various works of John Kenneth Galbraith, particularly *The New Industrial State*, op. cit.

16 The Politics of the Middle Class in a National Crisis: The Case of Watergate*

Arthur J. Vidich

OF LAWS AND MEN

Through July and August of 1974, during Watergate, major political constituencies in the United States withdrew support from a popularly elected president and his inner governing circle. Voters who had voted for President Nixon considered their vote to have been fraudulently claimed and felt betrayed by the candidate for whom they had voted. Other citizens and leaders who had not voted for Nixon no longer felt a commitment to respect the results of the election. The withdrawal of support and consent from the ruling circle of political leaders resulted in a virtual paralysis of governmental operations.

During the last stages of the paralysis in August, the sources of the legitimacy of governmental actions were difficult to locate. Governmental departments such as Defense, State, Health, Education and Welfare, and bureaus such as the FBI and CIA were presumably acting on their own cognizance since the president was discredited and most of the inner circle of government under whose direction existing policies had been set were either in jail or on their way to criminal prosecutions that would put them in jail. At the last moments of the Nixon presidency, the secretary of the armed forces, James Schlesinger, took it upon himself to screen any communications that might have come from the White House to the military services. Presumably he was

* Reprinted from *Social Research*, vol. 42, no. 4 (Winter 1975).

suspicious of a last-minute presidential attempt to save power by means of force. By so doing, however, Schlesinger arrogated to himself the direct powers of government and came perilously close to accomplishing what he was trying to avoid. The legitimacy of a duly elected president and his government was abandoned on the grounds that the president was possibly a criminal. The vacuum created by these events was filled by self-appointed guardians of authority whose claims to legitimacy rested on discrediting traditional forms of legitimation.

In democratic society the idea of the supremacy of the electoral mandate is basic to its legitimacy. Early in the development of capitalism, the bourgeoisie in its efforts to express its sense of self-worth made claims for participation in the political process. Except for such movements as Bonapartism, Nazism, and Fascism, the electoral affirmation and support of a government and its policies by the majority of its citizens has been thought necessary to the legitimacy of governance. Electoral legitimation has been distinguished from the mass support achieved by Fascism and Nazism because the latter used political processes that violated the institution of free elections. Popular elections involving competing parties have come to be thought of as the fundamental instrument for securing consent and for making claims to legitimacy.[1]

But in the history of capitalism and democracy, the electoral process has been constrained by a larger legitimating idea known as the "rule of law."[2] Legality, as represented in such documents as constitutions, bills of rights, and statutes supported by judicial procedures are in Weber's terms the basis upon which legitimacy is claimed under a system of rational legal authority. Thus legitimacy granted by the electoral process is limited and restricted by the parameters of the law. When engaging in actions for which routine legal acceptance cannot be expected, leaders have been careful to find in advance explicit legal justifications for such actions, or, if necessary, as for example in the Gulf of Tonkin resolution, to create laws in advance of the use of authority which might otherwise be regarded as of dubious legality. When legality has not been adhered to, recourse has been had to clandestine actions in agencies such as the CIA and FBI, or to the subcontracting of illegal work to private businesses such as the Mafia. Since these latter actions have been kept secret in the sense that it was difficult in pre-Watergate times to discuss them publicly, they could be thought to either not exist or to represent only an occasional lapse into illegality. Legitimacy is thus ultimately based on claims of legal rationality supported by rhetorical invocation of "government of laws, not of men."[3]

However, the rhetoric of the rule of law as indicated by secret governmental operations has been muddied by the growth of the administrative state and by the bureaucratization of the presidency. President Nixon and his inner circle seemed to act outside the framework of established law. Congressional investigators tried to act within the law in carrying out their investigations, but they engaged in unofficial "plea bargaining" with witnesses and the accused in order to facilitate their legal actions. Judges refused to accept the testimony of witnesses whom they knew had perjured themselves and made deals with other witnesses for reduced sentences in exchange for confessions. The president himself was pressured into resigning by some of his closest associates and friends. Finally, it appears that the resignation of the president may have involved informal agreements concerning the terms of the resignation and that the investigators may have been consulted about the acceptability of these terms. Illegal or extralegal actions were used to restore the rule of law. It would appear that the rule of law requires as a prop the rule of men.

Watergate revealed that the restoration of legitimacy could be granted only by men who as self-appointed guardians of authority choose to restore legitimate rule of law. Both the resignation under pressure and the restoration of legal authority revealed the previous absence of law.

LEGITIMATION PROBLEMS REVEALED BY WATERGATE

It is generally agreed that the Nixon administration had no legal justification for the bombing of Cambodia, the theft of Daniel Ellsberg's psychiatric files, the break-in of the Democratic Party's national offices in the Watergate building, the attempts to suppress the investigation of Watergate, and, finally, the efforts to conceal and destroy legal evidence related to the Watergate cover-up. Some of these illegal activities were ordered by the president himself. Others were ordered and executed by officials appointed by the president acting on the strength of his office. All of these acts were committed while Richard M. Nixon was president of the United States. None was challenged until after he was inaugurated for his second term of office, an election he won by one of the largest electoral majorities in modern times.[4] Most of these crimes were reported in the press but were played down and little noticed. Only after the Watergate break-in trial and the resignation of Elliot Richardson after the election did the public respond to facts that were already reported. In spite of or perhaps because of his alleged crimes, it is clear that Nixon convinced many citizens of his qualifications for the presidency. This fact alone calls for some explanation of the sources of legitimation of the American government in the actions of the leader himself.

Moreover, it was only because of the naive discovery of the Watergate break-in by a night watchman who took his job seriously and was helped in his work by the apparent overconfidence of the Watergate burglars that the train of events leading to the Watergate investigation was initiated. Similarly, Nixon's demise might never have occurred if he had not, because of the tapes, supplied the hard evidence to refute his own denials. Presumably, without the discovery of the break-in and the existence of the tapes, Richard Nixon could have remained president of the United States, the crisis of legitimacy created by Watergate would not have occurred, and the concept of "government of laws, not of men" would still be intact, at least for those who accept this conception. The maintenance of secrecy supports legitimacy and becomes a part of it. It would appear that the processes by which Watergate was brought to the attention of the governed are also a part of the problem of legitimacy. Mass communications, counterintelligence, mutual covert surveillance, propaganda and public opinion, while having no place in received theories of legitimation and delegitimation, must be made part of the analysis.

In the administrative state, mass communications and image

management (propaganda) are also branches of government which are not part of the traditional language of the "rule of law." Thus the rules and regulations (the ethics and morality) governing the competition for the attention of the public are neither specified nor codified. Competitive struggles to claim the right to the attention of constituencies and to define political issues are linked to free speech and free press, but can also include struggles to define and specify the grounds of legitimacy itself. The concepts of public opinion, intelligence, and political legitimacy are closely related.

Historically, the ideas of knowledge and of intellectual enlightenment have been associated with the slogans "freedom of speech" and "freedom of the press." The right to freely transmit information and news was thought of as a powerful instrument not only for resisting the tyranny of government but also for the creation of an educated political community. The safety and well-being of democracy were thus linked to an intellectually enlightened public. With the advent of mass media and highly complex institutions of opinion formation, the slogan "freedom of speech and press" has been extended to cover these newer media. However, the media are highly complex bureaucracies which specialize in gathering and transmitting news and information. As corporate structures, which are similar to business corporations, they have claimed under the legal fiction of the corporate individual equal rights to freedom of speech and press. The success of this claim has given to the media a powerful voice in supporting or denying the legitimacy of slogans.

The conflict between government and media includes vast administrative and organizational struggles to appropriate the power of slogans. The marketplace in which these struggles occur bears no relationship to the marketplace of free speech as conceived by liberals in the nineteenth century. The administrative and organizational apparatus employed in these struggles is not part of any tradition of rule of law as related to constitutionalism.

The absence of formal rules for the regulation of competition between government and media has meant that the relationship between these two institutions is regulated by other means. At times, their representatives may negotiate formal contracts, but at other times the relationship may rest on informal understandings, threats, bribes, and blackmail. Thus, in both government and the institutions of the mass media, there is a backstage of administrative process which is managed by political and administrative bureaucrats who make laws and break them and at the same time manage the appearance of legality.[5] So long as frontstage and backstage are kept apart—in our terms, so long as the propaganda remains intact—crises of legitimacy are not likely to occur.[6]

Backstage political processes may be conveniently referred to as the invisible government.[7] In the invisible government, relations among leaders are based on powerful forms of clique group loyalty. The inner clique or cliques, whose existence in the Nixon administration were so fully revealed during the Watergate investigations, play an autonomous—that is, not legitimated—role in the governing process. Because they can strengthen the appearances of frontstage politics, their role can include the maintenance of beliefs in legitimacy. A key question in the study of the problem of legitimacy is: What are the circumstances under which front- and backstage are broken down sufficiently to reveal to believers that their faith has not been justified?

An answer to this question involves several political processes whose examination may shed some light on the problems of legitimation in modern industrial, bureaucratic society:

– On what grounds do the groups, classes, and individuals who are the governed grant consent to be governed? We do not assume that all groups grant consent for the same reason—that is, there do not necessarily exist overarching legitimacy symbols and ideologies.
– Who among the totality of political actors will assume responsibility for exposing backstage politics to the point of threatening the faith of large numbers of citizens?
– Once political faith is destroyed, what processes are available for its recreation, and who will elect those who administer the restoration?

VARIETIES OF CONSENT

If the values governing consent are different for different groups, it follows that assessments of what is legitimate government and what illegitimate will also vary among different constituencies. In this brief essay I cannot discuss the full array of groups in American society, so I will limit the discussion to the older middle classes, the industrial and factory working classes, and the new middle classes.[8]

The Old Middle Classes

Throughout the course of Nixon's impeachment proceedings, the opinion polls reported a stable 25 percent of the electorate to be in support of the president and his government. For these citizens, legality or illegality was not at issue in their acceptance of Nixon. Neither the admission of outright lies nor attempts to cover up lies were sufficient to disabuse them. At the time, the summer of 1974, analysts believed that this constituency was made up of middle-American middle classes whose loyalty was to conservatism and to the Republican party.[9] My own studies, with Joseph Bensman, of American society confirm this interpretation.[10] We called this group the "old middle classes" to distinguish them from the new middle classes, who are bureaucrats, managers, administrators, and professionals employed in public and private bureaucracies.[11]

The political experience of the old middle classes is most likely to have been shaped in towns, smaller cities, and county governments. In our study of Springdale, we found that this group under the leadership of Jones routinely had recourse to the use of extralegal measures in local politics. In a later essay,[12] we described the position of the old middle class relative to newer cultural and political movements in American society and pointed out that they could be both defensive and at times desperate because of their fear of losing control. We would argue that Nixon represented the conservatism and Republicanism of this older-middle-class tradition and simply enacted on the national stage the political style Jones enacted in Springdale. Thus, for them, Nixon's "criminal" conduct did not depart from tradition but upheld basic

American moral values. As a result, Nixon's conduct did not call for reactions of moral revulsion or withdrawal of credence but required support and loyalty in the face of adversity. Defense of party and patronage and of the American system were more important as issues than mere legality or illegality.

In this view, victory at the polls guarantees four years of rule and grants to the victors the choice of political means. Surely, many in the older generation of the Republican old middle class could remember their defeats at the hands of Franklin D. Roosevelt in the 1930s and 1940s. They remember having suffered the "regulation of business," the introduction of the welfare state, and the attempted packing of the Supreme Court. Many regarded Roosevelt to have exceeded the legal limits of the presidency and thought him to be a criminal. Yet they would say that they accepted the electoral process as the source of governmental legitimacy and did not run Roosevelt out of the White House. They would agree with Nixon, who throughout Watergate seemed to be saying, "I won the election, why can't I be president for four years?"

Legitimacy based on party victory rests upon mutual acceptance by opposing parties of the results of elections.[13] Victors, in this tradition, are free to choose political means, including those used to gain victory. Losers do not accept the legitimacy of the rule of the victors, but agree only to accept their own defeat on the grounds that they will have a chance to try for victory at a later time. Legitimacy for both winners and losers resides in the hope of future victories.[14] Crises of legitimacy are avoided or forestalled because all contenders for power can hope that power will be theirs in the future. The expectation of future victory results in political self-restraint, unwillingness to use violence to gain power, and acceptance of the authority of the victors. Thus Nixon did not use force to retain power because he could entertain the hope of a political comeback.

The Industrial and Factory Working Classes

In their daily work, industrial and factory workers (hard hats), as distinguished from service and white-collar employees, tend to confront inert objects rather than people or paper. Their routine work activities involve neither psychological sensitivity to clients nor bookish or literary kinds of intellectuality. For the most part these workers, except for some younger ones who have had college educations, are defensive with respect to their abilities to understand the complexities of the culture and politics of modern industrial society. They are likely to prefer clear-cut political choices that enable them to take a political stand without the need for knowledge in depth. As hard hats, they are likely to be suspicious and perhaps resentful of the wordiness and intellectual sophistication of "egg heads." George Meany, president of the AFL-CIO, has embodied the attitude and style of political gruffness and bluntness that is representative of the communicative level preferred by these workers.

President Nixon, as part of his political strategy, addressed the hard hats on their terms. He also made direct advances to George Meany and gained his political support. His appeals to workers consisted in clear definitions of the meaning of loyalty and patriotism to the nation, and included an image of a tough president who opened the White House to hard hats at the expense of intellectuals. This working-class constituency, relatively new to the Republican Party, was one of Nixon's creative innovations which, incidently, confounded both the Democratic Party and the socialist and Marxist political left. Later, when he recognized that he had been taken, it was also a source of embarrassment to George Meany.

I exclude the white-collar working and service classes from this analysis because they have a much greater familiarity with the inner workings of bureaucracies and because to them "paper and pencil work" comes easily. Bureaucratic procedures such as filing, pre- and postdating letters, rigging tax returns, destroying correspondence, fixing conferences, placing blame on scapegoats, sandbagging, stonewalling, protecting the boss and so forth are all part of everyday work experiences. In their case, the revelations about the inner workings of the White House were recognizable, comprehensible, and believable. For this group, a critical point in the erosion of the president's credibility occurred when Rose Mary Woods, in a photo reproduced in newspapers throughout the country, demonstrated how she accidentally destroyed a portion of a tape while transcribing it. Miss Woods was shown operating the transcribing device with one leg fully extended and operating a telephone with one arm fully extended in the opposite direction. The critical eighteen minutes of erased tape were attributed to this maneuver. Secretaries and office workers would know from their daily work that this pose was unbelievable. A difference in an ability to see (through) a rigged scenario suggests the difference in political skill between white-collar as opposed to industrial and factory workers. Such differences in political skills among the working groups in society suggests that even workers are not a unitary constituency whose grounds for granting or withdrawing consent are common.[15]

For the industrial and factory working classes the will to believe in the image of Nixon as a leader was built on themes such as: (a) the tough, shrewd, political tactician who held close reins over irresponsible congressmen; (b) the bold leader who would restore order to American society after the civil rights, racial, and student disorders which the Democratic Party had tolerated during the 1960s; (c) the rational administrator who as president was reasserting control over an overexpanded, frequently autonomous Federal bureaucracy; (d) the world statesman, tough on Communism, but unafraid to deal with the Communists in order to promote American interests. In short, major segments of the working class could place faith in Nixon and be assured that their political interests were protected.[16]

At the time the Watergate scandal began to unfold, the honeymoon between President Nixon and the workers was still in effect. However, as the investigations continued, seeds of doubt were sown and workers became less sure of their new-found political ally. The major feature of the Watergate investigations and the impeachment hearings was precisely that they lacked clarity, simplicity, and comprehensibility. They were highly technical and legalistic in form, and were frequently ambiguous and difficult to follow. To attempt to understand them required close and sustained attention, and even then it was difficult to follow the twists, turns, implications, and ramifications of the proceedings and the intentions of the antagonists. The working classes in particular were neither equipped to digest this material nor capable of easily judging truth and falsity. Nixon's outright denials and brazen efforts to conceal could appeal only to those who wished to avoid involvement in the political complexities of the situation. One must understand that what was later called his duplicity may have been a conscious effort on Nixon's part to retain a positive working-class public opinion by giving workers an opportunity to make a simple choice based on loyalty and patriotism. It was to this class more than to any other that Nixon offered a simple choice when he defended the presidency rather than himself. At this point Nixon's claim was to the sanctified legitimacy of the office, not to himself or the law.

The Watergate and cover-up investigations created confusion and uncertainty and perhaps even fear in the working classes. Since the basis of faith in Nixon rested on trust, the violation of trust resulted in feelings of betrayal and a moral crisis for believers, including political disenchantment and reversion to more customary forms of cynicism—"all politicians are crooks"—characteristic of America's working classes. However, though the disenchantment of the working classes came late, it represented a major source of delegitimation of the Nixon administration. The meaning of this delegitimation must be made clear.

The working classes accepted the legitimacy of Nixon and his government because Nixon recognized and accepted them and, equally importantly, relieved them of the responsibility for understanding the processes of government. Thus a group's willingness to be co-opted cognitively and spiritually (for whatever reason) may be a basis for the consent necessary for political legitimacy. However, this type of legitimacy is effective only so long as the co-optation, the will to believe, is not violated by a shattering of the faith, by the feeling of having been double-crossed. When faith is shattered, withdrawal from co-optation occurs.

However, withdrawal from the co-optation left the working classes in the same position they had been in before— politically powerless—until some other leader or agency offered to co-opt them. The critical factor, then, is not that the government needs acceptance of its legitimacy from the working classes but rather the kinds of political roles that are assigned to them by the ruling elite. Thus there need not be a *common* belief in the rule of law or rational–legal legitimacy as a prerequisite for the operations of modern governments. Other, short-term bases for legitimacy may be created by political leaders when it is convenient for them to do so, or such belief may be simply regarded as unnecessary regardless of basic ideology or belief.

The New Middle Classes

The new middle classes are different from the bourgeoisie identified with the nineteenth-century development of democratic institutions as described by Marx. This bourgeoisie made its claim to political participation on the strength of its new industrial capital and on the economic power which accrued to it as a result of the success of capitalist business enterprise. The new middle classes neither base their social and political position on ownership of business capital, nor do they necessarily commit themselves to ideologies of capitalism. Their claim to status and income is based on education, skilled expertise in the tasks required of large-scale bureaucracies and professions, and their ability to participate through their occupational roles in decision-making that affects the society as a whole. One of its problems has been to find a political role that would be consistent with a moderately successful, educated, and cultivated self-image.

As the educated elite of the society, they hold key technocratic positions in some of the older as well as newer public institutions. The university is one of the older institutions that have become major sources of their support. Through the university and university-related institutions such as institutes of higher learning and think tanks, they have had access to policy-makers in education, defense, planning, and public opinion. More importantly, however, modern institutions of public opinion have not only been a major source of economic support but also a crucial channel of access to information-consuming publics. Thus news commentators, foreign correspondents, journalists, editors of scholarly and unscholarly magazines, public-opinion pollsters, advertising men and public-relations counsels contribute to the formation of public opinion. In an epoch when the educated can believe in the social construction of reality, the importance and effectiveness of knowledge and propaganda cannot be underestimated. The new middle classes in part have made their claims to privileged political participation on the mystique of controlling knowledge and intelligence.

The idea of natural law, of God and divine justice, and of Adam Smith's free market as the basis of economic justice are not parts of their ideology. Bentham's slogan, "the greatest good for the greatest number," is likely to be invoked when it is recognized that a particular policy involves a clash of interests. The concept of the public interest is not regarded as transcendent but rather as a link to ideologies of democratic pluralism and to the possibility of a managed balance of social and economic justice by the operators of the bureaucratized corporate society. The public interest is also the slogan which justifies claims to the privileged role of technical intelligence in politics.

The rise in political importance of the educated new middle class has been associated with the growth in organizational and bureaucratic complexity of the opinion, propaganda, and communications industries. As an occupational group, it monopolizes technologies of production in symbol-making industries and is the source of supply for the consumers of opinion and communication.[17]

The educated elites of the new middle classes are still in the process of attempting to find ideologies to support and justify their ascendency and their claims to political participation. Robert Lilienfeld describes the ideology of systems theorists who make their claim to authority on the grounds of scientific rationality applied to societal administration. For systems theorists, the public interest is represented by the rational objectivity inherent in the logics of the system. Peter Ludz[18] describes the application of this ideology to Eastern European nations where the ruling administrative classes are attempting to replace outmoded revolutionary ideologies with ideologies of systems functions. If the system can be said to be functionally interrelated at all managerial levels, then all participants ought to share in the operation of society. Thus the unanticipated growth of the state bureaucracy in socialist countries is solved as a problem because the rewards of state power ought to be distributed to participants at all levels in the social system. The result would be a withering away of the state and fulfillment of a revolutionary promise.[19] Another example is the work of John Kenneth Galbraith, who, writing from the perspective of liberalism, came close to supplying an ideology for state economic planners when he described the functions of the technostructure in *The New Industrial State*. Other similar claims have been made by those who have proclaimed the end of ideology in postindustrial society. As a substitute for the end of ideology, they have proposed rational planning based on social–scientific analysis of social indicators by social scientists. Their claim to predict the future through futurology is a claim for authority based on a mystique of foreknowledge. The efforts of all these theorists are attempts to supply an ideological underpinning to the ascendency of what Djilas called for Eastern Europe the new class[20] and what we refer to here as the new middle class. A key dimension of Watergate was the relationship between this class and the Nixon administration.

In contrast with the 1968 election, when Richard Nixon did not have the support of this class, a substantial portion of it, including university professors and journalists and writers, voted for him in 1972. By 1972, President Nixon had recast his image from one based upon his defeat of Helen Gahagan Douglas and his prosecution of Alger Hiss to an image of the masterful professional politician who could be trusted with the administration of domestic and international affairs in contrast with his opponent, George McGovern, who appeared naive, disorganized, uncertain, and overly responsive to hippies and student radicals. Thus, this class could identify Nixon as an astute political bureaucrat even though this claim to rule violated some elements of such ideologies as pluralism, futurology, and technical planning rationality. It was not until the Watergate exposures, however, that this class, much like the working classes, began to feel the sense of betrayal and the loss of trust which became the basis for a reassertion of its sense of political morality independently from its occupational ideologies.

THE POLITICAL BUREAUCRAT AND THE MANAGEMENT OF IDEOLOGY

In his actions as president of the United States, Richard M. Nixon not only rejected the claims of these newer-middle-class ideologies but also their claimants. He represented the ideology of the rational political bureaucrat whose *modus operandi* depends upon the blind loyalty of clique associates and not upon the acceptance of alternative ideologies. He used his own corps of managerial technocrats as a vehicle for his illegalities and his programs, but he did not ideologize them. In fact he did this while attacking governmental bureaucracy and the civil service. Thus the vast majority of the new middle class were psychologically, occupationally, and politically excluded from both participation and a sense of participation. The administration's techniques of media and opinion management were employed at the expense of the new middle classes.

The role of the new middle class in the legitimation process was revealed during the Watergate scandal and the resignation of President Nixon. It opposed Nixon because he excluded it from levels of political participation that it deemed consonant with its self-image.

President Nixon centralized the power of the presidency to a greater extent than previous presidents. He consolidated his power in five major areas of government and party operations.

First, foreign affairs were placed in the White House by the simple method of abandoning cold-war policies to which other Federal bureaucracies, especially the State Department and the Department of Defense, were still committed. By inaugurating détente as a policy and keeping its contours secret until dramatic public announcements could be made, Nixon immobilized other agencies; lacking information, they could not publicly debate the issue, let alone oppose the policy. Thus Nixon and Kissinger could dominate a major reversal of foreign policy largely without reference to the Federal bureaucracy or Congress.

Second, the Office of Management and Budget was set up within the executive branch as a watchdog agency designed to scrutinize government operations in all spheres.

Administratively, it stood between the president and his own cabinet members and was the device by which the president undercut their authority. The key administrative technique included in this by-passing of the traditional authority of the cabinet was to assign a representative of OMB (in effect a presidential agent) to policy-making positions in each department of government. The penetration of departments by a presidential agent who had direct access to the White House was a formalization of interorganizational clique control[21] over all branches of government, thus rendering impotent alternative sources of authority and policy.

Third, the systematic presidential practice of impounding congressionally approved expenditures deprived congressmen of one of their main sources of rewards to their constituents, that of bringing money into their districts and states. Impounding of funds weakened the position of congressmen in relation to their constituencies, weakened their bargaining position with lobbyists who had already paid for their share of funds that were blocked by impounding, and made them more dependent on the president for campaign funds and other patronage.

Fourth, revenue-sharing or the direct grants of Federal funds to state, town, and county governments on a prorated scale again deprived congressmen of the right to claim credit for Federal expenditures in their voting districts. In effect, traditional patronage rights to which congressmen had become accustomed were being claimed by the White House itself. This was a hardship for urban liberal congressmen who had grown accustomed to taking credit from blacks and other minority and disadvantaged constituencies for funds channeled through OEO, welfare programs, educational spending, federal support of urban renewal, housing, and so forth.

Fifth, the traditional campaign and electioneering apparatus of the Republican Party was circumvented and rendered impotent by the creation of the Committee to Re-elect the President (Creep). Again, Creep was controlled by the White House, and campaign contributions were channeled through Creep rather than through the party, which as a result had almost no role in the 1972 campaign.

Nixon's successful domination of the Federal bureaucracy,

Congress, and the Republican Party enabled him to centralize societal administration in a manner that can be compared with the situation in Russia when the secretaryship of the Communist Party and governmental administration are combined in one person. Such centralization makes possible the orchestration of administrative actions related to widely disparate sectors of society. Not only does society appear to be managed with some measure of rationality, but it becomes apparent to some of those who are so managed that they have been excluded from participation by the processes of management. It is quite obvious that this process was not complete by the time of Watergate or there would not have been a Watergate crisis. But it is also obvious that the process was well underway.

However, since not all groups claim their right to participate, Nixon's policies of exclusion did not affect all groups equally. For purposes of this analysis I will mention only those groups on which Nixon's policies had a negative effect. The excluded groups included the following.

First, Congress, because legislative and patronage initiatives were monopolized by the White House. Congressmen were offered the alternative of accepting the White House policy or being penalized for rejecting it.

Second, bureaucrats in almost all branches of government, because they discovered they were surrounded by Nixon men in their own bureaus. Bureaucrats could either accept their impotence or could fight back by counterspying on the White House (e.g., Department of Defense and the CIA), or by sabotaging White House policy by legalism, delay, news leaks, and planned inefficiencies.

Third, the press, because it was denied access to the policy-making secrets of the White House and, when it attempted to pierce the managed veil, was denounced as the tool of an un-American, eastern radical establishment and subjected to threats of loss of licenses and of prosecutions for tax evasion. So tight was White House control over news releases and news leaks that the press corps was almost reduced to an agitprop branch of government.

Fourth, universities and university-based consultants had their funds sharply curtailed and their services were not utilized. This was a particularly stunning blow to many

university professors and administrators who had been supporters of government policies throughout the cold-war
period. President Nixon's failure to defend them even after
they defended government-supported operations in the universities against radical students left them free and resentful.

Fifth, new middle classes, which had grown accustomed
to being recipients of educational, cultural, transportation,
and welfare benefits, because the White House redirected
these funds to another class of recipients under its program
of revenue-sharing.

President Nixon's politics of exclusion were carried out
largely within the framework of the law. The use of organized power cliques, employment of persons wholly dependent on the president, use of budgetary methods to destroy
competition, reversals of policy to by-pass existing centers of
authority, and administrative reorganizations to redistribute
power were legal methods of administration. Where the
success of these policies depended on bureaucratic technique,
no laws existed which could be invoked against the administrative methods used. At the level of governmental operations President Nixon's extraordinary success as a political
bureaucrat reduced his opposition to impotence. If President Nixon had continued to manage the society under his
terms, there would have been no necessity for a government of law or of rational legitimacy. All that would have
been required was an effective control of public opinion.[22]

THE FAILURE OF NIXON'S CLAIM TO LEGITIMACY

The evidence from the Watergate example shows that industrial, bureaucratic society functions without a dominant
ideology of legitimation based on rational–legal authority.
However, while arguing against the Weberian concept of
rational–legal legitimacy as the basis of modern society, I
have also noted the existence of a multiplicity of other ideologies and bases of legitimacy that can coexist and occasionally merge with each other. Class, occupational, and
educational interests are alternative bases for ideologies which
can coexist with the "rule of law" as legitimating ideologies.
Even the idea of "administrative necessity" which replaces

ideological justification can be the basis for an alternative ideology.

The basis of legitimacy in modern society need not be only the rule of law—rational–legal authority, so defined— but can be defined separately to meet the aspirations of new classes, elites, and occupations. Thus modern legitimacy can be based on managerial or scientific necessity, a special technique or function, special kinds of knowledge (scientific systems, futurology, dialectics), judgment and political intelligence, and morality, to mention only a few.

President Nixon attempted to base his ideology of legitimacy on practical political intelligence while subverting the rule of law, even while he preserved its public forms. He also exalted the charisma of his office, the presidency, over and above the rule of law. Ultimately, President Nixon, the masterful politician, demanded the *trust* of others on the basis of his political know-how supported in part by some red-neck, Protestant, practical morality (if it works, it's good). He supported this claim by simultaneously attempting to withdraw legitimacy from other claimants who based their claims on science, systems analysis, and universal morals. His claim was sustained by the appearance of success, carefully managed by stage managers and image makers.

Part of President Nixon's success was based on his ability to make his enemies and opponents appear to be incompetent, bumbling, or foolish—above all, incapable of operating the American political system because they were too idealistic, unable to create efficient organizations, not politically hard-headed, too ideological or too flabby in their liberalism. By his formula for legitimation, success could only breed success, and it appeared that in 1972 the majority of Americans were prepared to accept both the appearances of success and the legitimacy claims.

In terms of this argument, President Nixon's *failure* can be attributed to the appearance of incompetence, ambivalence, and hesitancy in his political mismanagement of the Watergate cover-up. By revealing incompetence and an inability to cope with his opponents and enemies, he violated his own claim to legitimacy based on mastery of politics. This failure made it necessary for President Nixon to introduce into his political style complexity, evasion, defensiveness, and trickiness, thus violating his promise of simplicity and confidence. Loss of his claim to trust was experienced as a betrayal by many who had accepted the claims, especially his new working- and middle-class constituencies. This gave a new chance to all those with competing legitimacy claims to press their claims to the newly created audiences of the betrayed who apparently were prepared to shift from a legit-imacy ideology based on practical political success to a legit-imacy ideology based on morality.

But the idea of the rule of law and even perhaps the notion of basic inalienable rights had some deeper resonances during the late stages of Watergate. It may take enormous amounts of immorality and criminality to evoke these resonances, but when evoked they resulted in an extremely intense reaction against Nixon by a majority of the citizens. In this extreme instance, the individual citizen perhaps feels or sees that his own political fate may indeed be connected to an ideol-ogy of the rule of law.

THE PROCESS OF RELEGITIMATION

The forces at work in the resignation of President Nixon involved more than legal and judicial processes. They in-cluded not only a clash of class and political-party interests but also a significant role for the opinion and media indus-tries. Moreover, class and party interests intersected within these industries when there was a mutuality of interests between them. These interests included claims to power, protection of jobs, and the preservation of a sense of self-worth and self-mastery in the face of emasculation by higher bureaucrats.[23] The question is, how were threats to these interests transformed into a withdrawal of consent?

Those who claim a right to grant legitimacy are limited to those who have access to the attention of publics. In this perspective, the concept of legitimate authority has a much narrower meaning than is usually attributed to it in conven-tional theory. Democratic, pluralist, and radical-left theo-ries of legitimation represent no more than the ideologies of specific interest groups who make their claim to partici-pation on the strength of these ideologies. Thus the new middle classes connected to the knowledge and opinion industries make their claims with ideologies that claim privileged participation for themselves. This phenomenon has been commonplace in the history of class ideologies, but it is unique in modern society because its claimants are the professors, academicians, journalists, writers, opinion specialists, social scientists, and others who play special roles in the historically unique institutions of opinion, communication, and knowledge dissemination—that is, the institutions through which claims and counterclaims to legitimacy are made. The concept of legitimation is thus restricted to those groups capable of either making a claim or refusing to accept the claims of others. Ordinarily these claims have been made at the time of elections, and elections have been thought to validate the claims. Watergate represents a rejection of the legitimacy of the electoral claim without a testing of the legality of the rejection in an impeachment process.

The work of the media industries in their reporting of the congressional investigations destroyed Nixon's legitimacy not by attacking policy but by attacking the moral tone and illegalities of his administration. The revelation of backstage bureaucratic acts such as spying, lying, sabotage, intimidation, bribery, pay-offs, co-optation, stonewalling, blackmail, and so forth were exposed to public view. Exposure of these bureaucratic ethics and morality by the press created new constituencies of nonbelievers in the legitimacy of political institutions. Nixon, too, became aware that the grounds for his claim to legitimacy had shifted from electoral victory and political mastery to the ethics and morality of his bureaucratic conduct when he felt obliged to declare to the nation, "I am not a crook." In making this statement, he indicated his acceptance of his opponents' rules of legitimation. His acceptance gave courage and conviction to the press that their standards of legitimacy were morally correct and justified.

Equally important was acceptance by Nixon and his circle of opinion pollsters' reports throughout the summer of 1974 that only 25 percent of the public supported the government. Nixon attempted to redress this low percentage rating by engaging in dramatic foreign-policy activities designed to make a claim to Americans that protection of national interests by the master diplomat was sufficient grounds for legitimacy, but because of détente no clear international enemy existed and sentiments of nationalism based on national security appeared not to carry weight in support of this claim. In the late stages of Watergate, no claims other than morality and legality were effective. Upon resigning, President Nixon justified his resignation on the grounds that he had lost his support in Congress. In his terms, he had lost his political base. In our terms, he had lost his legitimacy because he had accepted the claims to legitimacy of others.

In Latin American countries, Nixon's resignation would be regarded as a *golpe*—a coup d'etat—and another political party would take power. As an American-style *golpe*, Watergate did not have this result. Legality was maintained by the ascension of a previously appointed vice-president.

Apart from this thin but important observation of the rules of legality, we may ask where it was that legality resided before and during the *golpe*. The answer to this question seems to be that it inhered in those people, such as Alexander Haig,[24] who prepared President Nixon to accept his own resignation, and the circle of Gerald Ford's friends, who appointed themselves to plan and manage governmental operations in anticipation of President Nixon's resignation.[25] When Vice-President Ford became involved in his friends' plans to inaugurate him and chart the course of his administration, he acted on the basis of a claim to future legitimacy: the legitimacy of his actions rested upon the expectation of Nixon's resignation. All of these actions were the actions of our then-existing invisible self-legitimating government.

During the congressional investigations, the impeachment hearings, and the resignation, no challenge to the legitimacy claims of others was made by either left revolutionary groups, militarists, or conservative businessmen. No attempt was made to seize the reins of government and rule on the basis of another set of claims. In point of fact, all of these groups were united by anti-Nixon ideology that had as its central tenet the desirability of removing him from office. Yet throughout the period of investigations and the paralysis of executive leadership, the government continued to function at the level of its bureaucratic mechanics. No class or group was prepared to press a counterclaim, even though there was a vast disenchantment with the members of the ruling elite. While the symbols of governmental legitimacy had been destroyed, and Nixon's specific claims were rejected, no new ones replaced them. The delegitimation of past symbols appears to be the only basis upon which the citizenry is prepared to consent to be governed. It is in this negative sense, perhaps, that the new middle class can achieve an ultimate sense of its self-worth and its sense of importance in the governing of modern society.

President Ford has made his appeals for support on the basis of candor, honesty, and political accessibility, replacing the appeals of intelligence and political practicality used by Nixon prior to Watergate. He has stressed the morality and legality of his presidential actions, and he has followed a policy of allowing full disclosure of past immoralities and illegalities in such agencies as the CIA, FBI, and Department of Justice. The American public seems to have accepted President Ford's claim, and journalists have been content to focus their attention on past indiscretions and illegalities. Thus President Ford, up to October 1975, has been able to govern with a relatively high public-opinion rating and with relatively little backstage scrutiny by the press. The legitimacy of government has been temporarily restored simply because President Ford's claims have not been rejected, for whatever reasons.

RADICALISM, MORALITY AND LEGITIMACY

Ideologists of the left, even when they claim descent from Marx, have abandoned the idea of economic class and class-based ideologies. For them, class has been replaced by the values of science and technology as central categories of analysis. Ideologies of acceptance or rejection of these values define for them the scope of legitimacy problems of late capitalism. Since science and technology are spheres of activity managed by academicians, administrators, bureaucrats, and technocrats, the left criticism is an attack on the political role of the right and middle sectors of the new middle classes. Thus left ideologists support those within the middle classes like youth, women, and communitarians who reject the results of modern science and technology. Their overall attacks on the social structures of late capitalistic societies have stressed the irrationalities of the productive and distributive systems. Because of these irrationalities they have called for a delegitimation of prevailing capitalistic institutions and governing methods. All of these political approaches are premised on the assumption that institutional and societal rationality are achievable by other means (a higher rationality than even that of science—perhaps the dialectic) and that these alternative approaches would produce results that would better serve society (the public interest).

Commitment to the ideology of a higher rationality has influenced their attitude toward violence and revolution. The disorder, confusion, and uncertainty of revolutionary violence run counter to order and rationality. It is perhaps for this reason that critical sociologists have not followed the politically activist dimensions of Marxism, but have confined their energies to a criticism of the irrationalities of late capitalism. However, even the revolutionary left in its own way is committed to a rational reconstruction of society for the purpose of fulfillment of fundamental human needs not now being met by late capitalism. Thus their rationality includes an attempt at an even more comprehensive rational organization of society than the rationality of those who only criticize. However, in the case of the revolutionary left, the rational organization of society is deferred until after the revolution.

The differences in ideological claims for privileged political participation made by the various sectors of the middle classes conceal the ideological similarities among them. As the educated, intellectual sector of society, the middle classes have stressed the functional necessity of rationality in governance. The rationality of science and technology has been absorbed into a legitimacy claim for the class itself. When science and technology are regarded as antirational in their consequences—that is, producing socially undesirable effects—resort is had to the moral condemnation of the bearers of science and technology. When use of legal rationality by government results in political defeats that retard class ascendency or class interests, legal rationality is either repressive or is regarded as immoral in its consequences. Terms such as rationality, irrationality, legality, and repressiveness stand as code indices for a belief by these classes that they are the moral arbiters of society. They are the definers of rationality and the designers of the future ideal society. Claims to moral righteousness thus relativize and make arbitrary the traditional rhetorics of legitimacy based on "rule of law," legality, and electoral results.[26]

The combining of rationality and morality as conditions for acceptance of governmental legitimacy has posed problems for the bureaucratic state because the moral codes that are invoked cannot be adhered to by the political bureaucrat who holds the power of government in his hands. At one extreme the Weatherman Underground Organization claims moral justification for its armed attacks on the institutions of government,[27] and on the other hand the CIA has justified to itself the moral necessity of spying on other branches of government. The arrogation of the moral authority to claim legitimacy for all varieties of political action places the politician in a defensive position because it constrains him to appear to be moral under circumstances where political choice involves moral compromises. Under these rules of politics the legitimacy of rulers can be challenged easily.

But, while there are a multitude of ways in which legitimacy can be challenged in modern society, consent and belief in legitimacy or illegitimacy are not required from all groups. The claims for legitimacy made by dissident groups— whether based on moral, radical, or reactionary ideologies— do not necessarily destroy a system of legitimacy or societal structure. Thus the attribution of absolute requirements for assent and universal legitimacy assumed to be necessary by some critical sociologists is more a product of their own need to believe and their own need for self-legitimation than it is an attribute of the social system.

The amount of withdrawal of consent necessary to overturn a system is substantial and would depend not only on the strategic position, numbers, and strength of dissidents, but also on the capacity of the system to maintain a minimal level of routine operations if only based on habit and inertia. It is in this sense that one can speak of legitimacy as mechanical or routinized in contemporary industrial–bureaucratic societies.

Notes

1. For a cogent statement of this position, see Hans J. Morgenthau, "Decline of Democratic Government," *The New Republic*, CLXXI (Nov. 9, 1974), 13–18.
2. For a contemporary version of this statement, see John R. Silber, "The Thicket of Law and the Marsh of Conscience," *Harvard Magazine*, November, 1974, pp. 14–18.
3. "Our constitution works; our great Republic is a government of laws and not of men," stated Gerald Ford upon assuming the presidency.
4. The fact that the Democratic Party failed to make an issue of the Watergate break-in during the election would suggest that its leaders were neither morally outraged nor regarded it as an issue. Presumably this form of interparty spying is regarded as the norm in Washington.
5. Jonathan Schell's series of six essays in *The New Yorker*, June–July 1975, presents a thorough recapitulation of the illegal and extralegal underpinnings of Nixon's presidency. By his reassessment of almost all of Nixon's private presidential actions after the fact of the exposures, Schell presents in combination the secret and official sides of government. His simultaneous juxtaposition of rhetoric and reality within the Nixon administration reveals the two faces of the rule of law. A similar analysis of the mass-media industry has not yet appeared, although David Halberstam has laid out the contours for such an analysis in "Press and Prejudice: How Our Last Three Presidents Got the Newsmen They Deserved," *Esquire*, LXXXI (April 1974), 109–114.
6. At least some members of the journalism profession were chastened by the power of the press in penetrating government operations during the Watergate affair. See Katharine Graham. "The Press after Watergate: Getting Down to New Business," *New York*, Nov. 4, 1974, pp. 69–72, where the point is made that Congress allowed the press to do its investigative work and that the journalists overly enjoyed it because they felt that Nixon had deceived and tricked them. This author argues that the press damaged itself by overstepping its role, but offers no clear definition of what its role is or should be.
7. See Arthur J. Vidich and Joseph Bensman, *Small Town in Mass Society*, rev. ed. (Princeton NJ: Princeton University Press, 1968), chap. 9, for a description and analysis of this form of government.
8. While it would be helpful to examine the political ideologies of the social and economic upper classes, they are less well known now than they were thirty or forty years ago because since then their

economic and social commitments and identifications have become internationalized and therefore their conceptions of legitimacy may transcend the nation-state.

9. These are the remnants of the old middle classes described in C. Wright Mills, *White Collar* (New York: Oxford University Press, 1951).

10. Vidich and Bensman, *Small Town in Mass Society*; and Joseph Bensman and Arthur J. Vidich, *The New American Society* (Chicago: Quadrangle Books, 1971).

11. For futher clarification of the distinction between these two groups, see our debate with Ivan Light in "Recent Developments in American Society: Reply to Ivan Light," *Theory and Society*, II (1975), 125–133.

12. See Vidich and Bensman, *Small Town in Mass Society*, chap. 12, "A Theory of the American Community," pp. 317–347.

13. There is some indication that Nixon felt cheated by his loss to John F. Kennedy in the 1960 election. In that election, the last votes to be counted were Mayor Daley's votes in Cook County, Illinois, and the absentee ballots in the state of California. The election hinged on how these votes would be counted because they would determine the electoral votes of both states. The California vote went to Nixon and the Illinois vote to Kennedy, so that the election was won for Kennedy by the Cook County results. Nixon apparently agreed not to challenge the legality of these results and accepted his defeat, though not without bitterness.

14. This system places heavy emphasis on the politics of means. Nixon and his inner group never thought of themselves as having committed crimes. They operated on the principle of a higher morality in the cause of saving the country from its enemies. Gordon Liddy, one of the Watergate conspirators, stated this position most fully in "Gordon Liddy: A Patriot Speaks," *Harpers*, CCIL (October 1974), 45–51, where he invokes the revolutionary spirit and the lawlessness of the founding fathers to justify his moral duty to protect American values.

15. Even here, however, one could argue that knowledge of the inner operations of bureaucracy does not automatically account for the political disenchantment of white-collar, bureaucratically employed groups. It is possible that each individual regards his own work situation as unique and, as a result, fails to generalize his experience as the norm rather than the exception. Psychological processes of particularization prevent an awareness of the general phenomenon and enable the individual to preserve illusions about the nature of political bureaucracies. When such beliefs in exceptionalism are violated as was the case during Watergate, political disenchantment can be prevented only by a purge of those who by their actions have threatened the illusions. The purge restores credence and reconfirms the belief in exceptionalism.

16. The acceptance of President Nixon on these terms was characteristic of other groups as well. By November 1972, the belief in Nixon's political mastery was held by most Americans.

17. To the extent that there are social and occupational relations between members of this class, their influence may be extended through the informal socializing they carry out with each other. Thus we have the phenomena of literary establishments, writers' cliques, *samizdat* journalism, "fixed" reviews, orchestrated literary attacks, and so forth. For a time, the CIA organized and rationalized all these methods for coordinating the viewpoints of the media and communications industries. Because the CIA's activities were unsuspected, it was able to coordinate opinion more effectively than the Soviet Union's Agitprop, which lacks a credible front.

18. Robert Lillienfeld, "Systems Theory as an Ideology," p. 637–660, and Peter Ludz, "Marxism and Systems Theory," p. 661–674 in *Social Research*, vol. 42, no. 4, Winter, 1975. See also Peter C. Ludz, *The Changing Party Elite in East Germany* (Cambridge: The MIT Press, 1972), especially Part IV, for a comprehensive discussion of East European managerial ideologies.

19. But of course bureaucracy would replace the state.

20. Milovan Djilas, *The New Class* (New York: Praeger, 1957).

21. See Bensman and Vidich, *The New American Society*, pp. 91–103, for a description of the characteristics of interinstitutional power cliques and the coordination of bureaucracies by cliques.

22. In the Soviet Union, the knowledge and communications industries have been under central government control since shortly after the revolution. In the Soviet political system, control of these industries at the level of influencing the political "line" has indicated both who is in power and whose power is likely to be legitimated. In the United States, as shown by Watergate, these industries may play an independent role and are not wholly controlled by the central government.

23. In this respect, see David Halberstam's comparative analysis (in "Press and Prejudice," op. cit.) of John F. Kennedy, Lyndon B. Johnson, and Richard M. Nixon in their relations with the press. Halberstam argues that Kennedy succeeded in controlling the press by appealing to the vanity of the members of the press corps, and that the press protected Kennedy from exposure because Kennedy supported the journalists' image of their own importance. Nixon, apparently, was incapable of performing this kind of psychological bribery. As a result, Kennedy was a popular president, but we know much less about the operations of his government than we do of the Nixon administration. President Ford is following the unique policy of attempting to bribe the press by giving it an oversupply of information about past secret governmental operations, thereby directing its attention away from the actions of his own government. The press appears to have accepted this bribe because it offers unlimited opportunities for headlines and by-lines.

24. See Theodore H. White, *Breach of Faith: The Fall of Richard Nixon* (New York: Atheneum, 1975) for documentation of the role of Alexander Haig. White claims that Haig managed the country during the weeks preceding Nixon's resignation.

25. See *The New York Times*, Aug. 26, 1974, p. 1, for James M. Naughton's story "The Change in Presidents: Plans Began Months Ago," where the activities of the group headed by Philip W. Buchen are described in detail.
26. John R. Silber, in "The Thicket of Law and the Marsh of Conscience," takes this position when he argues that President Ford's unilateral pardon of former president Richard M. Nixon could have been used as an occasion for the restoration of the rule of law if Nixon had pleaded guilty prior to the pardon. He writes (p. 17): "Mr. Ford has told us that only he could write 'The End' on what he called the American tragedy of Watergate. Mr. Ford is wrong, for only the law can put an end to Watergate. But that end would be swiftly accomplished even now, were Mr. Nixon to sit down with the Prosecutor, agree on charges, plead guilty and thus complete the legal process. ... As soon as Mr. Nixon admits his guilt to properly drawn charges, President Ford's pardon restores our expectation of equal justice under law and mercifully closes the book of Watergate for Mr. Nixon." Professor Silber seems to be unaware that he has granted to Nixon the power to restore the rule of law. In his terms, because Nixon has not confessed to his crimes we do not have a rule of law. This explanation is excessively simple. It also has the disadvantage that it places Professor Silber in the position of being the moral arbiter of President Nixon's actions.
27. "The Weather underground organization is responsible for over 25 armed actions against the enemy. ... This includes the attack on the Pentagon in 1972 and on the State Department in 1975. Ten actions were directed against the repressive apparatus: courts, prisons, and in support of Black Liberation. This includes attacks on New York City Police Headquarters. ... Together they have resulted in approximately $10 million damage to the imperialists and a significant blow to their arrogance. ..." (*Osawatomie*, No. 2 [Summer 1975], p. 2).

17 Class and Politics in an Epoch of Declining Abundance*

Arthur J. Vidich

Historically, America has represented itself as an open society providing the promise and frequently the actuality of opportunity for almost all groups and classes. The cheap land of the American frontier and one hundred and fifty years of industrialization have supported a continuously expanding economy capable of absorbing generations of immigrants and supporting the mobility aspirations of almost all classes and groups except the blacks. Now, for the first time in American history there is the prospect for a long-term decline in the rate of economic growth and expansion, and hence, an abrogation of the promise that to many constituted the essential character of America. This change is related in part to such long-term trends as:

1. The increasing age of our capital base and increasing competition from more efficient producers in other parts of the world.
2. Increasing dependency on monopoly-determined high-cost petroleum imports necessitated in part by over-utilization in the past of low-cost domestic petroleum.
3. The rising cost of agricultural land relative to its productivity, caused in part by massive investments in land by international corporations, by holders of cheap dollars in dollar rich countries, and by Middle-Eastern and Latin American investors.
4. Fundamental changes in attitudes toward work resulting in replacement of the older work ethic based on a production mentality with a consumption mentality

---

* Reprinted from *Social Problems*, vol. 27, no. 5 (1980).

linked to a desire to achieve a given life-style at a chosen level without regard to the value of work and mobility *per se.*

DECLINES IN U.S. AUTONOMY AND ECONOMIC VITALITY

Seen in long-term perspectives, these trends are part of a worldwide sociocultural process. For the past several hundred years, the new world—especially the United States—has been at the center of world civilization. The apex of American power was probably reached between World War II and the beginnings of detente. Now it appears that this nation is losing some of the advantages accrued when its industrialization took place in a large virgin territory and many of its new inhabitants brought with them social and psychological predispositions which released vast stores of human energy into economic activities. These initial advantages are now not so great, as other societies and civilizations move toward a new center, or perhaps to a world with no center.

The dependence of the United States on an uncontrolled and perhaps uncontrollable world economy has for the first time in this century placed it in the position where it can no longer operate on the assumption of an autonomous national economy, directable without outside constraints. The internationalized world economy, which was in part created by the United States, now subjects its internal social and economic life to extrinsic processes.

Even from a purely economic point of view, not all individuals and groups are equally effected by inflation, unemployment and decreases in the rates of expansion. With regard to inflation, some groups have neither cost nor income elasticity, while others may have both. It is also possible for groups to have income but not cost elasticity, or vice versa, and, of course, different groups may have varying degrees of cost and income elasticity. Unemployment and under-employment may effect some ages, occupations, ethnic groups or races more than others, depending upon how particular industries or businesses are related to contractions or expansions of different sectors of the economy. Ethnic groups or races typically associated with declining industries may suffer, while others associated with expanding markets may benefit. Property-owning classes may experience losses or gains depending on the profile of their investment port-folios; those with investments in industries related to nu-clear energy may suffer losses while others who own rights in land or shares in oil companies may be beneficiaries of great increases in both demand and prices. The effects of inflation, unemployment or economic contraction do not have the same effects all across the social structure.

It would be ideal to analyze all the market situations of the multiplicity of groups and classes making up America, but in this essay we can only point to the effects the econ-omic trends noted above will have on a few. Our discussion will examine some sectors of the *upper* and *middle classes* and some *economically marginal groups*, and will focus on the fol-lowing questions.

1. Which groups and classes are most apt to bear the bur-den of unemployment, inflation and decreases in the rates of economic expansion?
2. What kinds of tensions and conflicts—and social resent-ments and hostilities—are apt to arise as result of the differential distribution of the economic burden?
3. What are the long-term prospects that American society will alter its dominant public ideology of maintaining an open society with opportunity for all?

EFFECTS ON THE UPPER CLASSES: OLDER AND NEWER

Some portions of the upper classes—for the most part the *older* upper classes whose original wealth was based on land grants, shipping, railways and post-Civil War heavy indus-try—continue to own land or have stocks or other resources in heavy industry, utilities and minerals. They are insulated from the negative effects of inflation and also from declines in the rate of expansion, as long as they are able to retain the benefits of tax and inheritance laws and interest poli-

cies usually written with their well-being in mind. The value
of their assets and income moves in phase with inflationary
rates and may exceed those rates if the value of real property, minerals and commodities rises at faster rates than
inflation. To the extent that these wealth holders have diversified their portfolios to include fossil fuels and minerals,
they are hedged against almost all short- and long-term economic fluctuations. Their economic position is stable in the
sense that it can only be altered by a change in the fundamental character of capitalism itself.

The economic stability of this sector of the upper class
could be threatened if social unrest and then political instability developed from dramatic downturns in the life situations of other groups. If economic decline or stagnation
erode the economic positions of the lower and the middle
classes to breaking point, the result could be large-scale social
discontent and political dissatisfaction among classes which
hitherto have always shared a basic commitment to the
American economic system. Such erosion of political commitment could be exploited by political parvenus—populist
and charismatic figures—promising easy solutions to the
economic and status problems of threatened groups. Under
such circumstances the old aristocracy of America and its
descendants, people who live off unearned income and who
have been instrumental in setting the cultural tone of the
country, may find it necessary to make bargains with new
political brokers who promise to protect their economic privileges. Their efforts to maintain their market advantages would
be increasingly dependent on precisely those political means
(e.g., favorable tax and inheritance legislation) that they do
not have personally and can only purchase from lobbyists
and legislators, who in their own quest for an economic or
political *quid pro quo* are likely to exact a high price. Should
this occur, an historic American economic sinecure based
on control and ownership of natural resources would be
transformed into a precariously protected political privilege.
The phenomenon of the politically protected sinecure may
arrive in America to create not a class of kept noblemen, as
has been the case in Europe for a long time, but rather a
nobility of the economically functionless epigoni of those
Anglo-Saxon Puritans whose original economic success

undermined the ideological foundations of the Puritan character that is today so heavily prized. Of course, if it is politically protected, such a class can sustain itself as long as the
economic system is willing to support it in the life-style to
which it has been accustomed. But if and when this class
begins to slide, its defensive political responses will rever-
berate throughout the society.

These *older* upper classes are to be distinguished from the
newer upper classes whose economic base is in mass communications, in electronics or aircraft industries with government contracts, and especially in oil and related machine-tool
products. Texas oil millionaires are an important segment
of the newer upper classes who have partly shoved aside
the older ones. While the wealth of the new does not always
distinguish them from the old, they are different in having
been tied from the beginning to politically determined market
privileges in a society in which—since the New Deal and
the beginnings of Keynesianism—government contracts, fran-
chises, subsidies and tax write-offs have become a prerequisite for access to market opportunities. From the beginning,
therefore, they have been identified with politics openly and
conspicuously and have played perhaps the most significant
role in influencing the executive and legislative branches;
they were in fact the first to rationalize and accredit the
arts of lobbying and to organize lobbying as the major
"nongovernmental" industry in Washington, D.C.

These business and industrial interests have now come to
be associated with the interests of regions, cities and, sometimes, occupational groups; what is good for the automotive
industry is good for Detroit, and what is good for Detroit is
good for the automobile unions. The special interests of
business and industry are thus supported by constituencies
that see their own interests linked to those of particular
segments of the business classes. We now have a type of "bread-
and-butter unionism" that has become society-wide, in which
all groups are conscious of where their interests reside, and—
barring the rare outbreak of altruistic idealism—respond only
in terms of those interests. In this new sort of political
economy, self-interest and instrumental rationality guide the
actions of all organized groups and each group seeks political alliances with all others that will be to their mutual ben-

efit. Thus, the political role of the new upper classes is not only conspicuous, it has also been accepted by large parts of society as a "necessary" part of the system. Even more important, however, is that the newer politically active upper classes are tied in an infinite number of ways to the managers, administrators and employees of industry who, in turn, see their own fate as being tied to that of business. These relationships—termed people's capitalism in the 1950s and 1960s—provide a source of political stability that might otherwise be threatened by advancing inflation and declining abundance. The political–economic administrative apparatus created as part of New Deal Keynesianism in the 1930s is now a foundation for political stability in its own right and serves to mute if not absorb some social resentment.

Those parts of the upper classes whose sources of wealth are based in petroleum are a special case because petroleum is a resource that now links the older and the new upper classes – particularly some parts of the Eastern establishment with the newer Texas and Southwestern oil fortunes. Because of the crucial role of petroleum in world industrialization and because the competition for its control is also international, the upper classes whose fortunes are based on oil have been obliged to limit and regulate their own domestic competition in order to be able to work together to enhance their positions on the world competitive market. A common interest in the prices and supplies of world oil thus connects one sector of the newer and older upper classes in the United States, creating a group uniquely apart from and above the rest of the upper class because its ability to influence the production and distribution of crude and refined petroleum on a world scale gives it tremendous power abo e and beyond the level of national governments. Part of the power of this group is based on its contracts and relationships with OPEC countries and with monarchs who are themselves even newer members of this now transnational class. And because their position is dependent on these foreign contracts and relationships, oil companies and their executives have a highly developed sense of international politics and a class identification both freeing them from some domestic political constraints and increasing their domestic political power. They may find themselves, willingly or unwillingly, in the role of political brokers between those who control the supply and those who determine its allocation for consumption. This type of independent political position is similar to that Lincoln Steffens described; the political "boss" in late nineteenth and early twentieth century American cities who was highly visible, highly resented and all-powerful. Theirs is, however, a kind of supra-institutional position which encourages ruthlessness, political experimentation and—above all—the use of extreme measures when necessary in order to protect narrow class interests. The internationalization of the world economic "order" and the destruction of the institutional framework of Keynesianism has opened up a new frontier for American laissez-faire capitalism.

In a period of declining rates of expansion, the upper classes are increasingly likely to resort to political means to protect and enhance their market positions. Moreover, such efforts are facilitated by the inability of political leaders to restrict and limit the predatory pricing activities of oil companies and OPEC. In addition, political leaders find it difficult to mobilize public opinion against them because the public is itself made up of a complex mix of groups already perceiving their own interests as being partly linked to business and industry. The public hopes that it might partly gain from the overall opportunities made available by the business system; people's capitalism enlarges the size of the predatory group. The result has been that the business managers of the newer upper classes gain a preponderant influence in governmental policy making, especially with regard to energy agencies. Political leaders, unable to organize and manage public resentment against the predatory groups, experience a political paralysis that leaves the field even more open to economic interests to legislate economic, welfare and social policy by pricing decisions. The paralysis of government and the high-handed methods of oil interests have led to increasing resentment of oil companies and of OPEC and to some advocacy for public ownership of oil resources. The more that governance is managed by this method, as both inflation and unemployment increase, the more the political economy is likely to disadvantage the poor, economically marginal blacks, marginal youth, welfare classes and workers who are not organized to resist.

EFFECTS ON ECONOMICALLY MARGINAL AND LOW-INCOME GROUPS

By low-income and economically marginal groups, we refer to all those (a) whose income is pegged at or near the minimum wage, (b) whose jobs are outside the organized labor force, (c) whose work is contingent upon day-to-day or week-to-week contracts, or (d) whose sole source of income is some form of welfare. Because their absolute income is low, economically marginal groups have the least income and cost elasticity; compared to other groups a larger percentage of their income is spent on such inflation-related necessities as food, clothing and shelter, and their incomes are the least likely to be indexed to inflationary rises. The specific sectors of the population in this category include a mixed racial and ethnic aggregate of impoverished urban and rural immigrants, traditionally poor indigenous Americans, the welfare classes (including some portions of age social-security recipients), and those portions of youth who have not found a point of entry into the job market.

These groups are disproportionately penalized by inflation, unemployment and declines in opportunity resulting from decreasing rates of economic expansion. The wages of unorganized workers do not keep pace with rising costs, and part-time and hourly wage workers have fewer opportunities for working extra hours or holding second jobs. Welfare remittances decline in value as inflation and rents increase, and the welfare classes find it more difficult to secure financial aid and social services as critics cut back on welfare budgets in periods of urban economic crisis. Both rural and urban poor become increasingly marginal to job and welfare markets and are steadily disenfranchised from society, with the result that the economy comes to produce an ever-enlarging group of internally displaced persons with no recourse other than some form of social and economic descent. Yet the lack of militancy on the part of these groups is a startling fact. Youth crime may be an expression of resentment, but it can also be a source of income. Similarly, small-scale white-collar crime may serve similar purposes for other groups who "sublimate" their hostility by finding ways to beat the system.

When such a descent occurs for these groups, it is not likely to be supported by the kinds of survival "cushions" that existed during the depression of the 1930s—return to the family homestead or to relatives on the farm. (Although there is the possibility of a certain amount of doubling-up in urban apartments, and of adult sons and daughters insisting on a prolonged stay in the homes of their more economically comfo ble parents.) The older ethnic ghetto, in the past a welf re system in its own right, also no longer exists. The older political party patronage systems have been displaced by state and federal welfare bureaucracies, and the newer black and Hispanic ghettoes have not developed internal systems of mutual aid because such cultural traditions of benevolence have been based on family ideology rather than community institutions. Transiency, as in the world of the hobo and bum, is tolerated less today by urban and state police, who are under political pressure to keep the municipal and state public image of "downtown" areas favorable for tourism and industry. As the poverty of some city dwellers increases, its visibility will be less tolerated by those committed to urban renewal of downtown areas and by property owners whose real-estate values are threatened by the presence of the visibly destitute: beggars, prostitutes, scavengers, bag ladies and others who pollute the visual harmony and aesthetic beauty of the urban landscape. Of course it is understood that the chronic poor do not have high expectations in the first place, and that their income and status decline is measured from such a low starting point that it can barely be called a descent. While this is true, it must also be remembered that the relative ascent of other groups is much greater. The poor may be more aware of their descent when they compare it to with the upward mobility of other groups. But again the absence of militancy is remarkable; the militancy of the 1960s seems not only to have been premature, but also may rob this decade's disfavored groups of a chance to repeat that militancy so soon after its prior expression.

Those whose only source of income is social-security benefits are said to be protected by a system of indexed social-security payments designed to reflect rates of inflation. However, such indexing lags behind and does not really compensate for rises in rents, taxes and other inflationary costs because the discretionary income of those who are wholly dependent on social security is marginal in the first place. Even as the economic position of these classes is eroded by inflation their costs to society are still high; medicare and medicaid benefits may save patients and prevent bankruptcy, but primarily they benefit the professional middle classes whose jobs are related to hospitals, nursing homes and medicine. These social-security classes will be more resented by the salaried middle-income groups whose income taxes increase proportionately to meet the increased costs of indexing and medical care. The salaried middle groups have continued to ask why they should bear the burden of supporting the aged and to inquire, "Who will pay for my indexed social-security benefits when I retire?" Congressmen may find it difficult not to listen to their complaints, and the social-security classes may begin to lose some of the political power that up to now has supported their indexed payments.

The "youthful disadvantaged" have actually become older and older in our present society. In some cases, youths may not enter the job market until the age of thirty or even later, while other, poorer young people may enter the labor force even before they are teenagers. We can speak of a class of economically marginal youth, but must recognize that it includes a complex aggregate of the uneducated and unpropertied—a substantial fraction of the population—which in the very nature of the developing occupational and economic system, is not able to make an effective occupational claim.

The life chances of any new generation will be partly governed by levels of opportunity and rates of economic expansion prevailing at the time it enters the job market. In periods of rising unemployment and decreasing expansion, penetration of that market becomes more difficult. The newest generation of lower-class youth have for the past ten years found it increasingly difficult to gain a foothold in that market. Significant numbers of youth reached maturity are either excluded from the market altogether or have been included only partially and occasionally. If the current recession results in an even greater rise in unemployment, the already dangerously large army of unemployed youth will be joined by both those now coming of age and by those who, because they are young and without seniority, will be the first to be laid off. It is quite certain, then, that youth will bear a disproportionate high share of the burden of unemployment and economic constriction.

The unemployed youth of the present generation are comparable to the unemployed youth generation of the 1930s only in the sense that their social and psychological predispositions toward society will remain with them as they pass through the social structure over the course of their life spans. But this generation's youth are in a worse situation than that of their predecessors, at least in the sense that unskilled minority youth seem to have become part of a permanent underclass with no hope of being redeemed by rising employment. Unless a major effort is made now to incorporate them into society they are likely to be a permanently disaffected group who will find it difficult to make ideological and career adjustments. If no legitimate political or economic means are found to solve their job and career problems, they are likely to find their own solutions in marginal and illegal activities or in forms of deviant and self-destructive conduct which will have deleterious effects on the quality of civic life at all levels and in all regions.

Increasingly the marginal welfare and youth classes will be cut off from the mainstream of society and will become a subproletariat based on minimal consumption and segmented social participation. Insofar as they lack skills or motivation there will be no way to incorporate them into the system. Insofar as the earth's land mass is saturated and the world no longer offers opportunities for rewarding adventure, mercenary employment, or promising emigration to overseas territories, they will have to be absorbed internally. They are likely to resent newer immigrant groups as competitors for nonexistent jobs, and they are likely to resent all those—such as the aged with fixed incomes or employed youth—who are secure. They are not likely to be committed to the American social and economic system and its values and will be open to whatever alternative private and political solutions arise. The social control of their resentments will be a continuing and increasing problem for the political managers of society.

EFFECTS ON THE MIDDLE GROUPS

The middle groups in the society are numerically dominant and are at present the most committed to the system. Their social privileges and rewards in income, position, profession, occupation, leisure, and medical and retirement benefits were secured during the period of economic expansion between 1950 and 1975, but they are by no means a unitary group. They are continuously subdivided into smaller and smaller segments at various skill, occupational, professional, industrial, agricultural and life-style levels, which are in turn subdivided even further by ethnic, racial and regional variations. The middle-class segment can include such diverse categories as skilled workers, teachers, professionals, managers, clerks and administrators. Their only common characteristic is their commitment to the system which has provided them with their good life.

At another level they can be differentiated with respect to their cost and price elasticity in relation to inflation. For example, professionals and industrial workers whose fees or contracts are tied to inflationary indices suffer inflation less than those whose incomes are not. Those who own real property, especially their own homes or income-producing paper, can regard such investments as a hedge against further inflation, and the changing rates of interest. Yet large sectors of the middle group live off relatively inelastic sources of income and suffer the deprivations of inflation in varying degrees depending on family size, ages of children, accrued equity and the number of family wage earners. Although these middle groups may be variously disadvantaged or advantaged by inflation they all share an awareness that they must adapt and adjust to it in order to try to shield themselves from its most serious consequences. In an effort to cope with inflation, they attempt to enchance their chances to maintain or increase living standards which were set well in advance of the inflationary spirals of 1974 and 1978–90. In the 1980s a powerful sense of market rationality drove the middle classes into an orgy of speculative activity in real estate, government bonds, precious metals and stones, and antiques and other price-elastic investments. Such economically defensive speculations exacerbate the problem of inflation because their cumulative effect is to increase inflation by increasing prices in transfer goods in the hope of beating the system. But a depression such as that which occurred in the early 1990s leaves the last purchaser "holding the bag." On the other hand, some people in this group attempt to hold their own by working overtime, taking second jobs or by pooling the resources of household members. For them, status and economic defensiveness become a dominant practical and psychological orientation to the world.

At a political level their efforts to defend themselves against inflation and depression are expressed as strident opposition to increases in taxes by supporting cutbacks in those social expenditures from which they do not directly benefit, and by a strong defense of established gains. At all levels they are prepared to displace the costs of inflation and unemployment on groups other than their own. The numerical size of special-interest groups becomes smaller and smaller as each group takes a more radically self-interested attitude. This middle sector is engaged in a vast competitive struggle within itself as well as with the rest of society to protect its present position from erosion. Those whose market positions within the middle classes are the weakest—that is, those who are vulnerable to cutbacks in the public payroll or to layoffs in industry—may join the unemployed and suffer economic disaster and social humiliation. As the competitive struggle to protect one's market position increases, the middle classes become less liberal, less able to take a civic or social attitude, and more subject to political appeals that offer easy, often irrational, solutions to personal economic problems.

Three occupational subsegments of the middle classes are worthy of special discussion because their occupations give them a special relationship to the processes and consequences of inflation and depression. These are (1) business managers and political administrators who deal with pricing policies and labor costs, (2) small- and medium-sized businessmen who attempt to anticipate future prices and costs relative to their own business operations, and (3) intellectuals and academicians who either try to understand these social processes or devise policies for dealing with them.

Business managers and political administrators directly confront the effects of inflation and depression on labor costs, production expenditures and budgets. In addition they are in a crucial position to influence pricing and investment policies, chart the value of labor, and advise management on overall policy. Their decisions have a direct influence on the distribution of the economic burden across the spectrum of society. Of course managers and administrators must work within the constraints of corporate, organizational and political policy and are not free of pressures from others, including political and labor leaders. They owe their own jobs to corporate owners and politicians and they are indebted to labor leaders who assure them a disciplined labor force. They are obliged to respond favorably to those pressure groups upon which they are most dependent. Consumers of their products (services in the case of government bureaucracies and educational institutions, and commodities in the case of industry) do not constitute an organized group capable of either engaging in boycotts or withdrawing consumption functions. Thus, managers and administrators respond in terms of the requirements of their own immediate situation. As a result, their responses to the pressure of special interests almost always mean price rises or reductions in services to consumers. Because no social instrument exists to coordinate their independent actions, each acts in terms of personal expectations of the responses of counterparts in other organizations and administrations. Other-directed, they respond solely in terms of their relevant other and are collectively affirmed in their decisions by the similar responses of the other. Thus, although the managerial and administrative classes hold decision-making jobs, there is neither social nor psychological machinery to coordinate their individual decisions and hence their collective economic consequences.

Many *small- and medium-sized businesses*—such as private owners of retail outlets, service establishments, subcontractors, franchise operators, and small medical groups—have actually become larger and larger even though this is not immediately evident because we tend to measure them against giant corporations rather than against their own past size. Collectively such enterprises actually account for a significant portion of the total volume of business, and they can make an important contribution to inflation because their prices can be highly elastic in relation to their costs. Yet, they attempt to move their incomes in phase with or faster than rates of inflation; and to the extent that they try to adapt rationally, they raise prices and fees in anticipation of actual rises in their own costs—thus exacerbating inflation by gaining temporary windfall profits. Furthermore, because these businessmen are continuously buying and selling, they are highly attuned to daily fluctuations in the value of the dollar or of stocks and bonds, and in costs, interest rates, prices and fees. They therefore become aware that their income and profits are as much a result of price fluctuations and fluctuations in the so-called money market as of the productive value of their services or the merchandise they sell. Their professional and merchandizing activities then, take on a purely business quality, with the further result that every increase in prices intensifies their sensitivity to additional speculative and price opportunities. This not only results in further inflation, it also leads to the growing resentment of groups in society who are dependent upon them for their goods and services, and who are unable to pass on price increases or escape from them in any other way. Whatever hatred of and hostility toward big business that exists is paralleled by an even greater resentment against the small- and medium-sized business classes whose success is immediately visible to all other groups below them. The visible success of the petit bourgeoisie heightens their working-class customers' inability to defend themselves against their own sufferings from the seemingly inexorable inflation and unemployment spiral. It is understandable that shoplifting and white-collar crime will become more prevalent, and looting and burning in crisis situations should not be unexpected.

Academicians and intellectuals are in some respects a special case. During the period of the late 1950s and especially 1960s they were major beneficiaries of the enormous expansion of the educational industry under the enlarged "welfare" state. From the beginning of President Johnson's administration to the middle of President Nixon's second term (1970), vast resources were invested in university construction, academic research and federal subsidization of professional salaries and student stipends. Government support of university libraries in turn lent new support to the publishing industry, and other federal programs provided financial aid to the arts, the humanities, and social-science research of all kinds. Some professors achieved semiautonomous positions within universities and even intellectuals without an institutional affiliation could at least survive if not flourish in the open marketplace. In the 1970s the decline of all of these areas of opportunity coincided with inflation and cutbacks in university budgets. The result has been demoralization of part of the professoriat and intensified efforts by university administrators to generate new business by opening up so-called "new career" opportunities and revitalizing professionally oriented programs. Such activity increased enrollments in business schools, law schools and medical and criminal justice programs, but also further demoralized the professoriat in the social sciences and humanities and the political and civic-minded intellectuals as well.

Ordinarily, academicians and political intellectuals would be the first to analyze and verbalize the social consequences and long-term societal implications of declining abundance, but it is another significant feature of the present situation that they have been slow to respond to these problems, if they can be said to have responded to them at all. Instead, they have focused their attention on the internal problems of their own professions and universities. The institutional absorption of many academic intellectuals in applied research and state-supported programs can make criticism more difficult, but academic intellectuals during the 1960s led the civil-rights and antiwar movements at a time when educational institutions were most heavily supported and subsidized by the very federal government whose policies they attacked.

The silence of the intellectuals at present seems to be related to a sense of helplessness as well as a change in their own career and intellectual situations. It is true many are now older by ten to fifteen years and so see life from the perspective of a tenured and entrenched civil service class. This fact alone would tend to narrow their vision of the world and discourage them from criticism at a time in life where such criticism would be of no advantage to them, and would have the negative effect of exposing them to the charge of antisocial or perhaps even un-American activity, in a period when the country is suffering considerable international losses as well as perplexing and seemingly unsolvable domestic crises. Newer professors, those who were still in graduate school ten years ago, must compete for positions and tenure with the established professoriat. If they do hold regular positions, many seem to direct much of their intellectual energies to the internal political affairs of the university; if they do not, many exhaust themselves in commuting from one part-time teaching position to another. The decline of political activism and of social criticism by the professors cannot be explained, however, primarily by their new career situations.

Much more important than such career considerations is the failure of social-science theory to supply an explanation of the present condition of American society in its own terms and in its relations with the world. It is now self-evident that the theoretical paradigms of the 1960s—especially structural functionalism and behaviorism in sociology and political science, and Keynesianism and monetarism in economics— lack any congruity with social reality, leaving social scientists without the tools and perspectives to orient themselves. They have responded to this intellectual disorientation either by seeking specific solutions to their own economic problems or by turning to older ideological questions. We now have— all at the same time—vast competitive struggles between universities for students and for government grants, intensive efforts to refinance and reorganize universities, and a proliferation of centers of both conservative and radical thought— each looking to past ideologies and social theories in order to understand the present. There have been very few efforts to understand the present in its own concrete terms. Behaving neither like Mannheim's "detached" or Schumpeter's "unemployed" intellectuals, academics and intellectuals today have generally responded as a middle class acting in terms of its own occupational and life-style interests. The intellectual stratum has neither articulated the causes of the present conditions nor offered solutions at the level of societal policy for the problems of the youth, the poor, the aged or for those other groups now undergoing the experience of economic disenfranchisement for the first time. Along with their partial economic disenfranchisement, the intellectuals have intellectually disenfranchised themselves.

FUTURE PROSPECTS

Over the next few years, if the depression continues at its present level and unemployment and underemployment increase because rates of economic expansion continue to decrease, more and more groups will be placed on the defensive in an effort to maintain existent or anticipated standards of living. And if in this respect the United States should become more economically autarchic, then a successful effort by one group or class to maintain or increase its economic share can only be accomplished at the expense of another group or class. Such competitiveness is then likely to be expressed at all institutional levels—in the open marketplace, the legislative struggles over the allocation of state and federal budgets, and in taxation, tariff, monetary and fiscal policies that influence the distribution of income and wealth. No area of life is likely to be free from such competition, and each group is increasingly likely to be aware of specifically who its direct competitors are. Yet, it is equally likely that there will be an increasingly large number of losers who see their losses as a direct result of the gains of others; this will be all the more the case as competing groups increase their levels of political sophistication, and with it their awareness that political means become economic determinants.

In a society highly fragmented by almost infinite subdivisions of groups based on differences of skill, occupation, class, life-style, race, religion, ethnicity and country of origin, the number of special interests and individual interests is almost too staggering to imagine. Yet as these groups become increasingly aware of their special interests, they may also organize for the purpose of protecting those interests. Each organized group can make its own claim on the system in order to protect, preserve or enhance its own interests, developing such ideologies as are necessary to justify its actions to itself and to others. The management of these interests is already the central political problem of the day. It is relatively easy as long as all or most groups continue to receive the shares, or at least the promise of shares, commensurate with their positions. But all political efforts to adjudicate the competing claims face a single dilemma—that is, how to meet the claims of groups who want more—or at least not less—in a period when it is impossible at an economic level to meet all the demands. When competition for shares increases because of a decline in shares, the competition between these groups and competitive struggles to gain political influence intensifies; political and economic constituencies are likely to split and mix in complex patterns that are not likely to follow class lines. The problem of political management of social resentment, intergroup hostility, hatred of leaders, and disgust with the system as a whole would seem to have no rational solution, because it appears to be impossible to make compromises that require some legitimate groups to make sacrifices while others benefit. The demands placed on the system are more than political leaders can satisfy by the economic and administrative means currently available to them.

Under these conditions, one test of political leadership will be its capacity to find noneconomic means for satisfying the competitive claims. Noneconomic means unfortunately often include such methods as discrimination and prejudice, scapegoating, an immoral equivalent to a "war on poverty," xenophobic nationalism, jingoism, red-baiting, anti-intellectualism and other even less palatable methods almost too frightful to contemplate in a highly international world. At times, international events beyond political leaders' direct control may, as in the case of the Ayatollah Khomeini or the Soviet invasion of Afghanistan, inadvertently supply us with a unifying scapegoat. Other noneconomic means include the formation of a system of coalition politics under which groups trade their votes for special favors promised in advance of elections. All such political bargaining for economic patronage essentially rests on promises to be delivered after the election. In the nature of the election system in the United States, there is always a pre-election inflation of promises which cannot be fulfilled by the successful candidate; with declining shares more promises will be broken, and it is likely that groups whose promises are not fulfilled will be less willing to wait the full four-year term of the presidency for their next chance to trade their votes for future promises. It will become more difficult to meet political mortgage obligations when outstanding promissory notes exceed available supplies of capital, although it is always possible that such notes may be renewed at shorter and shorter intervals.

Still another means is to exhort groups on the basis of civic values or Christian ideals to reduce their claims in the interests of the common good. This method, however has the evident weakness that it is difficult to define a common good for groups whose competition with each other includes different ideas of what is the common good, and in a society in which Puritan religious values have declined and narcissistic ideologies have captured the imagination of much of the youth.

Even the psychological means available to political leaders to coordinate mass psychology become more difficult; the multiplication of audiences makes it difficult to find slogans that can transcend the psychological boundaries of particular constituencies. Political management depends increasingly on the coordination of mass psychology; and when political leaders lose their credibility with the masses, the masses are prepared to replace them with new ones.

In some instances, such as that of President Nixon during Watergate, political leaders lose their ability to manage mass psychology; and its management then passes into the hands of the mass media. Yet the media are really not able to manage it either, because they have not yet developed a political line of their own—other than responding to audience responses. Perhaps the media can temporarily absorb resentments and hostilities by playing to the resentments and hostilities of all groups simultaneously and thus render some stability to mass psychology.

Pragmatically, the solution is likely to rest in the acceptance by all concerned groups of a slow and gradual decline in consumption standards and living styles. However, as long as the decline comes in small steps and slow stages, it will not be sufficiently noticeable to precipitate a general crisis, and no major group will feel that it is carrying an excessive burden relative to its immediate competitors. If this is to be the case, much of politics will concern itself with a form of de-escalation of economic and social expectations, and each step in the de-escalation will be fraught with political dangers from the resentment of groups regarding themselves as paying too high a price. There is some question whether the American political system can produce a leader who is capable of this type of social and economic orchestration, since the leaders themselves are part of the class and regional competition. But all such seemingly "unresolvable" processes can be rescued by a war, a depression or by some unexpected form of "good luck," although the latter is the hardest to imagine. What is more likely is that the conditions we have attempted to analyze will result in forms of political instability and/or a chronic sense of malaise with which American society has heretofore not had to contend.

None of the internal economic conditions we have discussed is independent of long-term changes in the United States' position in world economic and political affairs. The overarching cause of its problems is, thus, the world's having reached the marginal utility of national states to regulate and insure their own society's life conditions. This marginal utility of national economics is the result of significant changes in the international economic order. The great expansion in number and size of multinational corporations—beyond the controls of federal law, regulation and perhaps even nationalization—has resulted in an international laissez-faire economy reminiscent of that of the United States in the nineteenth century.

Within the framework of such laissez-faire internationalism, the postcolonial world has begun to assert its claim to price and market its own natural resources. The apotheosis of this postcolonial and civilizational (e.g., Islam) "nativistic" assertion finds its economic power in the historical accident of ownership of fossil-fuel beds vital to the industrial nations, including the United States. Other third-world countries possess primary extractive resources that the already industrialized countries increasingly compete to possess. The competition to control and market crucial national resources throughout the world has created new international oligopolies that render much economic theory and practice obsolete, because it rests on the assumption of an international order and on the presumption that the state will be the largest unit for economic management. Neither the internal nor the external economic problems of the United States are manageable within the framework of its own institutions. Like the countries of the old worlds, the United States is now becoming an old country. It remains to be seen how, under these conditions, this nation will use its power for the future reshaping and reorganizing of a world of inevitable frustrations in which it cannot prevail on its own terms.

Acknowledgements

I thank Harry Dahms, Macklin Trimnell, Karin Weyland and Abby Scher of the Graduate Faculty, New School for Social Research, New York for editorial and technical assistance during the preparation of this volume, and Paul Cantrell for preparation of the Index.

The essays appearing in this volume are printed with the permission of their original publishers:

Chapter 1, "The Discovery of the New Middle Classes" by Val Burris, reprinted with the permission of Martinus Nijhoff Publishers from *Theory and Society*, vol. 15 (1986), pp. 317–49. Copyright © 1986, Martinus Nijhoff Publishers.

Chapter 2, "The New Middle Class" by Emil Lederer and Jacob Marschak, reprinted with the permission of J. C. B. Mohr from "Der Neue Mittlestand" (The New Middle Class) *Grundriss der Sozialokonomik*, IX Abteilung I, Teil. Copyright © 1926, J. C. B. Mohr (Paul Siebeck).

Chapter 3, "Middle-Class Notions and Lower-Class Theory" by Hans Speier, reprinted with the permission of Yale University Press from Hans Speier, *German White Collar Workers and the Rise of Hitler*. Copyright © 1985, Yale University Press.

Chapter 4, "The Growth of the New Middle Class" by Anthony Giddens, reprinted with the permission of Harper Collins from Anthony Giddens, *The Class Structure of Advanced Societies*. Copyright © 1973, Anthony Giddens, reprinted by kind permission of the author.

Chapter 5, "The Status Sphere" by Hans H. Gerth and C. Wright Mills, reprinted with the permission of Harcourt Brace Jovanovich, Inc. from Hans H. Gerth and C. Wright Mills, *Character and Social Structure: The Psychology of Social Institutions*. Copyright © 1953, Harcourt Brace Jovanovich, Inc.

Chapters 6 and 7, "The Foundations of Social Rank and Respect" and "Bureaucracy and Masked Class Membership" by Hans Speier (originally titled "The Hierarchy and Masked Class Membership"), reprinted with the permission of Yale University Press from Hans Speier, *German White Collar Workers and the Rise of Hitler*. Copyright © 1985, Yale University Press.

Chapter 8, "Economic Class, Status and Personality" by Joseph Bensman and Arthur J. Vidich, reprinted with the permission of Quadrangle Books from Joseph Bensman and Arthur J. Vidich, *The New American Society*.

388 *Acknowledgements*

Notes on the Contributors

SERIES EDITORS

Robert Jackall is Willmott Family Professor of Sociology and Social Thought at Williams College. His most recent book is *Moral Mazes: The World of Corporate Managers.*

Arthur J. Vidich is Senior Lecturer and Professor Emeritus of Sociology and Anthropology at the Graduate Faculty, New School for Social Research. He is the co-author of *Small Town in Mass Society* and *American Society: The Welfare State and Beyond.*

Joseph Bensman (1922–86) was Professor of Sociology at the City University of New York and a Lecturer at the New School for Social Research. He is the author of *Dollars and Sense: Ideology, Ethics and the Meaning of Work in Profit and Non-Profit Organizations,* is coauthor of *Craft and Consciousness: Occupational Technique and the Development of World Images* and *Between Public and Private: Lost Boundaries of the Self.*

Vallon Burris is Professor of Sociology at the University of Oregon, Eugene. His areas of interest include social theory, social stratification and the role of the right wing in America. In addition to *The Crisis of the New Middle Class,* he regularly contributes to numerous journals and anthologies. He is also editor of *Critical Sociology,* and on the editorial boards of *Current Perspectives in Social Theory* and *Social Science Quarterly.*

Arthur S. Evans, Jr is Professor and Chair of the Department of Sociology and Social Psychology at Florida Atlantic University. He is coauthor of *Pearl City Florida: A Black Community Remembers.*

Hans H. Gerth (1908–78) was Professor of Sociology at the University of Wisconsin and, beginning in 1968, at the Frankfurt Institute for Social Research. He is author of *Burgerliche Intelligenz um 1800* and *The First International: Minutes of the Hague Congress of 1872.* He was C. Wright Mills' professor and collaborator in *Essays from Max Weber,* for which he wrote the introduction, and *Character and Social Structure: The Psychology of Social Institutions.* His essays are published posthumously in *Politics, Character and Culture, Perspectives from Hans Gerth.*

Anthony Giddens is Professor of Sociology at Cambridge University. He has published *Capitalism and Modern Social Theory* (1971), *New Rules of Sociological Method* (1976), *Profiles and Critiques in Social Theory* (1983), *The Constitution of Society: Outline of a Theory of Structuration* (1984) and *Social Theory Today* (1987) and has published many other sociological treatises.

Michael W. Hughey is Professor of Sociology, Moorhead State University, Moorhead, MN. He is the author of *Civil Religion and Modern Order: Theoretical and Historical Dimensions* and coeditor of a volume of essays entitled *The Ethnic Quest for Community: Searching for Roots in the Lonely Crowd.*

Emil Lederer (1882–1939) was a major economic theoretician of the German national economy during the Weimar period, and a colleague of Joseph Schumpeter and Alfred Weber. He became Dean of the Graduate Faculty of the New School for Social Research in 1933. Among his many writings are *Technical Progress and Unemployment: An Enquiry into Obstacles to Economic Expansion* (1938), *State of the Masses: The Threat to the Classless Society* (1939) and a collection of essays edited by Juergen Kocka, *Kapitalismus, Klassenfrukfur und Probleme der Demockratie in Deutschland, 1910–1940* (1979).

Jakob Marschak (1898–1977) taught at the New School for Social Research, the University of Chicago, Yale University and other universities in Europe and America. His publications include *Income, Employment and the Price Level: Lectures Given at the University of Chicago* (1951), *Kapitalbildung* (1936) and *Economic Information, Decision, and Prediction* (1974). In addition he has coauthored other publications, including *Economic Aspects of Atomic Power* (1950) and *Management in Russian Industry and Agriculture* (1944). He was a leading international economist who became president elect of the American Economic Association in 1977.

Hans Speier (1905–90) left Germany in 1933 to recruit the first faculty of the University in Exile, which later became the Graduate Faculty of the New School for Social Research. His first book, *Die Angelstellten vor dem Nationalsozialismus: Ein Beitrag zum Verstandis der Deutschen Sozialstruktur 1918–1933*, finished in 1933, was denied publication by the Nazi regime. It was published for the first time in German in 1977 and in 1986 appeared in English translation under the title, *German White Collar Workers and the Rise of Hitler.* His other books include *Social Order and the Risks of War; Force and Folly* and, in 1987, *The Truth in Hell and Other Essays on Politics and Culture: 1935–1987.*

Arthur J. Vidich is Senior Lecturer and Professor Emeritus of Sociology and Anthropology at the Graduate Faculty of the New School for Social Research. He is author of *The Political Impact of Colonial Administration* and coauthor of *Reflections on Community Studies* and *American Sociology: Worldly Rejections of Religion and Their Directions.*

C. Wright Mills (1916–62) was Professor of Sociology at Columbia University and is author of *The Sociological Imagination, The Power Elite* and *The Marxists,* and, with Hans H. Gerth, is coauthor of *Essays from Max Weber* and *Character and Social Structure: The Psychology of Social Institutions.*

Index

Note: indexed materials in endnotes to chapters are signaled by 'n.' after a page number, followed by the endnote number.

as an educated elite, 346–47; relation to Nixon, 348–49, 352; and symbolic delegitimation, 357; leftists against, 357. *See also* Civil servants, Salaried employees, White-collar workers

New Right: as a neo-populist revolt, 47–48

New working class: in social theory, 16, 121–26; as an historic bloc, 123, 125, 126; technical specialists in, 124–25; developed by French writers, 125–26; and white-collar workers, 209–10

New York City: middle class life-styles in, 292

Nixon, Richard M.: and Watergate, 8–9, 335, 342, 353–54, 383; and the new conservatism, 300–01; and the old middle classes, 310–12; attempts at suppression, 337–38; political polls on, 341, 355–56; and the working class, 343, 361n.16; and the new middle class, 348–49; centralized the presidency, 349–51; policies of exclusion, 351–52; claim to legitimacy, 353, 355–56; view of 1960 election, 361n.13; relations with press, 362n.23; pardon of, 363n.26; support of universities, 378–79.

Northeast (U.S.A): immigrant politics in, 306; and economic development, 317; Westerners disdain of, 321

Occupation: as a sociological concept, 92–93; as a basis of status, 135–36; and experience, 152; history of, 189; and managerial responsibilities, 189–90; and specialization, 191; and industrial production, 191–93; and distribution, 193–95; and marketing changes, 196; of blacks, 215, 217, 225; and life-style changes, 250; and life-style, 263–64, 269; new middle class monopolies of, 347

Occupational associations: and German politics, 5; and status claims, 6; among salaried employees, 29, 33, 68–79, 82,

84–86ns.10–13/19; of white-collar workers, 87–88, 96, 97; and class consciousness, 97–100; among professionals, 114. *See also* Unions

Old middle classes: decline of, 7, 28, 60, 103–04, 305–12; and Watergate, 8–9; relation to the new middle class, 25, 55, 57, 204, 326–28, 331–32, 341; support of German fascism, 43–44; as employers, 68–69; in the class structure, 103; inter-social comparisons of, 104; in the labor force, 190; and occupational functions, 197–98, 201, 202; and the new conservatism, 302, 311–16; general characteristics of, 302–05; social movements of, 307; patriotism among, 304, 308; and political confrontation, 308–12; and societal domination, 315–16, 328; nostalgia for the Holy Commonwealth, 316; political traditions among, 341–42

Opportunity: and business cycles, 162–66; and capital accumulation, 178

Orthodox Marxism: view of Marxist theory, 24; view of the new middle class, 25, 31, 32, 206–07; and social democrats, 25; view of class membership and consciousness, 32; on the size of proletariat, 34–35, 46–47; view of white-collar workers, 104; view of salaried workers, 123

Parties: and extra-legal interests, 354

Petty bourgeoisie: theorized decline of, 19; contradictions of, 23–24; as a mediator category, 25; theorized expansion of, 27; and fascism, 37, 39; and capitalist development, 103; hostility toward, 378

Political administrators: socio-economic situation of, 376–77

Political psychology: and inter-class relations, 7–8; of social strata, 208–11

Political sociology: the new middle class in, 15

Political theory: and stratification,